D1266521

The Populist Mind

THE AMERICAN HERITAGE SERIES

THE

American Heritage

Series

UNDER THE GENERAL EDITORSHIP OF

LEONARD W. LEVY AND ALFRED YOUNG

The Populist Mind

EDITED BY

NORMAN POLLACK

Wayne State University

THE BOBBS - MERRILL COMPANY, INC.

Indianapolis and New York

TO MY WIFE, NANCY

FOREWORD

Historians once confidently believed that they understood Populism. Almost unanimous in their sympathetic portrayal of the movement, they saw it as a lineal descendant of Jeffersonian and Jacksonian Democracy, a precursor of progressive reform. The standard interpretation of Populism—and it was the liberal's interpretation that prevailed—remained essentially static for several decades. Then the winds of revisionism swept the plains of Populist historiography.

Distinguished historians defaced the old image of the Populists as native radicals and democrats. They began to depict the movement as a retrogressive political force that sought to restore the lost and unrecoverable world of the yeoman farmer. They described the Populists as petty agrarian capitalists on-the-make, filled with deluded notions about the existence of a conspiracy of the "special interests" against the common people. The Populist emerged in revisionist writings as a prototype of the authoritarian personality who shrilly reflected anti-intellectual, anti-Semitic, and xenophobic ideas. He was the yokel who seized upon simplistic and unrealistic panaceas to redress his grievances. Thus, the harbinger of progressive reform, the symbolic epitome of American virtues, the underdog who had conscripted the loyalty of everyone devoted to social and economic justice had become the rustic reactionary who was a precursor of McCarthyism.

Professor Norman Pollack belongs to what might be called the counter-revisionist school of Populist historiography. His remarkable empathy for the Populists leads him to their defense and to what his critics regard as a romantic view of the meaning and character of their movement. It has been said that he has joined their Manichean universe and sees them as the embodiment of all that was true and just and good in their time. His own defense does not rest on his scrappy, pungent, and critical assault on the revisionists; it rests, rather, on the only foundation upon which a scholar can build: the evidence of the primary sources. This book, which is enlivened by Pollack's spirited introduction, is incomparably the fullest revelation of the Populist mind. It is a superlative collection of the primary sources, many of them reprinted for the first time. Regardless of whether one agrees with his interpretation or not, there is no denying that he has an unrivalled knowledge of the literature of his subject. He has culled his materials from newspapers, pamphlets, books, speeches, party proceedings and platforms, and from manuscript collections. He has brought us back, with an astonishing sense of immediacy, to what was being said and thought by the Populists in the South and in the West, on their lonely farms, and in their country stores, courthouse squares, conventions, picnic grounds, and meeting halls. Never before have students and scholars been presented with so rich, varied, and valuable a gathering of Populist documents. The reader can judge for himself whether or not the Populists were the humane, equalitarian, and progressive social force that Pollack claims; whether, as he asserts, they presented a sensible, realistic, and comprehensive program of reform that was addressed to specific and realistic grievances; and whether their place in American history is best understood by the revisionists or by those who, like Pollack, follow the traditional view in arguing that the Populist objective was to democratize industrial society.

This book is one of a series of which the aim is to provide the essential primary sources of the American experience, especially of American thought. The series, when completed, will constitute a documentary library of American history, filling a need long felt among scholars, students, libraries, and general readers for authoritative collections of original materials. Some volumes will illuminate the thought of significant individuals, such as James Madison or Louis Brandeis; some will deal with movements, such as those of the Antifederalists or the Populists; others will be organized around special themes, such as Puritan political thought, or American Catholic thought on social questions. Many volumes will take up the large number of subjects traditionally studied in American history for which, surprisingly, there are no documentary anthologies; others will pioneer in introducing new subjects of increasing importance to scholars and to the contemporary world. The series aspires to maintain the high standards demanded of contemporary editing, providing authentic texts, intelligently and unobtrusively edited. It will also have the distinction of presenting pieces of substantial length that give the full character and flavor of the original. The series will be the most comprehensive and authoritative of its kind.

Leonard W. Levy
Alfred Young

CONTENTS

PART ONE

THE GENERAL MOOD:

DEGRADATION, OPPRESSION,

DETERMINATION

PART TWO

THE POLITICS OF INEQUALITY:

SEVEN POPULIST VIEWS

PART THREE

JUSTICE FOR THE OUTCAST:

I

THE UNEMPLOYED

PART FOUR

JUSTICE FOR THE OUTCAST:

II

THE NEGRO

PART FIVE

THE BRUTALITY OF CAPITAL:
POPULIST SUPPORT FOR THE
WORKING CLASS

PART SIX

EPILOGUE: A TRANSFORMATION OF

SOCIAL VALUES

INTRODUCTION

The underlying current permeating every realm of Populist thought is man's quest for a just social order. By this, Populists meant a social order which not only eliminates poverty but develops and controls technology for the general well-being; one which not only insures widespread suffrage and a fair count but makes participation in the political process meaningful through directly confronting major social problems; and one which not only encourages an ethic of fellowship but goes a good deal further, calling for a transformation of values where the narrow urge for profit gives way to concern for the welfare of all. Whether in the areas of economics, politics or social values, there is a consistent and continuous humanitarian underpinning to their thinking. Populists challenged the strident materialism of their day and worked to achieve a democratized industrial system of humane working conditions and production for human needs. They sought to build a society, in sum, where the individual fulfills himself not at the expense of others but as a social being, and in so doing attains a higher form of individuality. (It is futile to single out specific documents in this volume to support the preceding statements, for the reader will find fully one half if not more of the sources touching directly on one or another of these points. The convergence of ethics and economics is striking throughout.)

According to the Populists freedom was not to be equated with unbridled individualism. Indeed, it was the very assertion of the competitive mentality, of the belief that some had the right to prosper while the remainder of Americans subsisted on a diet of misery, which Populists regarded as the stumbling block to that just social order. (See for example Parts Three and Four dealing with justice for the outcasts of society, for the all-embracing conception of equalitarianism.) Freedom, then, meant nothing less than a state of affairs where existing arrangements promoted, rather than hampered, human potentiality. (Several documents in Part One, notably the first editorial by the *Farmers' Alliance*, the first by the *Advocate*, and Lorenzo D. Lewelling's inaugural message, convey this viewpoint.) It was not sufficient that a few, or even a class, could enjoy the benefits of civilization; society was to be judged not by its apex but by its base. The quality of life of the *masses* was the index by which to measure social improvement. (Again, reference to this emphasis on the people occurs in many of the documents in Part One, especially beginning with Document 13.)

As its name suggests, Populism was people-oriented. It was not dollar-oriented, success-oriented, survival of the fittest-oriented, or whatever else the prevailing ideologies held up to industrial America. There was little of the self-conscious in the Populist enshrinement of the common man: He was not a sentimental construct but the ultimate basis for government and for the creation of wealth. (Perhaps the best place to note these more long-range arguments on political philosophy would be in the extended discussions contained in Part Two, specifically the writings of Peffer, Weaver, Davis, and Nugent.) Society must be attuned to *his* needs, or it ceases to be democratic. No man is free when all are not free. It is this heightened awareness of the human condition in the late nineteenth century which gave rise to the Populist movement, and which served to define the outline of its thought.

I

It should be noted from the start that this interpretation differs markedly from the critical estimate of Populism which was fashionable in the 1950's and which to some extent persists today. In 1951 Oscar Handlin, in a highly sophisticated analysis which appeared in the *Publications of the American Jewish Historical Society*, suggested that certain thought patterns in the late nineteenth century converged to produce an imagery of the Jews which in a later decade served as the basis for the themes found in American anti-Semitism. Since a source he relied on heavily derived from the Populist movement, his article was widely interpreted to mean that Populism was the source of anti-Semitism in the United States. Mr. Handlin later denied that this was his intent (see an exchange of letters between him and the present writer in the *Journal of American History* for March 1965), but at the time and through no fault of his own this conception of the anti-Semitism thesis had an immediate impact on the analysis of Populism. Historians reasoned, quite understandably, given their misreading of the thesis and their belief that all of his evidence pointed to Populist anti-Semitism (actually only one source out of 112 did), that if Populism was anti-Semitic it no longer deserved to be considered a democratic social force. By its very nature anti-Semitism is incompatible with a humanitarian outlook; the two cannot exist side by side. Even more, anti-Semitism suggests the presence of deeper anxieties which may be characterized in terms of an irrational perception of conditions, events, and people, and which takes the form of nativism, xenophobia, and conspiratorial delusions. The reasoning makes perfect sense, provided of course it has been shown that Populists were in fact anti-Semitic; but this had never been shown, and a new image of Populism was constructed—containing the traits listed above and a host of others—without foundation in anything except the faulty reading of Mr. Handlin's work and vivid imaginations.

Four years later Richard Hofstadter, writing in *The Age of Reform*, supplied further refinements to this new interpretation of Populism. Mr. Hofstadter wrote that the movement was unable to confront the facts of industrialism but sought instead to turn its back on social change in favor of the restoration of a golden age in the past. This retrogressive view of history insured the irrationality of Populist solutions. A movement cannot possibly ascertain the nature of its grievances and propose appropriate remedies when it refuses to recognize the changing circumstances of its environment. With this initial irrationality established, Mr. Hofstadter went on to show its more specific manifestations: the notions of a natural harmony of interests between all labor, which were predicated on the physiocratic doctrine of producer values; the belief in a dualistic version of social struggles, in which the agrarians were deliberately oppressed by the forces of industrial capitalism; and, inevitably, the adherence to conspiracy theories, with the Jews as the explanation of Populist discontent. For Mr. Hofstadter, Populism was indeed the source of American anti-Semitism. Finally, since the movement's perception was so out of focus, there was reason for believing that the agrarians may well have exaggerated their grievances, that perhaps times were not nearly so hard as they imagined, and hence that their protest was all the more irrational, being a response to nonexistent problems and to an American society which was beneficent and functioning smoothly. Under these circumstances it is difficult to take their protest seriously. Populists, like other Americans, were not really radical. Instead they were capitalists-on-the-make who wanted a larger share of the pie, but did not quite know how to express themselves. This tension in their thinking, moreover, was nothing new in the American reform tradition. Beginning with the Jacksonians, the history of the United States has witnessed examples of cranky radicals who talked of the money power but who were in reality not radical at all. Populism was one more instance of this endemic impulse in our past. Politically, the Populists were opportunists who were for sale to the highest bidders (in this case, the free-silver forces).

Mr. Hofstadter simultaneously denied the movement's humanistic, rational and radical dimensions. But he did more. Taking Populism as the model for the reform tradition itself, he suggested that intrinsic to radicalism were the host of illiberal factors already noted. In his exploration of the American past, Mr. Hofstadter finds that there has always been a fundamental consensus, and that any social protest which conceivably existed outside that consensus assumed irrational forms. Not only Populism but radicalism in general became the subject of critical scrutiny.

An influential collection of essays, *The New American Right*, edited by Daniel Bell, also appeared in 1955 as part of the continuing discussion. In some cases relying on what was taken to be the Handlin thesis, and reflecting many of the ideas expressed by Mr. Hofstadter, the authors of this volume used the term "populistic" to describe the authoritarian currents in American life. Explicit links were suggested between Populism and the proto-fascistic behavior that culminated with McCarthyism in the 1950's. The writers in Mr. Bell's book maintained that such behavior was an integral feature of lower-class social movements. The very stress placed on the masses by Populism was regarded as the dangerous element contained in large-scale movements, for such thinking erupted into anti-intellectualism, the search for conformity, and the glorification of mediocrity. One essayist in Mr. Bell's book, Seymour Martin Lipset, extended this line of reasoning in subsequent works directed to the concept of working-class authoritarianism.

Several other writers presented the same interpretation of Populism in the latter 1950's (Victor C. Ferkiss, for example, in 1957 wrote of the movement as the forerunner of American fascism in the *Western Political Quarterly*), and this revised estimate enjoyed, generally speaking, widespread acceptance. Although the image of Populism had been wholly transformed, few historians challenged this major departure from the writings of earlier scholars. The first two efforts caused considerable discussion. Also in 1957 John Higham, writing in the *Mississippi Valley Historical Review*, felt that the allegations undoubtedly had some merit but were carried to excessive lengths. Mr. Higham called for moderation and balance; if the Populists were anti-Semitic, so was American society as a whole during this era. The Populists were not alone in this regard. And C. Vann Woodward, in the Winter 1959–1960 issue of the *American Scholar*, went a step farther in evaluating the criticisms of Populism. He showed the historical inaccuracies contained in *The New American Right* essays, pointed out how Populists had extended political justice to the Negro in the South, and indicated that the new interpretation may have been a somewhat confused response to the threat of McCarthyism in the early 1950's.

Then the present writer, in a series of five articles and an intellectual history of midwestern Populism, developed a systematic and detailed critique of the negative writings on Populism and offered a treatment of the movement as a humane and progressive social force. Although it was an unpleasant task to investigate the findings of specific historians, there seemed to be no other way to clear the ground so that a fresh start could be made, particularly in light of the tenacity with which the new image was held by many in the profession. (It is safe to assume that further critical work is unnecessary and that scholars can resume the study of the movement for its own sake.) In the *Journal of Southern History* in 1960, I examined intensively Mr. Hofstadter's *The Age of Reform*, and contended that the book was an unwarranted denigration of Populism. Among the issues raised were the following: Mr. Hofstadter disregarded the vast monographic literature on the movement and hence presented a new interpretation without confronting the work of at least three decades of substantial scholarship; he had not studied the primary sources and indeed had based his views on very little evidence; he had not correctly used much of the little evidence he did offer; and he had done no more than read into the past his own notions and the disillusionment with radicalism of present-day intellectuals.

Writing in the *American Historical Review* for October 1962, I concluded on the basis of research into the primary sources on Populism in the state historical societies of Wisconsin, Minnesota, Nebraska, and Kansas, and in the Library of Congress, that the incidence of Populist anti-Semitism in the region associated with the charge was infinitesimal. Since the manuscript collections and newspapers included all those drawn upon by John D. Hicks in *The Populist Revolt* (1931), and others as well, this conclusion on the absence of anti-Semitism in the movement rested on a firm foundation. Significantly, Mr. Hicks had made no mention whatever of anti-Semitism in his excellent and comprehensive account.

In late 1962 the present writer's book, *The Populist Response to Industrial America*, was published. Reconstructing Populist thought almost exclusively from primary sources, I found that the movement's democratic character had if anything been underestimated by earlier historians. New dimensions to Populism were uncovered: its constructive stance toward industrialism, its concern for the underprivileged, its support of the working class, and its attempt to remain a radical social force within a political system that provided little opportunity for the expression of radicalism. All of these findings flatly contradicted the writings of Mr. Hofstadter and others.

At the close of 1964 the writer, in the *Journal of American History*, analyzed the evidence in Mr. Handlin's article on anti-Semitism. This became necessary because there was no other way to lay the idea of Populist anti-Semitism (and the cumulative charges leading to proto-fascism) to rest than to go to the source of the misconceptions, or at least to what was generally regarded as the source. And there was very real doubt on this point, for Mr. Handlin did not clarify his intent until after the critique was published. Since virtually every attack on Populism used Mr. Handlin's article as the starting point,

I had no choice but to examine every item he used and report the results. As noted above, only one work—Ignatius Donnelly's *Caesar's Column*—out of 112 sources had any bearing on Populist anti-Semitism, and five other items were barely relevant to the discussion but did not support such a thesis. (It was on this one novel by Donnelly which later writers fastened to indict the entire movement.) Yet Mr. Handlin ignored the whole other side of the book, where the values expressed were directly antithetical to anti-Semitism, and further, that the anti-Semitism in question took a highly ambiguous form. While Donnelly opposed wealthy Jews, he repudiated persecution in any form and voiced strong compassion for the Jewish people. Mr. Handlin made no effort to assess Donnelly's total career and utterances on the subject, even though Donnelly wrote other novels and left a voluminous set of papers, diaries, and editorials. (See my article in the *American Historical Review* for a summary of the Donnelly Papers at the Minnesota Historical Society, and my "Ignatius Donnelly on Human Rights: A Study of Two Novels," *Mid-America,* April 1965, for a discussion of his *Doctor Huguet,* which strongly defended Negro rights, and his *The Golden Bottle,* which notably revealed philo-Semitism.) The present writer's most recent formulation on the character of the denigration process, which I believe to be very much in the spirit of Mr. Woodward's analysis but more critical of the newer interpretation, can be found—along with contributions by Professors Handlin, Irwin Unger and J. Rogers Hollingsworth—in *Agricultural History* for April 1965.

Since 1962 there have been two other studies directly relevant to a discussion of the critical literature. The first, Martin Ridge's *Ignatius Donnelly: The Portrait of a Politician* (1962), is a fine biography which corrects prevailing misconceptions on its topic. The second, Walter T. K. Nugent's *The Tolerant Populists* (1963), finds from a thorough study of Populist mate-

rials in Kansas that the movement was not nativistic or anti-
Semitic.

Thus, if the reader not conversant with the current dialogue
expects to find incipient fascism in this collection of Populist
documents, he will be sadly disappointed. Such sentiments did
not occur in Populism itself. The documents assembled here
are unusually comprehensive in scope: from inarticulate farmers and national leaders, from West and South, from moderates
such as William A. Peffer and James B. Weaver and radical
sources such as the Topeka, Kansas, *Advocate*. With this brief
summary of the various interpretations stated, one can resume
the discussion of Populist thought.

II

It was suggested earlier that Populists were very much aware
of the human condition in late-nineteenth-century America. In
place of a society suffused with an equalitarian spirit, a society
which is responsive to the growth of all and oppresses none,
Populists pointed to the dispossessed farmer, the unemployed
worker, the so-called "tramp" moving from one town to the
next in search of work—that is, to an industrial capitalism running rampant, growing callous, and becoming each year more
antidemocratic. (See the farmers' own comments on poverty
and the fear of losing their farms in Part One, the remarks
on the unemployed in Part Five, and all of Part Three.) In
place of the free citizen deriving benefit from his labor
whether on the farm or in the factory, determining the policies
under which he is to be governed, and enjoying a sense of
dignity in his day-to-day life, Populists found man to be impoverished, voiceless, and degraded. (See especially Document
One.) Their critique of existing arrangements, therefore, went
beyond economic conditions to embrace the question of the
individual's plight, his dehumanization, and his loss of auton-

omy in a society which rapidly reduced him to a dependent state; dependent on someone else's decisions, someone else's laws, someone else's machinery, someone else's land. There seemed to be no place in America for the masses, except as the raw materials to be served up to the twin gods of Production and Profit.

While economics was usually their starting point, Populists reasoned that the economic, political and social dimensions to man's existence were integrally related. Hence, to express one-self freely in one area and not in the others was only a carica-ture of a democratic society. What is political democracy, they asked, without economic democracy? And what is either with-out a value system supporting a commitment to the common good? (Numerous documents in Part One and those in Part Six reflect this feeling.) Yet, Populists maintained, even this picture was too favorably drawn. For not one of these areas was truly democratic. One free channel would be at least something, would mean that partial reform stood a chance of spreading, and that the problems facing America were not so fundamental as to necessitate a reappraisal of the total social structure. But this possibility was no longer open. Nowhere on the landscape did Populists find the equalitarianism they sought, and because they did not, their thinking, their probing, their research, and their recommendations became increasingly enlarged, increasingly directed to the need for basic changes.

Their protest was a consequence of the times, not only of the 1890's but of the preceding two decades, where the rule and not the exception was all-pervasive hardship. That Popu-lists did not respond to non-existent grievances is underscored by virtually every study made of the movement. One need only read such sober appraisals as Alex M. Arnett's *The Populist Movement in Georgia* or C. Vann Woodward's *Origins of the New South* to see the poverty, malnutrition, broken fences and broken hearts stamped on every feature of southern Populism, or John D. Hicks' *The Populist Revolt* to see the consequences of declining crop prices in the Midwest (crop prices which at times were below the actual cost of production).

Prior to the rewriting of this portion of American history, with its denial that there were grounds for social protest in the United States, historians pointed to increased tenantry and sharecropping, and in the case of some farmers to dispossession from the land entirely; to an appreciating dollar, which made debts almost impossible to repay; and to the ever-present mortgage in the West, and even more pressing, the crop-lien system in the South, dragging men further and further below the surface of an independent existence. They pointed to combines, pools, trusts and monopolies in the manufacturing sector, which created artificially high prices in the domestic market through planned scarcity and the protection afforded by tariff barriers. They pointed to a railroad system in which discriminatory charges had eaten away all prospects the farmer had for breaking even, a railroad system which gave preferential treatment to favored shippers, dominated state legislatures, blackmailed towns into issuing bonds, held large tracts of land off the market, and refused to assume a proper share of the tax burden. And they pointed, on railroads, to the more serious problem of how the transportation network was contributing to a closed system for the distribution of goods.

Populists addressed themselves to each of these issues, as well as to others of a like character. They also expressed strong concern about the conditions of the industrial worker: wages driven down to the subsistence level, company towns, frequent unemployment, and the use of outright coercion in the form of Pinkertons, cooperative militias and imported strikebreakers to prevent the workers from forming unions to rectify their grievances. (The documents in Part Five are very much to the point.) And finally Populists looked with some misgivings at a political framework where basic problems were never aired, and if anything, were obscured by the raising of all manner of diversions, ranging from the "bloody shirt" of sectional antagonism to the cry of tariff as the salvation or the ruin of the nation. Populism was indeed a response to the times, but it was also something more: It was an attempt to transcend those times and, in the act of transcending the existing social context, to pose an alternative conception for the development of America. (See especially Documents Three, Four, and Six.)

As a response to the times Populism was not an endemic impulse but a historically specifiable movement. Before going still more deeply into the Populist position, it might be well to pause here in order to review the movement's history. This bare outline of political facts will tell us little about what Populists were thinking, but the background may help the reader to place Populism itself more clearly in the American past.

III

As a cohesive social and political force Populism existed from 1889 through the presidential campaign of 1896. It was thus of relatively short duration. But in that brief period Populism brought to a focus many of the grievances existing throughout the post-Civil War generation, summed up the principles of an entire century of reform thought insofar as these could be applied to the new conditions, and provided a springboard for future radical programs. Populism was, then, at one and the same time a consolidation, an awakening, and a blueprint for many subsequent radicals.

Yet since large-scale movements do not as a rule emerge fully fashioned overnight, it is necessary to look at the two decades preceding the St. Louis Conference of 1889, where Southern and Northern Alliance organizations explored the possibilities of union and a common set of reform goals. The 1870's and 1880's witnessed in rapid-fire succession a number of movements pointing the way to Populism. This does not mean that Populism was merely the culmination of continuing waves of agitation. For it went beyond its predecessors both in the comprehensiveness of its membership and in the character of its discussions of industrialism. But it nonetheless benefited from many of the ideas and personnel represented in these early experiences. One need only note the activities of James B. Weaver, the People's party nominee for president in 1892, and Ignatius Donnelly, the leader of Minnesota Populism, to see the continuities. Weaver, for example, was also the presidential candidate of the Greenback party in 1880.

To understand the currents feeding into Populism, one must trace the developments occurring in two separate regions, the western Middle West and the South; indeed not until after 1890 is it meaningful to speak of a unified movement, if even at that time, for distinctive regional problems remained. Hence, different agrarian groups sought solutions to their own problems, sometimes paralleling each other (for the basic transportation and financial grievances were similar), sometimes overlapping on national campaigns, but for the most part working alone while reaching many of the same conclusions.

In the Midwest the chief reform groups were the Granger, Greenback and Northern Alliance movements, spanning respectively the early and late 1870's and the 1880's. Each made a basic contribution to Populism. The Grangers supplied the emphasis on the effective regulation of railroads and of the operations of grain elevators. They also, as Solon J. Buck shows so well in *The Granger Movement,* were instrumental in furthering the interest in cooperative ventures, an activity which was central to the spectacular growth of the Alliances in the late 1880's. The Greenbackers furnished a heightened awareness of the financial question, calling for government rather than private control of the monetary and banking system. (The resistance of most Populists to free silver, as divorced from larger considerations dealing with the role of national banks, credit restrictions and the like, owes much to the Greenback

position. Ignatius Donnelly's *The American People's Money,*
which was published at the late date of 1895, reflects these
sentiments in opposition to free silver per se.) And the Greenbackers added another factor which later assumed importance
to the Populists. Through the Greenback-Labor campaigns of
1876, 1878 and 1880 one sees the agrarians coming into increasing contact with, and recognizing the problems of, the working
class. The Northern Alliance provided a general statement of
the demands of farmers and served, as did the other movements, as an educative force in the discussion of credit, interest
rates, grading practices of the wheat crop, and transportation
abuses.

In the South a series of groups—notably the Texas Alliance,
the Louisiana Farmers' Union, and the Agricultural Wheel in
Arkansas—arose in the late 1870's and early 1880's in response
to the conditions confronting the farmers. While these organizations were nonpartisan, they were far from being nonpolitical in character. Strongly oriented to issues, the agrarian
organizations of this period served as an important halfway
step in undermining the southern farmer's blind allegiance
to the Democratic party. To the extent that the Democrats
departed from agrarian demands—by 1890 this was expressed
as being measured by the Alliance yardstick—seeds of doubt
were planted about the necessity for supporting one-party rule
in the South. The point, then, is that although it was difficult
for southern whites to join the People's party in 1892 (because
Democrats charged this would undermine white supremacy),
this difficulty should not be seen as a sudden, traumatic experience. Farmers had already begun to follow this path in the
preceding decade, when they had turned to independent
organizations in order to exert pressure on state and national
policies.

To gain some idea of what farmers called for in the mid-
1880's, one might stop to examine in detail a representative
statement of their position. The Cleburne Demands which

emerged from the state convention of the Texas Alliance in 1886 were designed to "secure to our people freedom from the onerous and shameful abuses that the industrial classes are now suffering at the hands of arrogant capitalists and powerful corporations." The first demand called for "the recognition by incorporation of trade-unions, co-operative stores, and such other associations as may be organized by the industrial classes to improve their financial condition, or to promote their general welfare." The second, third, and fourth demands dealt with the problem of land monopoly—specifically, that the size of holdings in the public school lands be restricted, that "large bodies of land held by private individuals or corporations, for speculative purposes," bear their just share of the tax burden, and that foreign syndicates be prohibited from acquiring title to land. The fifth demand condemned "the dealing in futures of all agricultural products," and sought to make speculation open to swift conviction. The sixth demand, again aimed at large-scale holdings, stated that "all lands forfeited by railroads or other corporations, immediately revert to the government" to be set aside for sale to actual settlers. The seventh demand concerned a state matter, the removal "by force if necessary" of fences erected by the cattle companies on the public lands. The eighth demand sought "to compel corporations" to pay their county and state taxes, and the ninth insisted that the railroads "be assessed at the full nominal value of the stock" on which they claimed to declare dividends. The tenth and eleventh demands, because they reflect the financial arguments to come, deserve to be quoted in full:

10. We demand the rapid extinguishment of the public debt of the United States, by operating the mints to their fullest capacity in coining silver and gold, and the tendering of the same without discrimination to the public creditors of the nation, according to contract.

11. We demand the substitution of legal tender treasury notes

for the issue of the national banks; that the Congress of the United States regulate the amount of such issue, by giving to the country a per capita circulation that shall increase as the population and business interests of the country expand.

The twelfth and thirteenth demands once more relate to industrial labor, one calling for the "establishment of a national bureau of labor statistics" so that "a correct knowledge" of the condition of the working class can be achieved, and the other for laws "to compel corporations to pay their employees according to contract, in lawful money" and to give workers "a first lien upon the product of their labor to the full extent of their wages." The fourteenth demand, also foreshadowing subsequent reform doctrine, and indeed, actual legislation, concerns "the passage of an interstate commerce law, that shall secure the same rates of freight to all persons for the same kind of commodities, according to distance of haul, without regard to amount of shipment." This point continued with the demand "to prevent the granting of rebates; to prevent pooling freights to shut off competition; and to secure to the people the benefit of railroad transportation at reasonable cost." The fifteenth demand required the abolition of the convict-lease system. And the sixteenth demand, significantly (for this is only August 1886), proclaimed: "We recommend a call for a national labor conference, to which all labor organizations shall be invited to send representative men, to discuss such measures as may be of interest to the laboring classes." (The Cleburne Demands are contained in Nelson A. Dunning, *The Farmers' Alliance History and Agricultural Digest*, pp. 41–43, a rich source for the pre-Populist period, published in 1891.)

Extensive commentary is unnecessary here. It is clear that these demands range broadly over the antimonopolist front, revealing a willingness to confront directly the problems of industrialism. In this meeting, where farmers from eighty-four counties were present as delegates, one can see that agrarians, far from being ostrich-like in outlook, were armed with a comprehensive reform program, one directed to the welfare of farmers and workers alike.

Through a series of mergers, the Texas Alliance, the Louisiana Farmers' Union, and the Agricultural Wheel became in the late 1880's a single organization known as the National Farmers' Alliance and Industrial Union, or more familiarly as the Southern Alliance. Negro farmers had been organized into a separate group, the Colored Farmers' National Alliance and Co-operative Union, which worked closely with the Southern Alliance and sent delegates to the national reform meetings. Thus when the St. Louis Conference convened, there was already a brief history of organizational efforts and the discussion of issues. The two regional Alliances were not yet prepared to join together, but each adopted a platform (the Knights of Labor signing that of the Southern Alliance) which had much in common with the other's and with the earlier Cleburne Demands. One notable addition, found in the demands of the Northern Alliance and the Southern Alliance, was government ownership and operation of the railroads. (This position changed back and forth over the next three years: the Ocala Platform of 1890 and the Cincinnati Platform of 1891 called for government control and supervision, and if this "does not remove the abuse now existing," then government ownership, while the Omaha Platform of 1892 came out unequivocally for government ownership.) It is not surprising to find indications at St. Louis that southern agrarians were aware of the problems of labor. As was the case in the Midwest, they too knew the meaning of major strikes, such as those on the Texas railroads in the mid-1880's, and they too felt the impact of the Greenback-Labor and Union Labor parties, particularly in Alabama. When one adds the fact that industrial laborers in the South, especially in the mines and textile mills, were of recent rural background, it becomes clear that lines of communication had been established between farmers and workers.

The year 1890 marked an important turning point for the southern farmers. After successfully combatting the jute-bagging trust in the late 1880's, the Southern Alliance found itself in the 1890 state elections with greater political power than even it had anticipated. As a result regular Democrats, both to gain the organization's endorsement and to head off the threat of a third party, were unusually ready to stand up and be measured by the Alliance yardstick. (This was not always the case with the controversial sub-treasury plan calling for government warehouses to store non-perishable crops. The farmer was to obtain a loan from the government of up to eighty per cent of the value of his crops, at two per cent interest. Meanwhile the crops were to be marketed gradually throughout the year in order to prevent forced sales all at the same time.) Alliance-supported candidates swept into office and the farmers had reason to believe that their demands would be met *within* the one-party system. Men pledged to reform not only made up the majority of several state legislatures, but also included governors and congressmen.

Elation quickly turned to disillusionment as it became clear that many of the successful candidates had no intention whatever of honoring these pledges. The very notion of nonpartisanship was visibly shaken. Still, it was not certain in the minds of southern farmers that independency was the answer. At least another year and two more national conferences had to go by before the final step was taken. The penalties attached to breaking away from the Democratic party were severe, and agrarians had yet to learn that the cry of "Negro domination" masked the attempt of a small number of whites to maintain themselves in power.

The Ocala Convention of December 1890 was a move in the direction of unity between the two regions. This was due in no small measure to the patient work of the leaders of both organizations, notably Leonidas LaFayette Polk of the Southern Alliance, in breaking down sectional animosities. Each group had to be certain that the other was acting in earnest. And the concerted attack on the "bloody shirt" as being a tour de force designed to obscure the discussion of fundamental questions provided the needed reassurance. The Ocala Convention did not, however, settle the problem of third-party activity, and the next skirmish took place at Cincinnati in May 1891. Few southerners attended the latter meeting, but the determination of the western delegates was so great to provide the machinery for independency that the South had little choice but to accept or reject what would be a certainty at the next gathering of the reform forces. Stating that "the time has arrived for a crystallization of the political reform forces of our country and the formation of what should be known as the People's party of the United States of America," the Cincinnati Platform created the basis for action at St. Louis the following February 22. In the meantime times were hard and growing worse. Grievances could no longer be downed in the bewilderment of inexperience and the lethargy of year-in and year-out discouragement. In short, the ingredients were present. Even the all-important radical agrarian press was starting to make its appearance.

In July 1892 the People's party presented its articles of faith in the Omaha Platform (see Document 24), nominated James B. Weaver for the presidency, and waged a vigorous campaign on the national and state levels. This last was accomplished in the face of an almost total lack of funds and continuous harassment, up to and including the murder of Negro Populists in Georgia. Weaver received over one million popular votes, and his twenty-two electoral votes marked the first time since the Civil War that a third party had entered the electoral college. Still, many Populists regarded the results as disappointing. Lorenzo D. Lewelling and Davis H. Waite had been elected governors of Kansas and Colorado respectively, but their programs were blocked in the state legislatures. Hence a clear test of Populist leadership was not provided in these states. Elsewhere, Ignatius Donnelly was defeated in Minnesota, Thomas L. Nugent in Texas, and the Jeffersonian-Democratic candidate, Reuben F. Kolb, in Alabama. Kansans elected five Populists to Congress, but Thomas E. Watson was fraudulently counted out in Georgia. Aside from Alabama, not one state in the South gave James B. Weaver one quarter of its popular vote. On the other hand, one finds Populists received the following percentages of the vote in the tier of states reading down from North Dakota: North Dakota (48.96 per cent), South Dakota (37.58 per cent), Nebraska (41 per cent), and Kansas (48.44 per cent). The South may well have experienced the greater hardship and supplied the more colorful rhetoric, but it cannot be considered the backbone of the movement in 1892. What southern Populists *did* accomplish splendidly was to stand up to the shouts of "Negro domination" and defend the rights of Negroes to political justice.

But disappointment did not mean discouragement. There was a widespread feeling that the movement was gathering momentum. Populists felt that the severity of the depression in 1893 and 1894 had made their case for reform all the more relevant and compelling to larger numbers of people. Although there were few election contests in 1893, and these for minor offices, they did not let up in their campaign of education and agitation. This was no ordinary political movement. For Populists the goal was to work steadily toward mobilizing public opinion, and not simply to work frenetically at election time. By now the Populist newspapers were coming into their own as the vehicle for keeping reform issues before the people. Besides the major weeklies in Lincoln, Topeka, Atlanta, Raleigh, Dallas, and St. Paul, there were literally hundreds with very small circulation sprouting up throughout the South and the prairie states. These latter often failed within the year because of the pressures exerted by advertisers and the inability of farmers to pay for subscriptions, but in turn they were replaced by new papers and the cycle more often than not was repeated. In sum, Populism was a movement of great intellectual ferment: Farmers met at schoolhouses and in picnic groves to discuss issues, editors followed national events closely and commented extensively on government policies and economic conditions, and meetings were held to draft resolutions. All the while hard times grew progressively harder. Thus, although Populism had a brief history, as already stated, it sustained a level of enthusiasm, concern, and purpose in the lives of its members over the entire span of those years.

In 1894 the People's party vote increased by 42 per cent, reaching a total of one and one half million votes. But this gain created problems in its own right. First, the Democratic party could no longer ignore the threat posed by the new party; it could no longer discount the possibility that its status as a major party might be endangered. Well before the 1896 convention Western Democrats were moving in an increasingly radical direction, and in the South the Hogg, Northen and Tillman administrations (Texas, Georgia and South Carolina) were openly rebelling against the eastern wing of the party even during the 1892 campaign. Something had to be done to take the wind out of Populist sails, and the radicalizing of the Democratic party was an important response to this situation. To prevent discontent from becoming translated into a new political alignment, Democrats in the West and South began to give qualified endorsement to Populist demands (qualified in that they accepted partial features of more comprehensive programs). This meant that Populists were confronted with an agonizing dilemma. They could place their political organization above all else and turn their backs on the very measures they worked so hard to achieve, and which now had some prospects of success. Or they could place principle above party and hence risk the destruction of their organization. The dilemma was compounded by the realization that in 1894 the People's party had in all probability tapped its maximum sources of strength. Populists felt that unless the labor movement as a whole responded to their pleas for unity, the third party would never be more than just a third party, with all that this implied for the attainment of the reforms. This has been an age-old problem for radicals in America, given the way the two-party structure militates against the expression of dissent, and Populists too had this almost Hobson's choice to make.

Since the very essence of its political stance had been to emphasize principles rather than party, Populism watched as the transformation in the Democratic party took place, and in the 1896 campaign supported William Jennings Bryan. This was an especially bitter pill for southern Populists to swallow, for they now had to embrace the very party that had persecuted them and had brazenly stolen elections during the past four years. Yet it was a bitter pill for the westerners as well. Throughout 1895 and 1896 Populists in the latter region debated every aspect of the policy of fusion with the Democrats. They were not gulled by free silver. They did not want to abandon their total conception of reform, as contained in the Omaha Platform, and they reluctantly stressed free silver at the expense of government ownership of railroads and other demands only with the understanding that the financial question would be the first step toward the larger goals. Thus, few Populists desired fusion in 1896, and even those who favored this decision made clear their intent to preserve the movement intact. Widespread support from the American Federation of Labor did not materialize, the Knights of Labor was now a negligible order, and only Eugene Debs' American Railway Union stood by the Populists. At the People's party convention of 1896 radicals and the conservative elements alike (conservative only in the context of Populism, for they were to the left of the Democrats) accepted the inevitable. After 1896 a small number remained to pick up the broken pieces.

IV

The Populists addressed themselves to numerous concrete issues; theirs was very much a response to the times, but more, they attempted to transcend those times and pose an alternative line of development for American society. For Populists the blueprint for a just society could profit little from the present surroundings. Equalitarianism lay only in a remembrance of the past, and a vision of the future. And of the two, the second played a far more important part in their thinking. (See for example Document Three.) Populism was not a retrogressive social force. It did not seek to restore a lost world of yeoman farmers and village artisans; still less did it wallow in the self-pity of an agrarian mystique, of an idyllic, static, insulated, and isolated way of life based upon barter when necessary, and self-sufficiency at all other times. (This basic point is reflected in most of the documents in Parts One, Two, Five, and Six.)

The reverse was true. Of course Populists borrowed from the past, but they borrowed selectively. They could no more divorce themselves from their cultural heritage than could any other social movement which had historical roots in their society. Few if any movements rise and disappear in a vacuum. But to say that they borrowed from the past is not the same as saying they were imprisoned by the past. What they took was not a petrified pre-industrialism, but a set of political principles, principles which they believed could be applied at any point, present and future as well as past. (One finds that even the most tradition-oriented of the Populist leaders, James H. Davis, used Jeffersonian doctrine as a basis for controlling the railroads. See the selections from his book in Part

Two.) From Jefferson and Jackson came the recurring theme of "equal rights to all, and special privileges to none"; from these and other sources came the labor theory of value; and from the Constitution came the commerce clause and other passages sanctioning government regulation in the general interest. Beyond this Populists did not go, for their gaze was directed to what lay ahead, rather than to what lay behind. The past furnished a standard of right applicable to all stages of production, but it offered no guidance on the concrete application of that standard to changing conditions. That was the task for the present generation, and that, in the last analysis, was the significance of the Populist remedies.

In seeking to democratize rather than abolish industrialism, Populism was a progressive social force. Yet its orientation was progressive not only because it based its remedies on an accommodation to social change, but also because in pursuing these policies it adopted a highly affirmative stance. The two are difficult to separate. For to be forward-looking while not at the same time possessing confidence that men do have the power to remake their institutions and values is to be as helpless, as escapist, as the one who rests content with a restoration of the past. To acquiesce in social change does not, by itself, insure a progressive outlook. A more positive frame of mind is required, and this Populists had.

Woven into the texture of their thought was the insistence that men *could* consciously make their future. (The documents in Part One from the *Farmers' Alliance* and the *Advocate* particularly reflect this feeling.) Society is not an organism subject to its own laws. It is a human community subject to the laws of men. (See Donnelly's treatment of this in Part Six.) Populists contended that there is nothing inevitable about misery and squalor, nothing irreversible about the tendencies toward the concentration of wealth and the legitimation of corporate power; not the impersonal tendency but men themselves are responsible for contemporary society, and for this reason, men can—and, according to Populists, must—alter the course of that society in a humanistic direction. (This general theme appears time and again in the selections in Part Two and in the analysis of the unemployed in Part Three.) What stands out, then, about the Populist mind is an affirmation of man, a faith in man's capability to shape his own history. (Document Twenty-six eloquently states this point.)

This positive aspect of Populist thought is not exhausted by the fact that numerous concrete proposals were offered to attack existing problems. More important was the attitude behind their formulation, and ultimately, the attitude toward the relation between the individual and his government. In keeping with the emphasis on men rather than impersonal forces as the agents of social change, and more specifically, on men as the wielders of power and the source of legislation, Populists held that laws were not made in heaven but here on earth. There was nothing sacred about the status quo, or for that matter about the institutions which safeguarded that status quo. (Practically every document in Part One attacks existing arrangements, but see especially Governor Lewelling's vision of the future in Document Nineteen.) Populists did not repudiate the notion of law and order; in fact they stressed the point that all reform must come through proper constitutional means. But they did assert, indeed they never tired of asserting, that *existing* law was class law, intended to protect the rich at the expense of the poor, and that order meant in the contemporary context the imposition of legalized repression to prevent the broadening of that law. (All of the writers in Part Two take this position, as do the first three in Part Five and others in that part concerned with the Homestead and Pullman strikes and the Pinkerton system.) In short, law was a disguise for privilege and inequality, a reflection of dominant group needs, and because of that, continued the Populists, it could be changed to satisfy the larger needs of society. Thus Populist reforms stemmed from an attitude of healthy skepticism concerning the sacrosanct nature of government. Since government was no more than an instrument to be used for good or ill by the groups which controlled it, then let the farmers and workers organize to secure that control, and prevent further encroachments on the general welfare.

Yet Populists found even this to be entirely too negative. Government should be more than a neutral observer, a policeman collecting taxes and seeing to it that business goes on as usual. (See Document Two.) That would not begin to tap the potentialities of the instrument. Government, instead, must be a dynamic force in bringing about equality. It was created to *serve* man, and not simply to protect property or prevent individuals from cutting each other's throats. Thus, Populists contended, government must be a responsive tool, one which can actively intervene in the economy to regulate matters affecting the public interest, and when necessary own outright monopolies of this character, and can just as actively aid the underprivileged and work for a more equitable distribution of wealth.

With this predisposition in favor of using the powers of government, and this faith in man's capacity for social planning, it is not surprising to find that Populism was not a single-issue movement, whether that single issue be free silver or any other. The multiplicity of reforms was striking. Their realistic and experimental qualities were even more so. While the national platforms remained by and large the same during the course of the movement, this testifies less to any rigidity in Populist thought than to the persistence of the major problems of the period. Each plank, far from being an empty formula, was the product of intensive research and lively discussion. When Populists, for example, spoke of nationalizing the railroads, they supported their arguments with studies, some at first hand, of publicly owned railroads throughout the world. Indeed even detailed plans for alternative means of compensation were debated. Discussion of monetary policy was perhaps even more thorough; and so it went down the line of reforms. (The selections from the books by Peffer and Weaver, in Part Two, indicate the rational tone and factual character of Populist proposals.)

Theirs was a vital program, and subject to change as their own horizons extended. To see only the platforms is to see only the end results; underneath the surface, and even in the state platforms, one finds the very real intellectual ferment noted earlier. Whether in the picnic groves, the courthouse squares, the crossroad stores, both West and South, Populist orators spoke for two or three hours and oftentimes longer, not haranguing a crowd, but more often than not discussing issues by quoting long passages from census statistics, court decisions, and the writings of economists. (The speeches of Thomas L. Nugent in Part Two are excellent examples.) In fact, they took delight in using established sources to make their case, so as to forestall the charge of resorting to biased authorities. Many of these speeches still exist, some running to thirty closely packed pages. In a period of American history when the major parties studiously avoided the discussion of contemporary problems, Populism stood as an important educating force in the lives of many citizens.

The issues Populists raised were not confined to economic matters. True, the well-known trinity of land, transportation and money figured prominently in their proposals. Each in its own right, as has been observed very briefly above, summed up a complex of abuses: land monopolized by railroads and syndicates; the rise of tenant-farming; railroad charges based on drastically watered stocks; a national banking system which gave the banker sovereign powers over circulation and credit, and so on. Populists felt that until this stranglehold on the economy was broken, until land was made available to farming farmers rather than to speculators or to rentiers, until railroads were efficiently run, charged low rates, made their services available to all, and refrained from interfering in state and local legislation, until a uniform dollar was created and backed by the federal government itself, low interest rates provided, and the amount of money in circulation increased, there could be no headway made in the direction of social and political democracy.

But in addition to land, transportation and money, there was a further dimension to the Populists' economic demands, centering on the industrial system per se. While Populism was primarily an agrarian movement, it sought earnestly to appeal to, and enlist the support of, industrial workers and reformers connected with the movements for social justice. (See the documents in Part Five.) That it did not succeed in this effort cannot be permitted to obscure the non-agrarian, distinctly industrial component in Populist thinking. (See especially Document Six.) The Populist movement did more than make formal overtures to labor organizations. It fought their battles in Congress and the public forums, militantly defended the right to organize, rendered assistance during strikes, and presented labor's side in Populist newspapers and on the speaker's platform. The Populist condemnation of the Pinkerton system was but one indication of a broad sympathy for the working class.

It is less easy to pin down measures in the political and social realms. The currents of thought already discussed were not readily translatable into platform planks. The political demands might best be summarized in terms of the need to bring the government closer to the people, to insure that the people's sentiments are accurately recorded in a fair count (see Document Eighteen), and finally, to prevent these expressions from being sidetracked by corporate influence once they have reached the legislative halls. There were explicit planks on the direct election of senators, the secret ballot, and in some platforms, the initiative and referendum. But there was also discussion on the committee system, the power of the Speaker, and other matters pertaining to Congress (see for example Document Twenty-eight); the prevalence of corruption, intimidation and outright violence in state elections, particularly in southern states; the role of lobbyists, and how their activities could be curtailed; and most important, the extent to which the major political parties were even reflecting the interests of more than a very small segment of the population. Populists, then, stood for the principle of direct democracy, but they were less concerned with the mechanics for implementing it than with the power structure which reduced these mechanics to empty forms.

The social demands can be gathered not only from the moral and ethical underpinnings of Populist thought, but also from the way the movement reached out to embrace and aid the underdog and the submerged in American society, specifically, the worker and the Negro. (See Parts Three through Five.) In both cases, the reasoning was the same: The underprivileged were being disadvantaged by a common system, industrial capitalism; they were all assuming the same position at the bottom of the social structure, and were being kept divided so as not to coalesce in a united challenge to existing arrangements; finally, their only hope for effective action lay in the recognition of identical interests. The most difficult test of all, of course, came in the South. Judged by the standards of a later age, and even by some of the advanced Populist pronouncements on human rights, the movement will appear in a somewhat less than perfect light; but judged by the conduct of late nineteenth-century white America, the movement more than fulfilled its democratic stand. (This aspect is treated more extensively in the introduction to Part Four and in several of the headnotes contained in that part.) Populists, at great personal risk, defended the rights of Negroes, accorded them positions of responsibility within the People's party, and under circumstances where it would have been very easy to appeal to prejudice in order to gain votes, did the reverse by pleading for tolerance. Yet while they championed the cause of the Negro far more than did other southern whites of the period, and while they took the first step in challenging the system of segregation, they would not take the crucial second step: Populists came out firmly for full political equality, but did not support social equality. They were critical of their age, but could not quite transcend it, at least in this important consideration.*

With this overview of the Populist mind now completed, the present writer would like to direct a word to the reader. A great deal of work remains to be done, both in research and interpretation, before the Populist movement as a dynamic social force is fully understood. While the literature on Populism is voluminous, it is surprisingly uncreative in treating the character of Populist thought, and it is wholly inadequate in relating the movement to the industrial transformation in the United States. Thus, once the reader becomes thoroughly conversant with what has already been written, he faces the exciting prospect of breaking new ground in the area of intellectual history. It is hoped that this collection will stimulate efforts in that direction.

---

* Several paragraphs from the introduction appeared in a different form in my "Fear of Man: Populism, Authoritarianism, and the Historian," *Agricultural History,* XXXIX (April 1965).

CHRONOLOGY

1870's-1880's

Succession of movements in Midwest and South reflecting long-term agrarian grievances and proposing solutions which had an impact on Populism. Notably Granger, Greenback, and Northern Alliance movements in Midwest; Texas Alliance, Louisiana Farmers' Union, and Agricultural Wheel in South.

1886

Cleburne Demands, a comprehensive reform program, endorsed at state meeting of the Texas Alliance in August.

1887

Waco meeting of the Texas Alliance, where that organization merged with the Louisiana Farmers' Union to form the National Farmers' Alliance and Co-operative Union of America, under C. W. Macune.

Minneapolis convention of the Northern Alliance in October, which placed this previously weak organization on a more substantial and permanent footing through the collection of dues and the writing of strong financial and railroad planks. Seven states sent delegates, and from that point on the membership increased greatly.

1888

During the summer the Southern Alliance successfully opposed the jute-bagging trust. At a convention it determined to use cotton bagging and to maintain a boycott.

In December the National Farmers' Alliance and Co-operative Union held its convention in Meridian, Mississippi, at the same time as did the Agricultural Wheel, and both agreed on a merger. The organization was subsequently called the Farmers' and Laborers' Union of America.

1889

In March the *National Economist,* edited by C. W. Macune, began publication. It was the official organ of the Southern Alliance. (The *Progressive Farmer* in Raleigh, L. L. Polk's paper, had been in operation since 1886; the Lincoln *Farmers' Alliance* also began in 1889; and Thomas E. Watson's *People's Party Paper* in Atlanta started in October 1891.)

In November Harry Skinner presented a formulation of the sub-treasury plan in *Frank Leslie's Newspaper,* and Macune proposed an expanded version to the St. Louis Conference the following month.

In December the national conventions of the Southern Alliance, Northern Alliance, Farmers' Mutual Benefit Association, and the Colored Farmers' National Alliance and Co-operative Union met in St. Louis at the same time. The resulting St. Louis Conference, to which the Knights of Labor also sent delegates, did not produce a consolidation of the two major groups (this was never attained) but did bring about a basic agreement on reform principles. The Farmers' and Laborers' Union became the National Farmers' Alliance and Industrial Union.

1890

The National Reform Press Association, composed of nearly one thousand newspapers, was established.

In April Ignatius Donnelly's *Caesar's Column* was published.

In June the People's party of Kansas was formed at a meeting in Topeka, and in July the People's Independent ticket in Nebraska resulted from a meeting in Lincoln. Statewide organizations were also effected in South Dakota, North Dakota, Minnesota, and Colorado.

In the election, the People's party of Kansas won the lower house and sent William A. Peffer to the United States Senate. The Independent ticket gained a majority in both houses in Nebraska. In Georgia, Watson was elected to Congress.

There were seeming Alliance victories throughout the South: four governorships, eight state legislatures, numerous congressmen.

In December the Ocala Convention of the Southern Alliance moved a step closer to independent political action. The plan was to postpone a decision until February 1892, and a minority called for an earlier meeting.

1891

In May the dissident elements at Ocala, who wanted to come out definitely for a third party, met at Cincinnati in the National Union Conference. The convention call took in more than the Alliance as such, and hence numerous reformers were present. Few attended from the South. The Conference agreed to wait until the following February, but created a national executive committee to go ahead, if necessary, after that time.

In November the Southern Alliance met at Indianapolis. It was made clear at this meeting that the organization had accepted the idea of the third party.

In December a People's party caucus was formed in Congress, with Watson selected by the nine congressmen as their candidate for Speaker.

1892

In February numerous reform groups, headed by the Southern Alliance, gathered for the St. Louis Conference. While technically the meeting was to do no more than state their demands, it then reconvened to form the People's party.

In July the People's party approved the Omaha Platform and nominated James B. Weaver (Iowa) and James G. Field (Virginia) as its national candidates.

During the summer Weaver campaigned extensively. There was some fusion in the South between Populists and Republicans, notably in Alabama and Louisiana, while fusion in the West between Populists and Democrats was resorted to on any scale only in Kansas and North Dakota.

In the election Weaver received slightly more than one million votes, and twenty-two electoral votes. The center of his support lay in the prairie and mountain states.

1893

Through Populist pressures the Newberry Bill lowering railroad rates almost thirty per cent was passed in Nebraska, only to be invalidated by the courts at a later time.

In June Ignatius Donnelly, Henry D. Lloyd, and other Populists bolted the Chicago Antitrust Convention and called for the confiscation of all property owned by the trusts.

In December Davis H. Waite, Populist governor of Colorado, proposed to the state legislature that foreign silver coins be made legal tender in the state.

Also in December Governor Lorenzo D. Lewelling of Kansas issued his "Tramp Circular" on behalf of the underprivileged.

1894

In the summer Henry D. Lloyd's *Wealth Against Commonwealth* was published.

In July the Springfield Conference met to forge a farmer-labor coalition in Illinois. The conference rejected Thomas J.

Morgan's "Plank 10" on collectivization in favor of Lloyd's compromise proposal that the extent of "collective ownership" be determined by how much "the people elect to operate for the commonwealth." The meeting committed farmers and workers to support at least temporarily the People's party.

In the campaign there was less fusion in the West than in 1892, but more (with Republicans) in the South, particularly in North Carolina.

In the election the People's party vote increased to one and one-half million, but the result did not show in the actual number of seats won; instead many gaps were narrowed, and candidates oftentimes lost with higher votes than in 1892.

In December the St. Louis Conference was called to decide whether the Omaha Platform should be scrapped in favor of a focus on the silver issue. This policy was rejected, and the Omaha Platform was extended to include government ownership of all monopolies affecting the public interest.

1895

There were no concrete developments except the election for the state supreme court in Nebraska, in which the Populist nominee was defeated, and the mayoralty contest in Chicago, in which Bayard Holmes was defeated on a platform calling for far-reaching municipal reforms.

During the year the chief question confronting Populists was what attitude to take concerning the free-silver Democrats.

1896

In July the People's party convention at St. Louis endorsed the Democratic nominee, William Jennings Bryan, and nominated Thomas E. Watson as its own candidate for vice-president. The party's spirit and structure were shattered beyond recovery, although after the election the National Reform Press Association took the lead in trying to keep the movement intact.

1897

In February the National Reform Press Association met at Memphis to arrange for a People's party convention.

In July the Nashville Conference created the National Organization Committee as a separate organization to make certain that the national executive committee of the party would never again attempt a policy of fusion.

1898

In June the two committees met at Omaha to work out a compromise (the Omaha Contract), in which the national executive committee agreed to call a convention in 1900 before those of the major parties, and not to support fusion candidates.

In September one group which was still not satisfied with the Omaha Contract met in Cincinnati to formulate a radical platform and nominate candidates for 1900. From that point on, factional fights multiplied, and the People's party declined rapidly.

SELECTED BIBLIOGRAPHY

ORIGINAL SOURCES

There are, regrettably, only two comprehensive Populist manuscript collections: the Ignatius Donnelly Papers, Minnesota Historical Society, and the Henry D. Lloyd Papers, State Historical Society of Wisconsin. Fortunately, they complement each other, providing a perspective in depth on the grass-roots level in the case of the former, and the larger national picture, urban Populism and social reform currents in the latter. Because of their size, the importance to the movement of Donnelly and Lloyd, and the existence in the Donnelly collection of diaries, scrapbooks of newspaper clippings, speeches, and pamphlets, and in the Lloyd collection of miscellaneous holdings, these papers constitute the indispensable starting point for any study of midwestern Populism. There are no comparable manuscript collections for southern Populism. The place to begin, however, is the Southern Historical Collection in the University of North Carolina Library. It is unlikely that scholars will exhaust the superb holdings in this collection, but for the Populist period few manuscript sources have survived. The chief of these is the Marion Butler Papers, which are exceedingly rich on the 1896 campaign (when Butler was the People's party national chairman), but contain little for the preceding years. The Thomas E. Watson Papers, while important for his later career, have virtually nothing for the years 1889 to 1896. (It is a testimony to C. Vann Woodward's thoroughness that he was able to reconstruct so ably Watson's activities in the 1890's, for the papers themselves were of little help.) There are also smaller collections which should be consulted at Chapel Hill, such as the Cyrus Thompson Papers. Lesser collections throughout the West and South worth studying include the following: the Luhman H. Weller and Robert Schilling Papers, State Historical Society of Wisconsin; the William V. Allen, Samuel Max-

lvi *Selected Bibliography*

well, and Samuel M. Chapman Papers, and the Nebraska State Farmers' Alliance Records, Nebraska Historical Society; the Lorenzo D. Lewelling Papers (actually *Governor's Letterbooks,* CVIII–CX, and scattered folders), Kansas State Historical Society; the Rebecca L. Felton Papers, University of Georgia; the Robert McKee Papers, Alabama Department of Archives and History; and the O. D. Streeter Papers, University of Alabama. This is far from being an exhaustive list. Many collections could be named which the writer found to be of little consequence, such as the James B. Weaver Papers, Iowa Department of History and Archives, and more important, there are still others, not yet studied, which remain in private hands. Finally, in part to compensate for the scarcity of Populist sources, and in part because they shed valuable light in their own right, one would do well to research in non-Populist collections which bear on the movement, such as the William Jennings Bryan Papers, Library of Congress; the James S. Hogg Papers, The University of Texas; and the William J. Northen Scrapbooks, Georgia Department of Archives and History.

The Populist newspapers are a far more useful source for the detailed coverage of the movement. Not only do they provide editorial opinion and a report of the week-by-week events in the movement, but they very often print the texts of speeches, platforms, and local resolutions, and in the letters-to-the-editor column, tap the views of rank-and-file members. A good place to begin is with this core group of six major papers: *Farmers' Alliance* (Lincoln), *Advocate* (Topeka), *People's Party Paper* (Atlanta), *Southern Mercury* (Dallas), *Progressive Farmer* (Raleigh), and *National Economist* (Washington). Each has its own particular emphasis, and together they cover a wide range of problems, regional as well as national, facing the movement. Unfortunately, when one turns to the grass-roots level, few of the literally hundreds of Populist papers, particularly in the South, have come down to us. In state after state, this writer was able to locate only a smattering of county newspapers. The *Louisiana Populist* (Natchitoches) is one of several he has turned up. Another, and perhaps the most neglected source in southern Populism, is Marion Butler's *Caucasian,* published first at Clinton, North Carolina, and then at Goldsboro and Raleigh. The situation is better in the case of midwestern Populism, however, for both the Nebraska Historical Society and the Kansas State Historical Society have excellent collections. In the former, the *Custer County Beacon* (Broken Bow), the *Platte County Argus* (Columbus), and the *Saunders County New Era* (Wahoo) are particularly useful. Lastly, one cannot omit the *Representative* (St. Paul), for this was the colorful newspaper of Ignatius Donnelly.

The published works of Populists constitute a final category of primary sources. These works are generally difficult to obtain, and many have thus far not been discussed by historians. The more well-known ones include William A. Peffer's *The Farmer's Side* (New York: D. Appleton and Company, 1891), James B. Weaver's *A Call to Action* (Des Moines: Iowa Printing Company, 1892), Nelson A. Dunnning's *The Farmers' Alliance History and Agricultural Digest* (Washington: Alliance Publishing Company, 1891), W. Scott Morgan's *History of the Wheel and Alliance, and the Impending Revolution* (Fort Scott, Kansas: J. H. Rice and Sons, 1889), Thomas E. Watson's *The People's Party Campaign Book* (Author's Edition: n.p., n.d.), Henry D. Lloyd's *Wealth Against Commonwealth* (New York: Harper and Brothers, 1894), and such novels by Ignatius Donnelly as *Caesar's Column* (Chicago: F. J. Schulte, 1890), and *Doctor Huguet* (Chicago: F. J. Schulte, 1891). There is of course a whole body of pamphlets which should also be consulted. Good collections exist in the libraries of the Kansas State Historical Society, the University of Nebraska, and the North Carolina Collection at the University of North Carolina. Still another area meriting exploration is the national magazines. Populist leaders often wrote articles for the *Arena,* and an occasional piece for the *Forum, North American Review,* and the *Review of Reviews.* A reasonably complete list of Populist writings remains to be compiled.

COLLATERAL READING

By far the best introduction to the topic of Populism is John D. Hicks, *The Populist Revolt* (Minneapolis: University of Minnesota Press, 1931), which provides a competent summary of the monographic literature written in the 1920's, supplemented by the author's research into the political history of the movement. For a general account of southern Populism, see the excellent chapters in C. Vann Woodward, *Origins of the New South* (Baton Rouge: Louisiana State University Press, 1951). Labor and urban dimensions to Populism, as well as conflicts within the movement, are explored in depth and with great perception by Chester McArthur Destler, *American Radicalism, 1865–1901* (New London: Connecticut College Press, 1946). For an intellectual history of midwestern Populism, see Norman Pollack, *The Populist Response to Industrial America* (Cambridge: Harvard University Press, 1962).

With these four as background, one can then turn to studies on the state level. By far the best in this group is Alex M. Arnett, *The Populist Movement in Georgia* (New York: Columbia University Press, 1922). This should be supplemented by two earlier works: Robert P. Brooks, *The Agrarian Revolution in Georgia, 1865–1912* (Madison: University of Wisconsin Press, 1914), and Enoch M. Banks, *The Economics of Land Tenure in Georgia* (New York: Columbia University Press, 1905). For the remainder of the South see also the following: William D. Sheldon, *Populism in the Old Dominion* (Princeton: Princeton University Press, 1935); Roscoe C. Martin, *The People's Party in Texas* (Austin: University of Texas Press, 1933); Simeon A. Delap, *The Populist Party in North Carolina* (Durham: Trinity College Historical Society, 1922); John B. Clark, *Populism in Alabama* (Auburn: Auburn Printing Company, 1927), a poor study which has been superseded by William W. Rogers, *Agrarianism in Alabama, 1865–1896* (unpublished Ph.D. dissertation, University of North Carolina, 1959); Melvin J. White, "Populism in Louisiana During the Nineties," *Mississippi Valley Historical Review*, V (1918–1919), and Lucia E. Daniel, "The Louisiana People's Party," *Louisiana Historical Quarterly*, XXVI (1943), both superseded by a very good dissertation, William I. Hair, *The Agrarian Protest in Louisiana, 1877–1900* (unpublished Ph.D. dissertation, Louisiana State University, 1962); James A. Sharp, "The Farmers' Alliance and the People's Party in Tennessee," *East Tennessee Historical Society Publications*, X (1938); and Albert D. Kirwan, *A History of Mississippi Politics, 1876–1925* (unpublished Ph.D. dissertation, Duke University, 1947).

For studies on the state level in the Midwest, see Ernest D. Stewart, "The Populist Party in Indiana," *Indiana Magazine of History*, XV (1918), XVI (1919); Roy V. Scott, *The Agrarian Movement in Illinois, 1880–1896* (Urbana: University of Illinois Press, 1962); Herman C. Nixon, "The Populist Movement in Iowa," *Iowa Journal of History and Politics*, XXIV (1926); Elizabeth N. Barr, "The Populist Uprising," in William E. Connelly, ed., *A Standard History of Kansas and Kansans*, II (Chicago: Lewis Publishing Company, 1918), and Raymond C. Miller, "The Economic Background of Populism in Kansas," *Mississippi Valley Historical Review*, XI (1925). For Populism in the mountain states, see John R. Morris, *Davis Hanson Waite: The Ideology of a Western Populist* (unpublished Ph.D. dissertation, University of Colorado, 1965), and also an older and highly stimulating work, Leon W. Fuller, "Colorado's Revolt Against Capitalism," *Mississippi Valley Historical Review*, XXI (1934).

There are three very fine biographies of Populist leaders: C. Vann Woodward, *Tom Watson: Agrarian Rebel* (New York: The Macmillan Company, 1938); Martin Ridge, *Ignatius Donnelly: The Portrait of a Politician* (Chicago: University of Chicago Press, 1962); Chester McArthur Destler, *Henry Demarest Lloyd and the Empire of Reform* (Philadelphia: University of Pennsylvania Press, 1963). Other biographies include Fred E. Haynes, *James Baird Weaver* (Iowa City: The State Historical Society of Iowa, 1919); Daniel M. Robison, *Bob Taylor and the Agrarian Revolt in Tennessee* (Chapel Hill: University of North Carolina Press, 1935); Stuart Noblin, *Leonidas LaFayette Polk: Agrarian Crusader* (Chapel Hill: University of North Carolina Press, 1949); and a contemporary tribute with much useful information, ed. Catherine Nugent, *Life Work of Thomas L. Nugent* (Stephenville, Texas: Catherine Nugent, 1896). For an illuminating study of the 1896 campaign, with special emphasis on Marion Butler, see Robert F. Durden, *The Climax of Populism* (Lexington: University of Kentucky Press, 1965). Although not specifically on Populism, students of the movement should consult two recent books of unusual interest: Stanley L. Jones, *The Presidential Election of 1896* (Madison: University of Wisconsin Press, 1964); and Paolo E. Coletta, *William Jennings Bryan: Political Evangelist, 1860–1908* (Lincoln: University of

Nebraska Press, 1964).

It would be difficult to list all of the works on general background or on factors and conditions affecting the movement, for
this would require selected bibliographies on agricultural history,
the labor movement, the status of the Negro, mortgage indebtedness, and countless other topics. Let me simply set down a small
number of studies which I find to be significant. On the problems
of agriculture and the history of agricultural organizations, one
should begin with the numerous writings of Paul W. Gates and
James C. Malin, and from there go on to Solon J. Buck, *The
Granger Movement* (Cambridge: Harvard University Press, 1913);
Fred A. Shannon, *The Farmer's Last Frontier* (New York: Farrar
and Rinehart, 1945); Allan G. Bogue, *From Prairie to Corn Belt*
(Chicago: University of Chicago Press, 1963); Theodore Saloutos,
Farmer Movements in the South, 1865–1933 (Berkeley and Los
Angeles: University of California Press, 1960); and Howard R.
Lamar, *Dakota Territory, 1861–1899* (New Haven: Yale University
Press, 1956). For a personal account of hard times in the prairie
states, see John Ise, *Sod and Stubble* (New York: Wilson-Erickson,
1936). The role of Negroes in Populism has been summarized in
two articles by Jack Abramowitz: "The Negro in the Agrarian
Revolt," *Agricultural History*, XXIV (1950), and "The Negro in
the Populist Movement," *Journal of Negro History*, XXXVIII
(1953). This subject is also treated by C. Vann Woodward in the
two books mentioned above, and in his *The Strange Career of Jim
Crow* (New York: Oxford University Press, 1955). An extremely
important case study is Helen G. Edmonds, *The Negro and Fusion
Politics in North Carolina, 1894–1901* (Chapel Hill: University of
North Carolina Press, 1951). Excellent background is provided in
Vernon L. Wharton, *The Negro in Mississippi, 1865–1890* (Chapel
Hill: University of North Carolina Press, 1947), and in William
A. Mabry, *The Negro in North Carolina Politics Since Reconstruc-
tion* (Durham: Duke University Press, 1940). Turning to mort-
gages and the crop-lien system, one finds three noteworthy studies:
Allan G. Bogue, *Money at Interest* (Ithaca: Cornell University
Press, 1955); Thomas D. Clark, "Imperfect Competition in the
Southern Retail Trade after 1865," *Journal of Economic History*,
III (*Supplement*, 1943), and the same author's "The Furnishing

and Supply System in Southern Agriculture since 1865," *Journal
of Southern History*, XII (1946).

For the critical literature on Populism, see Oscar Handlin,
"American Views of the Jew at the Opening of the Twentieth
Century," *Publications of the American Jewish Historical Society*,
XL (1951); Richard Hofstadter, *The Age of Reform: From Bryan
to F.D.R.* (New York: Alfred A. Knopf, 1955); and Daniel Bell,
ed., *The New American Right* (New York: Criterion Books, 1955).
For criticisms of the critics, see C. Vann Woodward, "The Populist
Heritage and the Intellectual," *American Scholar*, XXIX (1959–
60); Walter T. K. Nugent, *The Tolerant Populists* (Chicago: University
of Chicago Press, 1963); and the following articles by
Norman Pollack: "Hofstadter on Populism: A Critique of 'The
Age of Reform,'" *Journal of Southern History*, XXVI (1960);
"The Myth of Populist Anti-Semitism," *American Historical Review*,
LXVIII (1962); "Handlin on Anti-Semitism: A Critique of
'American Views of the Jew,'" *Journal of American History*, LI
(1964); "Fear of Man: Populism, Authoritarianism and the Historian,"
Agricultural History, XXXIX (1965); and "Ignatius Donnelly
on Human Rights: A Study of Two Novels," *Mid-America*,
XLVII (1965).

EDITOR'S NOTE

The selections in this volume appear as in their original form. No attempt has been made to indicate errors. The customary *sic* has been dispensed with on idiosyncratic grounds: the present writer feels that it would be condescending to correct what others have expressed, particularly when the expressions eloquently state their deepest convictions. The only alterations occur in the case of poorly set type, say an inverted letter, or when the size of headings is changed for the sake of uniformity. As for editorial comment, it seemed advisable for two reasons to keep the headnotes to a minimum length. This provides more room for the selections themselves, and encourages the reader to offer his own interpretation, without this writer looking over his shoulder. Extensive commentary has been included, however, at the beginnings of Parts Three through Five, and in other places where this writer felt inclined to develop particular points, such as the sketches of Henry D. Lloyd and James B. Weaver. Finally, when a choice had to be made between a chapter standing alone in a larger work, and passages scattered throughout that work which brought together the total argument, this writer generally chose the latter. Summaries of the omitted portions are enclosed within brackets.

The Populist Mind

PART ONE

THE GENERAL MOOD:
DEGRADATION, OPPRESSION,
DETERMINATION

---

1. The Alienated Individual

At the heart of the Populist critique of industrial America was the contention that the social order destroyed man's sense of being human. Far from liberating the capacities of the individual, far from being responsive to his growth and well-being, society, the Populists maintained, was transforming men into unthinking creatures, into brutalized units of an exploitative productive system. This feeling was expressed in an editorial written by Jay Burrows, himself a prominent official in the Northern Alliance during its early days, for the *Farmers' Alliance* of Lincoln, Nebraska.

The materialism of to-day does all the time seggregate human lives. Take a man for instance who labors hard from fourteen to sixteen hours a day to obtain the bare necessaries of life. He eats his bacon and potatoes in a place which might rather be called a den than a home; and then, worn out, lies down and sleeps. He is brutalized both morally and physically. He has no ideas, only propensities. He has no beliefs, only instincts. He does not, often cannot, read. His contact with other

---

Reprinted from *Farmers' Alliance* (Lincoln), May 7, 1891. Nebraska Historical Society.

people is only the relation of servant to master, of a machine to its director. How can you reach this man, how kindle the divine spark which is torpid in his soul, when he knows that it is greed that enforces the material labor that is crushing him down, when he feels it is the wage system that is stealing the fruits of his toil and abasing and enslaving him? Here is Humanity's problem. It involves all other problems, and all modern life. . . . This man's name is Million. He is all about us. He constitutes half the population of the world. How is he to have more time and more energy to develop his faculties except by lessening his hours of labor and increasing his wages? Can this be done under the present system? Has there been a better system in the world? Does not the problem of humanity demand that there shall be a better system?

There *must* be a better one. . . . The tendency of the competitive system is to antagonize and disassociate men. The survival of the fittest is a satanic creed, applicable to the savage creation, perhaps, but only in the broadest sense to men.

Humanity must rise to its own needs, or the soul of man will flee, and the senses be left alone to reign.

The actual state of society to-day is a state of war, active irreconcilable war on every side, and in all things. Deny it if you can. Competition is only another name for war. It means slavery to millions—it means the sale of virtue for bread—it means for thousands upon thousands starvation, misery and death. After four thousand years of life is this the best that we can achieve? If so, who cares how soon the end may come?

2. Industrial Slavery

Speaking in late July 1894, in the midst of the depression and just after the unsuccessful Pullman strike, Lorenzo D. Lewelling, the

---

Reprinted from Lorenzo D. Lewelling, speech of July 28, 1894. Kansas State Historical Society.

Populist governor of Kansas, placed the prevailing discontent into the larger context of the operation of the industrial system. In this speech he ranged over a wide variety of topics—from a condemnation of the survival of the fittest mentality to remarks on the concentration of wealth and power in American society—and in so doing, called attention to many of the grievances voiced by the Populists. As a young man in Iowa, Lewelling—true to the fashion of many Populist leaders—had a rich and varied career: school teacher (he graduated from Whittier College), newspaperman, and farmer. Removing to Wichita in 1887, he became a businessman and, three years later, an active Populist. Lewelling had, by his own admission, experienced the hard times of an earlier period at first hand when forced to wander in search of work during the 1870's.

The trouble has been, we have so much regard for the rights of property that we have forgotten the liberties of the individual. We have had some illustration of that in the great strike at Chicago and a number of other illustrations. I claim it is the business of the Government to make it possible for me to live and sustain the life of my family. If the government don't do that, what better is the Government to me than a state of barbarism and everywhere we slay, and the slayer in turn is slain and so on the great theatre of life is one vast conspiracy all creatures from the worm to man in turn rob their fellows. That my fellow citizens is the law of natural selection the survival of the fittest. Not the survival of the fittest, but the survival of the strongest. It is time that man should rise above it. . . .

Now, there are 350,000 able-bodied men in Kansas and their average individual earnings last year and the year before were $500. per man. That is what they earned on an average, but I might imagine some of you people here in this audience saying, "Well, I didn't get my share even of the $500." And I don't think you did. What has become of that $500. you were to get? It has gone where the wang-a-doodle mourneth for its first born. It went to pay excessive freight rates on commodities which we bought and sold, and then it went to pay interest on your mortgages. Why, I might tell, and I know something about it from experience, that the people of Kansas are paying 6%, 8%, 10%, and some as high as 12 and 15% per annum. Then, what is to become of us, my fellow citizens? Where are we going to? Don't you see pretty clearly we are going into a hole every year?

Now our friends have told us that the only trouble about this country and our condition is a "lack of confidence." And I saw an old farmer the other day who said he had been to market with a load of wheat. He said he got $7.50 for the 30 bushels of wheat that he had taken to town, and he bought a couple of pairs of shoes for the children, and a calico dress for his wife, and then he felt confident he had gone dead broke. . . . Still he had to pay his mortgage—And when his neighbor sold another load of wheat and still another load, and put his money in the bank and kept on accumulating in order to pay off the mortgage and finally the bank broke and then he said he had lost his confidence, and his patience too, and swore by the Great Horn Spoon, that hereafter he would vote the Populist ticket and vote for the kind of bank that never breaks and that is the Postal Savings Bank that is advocated by the Populist platform. . . .

I say now, it is the duty of government to protect the weak, because the strong are able to protect themselves. . . .

I believe, and I say it freely, that the working men and women of this country, many of them, are simply today in the shackels of industrial slavery. . . .

I do not believe it is possible, ever under the shining sun, while the present financial system continues, for the debt of the people of Kansas to be paid. I do not believe it is possible that the debt of the United States Government can be paid while the present financial condition exists.

All we want is a little relief, a little remedy. . . . Why, I would take the Colorado contingent of the Industrial Army and set them out in Colorado to digging the silver from the native hills and making money out of it. Why, my Republican friends say, these men are idlers, and vagabonds, they don't want to work, yet the fact remains that out in Colorado they actually fought each other to obtain the picks and shovels with which to do work for the city in order that they might obtain a pittance to provide for themselves and families. When the mines shut down . . . there were 30,000 men thrown out of employment in ten days in Colorado. They didn't know what to do nor where to go. They began drifting across the country, they naturally tended towards the great centers of civilization and a great many of them brought up in Chicago and there they joined the immense multitude like the sands of the sea and they gathered themselves together on the lake shore. There were 5,000 assembled together discussing their ways and means. They said to the people, the passers by, to the authorities of Chicago, "Give us bread for we are starving, give us work or give us bread," but instead of bread they did not get the proverbial stone, but they were kicked out of the way by the heavy boots of the policeman, and next day the Chicago papers came out and said, "Oh, there's nothing like leather for dispersing a mob." The mob dispersed harmless and armless, without evil intentions to anyone, driven out of the way by the kicks of the police and that too under the shadow of the statute of Liberty which overlooks the lake shore. . . .

I ask you now, what can the poor man do today that comes to you and says, I have hands to work with, I have bodily strength, I am willing to give all those for a morsel of bread . . . but you say, "I have no work to give you." What is he to do then? . . . Senator Ingles [Ingalls] told us some two years ago, there are over a million men in the United States who are in that condition, and today the number is swelled to three million. Oh, is it any wonder there are common wealers? Is it

any wonder there are anarchists? There is no greater crime
breeder in the world than poverty . . . I came here this evening
asking you to join with me in the organization of a great anti-
poverty society. Will you do it? (Cheers and cries of yes.)
. . . . They say that I am a "calamity howler." If that is so,
I want to continue to howl until those conditions are improved. . . .

What do we see today? When labor is to be crucified. . . .
We see the President of the U.S. throwing an armed force
across the border into Illinois, and other states, without so
much as inquiring whether or not it will be agreeable to the
authorities of the state itself. Not only that, we find in close
alliance with the power of the Executive, the Courts of the
Land. . . .

While I have talked to you about the condition of the laborer, the condition of the farmers is about the same all over
Kansas, and I am specially glad to know the farmers to be in
hearty sympathy with the cause of labor. Down in Arkansas
City, they are bringing in supplies day by day to supply the
men striking on the railroad. And I understand the same thing
is done here. A friend of mine who is nominated for senator
on the populist ticket had the audacity, my friends, to contribute to the striking laborers of that town. Today he is ar-
raigned by the United States Court and summoned to Topeka
and placed on trial for aiding and abetting the strikers against
the government of the United States.—Think of it!

And I find also that injunctions are already issued against
working men to prevent them from expressing an opinion. It
is not your right or privilege my fellow citizens to make prose-
lytes, anymore. . . . Under the decision of the United States
Court you have no right to convince a man to your opinion.
You have no right to ask a man to quit work today, no matter
what the cause. This is the position that some of the United
States Courts have taken today. This is whither we are driven,
my fellow citizens. . . .

[As for the condition of the farmer:] His earnings are naught. Add several ciphers together and you will have the sum of his profits this year and last. Take his wheat, which is worth twenty-five cents a bushel, and costs forty cents to raise it. How is he going to come out this year? I will tell you something: did you know that forty-three per cent of the homes of Kansas have already passed into the hands of land lords? I heard a man standing up in the pulpit . . . and discoursing loud and long over the evictions of the Irish tenants across the water and I will tell you we have got in the State of Kansas 10,000 people who are made homeless every year by the foreclosure of mortgages and this has been going on for several years. . . .

One of the means of contraction of the currency is the holding of money in the bank's vaults. Why does the banker keep it in the bank vaults? Because he is afraid to loan it to you and me, because we may not pay it back. Why don't you put your money in the bank? You say you are afraid the bank will break. . . . You are both "skeered."

What is the remedy? Take the Postal Savings bank. You can put your money in there and the government is security for it. . . . The bank isn't afraid there will be a run and so the money is kept in circulation and business is stimulated. . . .

We look at the city in a mass and we forget the individual sufferer. But these have gone on multiplying in Kansas until today one-tenth of the entire population of the United States is brought face to face with poverty. Six million people in this land of plenty are today suffering for bread. And I ask you again, is it any wonder that there are common wealers. Is it any wonder that there are anarchists, and I want to say further, we are traveling in the line of past history, we are in the same condition as a nation as that ancient Rome, when the currency of the people was contracted. . . . Remember when the currency contracts, your debts remain the same, only they get bigger, that is the law. A few years ago, a bushel of wheat would pay a dollar of your mortgage. Today it takes four bushel. . . .

And yet, the people down there in Rome said the same thing that the Republicans said to us last year . . . "Stand up for Rome." Rome was rich, and great and powerful. Rome was wonderful in her commercial importance and supremicy. Yet, remember my friends, that underneath the City of Rome in that great day of prosperity were the grinning skulls and bleaching bones of more than six millions of paupers and laborers who had been driven to despondency and death by the same conditions which seem—.

I ask you in Honor, are we not tending in the same direction? And shall the future historian say of you and me that we as a nation of free men, have you submitted to this despotism of greed until the star of our liberty has sunk into night? . . .

Relief will come, I believe this inspiration will be found in every heart. I believe the effort will be made by the people. Already great labor organizations are uniting themselves for battle, welded together in conduct and purpose and action. . . . Our path will be in conflict, but it will also be conquest. It must be so! The demands of the people will be heard. They must be heard.

It seems to me my friends that the dead sea of civilization grows wider year by year. That the yawning gulf between Dives and Lazarus becomes more and more impassible. On one side Gould and Vanderbilt—I have a list here of eighteen names ranging in wealth from twenty to a hundred and twenty-five millions of dollars, and yet, I say to you my fellow citizens that no man in America ever had the genious or brain to earn a million dollars honestly. He can't do it while the sun shines. Think of a man working at a dollar a day earning a million dollars! How long do you suppose it would take him.

I say we have the Goulds and Vanderbilts and Rockafellers on the one side—Why, Vanderbilt once deposited $50,000,000

of government bonds. How much money was that? The interest amounted to $5,000. About $3.50 a minute. . . . "Money is
power." That is what we are taught in school, but I tell you
today "power is money." The Goulds, Rockerfellers and Vanderbilt on the one side—Mr. Rockafeller, a great man, a rich
man. He owns a hundred acres over there on the Hudson
River. . . . They tore the old mansion down and built in its
place a private American residence that cost three million dollars. . . . And built a stable that cost thirty thousand dollars.
. . . This American simplicity. I don't blame Mr. Rockafeller
for doing this, he simply lives up to the custom of the times.
They say Mr. Rockafeller is a good man. Down here at Hutch-
ingson, a minister of the gospel preached to his hearers one
Sunday and told them what a great man Mr. Rockafeller was
because he contributed so liberally to the church, and because
he had established an institution of learning in Chicago. . . .

I simply say these men are arrayed on the one hand, and on
the other the industrial army. . . . 30,000 tenants annually
ejected in New York City. One tenth of all who die burried
in the potter's field. 10,000 farmers made homeless in Kansas
every year. . . . The great throbbing centers of civilization
seem to me to be dead to the instincts of humanity. . . .

The People's party has stepped into the breach between the
classes to demand justice for the poor as well as to the rich
and for every man. The machinery of government has been
arrayed against us. It seems to me that the Courts and Judges
of this country have become the mere tools and vassals and
jumping-jacks of the great corporations that pull the string
while the courts and judges dance. . . . So, these great corporations are forces against which we are to contend, but I am
willing . . . to place truth against the world. . . .

Men are nothing in a great contest of the people like this.
It matters not who is the leader so that all the people stand
together united for the great principles of humanity.

3. The Common Property of All

For Populists the impoverishment of the individual was all the more
inexcusable, all the more unnecessary, because America had the
productive potential for attaining conditions of abundance. It was
not industrialism but the social context in which technological
forces operated which was at fault. That social context was dedi-
cated to profits not men, Populists argued, and served to create the
very poverty that the machine could overcome. Frank Doster, a
prominent Kansas Populist and later the Chief Justice of the Kansas Supreme Court, developed this view in a speech at Topeka on
Labor Day, 1894.

Everything which goes to sustain his physical life, which enables him to conduct his daily toil, which makes existence
possible in this fierce competitive strife have become the
monopoly of others—others to whom he sustains only the
harshest and most exacting kind of contract relations. Formerly
the tools of agriculture were the wagon and the plow; the tools
of the worker in wood his plane and chisel and saw; the tools
of the worker in iron his hammer and anvil and forge; and
they were sufficient for all the purposes of industrial life. Now
the terrible elements of physical nature which the gods can
scarce bridle or control—steam, electricity, compressed air—
are utilized to do the work of man. But these, the common
property of all, have been made the monopoly of the few,
have been turned aside from the beneficent ends for which
designed, to serve the selfish purposes of avarice and greed.
In the face of the power exerted by the monopolists of these
tremendous engines of industry and commerce the republican

Reprinted from *Advocate* (Topeka), Sept. 19, 1894. Kansas State Historical Society.

and democratic parties stand paralyzed—hypnotized as it were, unable to control it or give it direction and shape for common good.

Against the tyrannical exercise of this power the People's Party in behalf of the laborers of the land protests. The failure to adapt the legislation of the country to the strange conditions which this new life has forced upon us is the cause in greater part of our industrial ills.

. . . The Populist Party proposes as the only means to the desired end to utilize the power of the combined whole, to bring the power of the social mass to bear upon the rebellious individuals who thus menace the peace and safety of the state. It says that the subjects of those monopolies and trusts are public in their nature, and that the powers exercised through them are in reality the functions and agencies of government itself. It would have the government, that is, the people, assert their rightful dominion over the same, and as the philosophic basis of its claim it prescribes at least two political formulae: One that it is the business of the government to do that for the individual which he can not successfully do for himself, and which other individuals will not do for him upon just and equitable terms; the other, that the industrial system of a nation, like its political system, should be a government of and for and by the people alone.

4. The "Modern Condition"

The disparity between the potentiality and the actual accomplishments of the industrial system long attracted the notice of the Topeka *Advocate,* the leading Populist newspaper in Kansas. In the following editorial, the *Advocate,* focusing on the use of labor-

Reprinted from *Advocate* (Topeka), April 11, 1894. Kansas State Historical Society.

saving machinery, suggests that this disparity will increase rather than diminish, that men will become even more displaceable, as industrial capitalism continues.

Has society, as a whole, derived the benefits from the use of labor-saving machinery that it might have done under a different system? We think not. Under the prevailing system the capitalist has been the chief beneficiary. . . .

When a labor-saving machine was invented, instead of using it to displace men, it should have been used to reduce the hours of labor, thereby continuing the opportunities of all to provide the comforts and luxuries of life for every member of society. . . .

Let us admit, for our present purpose, that there is more of everything produced than the necessities of the people require. The fact that all are not supplied, then, shows that there is something wrong in our system. . . . Look at the multitudes who have been but recently thrown out of employment, and whose families have been destitute in consequence. . . . It is cruel, it is inhuman, to attribute these conditions to laziness, drunkenness and incompetency. They are the natural product of a false and vicious system by which the few grow rich beyond all human need, and the many are doomed to eternal poverty and want. One of the causes of this "modern condition" is the monopoly of machinery and other means of production and distribution by which the few are benefited and the many are deprived of fair opportunities in life.

Contrast this "modern condition" with what might be attained by a proper use of the instrumentalities of modern production and distribution. Suppose, as we propose, that machinery, instead of being used to displace labor, were used to diminish the hours that each should be employed. This would apply to the farmer, as well as to the man who works in the shop, under a proper distribution of labor. Under such a system, no one who has the disposition to work would need to be idle. . . .

Work should be so distributed that each should do his share and receive the reward of his labor. Work enough should be done to supply the demand of the whole people for every comfort and luxury of life; and the time not required for such production should be devoted to rest, to mental culture, to social intercourse and recreation.

5. Landlords and Tenants

An unknown farmer from North Platte, Nebraska, strongly dissents from the thesis that overproduction has been responsible for agrarian discontent. In this letter to the editor of the *Farmers' Alliance,* he calls for a movement of farmers and workers—this, in the infancy of Populism—to bring an end to monopolistic practices.

The farmers know well that if they had got the benefit of everything they have produced since they have been farming, there would be no need for them to be in debt now.

The laborer knows that if he had been paid the value of his services he could now have a home of his own. . . .

The man hunting work knows there is plenty of work to do. He sees there is no "over-production" to cause men to be idle. For if he sees the elevators and cribs full of corn in Illinois, at the same time he knows of the hungry stock and hungry people in the west. And before when he saw the west over-loaded with corn, which the people had to burn because they could get no coal, at the same time he knew of the thousands of tons of coal banked in Illinois; of 20,000 hungry and idle miners. . . .

We do not take our enemy's explanation any more. We look away from home. We see the farmers and laborers, the wealth producers of every section of our country, getting poorer each

Reprinted from J.M.C. to the editor, *Farmers' Alliance* (Lincoln), March 21, 1891. Nebraska Historical Society.

year, and the monopolists and money changers waxing richer and richer.

Then we think that the manipulation of money and monopoly are the causes which bring about this state of affairs. Who says we are not right? . . .

Our platform is broad enough for every farmer, mechanic and laborer; for every Union Labor, United Knight of Labor and Alliance man in the country to stand on and to fight for. . . .

We cannot boast that this country allows each man a home because we are tenants and can hardly make enough to pay rent; we can no longer send help to the tenants of Ireland because we are in the same conditions; we have been reduced from freeholders to a class of cringing renters. The lands must be used and our landlords can exact whatever they ask. . . . Let me say we cannot "regulate" the railroads and usurers because we can not get out of their power. Already this monstrous landlord and tenant system is getting to assume threatening attitude and it is not unreasonable to suppose that our land shall be taken even before we get the other monops under control.

Already the people are familiar with the fact that great bodies of land are held by individuals and that the mortgages are the proper means to take the lands and homes out of the hands of the bread-winners and gather it into the hands of individuals.

6. On Economic Trends

The selections which follow represent editorial comments in the *Farmers' Alliance* on the nature of industrial capitalism. Common to all five is the position that competition has led to monopoly, and that in the process, the laboring population is being reduced to the

Reprinted from *Farmers' Alliance* (Lincoln), Sept. 6, 1890, Feb. 28, 1891, two from Oct. 22, 1891, March 3, 1892. Nebraska Historical Society.

subsistence level of living. Throughout the discussion runs the theme that such a society is defective at its very core, and hence, that a fundamental alteration of that society is necessary.

I

There is now being fought in Nebraska the fiercest political battle ever known in the history of the state. Upon its decision hangs something more than the mere choice between two masters; but a choice, rather, as between principle and party, right and wrong, justice and injustice, liberty and slavery. It is a conflict between plutocracy on the one hand and the people on the other. Between millionaires and the masses. Between the money bags of the east and the corn and wheat and beef and pork of the west. Between the insatiable greed of organized wealth and the rights of the great plain people, as vouchsafed by the constitution.

It is idle to educe proofs. The simple fact that, despite a generation of hard toil, the people are poor today, mortgage-ridden and distressed, is sufficient evidence that the whole system under which they have lived is a lie and an imposture. They have produced but they possess not. They have amassed wealth for other people to enjoy while they themselves are almost without the necessaries of life. They have builded palaces for the rich while they themselves live in sod houses, and so far from luxury, are denied even the common comforts of life, which no one on earth has a right to enjoy to the exclusion of him that earned them.

The present cruelly unjust system, therefore, is fast working the hopeless pauperization and degradation of the toiling masses. The great middle class, including the farmer, is gradually being undermined and destroyed. It has been boastingly said that there will yet be two classes in this country, the very rich and the very poor; in other words, the master and the servant. To this end, legislation both state and national has directly tended, consciously or unconsciously, since 1861. And in keeping herewith, whereas the farmers owned nearly three-fourths of the aggregate wealth of the whole country in 1850, they barely own one-fourth of it in 1890. . . .

At the present time, twenty-five billions of dollars, or just half the entire wealth of the nation, are in the hands of twenty-five thousand aristocrats, while three-fifths of the whole wealth is cornered by thirty thousand persons out of a total population of sixty-five millions! Comment is unnecessary. Too plain is it to the patriotic vision that our country is fast going the way of Egypt, of Greece, of Rome, that is, to the certain death that awaits all nations alike when the wealth of all falls into the hands of the grasping few. Then is liberty at an end, and then, as in all the despotisms of the past, a nation of brow-beaten slaves will produce wealth for a handful of soulless tyrants to possess and enjoy.

The impending struggle, then, not only involves the safety of our homes, but the cause of liberty as well; the preservation of our free institutions, the very existence of our beloved country. Confronted by such dangers, and with such a stake hanging in the balance, what is the duty of the present hour? . . . It is to keep our eyes unwaveringly set on the *main issue,* the rights and liberties of the people as against the arrogant encroachments of the money power. It is to firmly and persistently demand a just and adequate solution of the problems of money, land, and transportation, that industry may be fostered and all labor fully rewarded. It is to check by every lawful means the future concentration of wealth, and to destroy forever the iniquitous domination of railroad and other corporate power in the politics of our state and nation.

II

The plutocracy of to-day is the logical result of the individual freedom which we have always considered the pride of our system. The theory of our government has been and is that the individual should possess the very greatest degree of liberty consistent, not with the greatest good of the greatest number, but with the very least legal restraint compatible with law and order. Individual enterprise was allowed unlimited scope. From this beginning the present development has been reached. Individual enterprise grew until its realistic achievements excelled the most extravagant dreams of song or story. When the possibilities of its conceptions passed the bounds of individual achievement accretions of other individuals took place. . . . An artificial individual was created . . . and was named the corporation. This individual, the creation of the law, soon began to bend to its uses the forms and powers of the law. While in its nature and development it is only the original and cherished principle of individual liberty, it has absorbed the liberties of the community and usurped the power of the agency that created it. By its gigantic combinations, its control of the money of the nation, by its gradual building up of a system of indebtedness of colossal magnitude, making every agency of exchange tributary to it, it has turned toward its coffers every golden stream—diverted into its treasuries the revenues of the nation. By it the toiling millions have been made the tools of a few plutocrats.

. . . The blind selfishness that led the slaveholder to demand a larger dominion for the safety of his peculiar institution, leads the plutocratic millionaire to demand larger expansion for his already over-grown privileges. The greed that a thousand slaves would not satisfy two hundred millions in bonds will not appease. Individualism incorporated has gone wild. . . .

The corporation has absorbed the community. The community must now absorb the corporation—must merge itself into it. Society must enlarge itself to the breadth of humanity. A stage must be reached in which each will be for all and all for each. The welfare of the individual must be the object and end of all effort.

III

The number unemployed is made to grow constantly greater and wages less by the pressure of poverty, our employing and distributing system being an autocrat-producing, mass-enslaving, pauper-manufacturing system.

The beautiful economic law of the competitive system reduces wages by an iron rule to the lowest level (at last) on which the workers can live and rear children to recruit their ranks. Observe, by this law the profit to the idle capitalist is made to increase with the increase of the number unemployed. His wealth depends upon their destitution; his fortune grows relatively as the poverty of the poor makes them powerless. . . . To make him a millionaire thousands must be over burdened, filled with anxiety, deprived of a share that they produce, and suffer from constant deprivation.

Why is all this necessary? It is not necessary. By the aid of invention, machinery and free motive power the work of the world can be performed in about half the time, with less than half the labor that was formerly necessary. . . .

The robber must be made to disgorge. The monopolist must be forced to yield room. The money-loaner must be dethroned and driven to labor for himself. The means of production must be placed in possession of the people. And to secure these reforms the people's independent party is organized.

IV

The laws which lead to all oppression, and the privation and suffering it causes, are class laws, laws which give monopolies, special privileges and immunities to a part of the people, making the rest in consequence subject to them. . . .

The people's party has sprung into existence not to make the black man free, but to emancipate all men; not to secure political freedom to a class, but to gain for all *industrial* freedom, without which there can be no political freedom; no lasting people's government. It stands upon the declaration that "all men are created equal," having equal right to live, labor and enjoy the fruits of their labor. It teaches that none should have power to enjoy without labor. It demands equal opportunities and exact justice in business for each individual, and proposes to abolish all monopolistic privileges and power. It is the first party that has comprehended the great question of injustice and proposed an adequate remedy for the evils of society. It is a grand new party which shall bind together the people for mutual help as well as defense, a party organized to dethrone the money kings, the monopolist despots, the ruling class; and which shall make of this nation an industrial democracy in which each citizen shall have an equal interest, and his own home secured.

V

Now what is life and so-called liberty if the means of subsistence are monopolized? Hunger-scourged, the dependent laborers must accept the wages that independent employers choose to offer, and the wages are made so low that the dependent cannot become independent. More are reduced to dependence than rise to independence. The army begging work is every year increasing, the small capitalist is being crowded down into the ranks of the wage earners by bigger, richer business rivals, and capital is concentrating and drawing to itself all power. Half a million poor emigrants from Europe are also each year pressing into our work-begging dependent class and the steadily increasing competition can no longer be relieved by going west. All land which the poor can make a living on is taken.

Railroad kings have also risen with power under present law to exact slavish and impoverishing tribute from all, and gold, by devilish inventive genius, has been made to fetter and

rob and rob and ruin at the will of the bankers, and the creditor and capitalist class.

The people, the producing classes, have arisen; they have
spoken; and they will perform.

7. Farm Poverty

A Texas farmer, while calling merely for an activated Grange in
1890, discusses the kinds of conditions which prompted farmers
to adopt an increasingly radical position. The writer points out that
tenantry is rising and that agriculture, despite the hard work of
farmers and abundant crops, is engaged in at a loss.

Most men that I talk with thinks the Grange will have to rise
and come again, though the same old Tale of years, is the
Cotton Gone, the money is all gone, two. one great Discour-
agin fact here is so many Farmers dont own theire Farms I
cant tell the per cent But here in the Eastern part of Falls,
and Western part of Limestone is a greate Nomber of them. . . .

Every agent, pedler and Every profession of men is Fleec-
ing the Farmer, and by the time the World Gets their Liveing
out of the *Farmer* as we have to Feed the World We the
Farmer has nothing Left, but a Bear Hard Liveing[.] I live
in the midst of a thick Heavey populated county of Farmers
6 miles from any Town and talk Freely with them as to how
much they make[.] And all tell me the same Hard Tale money
all gone. . . .

We have a working Energetic people that would improve
if they could and Farmers in these two countys is successfull
in Farming. we all make it but some way we cant Keepe it. I

J. C. Peoples to A. W. Buchanan, Dec. 12, 1890. J. A. Rose Papers,
The University of Texas Library, Texas Archives Division.

want yout to write to me and tell me what is the matter Can
our Legislator do any thing That will give us any Reliefe. I am
Greatly discouraged in Farming[.]

8. Imperial Tendencies

Thomas E. Watson was the leader of Georgia Populism. He was
also a good deal more; he was one of the half dozen nationally
prominent figures in the movement. Watson's activities made him,
particularly after the death of Leonidas LaFayette Polk in 1892, the
center of reform ferment in the southeast. That he was a congressman (and head of the independent caucus in Congress in 1891–
1892) is merely one aspect of his career. Perhaps more important
to the Populist movement in the long run was Watson's strong
commitment to educating the masses, both Negro and white, on
the political and economic problems of the period. It was his belief
that the people themselves must take the initiative in shaping a
more democratic society. When Watson stated in December 1891
that Populism was "a movement of the masses, an uprising of the
people, and they and not the politicians will direct it," he was expressing that dimension to his activities which was of greatest significance. As editor of the *People's Party Paper,* as author of
campaign books for the party, as speaker day in and day out, he
sustained the momentum of Populism in his state even in years
when there were no elections, and he activated the masses to think
and to discuss the issues.

After his first term in Congress, Watson was flagrantly counted
out in the next two elections. As C. Vann Woodward shows, Watson's opponent in 1892 received twice as many votes in Augusta
as there were legal voters, and this performance was more than
duplicated in the succeeding election. And yet, Watson persisted

---

Reprinted from *People's Party Paper* (Atlanta), April 14, 1893. Library of Congress.

in the face of such fraud and intimidation to continue the work of agitation. He shared the speaker's platform with Negroes, attacked the corporations in editorials, sought while still in Congress to abolish the Pinkerton system, introduced the resolution providing for rural free delivery, and was in the forefront in calling attention to national problems. He prepared the way very early for independency in the South by taking an active part in the fight against the jute-bagging trust in the late 1880's, and in so doing, helped the Alliance movement gain a sense of its emerging power. Watson also prepared the way for a break with the Democratic party by challenging Henry Grady's New South ideology and its glowing picture of industrial progress made possible by northern capital and one-party rule. When Watson ran as the People's party vice-presidential candidate in 1896, he was once again upholding the view that independent political action was a necessity, and was once again using a political campaign as the vehicle to acquaint the people with the issues.

Then, after the new century began, Watson became his own worst enemy. There is still no fully adequate explanation for what happened to him, and perhaps there never will be. But whatever the explanation, it is clear that he reversed himself on the very humanitarian issues he fought so hard for during the vital years of Populism. His subsequent stand became a living denial of all that distinguished the early Tom Watson, particularly his defense of Negro rights. Before the decade ended, anti-Negro and anti-Catholic feeling permeated his outlook, and to this was added, during the Leo Frank case of 1913–1915, a strongly anti-Semitic stand. He later went on to the United States Senate, and was still something of an economic radical, but this was a man the pre-1900 Tom Watson would not have known, and indeed would have bitterly opposed. In the Populist period he was the leader of the underprivileged of both races, and always at great sacrifice to his own personal career.

In this first selection from Watson's speeches and writings, one finds him deploring the condition of the individual and contending that the United States is fast taking on the traits of a feudal society. This editorial was prompted by a court decision directed against the strike of the locomotive engineers.

This Government was founded upon the distinct proposition that Royalty was a tyrrany and a humbug, and that the ways of Royalty brought pride, luxury and corruption to the higher classes, while they brought poverty, suffering and degradation to the great mass of the underprivileged. . . .

Having become an empire in territory, and in wealth, and in power, we seek to become an empire in outward appearance, in the display of armies and navies, in the geegaws of royal ceremonial and observances, and in the maintenance of splendid embassies at foreign capitals.

Who shall gather round himself the servile attentions, the abject flatteries, and the degrading prostrations of the court circle?

Why, the President, of course; the man whom our masters, the corporations, set up over us.

Who shall constitute our cod-fish aristocracy? Why, the millionaires, of course; the men whose purses pay the bills for stuffing ballot boxes, the men who dictate the class legislation on which they fatten, the men who are swiftly laying the foundation, in this country, for a more brutal and godless and rapacious nobility than ever rode, lance in rest, over the peasantry of Feudal Europe.

For the first time in one hundred years, it is boldly announced that we have slyly gone forward until we have a navy of Battle-ships superior, in some respects, to anything that floats.

For the first time it is announced that we can go twenty-one hundred miles into the ocean and seize upon Islands which do not belong to us and are not necessary to us.

. . . For the first time it is boldly declared, by Judicial decision, that organized Capital can coerce Labor, and that organized Labor is forbidden to make effective protest. The old baronial right to "bind a laborer to the soil" finds its twin-brother in this modern corporation right to bind the laborer to his Engine.

For the blindest can see that if an Engineer can be bound to his engine, willing or unwilling, the weaver can be likewise bound to the loom, the clerk to the counter, the herdsman to his herd, the carpenter to his bench and the miner to his pick.

Thus does the individual right sink, while the corporate right mounts up. The very essence of a Republic is the right of the individual. The very essence of monarchy is the subjugation of the individual.

In all essential respects, therefore, the Republic of our fathers is dead. The remnants of its form, its outward semblance, may be left, but its animating spirit is gone.

In all vital things and in every controlling tendency we have an Empire, proud of the servility with which it apes the royal customs it once despised, and shamelessly constant in plundering the people it once pretended to love.

Day by day the power of the individual sinks. Day by day the power of the classes, of the corporations, rises. And every loss to the individual is a loss to the Republic, while every gain of the corporations rivets a fresh link in the chain of the modern Feudalism.

9. Modern Feudalism

The thesis that American society was fast approximating the conditions of feudalism was heard on numerous occasions before W. J. Ghent published *Our Benevolent Feudalism* in 1902. Here, in a

---

William Sage to Henry D. Lloyd, April [no day], 1895. Lloyd Papers, State Historical Society of Wisconsin.

letter from one of Henry Demarest Lloyd's correspondents, is but another expression of the feeling that the United States had a clearly defined power structure and one which was incompatible with democratic government.

We are living in a state of modern feudalism under a Commercial despotism more powerful than those other despotisms of the past, because with the advent of steam and electricity its power for injury is greater.

This state of affairs will last until the majority of the people realize their true condition and are not misled, by the waving of the american flag, into the belief that they actually live in a Republic "where *all* have an equal chance"—not intimidated by the fear of being called a "*socialist*." Your work will certainly aid them.

Which will come first the "enlightenment" or the end of the Republic is the question. One or the other must come within fifty years—perhaps much sooner.

I sometimes think that in the destiny of nations it is not *our* lot to be the *enduring* Republic but rather the "terrible example" to show future "free" Governments that they cannot possibly exist except on a foundation of actual freedom—The ownership of all the nations wealth by the people.

10. The Corporation Versus Civil Liberty

James H. Davis, the most effective Populist lecturer in Texas, did indeed earn his nickname of "Cyclone" on the campaign trail and off. He was among other things a school teacher and lawyer, but was at all times, as C. Vann Woodward points out, "a born dis-

Reprinted from James H. Davis, *A Political Revelation* (Dallas: The Advance Publishing Company, 1894), pp. 242, 244-245, 251.

senter," a towering man who never tired of expounding Jeffersonian doctrine on the platform and in his writings. In this brief excerpt from *A Political Revelation,* Davis comments on the nature of corporations.

These corporations, being artificial creations invested with authority to act as natural persons, they are moved only by an exhaustless greed for lucre, without one human sympathy.

They are permitted to acquire land, the great source and support of life, and with the mighty power of the capital which they concentrate, to speculate in its price, at the expense of natural persons.

The continuation of their existence, and their responsibility for their obligations, which is limited to capital invested, gives them a fearful advantage over natural persons, pursuing them with the same objects.

Being soulless, artificial and intangible, they act only through created agencies. Thus natural persons who own and move their power, look to them only for an increase of gains, and feel no personal concern for the moral quality of the acts which produce money.

Their power enables them to render abortive the individual efforts of labor for just remuneration, when invested in competing enterprises.

Surely we should expect strong reasons to authorize the continuance and increase of such a gigantic man-power, with soulless existence, moving, acting and dealing in the walks of men.

. . . In proportion as men are educated, and encouraged by their government to look alone to their individual intelligence and energy in providing for themselves, just to that extent is the spirit of civil liberty fostered and protected. On the other hand, just in proportion as the organic structure or practices of a government, permit or extend paternal aid in helping the individual man, that aid will in some way be appropriated for the benefit of the few and not the many. That aid will, through circumstance, artifice, favoritism or fraud, be used to increase the gains of capital and not the wages of labor; and while building up a depraved lust for place and power in the few, it will render discontented with their lot those who labor for their bread.

We live in an era when homely truths like these, such as would have been boldly spoken fifty years ago, without being questioned, are now whispered with bated breath, and that he who speaks plainly of the bad influence of this artificial power among natural persons, incurs the risk of being suspected of communism. But if there is any truth valuable to be known, next to that which will effect us after death, it is that which effects our freedom here; and civil liberty is never in such deadly peril as when men deceive themselves as to its dangers.

No one will deny that the harsh and inflexible rules with which corporate power administers its capital and directs its agencies, are such as no manly and generous mind would sanction. The individual is merged in the money-machine of which he is an integral part, and the morality of its action is the morality of the company, not his; nor is he unhappy over it so long as it produces gain. Thus its reacting influence on the man, corrupts and degrades, until at last a sort of financial self-respect will constrain him first to excuse, and then to defend all the means, no matter how corrupt, which were used to bring him a fortune.

. . . I believe that civil liberty is in jeopardy when the aspirations of men are suppressed or exercised by the sufferance of these artificial creations, controlling almost boundless wealth, whose influence is vast enough to shape the laws of the government which created them, and which, knowing no such thing as humanity or patriotism, recognize no duty except that of increasing their wealth and power.

11. The Dangers of Monopoly

W. Scott Morgan's subtitle to his history of the Agricultural Wheel and the Southern Alliance, *The Impending Revolution,* promises a greater militancy than the volume actually contains. Yet there are several strongly worded indictments of monopolistic practices, as this selection indicates. Here, as early as 1889, Morgan also captured a sense of the groundswell of discontent and the desire for change among the farmers.

. . . The agricultural masses, the most numerous and important of any class of people forming the great body of the republic, and whose interests are identical, are kept divided upon the great issues which affect their welfare. They are robbed by an infamous system of finance; they are plundered by transportation companies; they are imposed upon by an unjust system of tariff laws; they are deprived of their lands and other property by an iniquitous system of usury; they are fleeced by the exorbitant exactions of numerous trusts; they are preyed upon by the merchants, imposed upon by the lawyers, misled by the politician and seem to be regarded as the legitimate prey of all other classes. Monopoly names the price of what they have to sell, and charges them what it pleases for what they are compelled to buy. The farmer may hold his crop in vain, for when he does put it on the market he finds that the same manipulators govern and fix the price of his products. Individual effort is fruitless. The relentless, remorseless and unyielding grasp of monopoly is upon every avenue of trade and commerce. Extortion is demanded with an audacity that was never surpassed by the Dick Turpins or Jack Ketches of English

---

Reprinted from W. Scott Morgan, *History of the Wheel and Alliance, and the Impending Revolution* (Fort Scott, Kansas: J. H. Rice & Sons, 1889), pp. 15-18.

highways. They lay tribute with as much authority as the vassal lords and princes of feudal times. If they are asked what right they have to do this, their answer would be the same as the highwayman's: "Because we can. It is a private affair of our own." When this state of affairs exists throughout the whole country; when these modern barons are levying tribute on everything the farmer sells and all that he buys, is it to be wondered at, that the law of self-preservation is forcing him to unite with his fellow sufferers to repel these encroachments upon his rights? Is it expected that he is to apologize for making a united effort to repel the invader? The organization of farmers is the outgrowth of an invasion of their natural rights. Such an organization was that of the Grange. If it only partially succeeded, it was not on account of a lack of honest effort, but because it did not go far enough to reach the root of the evils of which it complained. It sought to correct existing abuses by abolishing the middle-man. This would afford but partial relief. The man who was in sight suffered, but the hidden enemy laughed in derision. It disarmed itself by prohibiting political discussion. The root of the evil lay in the laws. Monopolies exist by law, are chartered by law, and should be controlled by law. A trust is a conspiracy against legitimate trade. It is against the interests of the people and the welfare of the public. It is demoralizing in its influence, inconsistent with free institutions and dangerous to our liberties. To participate in a trust should be a crime subject to severe punishment. Trust is only another name for monopoly. Monopoly is wielding a greater power in the government than the people. While general discontent prevails, the masses of the people who suffer all the evils of class legislation have been disunited, and charging each other with being the cause of their ills. But the light of a new era is dawning. The farmers have begun to realize that a law that is good for one of them is beneficial to all; that their interests are identical, and that the only hope of reform is to lay down all prejudice and make

a united effort. In the North, in the South, everywhere, the
farmers are organizing. They are adopting systems of trade
and studying questions of political economy as they never did
before. Mistakes may occur, as no doubt they will. Their track
may be strewn with wrecks of failures; but they will move on;
they cannot do otherwise; self-preservation drives them to
unity of action. . . .

The independent manhood of the country is rising up in
defense of its liberties. An army of oppressed producers are
organizing for victory. They are marshalling their hosts on the
hilltops of freedom. Upon their banner they have inscribed:
"Liberty, Justice and Equality." A million hearts are beating
in response to this sentiment, and millions of arms are ready
to defend it. The march of this mighty army is already felt by
the enemy, intrenched behind the fortresses of King Mammon.
With flying banners and an irresistible force, they are moving,
inspired with a confidence that says the victory is already
won. The Wheel and Alliance stand to-day like a young army
flushed with victory, without regret for the past, or fear for
the future. Let us fondly hope that their mission may be accomplished, and peace, prosperity and happiness may be the
inheritance which they bequeath to future generations.

12. Six Farmers Confront the Hard Times

The sense of degradation keenly felt by many Populists was more
than an awareness of not having attained equal rights and human

---

Halvor Harris to Ignatius Donnelly, Jan. 29, 1891, Donnelly Papers,
Minnesota Historical Society; W. M. Taylor to editor, *Farmers' Alliance*
(Lincoln), Jan. 10, 1891, Nebraska Historical Society; W. T. McCulloch
to Donnelly, April [no day] 1892, Donnelly Papers; M. F. Blankenship to
editor, *Custer County Beacon* (Broken Bow, Neb.), March 24, 1892,
Nebraska Historical Society; Susan Orcutt to Lorenzo D. Lewelling,
June 29, 1894, Lewelling Papers, Kansas State Historical Society; W. R.
Christy to L. P. Broad, Dec. 28, 1894, Lewelling Papers.

dignity. For them, there were even more pressing problems: the hard facts of daily survival. Men felt degraded because they were slowly starving, were losing their homes, were experiencing directly in their own lives the deprivations created by the existing system, deprivations which served as the basis for their larger and more philosophic critique. Thus, it is important to note that loss of meaning in one's life was not only a philosophic grievance, but an economic reality. In the six letters which follow, the reasons are revealed for such demands as the return of excessive railroad lands to the people, the need for a readily available supply of credit at low interest rates, and government aid to those who are living on the marginal lands of drought-stricken areas. The first is from a farmer in Bigwoods, Minnesota; the second, which points out that many farmers are being dispossessed, is written by a Nebraskan to his state's leading radical agrarian paper; the third, a more generalized complaint against tenantry, comes from the president of the Griggs county Alliance in Jessie, North Dakota; the fourth is by one who had already lost his farm in Custer county, Nebraska, and was now starting again in the Oklahoma Territory; and the last two are from western Kansas.

I

In the minds of the forlorne and the unprotected Poor People of this and other states I might say I am one of those Poor and unprotected. One of those which have settled upon the socalled Indemnity Land of the Minn St Paul and Manitoba now the great Northern. I settled on this Land in good Faith Built House and Barn Broken up Part of the Land. Spent years of hard Labor in grubing fencing and Improving are they going to drive us out like tresspassers wife and children a sickly wife with Poor Health enough Before and give us away to the Corporations how can we support them. When we are robed of our means.   they will shurely not stand this   we must Decay and Die from Woe and Sorow We are Loyal Citicens

and do Not Intend to Intrude on any R.R. Corporation   we
Believed and still do Believe that the RR Co has got No Legal
title to this Land in question   We Love our wife and children
just as Dearly as any of you But how can we protect them
give them education as they should wen we are driven from
sea to sea. . . .

II

This season is without a parallel in this part of the country.
The hot winds burned up the entire crop, leaving thousands
of families wholly destitute, many of whom might have been
able to run through this crisis had it not been for the galling
yoke put on them by the money loaners and sharks—not by
charging 7 per cent. per annum, which is the lawful rate of
interest, or even 10 per cent., but the unlawful and inhuman
country destroying rate of 3 per cent. a month, some going
still farther and charging 50 per cent per annum. We are
cursed, many of us financially, beyond redemption, not by the
hot winds so much as by the swindling games of the bankers
and money loaners, who have taken the money and now are
after the property, leaving the farmer moneyless and homeless. . . . I have borrowed for example $1,000. I pay $25 besides to the commission man. I give my note and second mortgage of 3 per cent of the $1,000, which is $30 more. Then I
pay 7 per cent. on the $1,000 to the actual loaner. Then be-
sides all this I pay for appraising the land, abstract, recording,
etc., so when I have secured my loan I am out the first year
$150. Yet I am told by the agent who loans me the money, he
can't stand to loan at such low rates. This is on the farm, but
now comes the chattel loan. I must have $50 to save myself.
I get the money; my note is made payable in thirty or sixty
days for $35, secured by chattel of two horses, harness and
wagon, about five times the value of the note. The time comes
to pay, I ask for a few days. No I can't wait; must have the

money. If I can't get the money, I have the extreme pleasure of seeing my property taken and sold by this iron handed money loaner while my family and I suffer.

III

As We are about to have our first great Battle in this State between Corporate Greed, and the great Plain People, the Strugle will be a Desperate one, and must be fought to a finish. Determining, whether it shall be Masters, and Slaves, or a free People. in fact as well as in Name. And few, Reading thinking Men in America, Deny the Slavery of the Masses. to the Money Power of our Country, and a large Portion of our People, having lost all faith in our present Political Parties. for any Reforms. that would wrest the Masses of our People from Corporate Greed. Or give them any Rights, that Corporate Greed would have to respect It does not appear, that we are Destined to Slavery of one Kind or another, For the Slavery of to Day. Is but of a little different Kind from that of old. While in former Days it was necessary, that the Masters Keep within reach of their Slaves. in order to reap the Profits of their Toil. . . . And there is no Denying. that the Masses have literally slept, the Sleep that brings on Tenantry and Serfdom. and the Partizan Hireling Press have depended upon our Ignorance, and their Power to fool us, and have taken unto themselves. leases, for Prevarication. Missrepresentation and Slander. which is a Menace. to the Moral. Social and financial welfare of every Honest Citizen, and Bodes the Destruction of this Republic. and our People must be put on their guard. Taught not, only the remedy but how to apply it, in order to rid our Land of this Blighting. Blasting Curse, which is undermining. Honest true Manhood in every Department of Life. where they Will not be made Jumping Jacks, at their Beck or call.

IV

I had a mortgage on my team, like all my brother farmers, of $64.50. I was given to understand that this must be paid. To borrow money was out of the question. Nothing was left for me to do but haul off corn, hogs, etc., and pay it. I went to work, hauled off my corn and hogs and sold my hay and paid it. I had made calculations and found I would have no feed, seed, or even bread and meat. . . . I did not know what to do. I received a letter from my uncle in Oklahoma, stating there was plenty of work here at good wages. There was no work, as you all know, in Custer county. After taking all things in careful consideration I concluded I would come to Oklahoma where I could get work. Before reaching this conclusion it cost me many a bitter tear and sleepless night.

V

I take my Pen In hand to let you know that we are Starving to death   It is Pretty hard to do without any thing to Eat hear in this God for saken country we would of had Plenty to Eat if the hail hadent cut our rye down and ruined our corn and Potatoes   I had the Prettiest Garden that you Ever seen and the hail ruined It and I have nothing to look at   My Husband went a way to find work and came home last night and told me that we would have to Starve   he has bin in ten countys and did not Get no work   It is Pretty hard for a woman to do with out any thing to Eat when She dosent no what minute She will be confined to bed   If I was In Iowa I would be all right   I was born there and raised there   I havent had nothing to Eat to day and It is three oclock[.]

VI

We are worried over what our Poor People of our county are to do for fuel to keep them warm this winter. . . . there are at least ⅔ of the People that have to depend on Cow chips for fuel & as the cattle had to be Sold off verry close that its been difficult to get them. Some have went as far as 13 miles to get them. the thermometer this morning was 16 below zero & .4 or 5 inches of snow on the ground, under those circumstances what are the People to do. at this time our coal dealers have not all told more than 100 bushels of coal on hand & it cant be bought for less than 40¢ per hundred in Less than ton lots.

13. An Uprising of the People

In the following early statement, before the People's party was anything more than a loose gathering of independent elements, the *Farmers' Alliance* proclaimed the need for challenging the structure of power and the distribution of wealth in the United States. Farmers and workers, it reasoned, must stand together if that challenge was to be an effective one.

At no period in the history of the United States has there been such an uprising of the agricultural and wage-earning people of the country to assert their rights and regain their waxing liberty of shaping the laws and affairs of state and national government. A lapsed vigilance at the close of a terrible war allowed class legislators to frame the laws controlling the financial affairs of the country to such an extent that a plutocracy of cruel, unfeeling millionaires have grown up and are attempting to seize the government and reduce the soverign people to a state of vassalage. . . . From the gulf to the moun-

Farmers' Alliance (Lincoln), Sept. 6, 1890. Nebraska Historical Society.

tains, over the field of Kansas, Nebraska, Iowa and Dakota the tread of the marching hosts of independents are moving against the ramparts of monopoly, greed and plutocracy. . . . There must be a change and a bettering of the condition of the wage-earner and the producer, and that change can only be gained by the victory of the independents. In the language of Douglass, there are to day but two parties, "Patriots and traitors." The traitors long held sway in legislative halls of state and nation. Over forty plutocrats are in the United States senate to day, and no measure of relief to the people is allowed to pass that body only by the strongest pressure. . . . The attempted seizure of the government by plutocrats and plutocracy must be throttled, *shall be throttled,* by free American independents.

14. A Great Political Protest

The *Alliance-Independent,* in reality the *Farmers' Alliance* with a new name and editor, continued that paper's critique of the profit system as it then operated. Running through its commentary is the belief in a labor theory of value, and in a social system where great accumulations of wealth are not permitted. As the third editorial suggests, it was felt not only that such accumulations led to poverty for the many, but more importantly, that this substandard condition of existence itself was indispensible to the continuation of existing arrangements. Accordingly, the *Alliance-Independent* called for a coalition of the farmers and workers not simply on the grounds of abstract sympathy for each other's plight, but as a practical necessity based upon grievances held in common.

Alliance-Independent (Lincoln), Jan. 11, 1894, August 11, 1892, August 11, 1892. Nebraska Historical Society.

I

How is it that the products of labor are in the hands of those who do not need them and will not use them, and the money too, while the people who produced all the goods have not money, or were found with insufficient money to buy back their products?

It is because all production and the work of getting goods to market is carried on by the net profit method that labor, labor products and money do not pass in equal value exchange, and trade preserve an equilibrium of forces. The men who work for wages must earn their wages and more, that is, a profit for their employers; and if a capitalist stands behind the employer the wage-earner must earn another profit for him. Hardly anything is put on the market without adding one or more profits to the whole labor cost. The landlords must first have a net profit; the capitalists must have dividends on their stock, and the money loaners must have interest. Rent, profits, interest, these have been drawn off in the shape of money; and every dollar so drawn from the producers and accumulated has tended to glut the markets, has taken from the wealth producers power to draw out of the market, and has given to the usurer or monopolist class power to buy up land, capital railroads, mines, etc., and to so increase their power [to] the people's dependence. Rent, profits, interest, destroy the harmony of the commercial world. They are the sole cause of panics and periods of business depression. They are monopoly tribute paid to veritable kings, taxation without representation; and they furnish present monopolists an ever-increasing enslaving power.

II

Why have men gone into the independent movement? . . . It is the conviction that has been forced upon them that the old parties have both passed beyond the control of the people into the hands of designing capitalists and corporations, whose end and aim in life is to control legislation in their own selfish interests.

. . . It may seem plausible to say that you cannot legislate a man rich or poor, but no man can deny that the capitalists of this country guard the legislation of [the] country with the utmost care, lest some of their wealth be legislated from their over-full coffers into the needy hands of the common people.

The organization of the people's party, as well as its wonderful growth, is a great political protest from the masses of the country against the management of public affairs solely in the interests of the few and against the interests of the many. It is a breaking away from false leaders when their perfidy has been discovered; it is the unspoken curse of the downtrodden as they rise up to strike their oppressors. The grounds for the present political uprising, far exceed the reasons which justified the American rebellion against British oppression in 1776.

III

The few for whom the many toil object to the American workman's standard of living. They want men in gangs, men "known only by their number," men wifeless and childless, men who will live in hovels and on offal. . . .

In the condition of the labor market today, the laborer without an organization is at the mercy of an organized capital that knows no mercy. And capital's combines have issued the edict that labor organizations must be destroyed. They have begun the war on them at Homestead, at Coeur Alene—where not?

And the war means that they purpose firmly riveting the chains of industrial slavery on every man and woman whose life and daily bread depends upon a daily wage. . . .

The farmer who feeds the city laborer is no longer on the side of the man who would reduce the purchasing power of the laborer by reducing his wages. Not in vain have the workers of town and country touched hands in fraternal greeting. At last they know one another. At last they recognize their common interests.

15. The Classes Against the Masses

The first of the following three editorials from the Populist newspaper in Columbus, Nebraska, expresses the belief that men can, through their own efforts, bring about changes in society and a bettering of conditions. For the *Platte County Argus,* the potentiality of political processes was enormous, provided the masses banded together to make their wishes felt. Coming on the eve of the 1896 campaign, the editorial conveys a sense of urgency, a sense that this was indeed a struggle between two competing classes. The theme of the need for common action was again stated by this paper three months later. And then, just before the campaign came to a close, the paper issued a scathing indictment of the powers of corporations, linking these to the widespread impoverishment throughout the country. Yet, while this newspaper repudiated the existing form of industrial capitalism and the values of social Darwinism, the concluding remarks make clear that it did not repudiate industrialism per se.

I

Politics, stripped of all its glittering generalities, simply means the manipulation of public affairs in such a manner so that

Platte County Argus (Columbus, Neb.), June 4, Sept. 3, Oct. 15, 1896. Nebraska Historical Society.

those who make politics their profession can direct the channels of trade—the distribution of wealth—to their special benefit. . . .

Politics can cause this country to bloom and blossom like the rose; it can make our people, generally speaking, prosperous, happy and contented, or it can stagnate every kind of enterprise, reduce the masses to want and misery and cause our people to become restless, desperate and blood-thirsty.

. . . We are on the eve of an important election. The classes, with their fabulous wealth, debauched newspapers and news monopolies, mysterious and powerful corporations, syndicates, trusts, a prostituted judiciary, corrupted legislators and hundreds of thousands [of] subservient office-holders, all to do their evil, mercenary and selfish bidding, is arrayed against the industrial masses. It is an irreconcilable conflict: a victory will be won by one side or the other. The people who desire to see this republic remain "the land of the free and the home of the brave" must unite their forces, and devote a reasonable portion of their time to politics.

The organized money power and corporate influences are working night and day, and are determined to perpetuate their cruel, heartless mortgage on the industry and individual efforts of our countrymen.

II

To avoid further degeneration, humiliation and violence, personal and class rule must cease. . . . The conflict between the common people and the overbearing, despotic, insulting monied aristocracy, who have set themselves up as our dictators, is inevitable, and the longer the crisis is put off the more fearful will be the struggle.

There is now an opportunity for every loyal American citizen to stand up for his country, to stand like men for the common people everywhere. Why hang around plutocracy, cringing and begging for the crumbs that fall from the tables groaning under the burden of the good things which your own hands provided, yet which you are unable to have? . . . Let us stand by one another in the struggle to maintain that grand principle incorporated in the declaration of independence, the right to life, liberty and the pursuit of happiness for all men.

III

No matter for what corporations were organized, nor what they have or may have accomplished in the past, all men today know that they are great engines of oppression. They have crushed individual efforts and hopes for a competent and independent living; they lift up the rich and crush down the poor. They will tolerate but two kinds of people—millionaires and paupers. They believe in but two kinds of homes—palaces and hovels. They have annulled the natural laws of supply and demand. They are fast monopolizing every avenue of industry or employment. The so-called great men who operate them, as a class, are moral cowards and public plunderers. They are everlastingly at war with the spirit of our republican form of government. . . . They have peverted the code of morals and stand up like the hypocrites of olden times and thank God they are not like other men are. They have the power to impoverish the farms, make millions of good men tramps; to reduce their employees to silent slaves; to ruin great cities; to plunge a happy and prosperous nation into sorrow and bankruptcy; to break the spirit of our young men and blast the virtue of our maidens. These things they have done, are doing and can do in defiance of law.

The people do not want to tear up the railroads nor pull down the factories. They do not complain of the palatial homes of others. They want to build up and make better everything. They rejoice in the life of ease and luxury of all good people, but even a worm will writhe and struggle when stepped upon, and surely, if Americans cannot be anything higher, they can be a nation of worms.

16. The Death Struggle of Our Liberties

The secretary of the Farmers' State Alliance of Texas, Fanny Leake, corresponded actively with Alliance members on the need to protest against the hard times they were facing. Of the four items which follow, the first two are militant notes of encouragement, the third is a printed address of the Alliance-Populist members of the state legislature directed to rank-and-file Alliancemen (and probably written by Mrs. Leake), and the fourth is her own pencilled notation at the bottom of a copy of a letter, asserting that men can and must control the political process to improve society.

I

Impress it on each to work as in a death struggle, for truly it is the death struggle of our liberties. I dont see how we dare look up at the "Stars & Stripes" if we make no effort to keep them waving over a *free* people, if we sit & *drift* & let our flag trail into a slavery more oppressive than African slavery.

II

We *must win*, we *dare not* lose, or all human rights & human liberty will go down in the blackness of darkness, and our children and children's children will rise to curse our memory.

Fanny Leake to unidentified persons, Oct. 23, August 4, 1895, printed letter dated Jan. 1895, all contained in Gillespie County Alliance Minutes, 1886–1896. The University of Texas Library, Texas Archives Division.

III

To-day with *armies* of beggars, our highways of tramps, our cities of starving and half naked women and children, and our women and children on the farms, picking "overproduction" cotton in an overproduction of cotton rags, their homes rotting down over their heads for lack of paint to preserve them, and then *dare* we *sit longer idle?*

IV

Corrupting legislation made us poor & only correct legislation *can* restore prosperity; therefore, the poorer we are the greater the necessity to cling together & keep strong the only order whose aim it is to investigate *what* legislation made us poor, what legislation we need to restore prosperity, and how best to secure that legislation. We *must* build up or *perish*.

17. Not the Platform of One But of All

For Thomas E. Watson, the People's party convention at St. Louis in February 1892 signaled the start of a national reform movement which for the first time would unite farmers with the working class. His views on the significance of that coming election, and on the class differences involved, are dramatically stated in this editorial.

The platform adopted at St. Louis is not now the platform of the farmers alone, it is the platform of all the industrial organizations of the country. It is one upon which both country

---

Reprinted from *People's Party Paper* (Atlanta), March 10, 1892. Library of Congress.

and city producers can stand; upon which they do stand, and which they have declared through their accredited delegates is wholly satisfactory to each and all.

We wonder if the people generally understand the full significance of this fact? Do our friends understand it? Do our enemies appreciate its meaning? If so, then the coming contest will be sharp indeed. There will be neither asking or giving of quarter, for upon both sides there will be the consciousness that the contending forces are not unequally matched, and that as they represent totally different and opposing ideas and theories, there can be but one settlement of the matter at issue, and that it must come through the utter overthrow of the one or the other of the parties to the contest.

Never before in the history of the world was there arrayed at the ballot box the contending forces of Democracy and Plutocracy. Upon the field of battle, behind barricades in the streets of cities, about the scaffold and the guilotine they have met, but never at the ballot box, as they will do next October and November.

And on which side shall you be found who read these lines?

Will you stand with the people, within the party of the people, by the side of the other wealth producers of the nation—from city and country? or will you stand facing them, and from the plutocratic ranks fire a ballot in support of old parties and their policies of disorganization, despotism and death?

This is a contest of the common people against the allied money powers of the world.

The motto of the monopolists is "divide and conquer."

Every effort possible is being put forth by both the Republican and Democratic leaders to keep the voters out of the new party. They know that if the people flock to the new party the reign of plutocracy is done. They know that if they can but revive sectionalism they can retain their power over the people. They know that if they can induce the South to now reject the overtures of the West, never again will the people be united as one people, but that they can continue to play one section against the other and rob the people of both in the future as they have done in the past.

Now is the time to speak out and let your friends and your enemies alike know where you stand.

The lines are being drawn; you can not longer stand doubting and undecided. Speak out and let the world know where you are to be found.

Your voice may be heard farther than you think. Each man has influence with another, and the united voice of many influence thousands and turn the tide of public opinion.

God hates a coward. Be men. Speak up.

On which side of the great contest are you going to be found?

If with those who compose the industrial organizations of your country—the wealth producers, the patriots—say so and fall into ranks. If with the plutocrats—the tories, the enemies of the common people—then have the courage to say that and take the place assigned you by the plutocratic bosses and those who contend for special privileges for the few as against equal justice to all.

The columns of the united wealth producers of the nation are preparing for the march and the battle. The roster is being made up. Upon the rolls of which army will your name be inscribed?

18. Augusta Democracy and Culture

Thomas E. Watson's account of the Democratic party's celebration in Augusta, following the monumental election frauds in 1892

Reprinted from *People's Party Paper* (Atlanta), Dec. 2, 1892. Library of Congress.

when he was defeated by John C. Black for reelection to Congress, is not without its humorous aspects. But, more important, Watson characterizes here the composition of the contending political parties, and in so doing, he explicitly views Populism as a movement of the poorer whites and Negroes.

Just after the November election, it was decided by the Democratic bosses of Augusta to celebrate their "grand victory."

This grand victory consisted mainly of voting the same men from five to twenty times. The other ingredients of the grand victory were whisky, bribes, intimidations and lies.

A grand victory of that sort needs celebrating. It might otherwise rot and begin to smell bad. So the Augusta bosses decided to celebrate. They got special rates from the railroads and bar-rooms, and put men to work to fix up mottoes, transparencies, etc., for the occasion.

Duly the crowds came. Duly the brass bands tooted. Duly the eloquent speeches were fired off to the reporters. Duly the procession got under way—as much of it as was sober enough to proceed. The ceremonies were not opened with prayer. The Democrats at first tried to pretend that they believed they were worth praying for, but they soon quit it. Ever since they howled at the preacher who tried to pray for the national Democratic convention at Chicago, they have dropped all gospel attachments.

Among the many mottoes and transparencies in the Augusta procession there were some which decency forbids me to mention. If there were any Democratic ladies who viewed the scene that night, they learned in a way not to be forgotten that the Augusta bosses have no respect for a lady.

The picture in which the Democrats expressed their hatred of Dr. S. F. Potts was the most filthy and obscene painting which was ever paraded in Georgia. How the decent Democratic gentlemen of that noble old city could have tolerated such an insult to themselves, their mothers, their wives, their daughters, is one of the mysteries of life.

How Mr. Black could ride in a procession which contained such vulgarities would be hard to understand if we did not already know how completely he has been captured and fastened within "the charmed circle" of the very ring of corrupt politicians which he used to denounce.

At the close of the transparencies came a wagon containing a coffin. It was represented as the coffin of Mr. Watson. Upon this coffin were seated two men who seemed to be drunk. They alternated in taking drinks of whisky from a bottle. The balance of the time was taken up in playing a game of cards on Mr. Watson's coffin.

In other words, the Democratic bosses, as an evidence of their "grand victory" over Mr. Watson, represented him as being dead and in his coffin while his Democratic victors were playing cards and drinking whisky on his supposed corpse.

This is the idea of the Democrats themselves. In their own way they display their conception of their work—and no words of mine could so completely prove their shame. When one citizen is proud of his disgrace, it is bad enough, God knows! But when a great party boasts of its crimes, and illustrates by pictures its own lack of decency, of morality, of respect for Christianity and Christian people, then, indeed, have we fallen upon evil times.

And poor Mr. Black! Where was he? Credible report says he was in his carriage immediately following the coffin of Mr. Watson. If he kept his eyes open he could see the men sitting on Mr. Watson's coffin drinking whisky. He could see their gambling over the supposed corpse. How much Mr. Black enjoyed the sight the newspapers do not say.

Ah, Brother Black! The time has been when no boss of the Augusta ring would have dared to thus insult you! The time has been when they had better sense than to put drunkenness and card-playing on a coffin in front of your carriage! The time has been when you would have sprung from that carriage and made the streets ring with your denunciations of that disgraceful insult to religion and morality.

But that time has passed, and your people know it. They know that you have joined the ring you abused. They know you owe your fraudulent majority to that ring. They know that you are the helpless captive of that ring. They know you dare not object to anything they do. They know that the doings in Augusta on the night of the celebration were in strict keeping with the methods of your campaign.

Ours is the party of the "poor whites and the negroes;" of the "rag-tag and bob-tail;" of the "ignorant" and of the "uncultured." Hence we obey the law; respect ourselves and our neighbors; do not violate the rules of public decency and do not burlesque the laws of God.

Yours is the party of "wealth and education;" of the "very best people;" of the "back-bone of society." Your leaders are "wise statesmen," while ours are only "demagogues." Your nominee for Congress was a "peerless gentleman," while ours was "an enemy to good government."

Perhaps this is the reason that we obey the laws while you trample them under foot. Perhaps this is the reason that we do not insult ladies, while you do. Perhaps this is the reason why we have conducted our campaign like gentlemen, while you have conducted yours in such disregard of honesty that even the fair-minded Democrats are disgusted. Perhaps this explains why our leaders stand more firmly fixed in our respect than ever before, while yours have fallen in the esteem even of their political friends.

In the "charmed circle" of ring politics, Mr. Black may live awhile longer, but in the hearts of the people he reigns no more.

Well may he shed bitter tears at the prayer-meeting. He has cause to weep. No man during these latter years has fallen as he did. He has set back the cause of morality in the Tenth district at least a dozen years. His whisky vote led the way, and its effects are seen all over the district.

Another such a "grand victory" will put the fight just about where the devil wants it.

The next time they "celebrate" in Augusta let them by all means have a picture of the "Old Boy" labeled thus, "One of our Best Workers."

No wonder Bob Toombs used to say to Bishop Pierce, "You fight the devil, George, and I'll fight the Democrats."

The man who hits the one will hear the other squeal.

T. E. W.

19. A Dream of the Future

Governor Lorenzo D. Lewelling of Kansas used the occasion of his inaugural address, January 9, 1893, to present not a blueprint for the next two years but rather a statement of the philosophy of Populism, and of what he hoped the role of Kansas would be in implementing that philosophy. In this speech, Lewelling characterizes the functions of government, and the rights of the people when government fails to fulfill those functions.

The survival of the fittest is the government of brutes and reptiles, and such philosophy must give place to a government which recognizes human brotherhood. It is the province of government to protect the weak, but the government to-day is resolved into a struggle of the masses with the classes for supremacy and bread, until business, home and personal integrity are trembling in the face of possible want in the family. Feed a tiger regularly and you tame and make him harmless,

Reprinted from *People's Party Paper* (Atlanta), Jan. 20, 1893. Library of Congress.

but hunger makes tigers of men. If it be true that the poor have no right to the property of the rich let it also be declared that the rich have no right to the property of the poor.

It is the mission of Kansas to protect and advance the moral and material interests of all its citizens. It is its especial duty at the present time to protect the producer from the ravages of combined wealth. National legislation has for twenty years fostered and protected the interests of the few, while it has left the South and West to supply the products with which to feed and clothe the world, and thus to become the servants of wealth.

The demand for free coinage has been refused. The national banks have been permitted to withdraw their circulation, and thus the interests of the East and West have been diverged until the passage of the McKinley bill culminated in their diversement. The purchasing power of the dollar has become so great [that] corn, wheat, beef, pork and cotton have scarcely commanded a price equal to the cost of production.

The instincts of patriotism have naturally rebelled against these unwarranted encroachments of the power of money. Sectional hatred has also been kept alive by the old powers, the better to enable them to control the products and make the producer contribute to the millionaire, and thus, while the producer labors in the field, the shop and the factory, the millionaire usurps his earnings and rides in gilded carriages with liveried servants.

To check and change these conditions for the good of all Kansas steps forth to-day, and while demanding the rights of the laborer and producer, she also presents the olive branch of peace and good will to the people of the South by sending to the National Congress a distinguished farmer and stock-raiser who was a Colonel in the Confederate army.

The problem of to-day is how to make the State subservient to the individual, rather than to become his master. Government is a voluntary union for the common good. It guarantees to the individual life, liberty, and the pursuit of happiness. The government then must make it possible for the citizen to enjoy liberty and pursue happiness. If the government fails of these things, it fails in its mission, it ceases to be of advantage to the citizen; he is absolved from his allegiance and is no longer held to the civil compact.

If old men go to the poor-house and young men go to prison, something is wrong with the economic system of the government.

What is the State to him who toils, if labor is denied him and his children cry for bread? What is the State to the farmer who wearily drags himself from dawn till dark to meet the stern necessities of the mortgage on the farm? What is the State to him if it sanctions usury and other legal forms by which his home is destroyed and his innocent ones become a prey to the fiends who lurk in the shadow of civilization? What is the State to the business man, early grown gray, broken in health and spirit by successive failures; anxiety like a boding owl his constant companion by day and the disturber of his dreams by night? How is life to be sustained, how is liberty to be enjoyed, how is happiness to be pursued under such adverse conditions as the State permits if it does not sanction? Is the State powerless against these conditions?

This is the generation which has come to the rescue. Those in distress who cry out from the darkness shall not be heard in vain. Conscience is in the saddle. We have leaped the bloody chasm and entered a contest for the protection of home, humanity, and the dignity of labor.

The grandeur of civilization shall be emphasized by the dawn of a new era in which the people shall reign, and if found necessary they will "expand the powers of government to solve the enigmas of the times." The people are greater than the law or the statutes, and when a nation sets its heart on doing a great and good thing it can find a legal way to do it.

I have a dream of the future. I have the evolution of an abiding faith in human government, and in the beautiful vision of a coming time I behold the abolition of poverty. A time is foreshadowed when the withered hand of want shall not be outstretched for charity; when liberty, equality and justice shall have permanent abiding places in the republic.

20. The Test of a Reformer

A simple, direct statement of what distinguished Populism from the major parties of the period is contained in a circular issued by the People's party executive committee of Los Angeles county. The emphasis here is placed on antimonopolism.

The People's Party is an outgrowth and development of the reform movements of the day; and is an effort to unite for political action all who recognize the evils of monopoly and the pernicious effect on the mass of the people of legislation dating from the Civil War—for which both of the leading political parties are responsible.

A review of the history of this legislation should convince every citizen that both political parties are guided and controlled by those who have created and profited by the monopolies now oppressing the people. . . .

It is impossible to frame a political platform that would receive the unqualified support of all; but this test should be applied: "Is it an honest attempt to suppress the monopolies, which recent legislation has fostered? Is it a sincere attempt at reform?" On this ground alone it should be judged; by the

---

Reprinted from circular of Los Angeles county committee of the People's party, Sept. 14, 1891. Ignatius Donnelly Papers. Minnesota Historical Society.

affirmative or negative it should stand or fall; and every American citizen should apply this simple test, and make it the standard of his allegiance to any political organization that asks his suffrage.

21. The Rise of the Common People

In a highly introspective and candid letter, a prominent People's party leader in Texas analyzes his reasons for leaving the Democratic party. Writing to John H. Reagan, the well-known senator and former congressman from Texas, W. M. Walton suggests that while the decision was a painful one to make, he was convinced that the older party was now denying its own heritage. After citing Democratic policy trends toward support of the gold standard and the national banks, Walton states in the portion which follows the positive case for Populism.

My belief that such would be the inevitable result caused me to break away from a party to which I had belonged all my life, and to which my fathers before me belonged for generations. I did not move rashly nor without maturest consideration. There was no defeated ambition, no heartburnings, no wish for place, position or power, but a simple desire to allign myself with organized men in view of a concerted effort to uphold and foster the best interests of the country, and to promote the welfare of the people under the principles of the constitution and a fair and impartial administration of all the laws, according to their letter and spirit. This party of men is yet young and constituted of the common people, who uprose

---

W. M. Walton to John H. Reagan, Feb. 25, 1896, Reagan Papers. The University of Texas Library, Texas Archives Division.

and broke from their necks the party collar and the party chains and shackles by which they were led and driven into mental and heart slavery by the recognition of a name that had lost its charm and virtue it used to represent. . . . Their utterings may be crude, "unlicked into shape and smoothness," but they are the utterings of honest men who love their country and have felt the goad of oppression, wrong and injustice, flowing from class legislation and a partial administration of the laws, whereby capital has been fostered and labor in all its departments discriminated against.

22. The Calamity Howler

Sometimes an intended epithet can be turned to good advantage. In the sole surviving issue of the Decatur, Texas, *Times*, one finds the way Populists not only accepted the label "calamity howler" but insisted that they had ample reason to howl and would continue to howl until their objectives had been attained.

Red-handed anarchy is fast developing in the soldiery of our beloved Republic, in the courts, the elections, in the legislatures and congress. The appeals of the producers for protection from vandalism of soulless corporations are mocked and treated with contempt. The dead remains of the old democratic motto "equal rights to all, and special favors to none" has been wrapped in the wet blanket of "vested rights" and laid in the little grove of partisan idolitry dug by the hands of ignorance, prejudice and intolerance, and the preachers and religious press have refused to officiate at its funeral or print its epitaph. . . . But we desist and thank our besmeared

---

Reprinted from *Times* (Decatur, Texas), March 22, 1893. Texas State Library.

friends—the enemy for the trueism calamity howler. We are that and will continue to be until [our] lost freedom is regained.

23. The Producer Must Retain What He Produces

The feeling that social protest was increasing is reflected in the first of the following editorials in the Topeka *Advocate*. Commenting on an article in the *American Banker* which gave qualified support to the income tax as a device to head off social revolution, the *Advocate* held that while such concessions were an encouraging sign, they would not be sufficient. In the second editorial, written some eight months earlier, this newspaper spelled out what it considered to be a comprehensive program of reform. Finally, in the third editorial, it explored the ramifications of public ownership. The *Advocate* indicated that the "gas-and-water" brand of socialism might well prompt reformers to entertain the possibility of taking further steps in the direction of government ownership.

I

Considering the source of these remarks and the place and circumstances of their utterance, they are peculiarly significant. Men who have had their eyes open have seen signs of impending disaster for a long time, but men of wealth have insisted upon remaining blind. It is a hopeful sign if they begin to permit themselves to see. If they would avert the revolution, however, they have something to do more than to pay an income tax. That is a very small matter. Monopoly of the

Reprinted from *Advocate* (Topeka), Apr. 3, 1895; Aug. 15, 1894; Nov. 22, 1893. Kansas State Historical Society.

resources of nature and of the means of production and distribution will have to come to an end. Robbery under sanction of law will have to stop. Equal rights and equal opportunities will have to become a reality. Military despotism will have to be done away with and courts will have to cease their usurpations. Conditions that will permit the producer of wealth to retain and enjoy that which he produces, will have to be established and maintained. There will be no security against revolution until these things are accomplished. It is in the air.

II

We propose the initiative and referendum as a means of wresting from a handful of pirates, gamblers and corporation attorneys the power they now exercise without question to determine the policy and conduct of public affairs for purposes of plunder, and of restoring that power to the masses of the people where it rightfully belongs.

We propose to take from the corporations the privilege of coining money and controlling its volume in their own interest, and restore this privilege to the people where the constitution places it, thereby insuring a volume of currency sufficient for the demands of our internal commerce, and not subject to exportation at the demand of foreign shylocks.

We propose that the people shall own and operate the railroads, telegraphs and telephones for their own interest and benefit; and that private corporations shall cease to monopolize these public functions for purposes of public plunder.

We propose that every monopoly, as soon as established, shall be seized by the people and used for the public good, instead of, as now, for private gain.

We propose to so change our system of taxation that land and natural resources of production cannot be held from use, or monopolized for purposes of speculation. Finally, we propose to so revolutionize our economic and social systems that labor shall enjoy what it produces.

III

The best features of our government to-day, national, state and municipal, are those which are purely socialistic. We would refer especially to our public school system and our postal system. There is not a feature of either that is not an exemplification of pure socialism. . . . Municipal ownership of waterworks, gas works, electric light plants, and other public utilities by which the people receive the maximum of service for a minimum of cost afford other examples of pure socialism, by which serious abuses are corrected and great benefits secured to the public. . . .

It is undoubtedly true that observing and studious Populists with such examples before them, have come to believe that a still wider extension of socialistic doctrines and practices would be beneficial to mankind. Looking about them they see nearly every industry monopolized by a corporation; and they are conscious of the robbery practiced upon them for private gain. . . . They have come to believe that many of the abuses to which they are subject might be remedied, and their condition be bettered by a proper exercise of the power of the government.

24. The Omaha Platform

The Omaha Platform of 1892 stands as the basic document in the literature of Populism. Taken as a whole, preamble and accom-

Reprinted from *National Economist* (Washington, D.C.), July 9, 1892, and in all of the leading Populist newspapers in the weeks following the convention. The *People's Party Paper* (Atlanta) often ran the entire document as late as 1893 and 1894.

panying resolutions as well as the planks themselves, the platform is a comprehensive statement of the Populist articles of faith. The preamble was written by Ignatius Donnelly, the leader of the movement in Minnesota and the northwest, and author two years earlier of *Caesar's Column.*

Assembled upon the 116th anniversary of the Declaration of Independence, the People's Party of America, in their first national convention, invoking upon their action the blessing of Almighty God, puts forth, in the name and on behalf of the people of this country, the following preamble and declaration of principles:—

The conditions which surround us best justify our cooperation: we meet in the midst of a nation brought to the verge of moral, political, and material ruin. Corruption dominates the ballot-box, the legislatures, the Congress, and touches even the ermine of the bench. The people are demoralized; most of the States have been compelled to isolate the voters at the polling-places to prevent universal intimidation or bribery. The newspapers are largely subsidized or muzzled; public opinion silenced; business prostrated; our homes covered with mortgages; labor impoverished; and the land concentrating in the hands of the capitalists. The urban workmen are denied the right of organization for self-protection; imported pauperized labor beats down their wages; a hireling standing army, unrecognized by our laws, is established to shoot them down, and they are rapidly degenerating into European conditions. The fruits of the toil of millions are boldly stolen to build up colossal fortunes for a few, unprecedented in the history of mankind; and the possessors of these, in turn, despise the republic and endanger liberty. From the same prolific womb of governmental injustice we breed the two great classes—tramps and millionaires.

The national power to create money is appropriated to enrich bondholders; a vast public debt, payable in legal tender currency, has been funded into gold-bearing bonds, thereby adding millions to the burdens of the people. Silver, which has been accepted as coin since the dawn of history, has been demonetized to add to the purchasing power of gold by decreasing the value of all forms of property as well as human labor; and the supply of currency is purposely abridged to fatten usurers, bankrupt enterprise, and enslave industry. A vast conspiracy against mankind has been organized on two continents, and it is rapidly taking possession of the world. If not met and overthrown at once, it forebodes terrible social convulsions, the destruction of civilization, or the establishment of an absolute despotism.

We have witnessed for more than a quarter of a century the struggles of the two great political parties for power and plunder, while grievous wrongs have been inflicted upon the suffering people. We charge that the controlling influences dominating both these parties have permitted the existing dreadful conditions to develop without serious effort to prevent or restrain them. Neither do they now promise us any substantial reform. They have agreed together to ignore in the coming campaign every issue but one. They propose to drown the outcries of a plundered people with the uproar of a sham battle over the tariff, so that capitalists, corporations, national banks, rings, trusts, watered stock, the demonetization of silver, and the oppressions of the usurers may all be lost sight of. They propose to sacrifice our homes, lives and children on the altar of mammon; to destroy the multitude in order to secure corruption funds from the millionaires.

Assembled on the anniversary of the birthday of the nation, and filled with the spirit of the grand general and chieftain who established our independence, we seek to restore the government of the Republic to the hands of "the plain people," with whose class it originated. We assert our purposes to be identical with the purposes of the National Constitution, "to form a more perfect union and establish justice, insure domestic tranquillity, provide for the common defence, promote the general welfare, and secure the blessings of liberty for ourselves and our posterity." We declare that this republic can only endure as a free government while built upon the love of the whole people for each other and for the nation; that it cannot be pinned together by bayonets; that the civil war is over, and that every passion and resentment which grew out of it must die with it; and that we must be in fact, as we are in name, one united brotherhood of freemen.

Our country finds itself confronted by conditions for which there is no precedent in the history of the world; our annual agricultural productions amount to billions of dollars in value, which must, within a few weeks or months, be exchanged for billions of dollars of commodities consumed in their production; the existing currency supply is wholly inadequate to make this exchange; the results are falling prices, the formation of combines and rings, the impoverishment of the producing class. We pledge ourselves, if given power, we will labor to correct these evils by wise and reasonable legislation, in accordance with the terms of our platform. We believe that the powers of government—in other words, of the people—should be expanded (as in the case of the postal service) as rapidly and as far as the good sense of an intelligent people and the teachings of experience shall justify, to the end that oppression, injustice, and poverty shall eventually cease in the land.

While our sympathies as a party of reform are naturally upon the side of every proposition which will tend to make men intelligent, virtuous, and temperate, we nevertheless regard these questions—important as they are—as secondary to the great issues now pressing for solution, and upon which not only our individual prosperity but the very existence of free institutions depends; and we ask all men to first help us to determine whether we are to have a republic to administer before we differ as to the conditions upon which it is to be

administered; believing that the forces of reform this day organized will never cease to move forward until every wrong
is remedied, and equal rights and equal privileges securely
established for all the men and women of this country.

We declare, therefore,—

First. That the union of the labor forces of the United States
this day consummated shall be permanent and perpetual; may
its spirit enter all hearts for the salvation of the republic and
the uplifting of mankind!

Second. Wealth belongs to him who creates it, and every
dollar taken from industry without an equivalent is robbery.
"If any will not work, neither shall he eat." The interests of
rural and civic labor are the same; their enemies are identical.

Third. We believe that the time has come when the railroad
corporations will either own the people or the people must
own the railroads; and, should the government enter upon
the work of owning and managing all railroads, we should
favor an amendment to the Constitution by which all persons
engaged in the government service shall be placed under a
civil service regulation of the most rigid character, so as to
prevent the increase of the power of the national administration by the use of such additional government employees.

First, *Money.* We demand a national currency, safe, sound,
and flexible, issued by the general government only, a full
legal tender for all debts, public and private, and that, without the use of banking corporations, a just, equitable, and
efficient means of distribution direct to the people, at a tax
not to exceed two per cent per annum, to be provided as set
forth in the sub-treasury plan of the Farmers' Alliance, or a
better system; also, by payments in discharge of its obligations
for public improvements.

(a) We demand free and unlimited coinage of silver and
gold at the present legal ratio of sixteen to one.

(b) We demand that the amount of circulating medium be
speedily increased to not less than fifty dollars per capita.

(c) We demand a graduated income tax.

(d) We believe that the money of the country should be kept as much as possible in the hands of the people, and hence we demand that all state and national revenues shall be limited to the necessary expenses of the government economically and honestly administered.

(e) We demand that postal savings banks be established by the government for the safe deposit of the earnings of the people and to facilitate exchange.

Second, *Transportation.* Transportation being a means of exchange and a public necessity, the government should own and operate the railroads in the interest of the people.

(a) The telegraph and telephone, like the post-office system, being a necessity for the transmission of news, should be owned and operated by the government in the interest of the people.

Third, *Land.* The land, including all the natural sources of wealth, is the heritage of the people, and should not be monopolized for speculative purposes, and alien ownership of land should be prohibited. All land now held by railroads and other corporations in excess of their actual needs, and all lands now owned by aliens, should be reclaimed by the government and held for actual settlers only.

RESOLUTIONS

Whereas, Other questions have been presented for our consideration, we hereby submit the following, not as a part of the platform of the People's party, but as resolutions expressive of the sentiment of this convention.

1. *Resolved,* That we demand a free ballot and a fair count in all elections, and pledge ourselves to secure it to every legal voter without federal intervention, through the adoption by the States of the unperverted Australian or secret ballot system.

2. *Resolved,* That the revenue derived from a graduated in-

come tax should be applied to the reduction of the burden of taxation now resting upon the domestic industries of this country.

3. *Resolved,* That we pledge our support to fair and liberal pensions to ex-Union soldiers and sailors.

4. *Resolved,* That we condemn the fallacy of protecting American labor under the present system, which opens our ports to the pauper and criminal classes of the world, and crowds out our wage-earners; and we denounce the present ineffective laws against contract labor, and demand the further restriction of undesirable immigration.

5. *Resolved,* That we cordially sympathize with the efforts of organized workingmen to shorten the hours of labor, and demand a rigid enforcement of the existing eight-hour law on government work, and ask that a penalty clause be added to the said law.

6. *Resolved,* That we regard the maintenance of a large standing army of mercenaries, known as the Pinkerton system, as a menace to our liberties, and we demand its abolition; and we condemn the recent invasion of the Territory of Wyoming by the hired assassins of plutocracy, assisted by federal officials.

7. *Resolved,* That we commend to the favorable consideration of the people and the reform press the legislative system known as the initiative and referendum.

8. *Resolved,* That we favor a constitutional provision limiting the office of President and Vice-President to one term, and providing for the election of senators of the United States by a direct vote of the people.

9. *Resolved,* That we oppose any subsidy or national aid to any private corporation for any purpose.

10. *Resolved,* That this convention sympathizes with the Knights of Labor and their righteous contest with the tyrannical combine of clothing manufacturers of Rochester, and declares it to be the duty of all who hate tyranny and oppression

to refuse to purchase the goods made by said manufacturers, or to patronize any merchants who sell such goods.

25. The Self-Interest of the Community

Henry Demarest Lloyd, like the other Populist leaders of his generation, had a long and continuous history of involvement in reform movements. That he is perhaps better remembered for other activities should not obscure his active role in Populism, and his belief that for the 1890's this movement was the ideal vehicle for achieving the community predicated on human welfare which he sought throughout his life. While his influence was centered chiefly in Chicago, hence placing him outside the main currents of grass-roots protest on the prairies and in the southern states, Lloyd nonetheless played a significant role in formulating national party policy, and in establishing lines of communication with industrial labor. His importance to Populism extended beyond the fact that he engaged in a dialogue with some more moderate leaders over the retention of the full Populist program, or that he was the People's party nominee for Congress in the Winnetka and North Shore area in 1894, or that he held the Illinois party together by presenting a skillful compromise in the Springfield Platform. For Lloyd stood out as the leading intellectual of the movement, and as the individual who best expressed its positive goal to democratize the industrial system. Because he gave unsparingly of his time, counsel and money to aid the reform forces, because the documentation he provided in *Wealth Against Commonwealth* gave the Populist attacks on Standard Oil and other corporations greater cogency, and for numerous other reasons not the least being the respect he commanded in the working class, Lloyd was recognized by his contemporaries as a preeminent figure among the radicals in American life. Only at the

---

Henry D. Lloyd to Edwin L. Shuman, May 28, 1896. Lloyd Papers, State Historical Society of Wisconsin.

close of the 1896 campaign, when he was one of the few who saw
that fusion with the Democrats had destroyed the movement, did
Lloyd become bitter and disillusioned about Populism. In those
weeks, he forgot the possibilities he himself found so attractive in
the earlier years of agitation, and to which he gave such eloquent
expression.

Lloyd had a truly cosmopolitan outlook. As a student at Columbia
in the 1860's, he read widely in philosophy, economics, and social
ethics. Although admitted to the New York State bar in 1869, Lloyd
felt that the practice of law would be less fulfilling than the practice
of reform, and became prominent—although in his mid-twenties—
in municipal reform and free-trade circles. Removing to Chicago in
1872, he began a thirteen-year association with the then less conservative *Chicago Tribune,* and for much of that time served as its
financial editor. Lloyd emerged from that experience not only as a
seasoned and radical reformer, but one who mastered the analytical
tools which made his later writings so incisive. Probably better
equipped than anyone to the left of the new school of economists,
Lloyd could and did carry the battle to monopolies in the early
1890's, beginning with A *Strike of Millionaires Against Miners*
(1890), more effectively than did the other reform intellectuals.

Yet Lloyd was cosmopolitan in a still more important sense than
that of being widely read and informed on economic principles and
methodology. He conceived of the industrial transformation in
worldwide dimensions, often comparing American developments
with occurrences in Western Europe, England, Australia, and New
Zealand. His trip to England in 1885, where he met with the outstanding socialists and labor officials of that country, and his subsequent correspondence with these and other radicals abroad,
indicate a breadth of understanding and interests almost without
parallel in our society at that time. Nor did Lloyd passively read
and accept what others were saying. For he brought to bear on the
welter of data coming to him a philosophic framework of his own,
which translated economic facts into moral concerns. Lloyd's thinking was always infused with one underlying goal: the realization

of an emancipated working class through industrial democracy. Much that he expressed was consciously derived from Emerson and Kant, but much was also his own unique synthesis of ethics and economics.

The first selection by Lloyd, a letter to Edwin L. Shuman, literary editor of the *Chicago Tribune*, calls for a political ethic which stands social Darwinism on its head. For Lloyd, society must strive for a higher form of individuality than one which places the weak at the mercy of the strong.

"Make no more giants, God; but perfect the race at once!"

I also am in favor of the survival of the strongest; and I think the intervention of the "artificial human idea" is not really artificial but as natural as the lower passions which it seeks to direct. And the "strongest." That, too, is a word which has two meanings. The whole idea of the State and of society does not seem to be the preservation of the weak but the preservation of the strong. Those who rely upon the grosser motives and powers seem to me to be really the weaker. Those whose inspiration is of a higher sort seem to me to be the stronger; and the net result of civilization has been to preserve the stronger from the insanities of the weaker and lower. Men like our great monopolizing capitalists of today are not the stronger unless lunatics are the stronger. Were the slave owners the stronger? Nor does it seem to me that this social process "tends to produce mediocrity." On the contrary, the tendency of social intervention seems to be to open the career to talent, in Napoleon's words; and that leaves the king-like Lincoln, who is hidden in the body of the people, free to emerge and rise. To me the secret of our times appears to be that society is about to apply the same civilizing process to another field of association—the field of industry. Human sympathy I do not make a supreme factor, but regard it as only one of the complex of forces. The whole problem can be argued out from the point of view of self-interest, putting the self-interest of the community against the self-interest of the individual; the self-interest of the better against the self-interest of the worse; and reading the survival of the strongest to mean the survival of the stronger virtues, not the stronger greed.

26. The Divinity of Humanity

Henry D. Lloyd's dream of attaining a social system which encouraged the growth of human potentiality can be seen in the speech he made closing the 1894 People's party campaign in Chicago. In this address to fifteen thousand people, Lloyd placed Populism into a context which transcended the hard times then existing, and which pointed to a more long-range transformation of social values.

The People's Party is more than the organized discontent of the people. It is the organized aspiration of the people for a fuller, nobler, richer, kindlier life for every man, woman, and child in the ranks of humanity. The price of liberty is something more than eternal vigilance. There must also be eternal advance. We can save the rights we have inherited from our fathers only by winning new ones to bequeath to our children. The air of our beloved America has been heavy for many years with the weary footfalls of the people—the workingmen tramping about, to find no doors open for them in the palaces of industry they built—the farmer surrendering first the produce of the year, and then his farm itself to market riggers and usurers; one-half the clerks, the salesmen, the skilled organizers of business set adrift, and the other half made to do

---

Reprinted from *Times* (Chicago), November 4, 1894.

double duty. . . . From the mountains of Colorado, the up-lands and lowlands of Georgia, and prairies of the Dakotas, Nebraska, Minnesota, Illinois, from the north, the south, the east, and the west, we can hear the march of these millions rising to join the people's party in order to make our govern-ment a people's government.

The people's party is not a passing cloud on the political sky. It is not a transient gust of popular discontent caused by bad crops or hard times. It is an uprising of principle, and the millions who have espoused these principles will not stop until they have become incorporated into the constitution of the government and the framework of society. The people's government . . . will rest on these two principles. 1) No use of public powers or public property for private profit. 2) The public have the right to use public powers for the public wel-fare to any extent the public demands. . . .

The first principle will put an end forever to all land grants, charters of railroads and of banks, gifts of public streets to profit-seeking gas, telephone, street railway syndicates. . . .

It [People's Party] is the only party that stands against the division of property . . . of the property of the people among the billionaires. . . .

The People's Party represents the mightiest hope that has ever stirred in the hearts of the masses—the hope of realizing and incarnating in the lives of the common people the fullness of the divinity of humanity.

PART TWO

THE POLITICS OF INEQUALITY:
SEVEN POPULIST VIEWS

---

27. The Farmer's Side

Despite the whiskers that made him a symbol for Populist radicalism among eastern cartoonists, William A. Peffer was somewhat
more conservative than is generally assumed. His reputation as a
judge and newspaper editor in Kansas, more than any advanced
views he may have held, was responsible for his selection as United
States senator after the Populist victory in Kansas in 1890. That his
ability was considerable, however, cannot be doubted, particularly
in analyzing the transportation and financial problems of the time.
In these selections from his major effort, *The Farmer's Side*, the
reader will find the kind of heavily documented arguments that
were characteristic of Populist books and pamphlets.

Briefly, while the world has been moving ahead with long and
rapid strides, while invention has multiplied machinery a thousand fold, giving every worker ten hands and increasing wealth
at marvelous rate; while the country has advanced without
parallel in the history of nations; while statisticians flood reports with bewildering figures; while politicians grow big with
patriotic conceptions and eloquent with fervid speech, the

Reprinted from William A. Peffer, *The Farmer's Side, His Troubles
and Their Remedy* (New York: D. Appleton and Company, 1891),
pp. 8-9, 21-29, 42, 47, 50-55, 68-74, 96-97, 99, 112-113, 116-123,
162-167, 190-194, 195.

men and women who do the manual work are growing relatively poorer, and the few who live off of the profits of other men's labor, or off of the interest on money, or rent on buildings and land, and they who gamble in labor's products and play with the fortunes of men as if they were foot-balls or dice, and to whom the toil and sweat of the poor have no more value than the drip of the roof, are growing richer. Advances in wages, real though they are, have not kept pace with the growing necessities of the working people. Is not the workman worthy of his hire? Ought not the producer to be first paid? Who may rightfully despoil him?

PROGRESS OF AGRICULTURE.

. . . The following table shows the progress of agriculture during the thirty years from 1850 to 1880:

TABLE VI

	1850.	1860.	1870.	1880.
Farms, number...........	1,449,073	2,044,077	2,659,985	4,008,907
Farms, acres in...........	293,560,614	407,212,538	407,735,041	536,081,835
Farms, value, dollars.....	3,271,575,426	6,645,045,007	9,262,803,861	10,197,096,776
Farm implements, value, $	151,587,638	246,118,141	336,878,429	406,520,055
Live stock, value, dollars..	544,180,516	1,089,329,915	1,525,276,457	1,500,464,609
Horses, number	4,336,719	6,249,174	7,145,370	10,357,488
Mules and asses, number..	559,331	1,151,148	1,125,415	1,812,808
Work oxen, number......	1,700,744	2,254,911	1,319,271	993,841
Milch cows, number......	6,385,094	8,585,735	8,935,332	12,443,120
Other cattle, number......	9,693,069	14,779,373	13,566,005	22,488,550
Sheep, number...........	21,723,220	22,471,275	28,477,951	35,192,074
Swine, number...........	30,354,213	33,512,867	25,134,569	47,681,700
Butter, pounds...........	313,345,306	459,681,372	514,092,683	777,250,287
Cheese, pounds...........	105,535,893	103,663,927	53,492,153	27,272,489
Corn, bushels............	592,071,104	838,792,742	760,944,549	1,754,591,676
Oats, bushels............	146,584,179	172,643,185	282,107,157	407,858,999
Wheat, bushels..........	100,485,944	173,104,924	287,745,626	459,483,137
Rye, bushels.............	14,188,813	21,101,380	16,918,795	19,831,595
Wool, pounds...........	52,516,959	60,264,913	100,102,387	155.681,751
Cotton, bales............	2,469,093	5,387,052	3,011,996	5,755,359
Hay, tons...............	13,838,642	19,083,896	27,316,048	35,205,712
Hops, pounds...........	3,497.029	10,991,996	25,456,669	26,546,378
Rice, pounds............	215,313,497	187,167,032	73.635,021	110,131,373
Tobacco, pounds.........	199,752,655	434,209,461	262,735,341	472,661,157
Irish potatoes, bushels.....	65,797,896	111,148,867	143,337.473	169,458,539
Sweet potatoes, bushels...	38,268,148	42,095.026	21,709,824	33,378,693

The average value of farms in 1850 was $2,257; in 1880 it was $2,543, and the average size of farms had decreased from 202 acres in 1850 to 134 acres in 1880. The average value of the acres included in farms was, in 1850, $11; in 1880 it was $19, an increase of $8 per acre, or 73 per cent in the whole period from 1850 to 1880. The increase in value of live stock during the thirty-year period was 176 per cent; of farm implements, 170 per cent; increase in pounds of butter, 148 per cent; bushels of corn, 196 per cent; oats, 178 per cent; wheat, 357 per cent; rye, 40 per cent; pounds of wool, 196 per cent; cotton, 133 per cent; tons of hay, 154 per cent; pounds of hops, 651 per cent; tobacco, 137 per cent; Irish potatoes, 158 per cent—making a general average increase on all these items of personal property equal to about 200 per cent. The prices of some articles named in the table were as follows in the years written:

	1850.	1880.
Corn	59 cts.	54 cts.
Wheat	$1 06	$1 24
Cotton	12 cts.	11½ cts.
Butter	12 cts. to 18 cts.	14 cts. to 30 cts.
Hops	8 cts. to 19 cts.	17 cts. to 39 cts.
Oats	37 cts. to 51 cts.	36 cts. to 49 cts.
Wool	30 cts. to 35 cts.	25 cts. to 45 cts.

Prices of the first three items are taken from table on page 312, Statistical Abstract of the United States for 1889; prices of the other four articles are taken from American Almanac, 1887, pages 100 to 102.

From these figures it is evident that, including the rise in value of land, increase of productive force by machinery, and fall in cost of transportation, the general average development and growth of agriculture during the period beginning with the year 1850 and ending with the year 1880 did not exceed 200 per cent. This is taken in gross—the gross increase, including all advances, excluding all increase or decrease in expense of carrying the business forward. Remember the figures. Agriculture grew in thirty years 200 per cent. Put in other, and perhaps plainer words, the farming industry of the country trebled itself in thirty years, while the general average increase for the whole country was 511 per cent during the same period.

The census figures for the period 1880 to 1890, so far as they relate to agriculture, have not yet been published; hence the data must be obtained from other sources. From tables published by the Department of Agriculture in 1889, by the Chicago Board of Trade recently, and from current market reports, the following facts and figures are taken, showing fairly the condition of agriculture during that time.

The average price of No. 2 red wheat in Chicago during the five years ending with 1883 was $1.11 a bushel; in the next period of five years, ending 1888, the average price of the same grade of wheat in the same market was 81 cents a bushel, a drop of 28½ per cent, although the wheat consumption of the country had fallen off 2½ per cent and the population had increased 15 per cent in the same time. Corn and live stock, cotton and wool are about 40 per cent lower than they were ten years ago. The annual average production of wheat in the United States in the years from 1871 to 1881, inclusive (eleven years), was 342,224,776 bushels. The average for the eight years 1880 to 1887 was 448,150,757 bushels, an increase of 30 per cent, just about equal to the increase of population during the same time. The annual average export of wheat during the years 1871 to 1882, inclusive (twelve years), was 95,345,889 bushels; and during the years of 1881 to 1887 (seven years) the average was 135,500,076 bushels, an increase of 42 per cent. This shows that our consumption of wheat during all the years from 1871 to 1889 did not increase as fast as the population by about 3 per cent, and the market reports show that the average price of wheat during the years from 1871 to 1881 was $1.05 a bushel, while the average since that time has been about 75 cents, a drop of 30 cents a bushel—28½ per cent.

Here are some figures showing wheat values during the years named:

	1875.	1887.	REDUCTION.
Average export value...........	$1 124	$0 89	$0 234
Average farm value, United States	1 00	681	319
No. 2 spring, Chicago..........	99 @ 1 04	75⅜ @ 78½	25
Average farm value, New York...	1 31	82	49
Average farm value, Ohio.......	1 09	75	34
Average farm value, Illinois.....	91	70	21
Average farm value, Nebraska...	64	53	11

The decline in average farm value of wheat has been very great since 1881, as follows, the average being that of all the States and Territories on the 1st of December of each year:

Years.	Prices.	Years.	Prices.
1881......$1 193		1886......$0 687	
1882...... 882		1887...... 681	
1883...... 91		1888...... 67	
1884...... 645		1889...... 68	
1885...... 771			

Wheat was lower in the United States in 1885 than it had been in forty years, and lower in England in 1886 than it had been in a hundred years. The average value of our wheat crops by the acre during the four years 1880 to 1883 was $11.77, and during the next four years it was $8.30½, a drop of 29½ per cent. Values of other grains and field products fell in about the same proportion during the same years.

While it is a little better with live stock, it is bad enough. During the four years 1880 to 1883 there were 6,446,637 head of cattle and calves, 24,992,328 hogs, 2,208,238 sheep, and 52,418 horses received at the stock yards in Chicago, valued at $723,938,329 in the aggregate; during the next four years the numbers were 8,297,037 cattle and calves, 24,479,115 hogs, 4,174,880 sheep, and 111,961 horses, valued at $704,372,033. The average value per animal during the first period was $20.98, and during the second period it was $19. The increase in number was 7 per cent, decrease in value 10 per cent, though the population of the country had increased 22 per cent during the eight years. These last percentages would be varied somewhat if the values of the different classes of animals were given separately, but the average drop in prices would be quite as much as these figures show.

On pages 304 to 314, inclusive, of the Statistical Abstract of the United States for 1889, figures are found for the following tables:

TABLE VII.—*Showing the average price of good and choice native steers per 100 pounds in the Chicago cattle market for each of the years written.*

	1884.	1885.	1886.	1887.	1888.	1889.
Steers...	$6 02	$5 25	$4 67½	$4 29	$4 70	$3 95

TABLE VIII.—*Showing the average prices of No. 2 red wheat, No. 2 corn mixed, and No. 2 oats in the Chicago market for the years written.*

YEAR.	WHEAT.	CORN.	OATS.
1881............	$1 31.8	$0 63.1	$0 45.9
1882............	1 27.8	80.1	51.9
1883............	1 17.5	65.1	42.9
1884............	97.5	60.8	36.0
1885............	96.4	53.1	35.9

YEAR.	WHEAT.	CORN.	OATS.
1886............	88.5	48.4	35.1
1887............	88.9	50.6	34.3
1888............	97.1	57.3	35.5
1889............	88.3	43.0	28.8

TABLE IX.—*Showing the average price of medium wool per pound for the month of January of each year, the average price per pound of middling cotton, the average price per barrel of mess pork, and tobacco leaf per pound in the New York market for the years written.*

YEAR.	MEDIUM WOOL.	MIDDLING COTTON.	MESS PORK.	TOBACCO LEAF.
1881............	$0 49	$0 12.03	$16 94	$0 8.3
1882............	46	11.56	19 79	8.5
1883............	43	11.88	16 59	8.6
1884............	40	10.88	16 48	9.1
1885............	33	10.45	11 58	9.9
1886............	36	9.28	10 63	7.8
1887............	38	10.21	15 00	8.7
1888............	35	10.03	15 10	8.3
1889............	38	....	12 57	8.8

These tables show that the prices of farm products have been falling since 1880. The prices of wheat and corn for 1890 were better than they had been for several years, but it was because of a short crop of those staples. When figures for the decade 1880 to 1890 are published, they will show a great falling off compared with those for the preceding ten years, and the average prices for the last half of the decade will show at least 20 per cent lower than those for the first half.

TABLE X.—*Showing the total production, acreage, and value of all the cereal crops—corn, wheat, rye, oats, barley, and buckwheat— in the United States from 1867 to 1888 (taken from page 290 of Statistical Abstract of the United States for 1889).*

CALENDAR YEAR.	TOTAL PRODUC- TION.	TOTAL AREA OF CROPS	TOTAL VALUE OF CROPS
	Bushels.	*Acres.*	*Dollars.*
1867.	1,329,729,400	65,636,444	1,284,037,300
1868.	1,450,789,000	66,715,926	1,110,500,583
1869.	1,491,612,100	69,457,762	1,101,884,188
1870.	1,629,027,600	69,254,016	997,423,018
1871.	1,528,776,100	65,061,951	911,845,441
1872.	1,664,331,600	68,280,197	874,594,459
1873.	1,538,892,891	74,112,137	919,217,273
1874.	1,454,180,200	80,051,289	1,015,530,570
1875.	2,032,235,300	86,863,178	1,030,277,099
1876.	1,963,422,100	93,920,619	935,008,844
1877.	2,178,934,646	93,150,286	1,035,571,078
1878.	2,302,254,950	100,956,260	913,975,920
1879.	2,437,482,300	102,260,950	1,245,127,719
1880.	2,718,193,501	120,926,286	1,361,497,704
1881.	2,066,029,570	123,388,070	1,470,957,200
1882.	2,699,394,496	126,568,529	1,469,693,393
1883.	2,629,319,088	130,633,556	1,280,765,937
1884.	2,992,880,000	136,292,766	1,184,311,520
1885.	3,015,439,000	135,876,080	1,143,146,759
1886.	2,842,579,000	141,859,656	1,162,161,910
1887.	2,660,457,000	141,821,315	1,204,289,370
1888.	3,209,742,000	146,281,000	1,320,255,398

Compare the years 1867 and 1887. Twice as many bushels in 1887 as in 1867, and more than twice as many acres cultivated, but the value of the crop is about $80,000,000 less. Comparing three-year periods, we have the following results:

TABLE XI.

PERIODS.	TOTAL PRODUCTION	TOTAL AREA OF CROPS	TOTAL VALUE OF CROPS
Three Years	*Bushels*	*Acres*	*Dollars*
1867, 1868, 1869..	4,272,130,500	201,810,132	3,496,422,071
1876, 1877, 1878..	6,444,611,696	288,027,165	2,884,555,842
1879, 1880, 1881..	7,221,705,371	346,575,306	4,077,582,623
1886, 1887, 1888..	8,712,778,000	429,961,971	3,686,706,678

Average price per bushel for the first period, 81¾ cents; for the second period, 44¾ cents; for the third period, 56½ cents; for the fourth period, 42¼ cents. (The rise from 1878 to 1881 will be explained farther on.) Taking the period (eleven years) 1867 to 1878, and we have an aggregate production of 20,564,185,887 bushels, worth $11,215,889,853, an average of 54½ cents per bushel. Taking the period of eleven years from 1878 to 1889, we have an aggregate production of 29,573,770,-905 bushels, worth $13,756,182,830, an average of 46½ cents per bushel, a general drop of 14⅔ per cent. This refers to all the cereals massed as one crop, and therefore may be deceptive more or less.

Comparisons of particular years show startling results sometimes, but it is not a trustworthy method for general purposes. For example: The average price of corn in 1869 was 75 cents, and for 1889 it was 28 cents, but little over one third as much. The price in 1873 was 39¾ cents, and in 1887 it was 41 cents. But, taking a long period of years together, the general tendency has been downward.

Table XII shows the average values of corn, wheat, and oats for each year from 1869 to 1889.

The Secretary of the Kansas State Board of Agriculture, in his report for the quarter ending March 31, 1890, shows, from a large number of reports from farmers of that State, that the average cost of producing a bushel of corn in Kansas is 21 cents. On the day his report was sent to press the average market price of corn in the State was 15 cents per bushel, and he says that if all of the corn crop of 1889—the largest ever grown in the State—had been sold at the then market price (15 cents a bushel), the aggregate loss on the crop would have been $15,000,000.

TABLE XII.

| YEAR. | AVERAGE VALUE PER BUSHEL. | | |
	CORN.	WHEAT.	OATS.
1869	$0 75.3	$0 94.1	$0 47.6
1870	54.9	104.2	43.3
1871	48.2	125.8	40.1
1872	39.8	124.0	33.6
1873	48.0	115.0	37.4
1874	64.7	94.1	52.0
1875	42.0	100.0	36.5
1876	37.0	103.6	35.1
1877	35.8	108.2	29.2
1878	31.8	77.7	24.6
1879	37.5	110.8	33.1
1880	39.6	95.1	36.0
1881	63.6	119.3	46.4
1882	48.5	88.4	37.5
1883	42.0	91.0	32.7
1884	36.0	65.0	28.0
1885	33.0	77.0	29.0
1886	36.6	68.7	29.8
1887	41.4	68.1	30.4
1888	38.1	87.3	33.3
1889	28.3	69.8	22.9

The President of the National Farmers' Alliance and Industrial Union, in a public address delivered in Washington city, April, 1891, and which was distributed extensively, made the following statements:

In 1850 our farmers owned over 70 per cent of the wealth of the country; in 1860 about 50 per cent; in 1880 about 33 per cent; and to-day they own less than 25 per cent, and yet they pay over 80 cents in every dollar that is collected in taxes.

From 1850 to 1860 farm values increased 101 per cent.

From 1860 to 1870 farm values increased 43 per cent.

From 1870 to 1880 farm values increased only 9 per cent.

Notwithstanding this alarming decline in farm values, the aggregate wealth of the country increased 45 per cent from 1870 to 1880, and the agricultural population increased over 29 per cent.

From 1850 to 1860 agriculture led manufacturing 10 per cent in increased value of products; from 1870 to 1880 manufacture led agriculture 27 per cent, showing a difference in favor of manufacturing of 37 per cent.

If a farmer had given a mortgage for $1,000 in 1870, he could have paid it with 1,050 bushels of corn. Ten to seventeen years later it would have taken, without interest, 2,702 bushels to have paid it, and so with his other crops. The farmer pays his debts with his labor. His crops cost him as much labor now as in 1870, but he receives only from one fourth to one half as much for them.

It is evident from what has been shown that the progress of agriculture, compared with other industries, has been less and less marked every decennial period since 1860. From 1880 to the present time farming as a business has not advanced. But that is not all. Farmers now need the use of ten dollars for one that was sufficient forty years ago. Then, when little was required, there was enough; now, when much is required, little or none is to be had. Farmers are poor, while manufacturers and bankers and railroad managers are rich. The wealth of the country is fast passing into the hands of a few rich persons, while the number of impoverished grows alarmingly larger every year.

[After a detailed analysis of census data on mortgage indebtedness, Peffer states:]

. . . Summarized, then, the situation is this: Farmers are passing through the "valley and shadow of death"; farming as a business is profitless; values of farm products have fallen 50 per cent since the great war, and farm values have depreciated 25 to 50 per cent during the last ten years; farmers are overwhelmed with debts secured by mortgages on their homes, unable in many instances to pay even the interest as it falls due, and unable to renew the loans because securities are weakening by reason of the general depression; many farmers are losing their homes under this dreadful blight, and the mortgage mill still grinds. We are in the hands of a merciless power; the people's homes are at stake.

[Discussing the plight of the worker—his alienation and impoverishment—Peffer suggests that labor is beginning to recognize a common interest with the farmers. For Peffer, money is becoming more important than men, and men are becoming transformed into machines.]

LABOR THE GREAT PROBLEM.

. . .We are steadily becoming a nation of hired men. It is time to recall the statement which no one disputes, but which most large employers ignore, "the workman is worthy of his hire." And "hire" means a fair, just, equitable reward for his toil. If he does all the work, surely he is entitled to a large share of the profits.

To value a machine higher than a man or a woman because it can work cheaper, is to place money above muscle, and to place money and labor in competition is to perpetuate the rule of caste.

. . . In many respects the same facts which apply to changes that have taken place in the condition of farmers apply to mechanics and to wage workers. Going back half a century, those of us who have lived that long remember distinctly that in every rural neighborhood the principal lines of mechanical work were represented by persons generally owning their own shops and dwellings. The wagon-maker, the blacksmith, the carpenter, the shoemaker, the tailor, the bricklayer, the stone-mason—all scattered about among the farmers. Now nothing of that kind is seen in the travel of a month over the country, but, instead thereof, in the cities we find mechanics for every grade massed in large numbers, where each one works separately at a particular part of the machine which he is making. In a wagon factory, for example, one man turns hubs, another bores the center opening, another mortises them, another is making spokes, another standards, another axles, another single-trees, and so on through all of the wood work. In the iron department one person cuts bars into proper lengths, another punches holes at the proper places; one is cutting rods, another is running threads on them, another making nuts, another heading bolts, and so on to the end. In a pile of a thousand or five thousand of these separate pieces any one of them will fit in its proper place in any one of the wagons made at that establishment. So it is in the shoe factory; so it is in every place where the finished product is made up of separate pieces. These people, from 500 to 3,500 at a place, go to their work at the blowing of a whistle or the ringing of a bell; they go to their meals and return by the same signs at stated times every working day. They are practically as much machines as the unconscious mechanical combinations to which they attend. By this process of absorption in large manufacturing establishments the individuality of the separate workers is virtually lost. The man who was once an individual citizen among the farmers is now part of a great manufacturing establishment in the city, doing his work with the same precision, the same regularity, the same method that an inanimate implement does. One of the necessary results of this change is that the mechanic and the wage worker have become largely dependent upon the business of his employer. If that fails from any cause the workers are temporarily out of employment. If any difference arises between the employer and the employés concerning their compensation, or concerning any other matter in which they are all interested, the employer has the advantage. In dull times, when work is scarce, the tendency is to reduce wages, which naturally affects the tempers as well as the pockets of the workers. These and other related circumstances breed a relation between the owner and the workers at the factory which in times of great excitement give to the employer a practical ownership of his work-people. When an economic question, in political discussions, is held up before the people as involving the rights of labor, and particularly in respect to their wages, it is a logical effect of the conditions that the workers should be appealed to to stand by the employer, because it is said whatever is to the interest of the employer will be to the interest of the employé, on the supposition that a good business for the owner of the factory will make more work and better wages for the men and women who do the work. In this way the manufacturer in charge of a large establishment wields a powerful influence over the persons in his employ. Aside from all this, it has been the rule ever since the relation of employer and employé was first established that the interest of the employer is for himself and not for his workman; that while he admits that the workman is worthy of his hire, yet he believes it to be his privilege to obtain labor at the lowest price. Labor has always been a commodity in the market for which employers bid just as dealers at an auction of dry goods—every one anxious to get what he desires at the lowest possible figure. So it is that work-people in all communities are nearly always within a few days, or at most a few weeks, of starvation; and it is probably because of this great and crushing fact that working men and women have united in organizations for their mutual protection. It has been the experience of American working people that, very soon after their absorption into large establishments became a fixed fact, at the first indications of discontent on account of the wages they were receiving, their employers at once looked about for foreign labor to take the place of that of citizens. This sort of thing began as far back as 1858. Then came on the great war, and in 1864 Congress was asked to authorize citizens of the United States to go into foreign countries and there employ work people and bring them to this country, holding a lien upon their wages and upon their homes, if they should obtain any, for the amount of money advanced in their importation. Such an act was passed July 4, 1864, but the people knew nothing of it until conditions afterward brought it out in public discussions of a bill to prohibit the importation of labor under contract. It was because of the effect of that act, largely, that Knights of Labor were organized about the year 1870. In 1877 came the great railroad strike, when millions of dollars' worth of property was destroyed in the city of Pittsburg. Strikes then followed in rapid succession, until at one time it was feared that striking of laboring people was going to be a mania. It has been discovered, however, that while these strikes have set on foot an extended investigation of the complaints of our working people, and their rights as citizens of the republic, their condition, compared with that of those who really control social and political affairs, is no better than it was at the beginning of the century. The employer still has the advantage, and he has it with practical completeness. He imports labor at his option, and he hires armed ruffians to stand guard at the gate while he drives out the citizen and escorts the alien in. The tendency is to concentrate still more and more in large establishments. By reference to the census reports of 1850, 1860, 1870, 1880, and 1890, it will be seen that while the number of manufacturing establishments has increased, there has been a gradual absorption of smaller ones into the larger; that, while more persons are employed in them, the number in each one has been greatly increased; that, while the amount of wages in the aggregate paid to employés has increased, compared with the amount of work that they do their wages is not as great now as it was at any former period. Besides that, it appears that every year the individuality of the working man is growing less and less distinct; he is becoming merged into the business of his employer; practically he is out of view. While he produces wealth in enormous amounts, it is found that his share of it, from some cause or other, is growing less and less relatively as the years come and go, while his employer grows richer and his influence in social and political affairs continually increases. Not only does the rich man to-day rule at home among his neighbors, but he rules in our national affairs. Money controls our legislation, it colors our judicial decisions, it manipulates parties, it controls policies. Manufacturers, bankers, railroad builders, and other capitalists dictated our present financial methods, and to-day their combined opposition is strong enough to defeat any measure proposing a change. It is that power which defeated the free-coinage bills that were proposed in the Fifty-first Congress; it is that power which defeats the reduction of excessive tariff duties; it is that power which holds within the hollow of its hand all the financial interests of the people. Wall Street is king. All of this makes the condition of the wage worker more and more dependent every year. He is beginning to see that the same influences which have brought bankruptcy to the farmer's door is taking away from him his home and preventing his neighbor from securing one. It is a fact, which most of the people who are not wage workers themselves have not yet learned, that it is more difficult now for a poor man to obtain a home than it has been at any time within the reach of memory. The writer hereof has heard many mechanics within the last two years state that their condition is growing worse and worse continually. He knows personally that many of them are wholly unable to meet obligations contracted in the purchase of their homes. Many homes have been sold from that class of people, because, from some reason inexplicable to them, they are growing less and less able every year to meet demands made upon them in this direction. The farmer and the wage worker are traveling the same road; they are both brought face to face with a perilous condition; they are both confronted with a merciless power which has brought disaster upon them both alike.

[This is followed by a commentary on the interrelatedness of mortgage indebtedness, overproduction, an appreciating dollar, and railroad land practices.]

SETTLEMENT OF THE NEW WEST.

. . . In connection with this subject [influence of dominant economic interests], the settlement of the new West is interesting. In the latter part of December, 1861, the banks of the country suspended specie payments. This was occasioned by the pressure brought to bear upon the Government for money because of the great war, which was then in progress. From that time until the present, as will appear more fully hereafter, the moneyed interests of the country dictated our financial legislation, obtaining all that they desired, or at least defeating all that was to them objectionable. In 1862 a large area of the public land was granted by Congress to the Union Pacific Railroad Company and auxiliaries, in all amounting to some twenty-eight million acres, and the next year to other roads as much more. With these grants began a system of disposing of the public lands in immense quantities to railroad companies by name. The extent of territory given to each road was measured by a limit extending out from ten to twenty miles on either side of the line as it should be finally located, the company receiving alternate sections, leaving the other half as public lands belonging to the Government. The railroad companies

at once undertook the settlement of the new region by bringing in immigrants from other parts of the world. Europe was
flooded with advertising literature, portraying in glowing
colors the wonderful fertility of this new unsettled region and
the marvelous facilities there for acquiring wealth by early
settlers. In order that this particular class of advertising might
be more effective, the railroad builders united with the manufacturers in asking Congress to enact a law authorizing the
making of contracts in foreign countries by American citizens
for labor.

The object of this enactment was twofold. First, upon the
part of manufacturers, to obtain cheaper labor than they were
then using, because a large number of the working people of
the country had gone into the army; second, the railroad builders wanted cheaper labor than they could employ in this country to build their roads through the new regions to be settled;
and in both of these respects the movement was eminently
successful. Large numbers of people were attracted by the
inducements offered, and in the course of a few years after the
war an area in the western part of our country larger than the
original thirteen States was settled and large portions of it
brought under cultivation. Farms were opened, towns were
built, churches and school-houses dotted the plains and hills,
and a post-office was established within easy reach of every
man's door. But in doing this it became necessary to make extended investments, both of credit and of money. The settlers
were generally poor; they were offered the railroad lands at
an average of about $3 an acre upon the payment of a small
portion cash—10 per cent or thereabouts—the rest in ten annual payments with interest at 7 to 10 per cent, giving a mortgage to the company as security for deferred payments. In
connection with this sort of railroad extension and settlement,
feeding roads were projected in all directions, and the people
who settled upon the lands to be supplied with the new roads
were asked to assist in the projects by voting municipal bonds.
This resulted in a large bonded indebtedness of the townships,

counties, and cities all through the West. The price which the railroad companies fixed upon the lands had the effect in law and in fact to raise the price of the reserved Government sections to two dollars and a half an acre. The homestead law did not apply anywhere within the limits of a railroad grant. Upon the public lands outside of the railroad limits any person authorized to make a homestead entry was entitled to locate, and for a few dollars (to pay fees and necessary expenses) he could obtain a quarter section of land and make a home upon it; but it required money to buy the lands within the railroad limits either from the company or from the Government, and a good deal of money for a poor man. The only way to obtain the money was to borrow it, and as a part of this scheme of settlement a vast system of money lending had been established, with agents in every town along the lines of the new roads engaged in the business of negotiating loans, advertising their work far and wide, so that the purchasers of lands from either the railroad company or from the Government within the limits of the grants need only apply to these money lenders, and for a commission to the "middle man" could obtain money from Eastern owners in any conceivable amount. It was not long until the whole country in the region of these new roads was mortgaged. While the lands were fertile they did not produce any more than other lands of equal fertility, and they were so far away from the markets of the country that transportation ate up from 60 to 75 per cent of the value of the crops. While a good deal could be produced upon these rich acres, still the profit margin was so small that there was really but little left in the end. Where a person took up a homestead claim and raised one good crop of wheat, he was considerably ahead in the world; but where he had to pay from two and a half to three dollars an acre, borrow the money, and pay 50 per cent interest upon it, renewed every year, he had a hard road to travel; it was with difficulty that even the best of the new farmers and the most economical among them were enabled to meet their engagements and save their homes. In a large majority of cases it became necessary to borrow more money in order to meet maturing obligations. Rates of interest were exorbitant, rates of transportation on the railroads were unreasonably high, taxes were excessive, salaries of officers were established by law and were uniformly high, while there was but little property and comparatively few tax payers at that early period in the settlement, so that the burdens of taxation fell heavily upon the few who were ready to be caught by the tax gatherer.

In connection with these proceedings it is proper to mention a fact which will be more fully elaborated further on, that while the burdens just mentioned were increasing other forces were operating to add to the difficulties in the farmers' way. The people were rapidly taking upon themselves new obligations, while, by reason of the contraction of currency, prices of farm products fell to a very low figure—in many cases below the cost line—and in a proportionate degree taxes and debts of all kinds increased relatively. While one hundred dollars were the same on paper in 1889 that they were in 1869, yet by reason of the fall in values of products out of which debts were to be paid the dollars grew just that much larger. It required twice as many bushels of wheat or of corn or of oats, twice as many pounds of cotton or tobacco or wool to pay a debt in 1887 as it did to pay a debt of the same amount in 1867. While dollars remained the same in name, they increased 100 per cent in value when compared with the property of the farmer out of which debts were to be paid; and while a bushel of wheat or of oats or of corn was the same in weight and in measure in 1887 that it was in 1867, yet it required twice as many bushels to pay the same amount of debt. The same principle holds good in all of the different obligations for which the farmers were liable, and is applicable to the only property with which they were supplied to pay their indebtedness. It became necessary under those conditions to renew loans, pay additional commissions, contract new obligations, until to-day we find that fully one third of the farms of the country, especially of the western part of the country, are under mortgage. In some counties from three fourths to seven eighths of the homes of the farmers are mortgaged for more than they would sell for under the hammer.

It is said frequently that the farmer himself is to blame for all of these misfortunes. If that were true it would afford no relief, but it is not true. The farmer has been the victim of a gigantic scheme of spoliation. Never before was such a vast aggregation of brains and money brought to bear to force men into labor for the benefit of a few. The railroad companies, after obtaining grants of land with which to build their roads, not only sold the lands to settlers and took mortgages for deferred payments, but, after beginning the work of building their roads, they issued bonds and put them upon the market, doubled their capital upon paper, compelling the people who patronized the roads to pay in enhanced cost of transportation all these additional burdens. The roads were built without any considerable amount of money upon the part of the original stockholders, and where any money had been invested in the first place, shrewd managers soon obtained control of the business and the property. So large a proportion of the public lands was taken up by these grants to corporations that there was practically very little land left for the homestead settler. It appears from an examination of the records that from the time our first land laws went into operation until the present time the amount of money received from sales of public lands does not exceed the amount of money received from customs duties on foreign goods imported into this country during the last year, while the lands granted to railroad companies directly, and to States for the purpose of building railroads indirectly, if sold at the Government price of $1.25 an acre, would be equal to three times as much as was received from sales of the public lands directly to actual settlers. The farmer was virtually compelled to do just what he has done. The railroad builder took the initiative. Close by his side was the money changer. The first took possession of the land, the other took possession of the farmer. One compelled the settler to pay the price fixed upon the railroad lands by the railroad company; the other compelled the settler on the public lands within the grant to pay the increased price, and to borrow money through him to make the payments on both. This system continued until the farmer, accommodating himself to prevailing conditions, was in the hands of his destroyers. Now we find the railroad companies capitalized for from five to eight times their assessed value, the farmer's home is mortgaged, the city lot is mortgaged, the city itself is mortgaged, the county is mortgaged, the township is mortgaged, and all to satisfy this over-reaching, soulless, merciless, conscienceless grasping of avarice. In the beginning of our history nearly all the people were farmers, and they made our laws; but as the national wealth increased they gradually dropped out and became hewers of wood and drawers of water to those that own or control large aggregations of wealth. They toiled while others took the increase; they sowed, but others reaped the harvest. It is avarice that despoiled the farmer. Usury absorbed his substance. He sweat gold, and the money changers coined it. And now, when misfortunes gather about and calamity overtakes him, he appeals to those he has enriched only to learn how poor and helpless he is alone.

[Peffer then goes on to develop an important argument: It is not high interest rates alone that are significant, but rather, high interest rates within the context of a contracted currency. In three chapters he discusses the acts of July 17 and August 5, 1861; February 25 and July 11, 1862; March 3, 1863; June 30, 1864; January 28 and March 3, 1865; April 12, 1866, and of course the National Bank Act of February 25, 1863, with the relevant sections of this last reprinted in full. Peffer continues with the following:]

. . . The banks suspended specie payments in the latter part of December, 1861, forcing the Government to rely upon its own resources exclusively for funds to carry on a great war, and from that time forward every dollar of money used by the Government and by the people in all of their multitudinous transactions was paper money. No gold or silver was used, except in the matter of the payment of customs dues and interest on the public debt, and the coin used for those particular purposes had to be purchased largely from men who made a business of buying and selling gold as men made a business of buying and selling wheat and corn, and when the war closed there was upward of $1,500,000,000 of the people's money afloat in business affairs without any coin whatever. Under the acts of 1865 and 1866, before cited, the Secretary of the Treasury began a wholesale withdrawal, and in the course of three years he had withdrawn from circulation over $800,-000,000. This question of whether the obligations of the people were to be changed after the war was submitted to a committee of Congress, at the head of which was Hon. John Sherman, of Ohio. A long report was made upon the subject, and in the report that distinguished financier shows very plainly, from the acts of Congress and from the manner of dealing among the people in their ordinary business, that there was at no time any disposition upon the part of Congress or of the people to pay anything except paper money for any of their obligations, unless there was a specific arrangement of that kind in the contract.

[Taking note of the credit-strengthening act of March 18, 1869, and the funding act of July 14, 1870 (and the amendatory act of January 20, 1871), Peffer states:]

. . . When the year 1873 came, and with it the general financial storm which swept away fortunes and impoverished millions of our people through a depreciation of the values of their property consequent upon an excessive contraction of the currency, while at the same time population had increased

15 per cent and the volume of business 40 to 50 per cent; when the business of the people required more money instead of less money for its proper transaction, and when, instead of having more they had 56 per cent less, Congress, by an act passed the 12th day of February, 1873, revised the coinage laws, dropping the silver dollar entirely out of the list of coins of the United States, at one stroke taking away from the people one half of their full legal-tender money. The same act provided that the gold dollar should be the unit of value.

[Finally, with the analysis of that act and subsequent legislation, as well as the inclusion of elaborate tables showing the decline of values in corn, wheat, rye, oats, barley, and buckwheat in the period 1867–1873, Peffer addresses himself to the contraction of the currency, using as the basis for his statements the reports of the Secretary of the Treasury. He concludes:]

. . . The contraction of the currency volume from the beginning of the fiscal year 1867 (July 1, 1866) to the first day of December, 1873, was $881,265,600, or 56 per cent, taking the figures first above given. While that process was going on the volume of business was constantly increasing, as the following brief exhibit shows:

Foreign commerce.

1866—$880,415,751.   1873—$1,270,705,643.

Wheat produced.

1869—260,146,900 bushels.   1873—281,254,700 bushels.

Corn produced.

1869—874,520,000 bushels.   1873—932,274,000 bushels.

Miles of railroads built.

1867—2,449 miles.   1873—4,097 miles.

From this state of facts it must be evident to all studious persons that a rate of interest equal to 10 per cent in 1866 was equal to 20 per cent in 1873. It was because of the withdrawal from circulation of so large a part of the currency that business became stagnant, trade paralyzed, and bankruptcy overtook the people. It was a perilous journey to take, but our statesmen entered upon it deliberately, plainly foreseeing and frankly foretelling the dreadful consequences, well knowing that ruin would follow in their wake. Creditors alone would profit by the wreckage, for they would absorb every dollar that debtors would lose. Nothing is better settled in political economy than that a long-continued diminution of the currency volume leads to disaster. This has been the universal experience of men. Our public men understood it well, and they gave warning of the coming destruction. . . .

THE BLAND SILVER LAW.

The people having discovered that silver dollars had been discarded by Congress (it seems that nobody—not even members of Congress nor the President who approved the bill— knew that it was intended to drop silver dollars from the coinage of the country), there was a strong demand for its restoration to its old place in our monetary system. The condition of the people was such that they had little patience with their law makers, and they demanded prompt relief. All that had been predicted concerning business prostration had come to pass; and when it was found that, in addition to the withdrawal of paper money, Congress had demonetized one of the coins that had descended to us as full legal-tender money from the fathers of the republic, a feeling of indignation grew aggressive among the people. A bill was introduced in Congress in 1876 to remedy the wrong which had been done, but its course was obstructed until early in 1878, when the temper of the people was recognized.

The silver bill—commonly known as the Bland Bill—which

was passed by both houses and vetoed by President Hayes, was reconsidered, passed again by both houses, and became a law February 28, 1878. It provided that the Secretary of the Treasury is authorized and directed to purchase, from time to time, silver bullion, at the market price thereof, not less than two million dollars' worth per month, nor more than four million dollars' worth per month, and cause the same to be coined monthly, as fast as so purchased, into standard dollars.

Resumption was supposed to have taken place on the first day of January, 1879, and on the 30th day of June following the banks had increased their notes to $329,691,697, and the increase was continued four years. At the end of the fiscal year 1882 (June 30th) the amount of bank notes out was $358,742,034. The increase from 1878 added $8,556,937 yearly to the circulation of the country, and the silver coinage under the act of 1878 added about $25,000,000 every year. Small as was the increase of the currency from these two sources, it gave stimulus to trade and prices grew better. Corn sold for 31.8 cents a bushel in 1878; in 1881 the price was 63.6, and in 1882 it was 48.5. Wheat rose from 77.7 cents in 1878 to 88.4 in 1882. (It had been $1.10 in 1879 and $1.19 in 1881.) Trade revived generally; all classes of people felt the good influences of what were believed to be evidences of returning prosperity. In 1882 the national banking law was reenacted, thus continuing the system another twenty years. Government bonds were worth 112 to 121, and banks began to withdraw their circulation, which process was steadily continued down to the present time. The amount of notes out on the 31st day of October, 1890, was $124,958,736.

The silver law authorized the Secretary of the Treasury to purchase $4,000,000 worth of silver bullion every month and coin it into standard dollars, but that officer and his successors persistently refused to go beyond the minimum limit of

the law—$2,000,000 worth—and the actual silver-dollar coin-
age amounted to a yearly average of only about $25,000,000,
less than the annual decrease of the volume of bank-note circulation. The only source of increase in the amount of money
in the country was gold coinage, an annual average of about
$25,000,000. But there has been no increase of the *circulation*.
The amount of money in *actual circulation* among the people
is not half as much per capita now as it was in 1878, when it
was $17.85. Senator Plumb, in a careful estimate presented
to the Senate on the 6th day of June, 1890, put the amount of
money "available for delivery or other use in the transaction
of the business of all the people" at $550,000,000, "or a trifle
over $8 per capita." He added: "If I were deciding this case
upon what I consider the best evidence, I would be bound to
say that I believed the money in actual circulation did not
much, if at all, exceed $500,000,000." While the business of the
people has doubled in the last twelve years, and the population has increased at least 30 per cent, our money volume has
shrunk from $17.85 per capita to $8. We had gone down far
below the danger line in 1878, and the way was strewn with
disaster; we have been since following the same perilous way,
going deeper and deeper in debt, until now Mr. Porter [Super-
intendent of the Bureau of the Census] tells us that during
the last ten years 9,000,000 mortgages were put on the lands
of our citizens—equal to one for every seven persons—and
the average mortgage is about $1,000. The private mortgage
debt of the people, judging from census reports thus far
published, probably amounts to between $3,000,000,000 and
$4,000,000,000 and the average interest rate to the borrower
is at least 10 per cent. The owner of the money does not demand or receive more than 7 per cent; the rest is taken by the
loan agent. The borrower pays 10 per cent, and has in thousands of cases, given separate mortgages for the excess above
legal rates, or above what the owner of the money receives.

THE HAND OF THE MONEY CHANGER IS ON US.

From this array of testimony the reader need have no difficulty in determining for himself "how we got here." The hand
of the money changer is upon us. Money dictates our financial
policy; money controls the business of the country; money is
despoiling the people. The author of *Twenty-eight Years in
Wall Street* boasts that in the wonderful commercial and industrial development of the age, and which, he says, exceeds
that of all past time since Herodotus wrote, Wall Street was a
prime factor. He claims, and truthfully too, that the power of
the men who assemble there to catch the driftwood of trade
is greater than that of monarchies. He says they "move the
money which controls the affairs of the world." We see plainly
that behind all the commercial villainies of the time this power
rests in placid security while the robbing of the toilers proceeds. These men of Wall Street, posing as missionaries con-
quering deserts and building republics, men piously assuming
universal dominion, religiously dictating the financial policies
of nations, moving in an atmosphere of radiant morals, self-
appointed philosophers teaching honor and honesty to an ignorant world, these men of fabulous fortunes built upon the
ruin of their fellows, are in fact the most audacious gamblers
in Christendom. The poor fool who with a few dollars opens
a faro bank or sets up a monte table in a country town is by
common consent an outlaw; every man's face is set against
him, and he is liable to arrest and imprisonment at any hour;
he is denied admittance to the houses of people who are clean;
even the street gamins pass him by as if he were a leper. No
man so little esteemed, no man so thoroughly loathed and
despised as this fellow, the common gambler. Yet here in the
very heart of the best civilization on earth, at the very center
of business life and activity, living in luxury and ease, renting
costly pews in splendid churches and hiring their worshiping
done; men petted and feasted by the rich and easy every-

where, with millions of dollars at their call, governments at their command, and a loyal people in their service; these men who produce nothing, who add not a dollar to the nation's wealth, who fatten on the failures of other men, whose acquisitions are only what their fellows have lost; these men without conscience, who believe they are specially commissioned to prey upon the people, who act as a sort of continuing self-appointed civil-service commission to examine candidates for important offices before their names are submitted to the voters; this pampered aristocracy living off the wreckage of commerce, who rake in a railroad, a state, or a nation with equal complacency; these men "whose private dwellings are more splendid than the public buildings," and whose "happy homes" are the fruit of other men's toil; these men who boast of their patriotism in lending a few millions of their ill-gotten gains to the government of their imperiled country at "12 per cent" interest, when thousands of farmers and wage workers of all sorts and conditions were voluntarily in the army at risk of life and home—all without question as to pay; these men masquerading as philanthropists and patriots while they are despoiling a nation and robbing the poor—these are the men who engineered the train that brought us where we are. They hold the bonds of nearly every State, county, city, and township in the Union; every railroad owes them more than it is worth. Corners in grain and other products of toil are the legitimate fruits of Wall Street methods. Every trust and combine made to rob the people had its origin in the example of Wall Street dealers. Touch any spring along the keyboard of commercial gambling and a Wall Street sign appears. This dangerous power which money gives is fast undermining the liberties of the people. It now has control of nearly half their homes, and is reaching out its clutching hands for the rest. This is the power we have to deal with. It is the giant evil of the time. Money is the great issue—all others pale into insignificance before this, the father of them.

[What follows is a good example of how Peffer uses a specific theme as a point of departure for analyzing larger trends, notably the concentration of wealth.]

STRINGENCY IN THE MONEY MARKET.

. . . This matter of a combination for political purposes of the industrial forces of the country is now being discussed in every county and in nearly every township and school district in the country. Farmers and working people of all classes are fast learning that their interests are identical. Men of great wealth, men having large estates, whether of one kind or of another, and men dealing in money, have always operated in common. They do not care anything about the platforms of parties provided they may name the candidates, and during all of the years since our great war began what is commonly known as the "money power" has had almost exclusive control of our financial legislation. Its footprints are seen in the statute books every year. Its views go out through the reports of the Secretaries of the Treasury, through inaugural addresses and messages of Presidents, through official documents of the heads of departments, through the columns of the metropolitan press, and through every channel which can operate to spread among the people the doctrine that men whose interests are involved in the accumulation of wealth must always be consulted when any sort of financial legislation is proposed. We have seen, very much to our astonishment, in late years that the public treasure is used as a fund by the highest officers of the Government to accommodate the temporary needs of men whose interests are directly at variance with those of the common people. Beginning with the great crash in 1873, and continuing down to the present time, the Secretary of the Treasury has been in the habit of visiting New York city and conferring with bankers and other capitalists there upon every occasion of what is termed a "stringency in the money market."

When there is trouble among speculators over there the Government officers are notified, the Secretary kindly goes among them, and asks how much of the people's money is needed to ease the situation. In the last report of the Secretary of the Treasury, bearing date December 1, 1890, at page xii to xiv, that officer calls attention to the course of his department in relation to the interests of the "money market" during a portion of the last year. He mentions the fact that there was a demand for money among the capitalists of New York (although in justice to the Secretary it must be said he did not state it in exactly the way it is here put), that after having tried to relieve the situation in July, 1890, by the purchasing of nearly seven million dollars' worth of bonds, he says, on page xxix: "It was soon apparent that these purchases were inadequate to meet existing conditions; therefore, on August 19, the department gave notice that 4½-per-cent bonds would be redeemed with interest to and including May 31, 1891; and two days later the circular of August 21 was published, inviting the surrender for redemption of twenty millions of those bonds, upon condition of the prepayment, after September 1, 1890, of all the interest to and including August 31, 1891, on the bonds so surrendered. Under this circular there were redeemed $20,060,700 4½-per-cents." Then he proceeds: "Notwithstanding the disbursements resulting from purchases and redemptions of bonds under the circulars of July 19 and August 21, the industrial and commercial interests of the country required that large additional amounts should be at once returned to the channels of trade." It appears from this last sentence that the Secretary had in mind, firmly fixed, the belief that it is the duty of the national Treasury to fly to the rescue of the "industrial and commercial interests of the country" whenever any disturbance in financial affairs indicates a money pressure in that particular part of the country where New York city is located; and this conviction, honest though it be, and from the Secretary's standpoint, purely patriotic and unobjectionable, yet, as the farmers and the workers view it, one of the most pernicious doctrines ever imbibed or taught by any American statesman, has become part of our financial policy. Think, dear reader, think; take one good long thought about the suggestion that whenever the men represented by "Wall Street," men engaged in the business of dealing in money because of the profits that come out of usury, men who have no more hesitancy in drawing a mortgage over a railroad system involving millions and millions of dollars, or over a county, or a State, or over the homes of millions of the people, than they have of sailing in a costly yacht on the calm waters of the ocean, or of eating a breakfast of "blue pointers," that when that class of men, after having brought upon themselves "stringency" through a gigantic system of the most brazen gambling, it is the duty of public officers to use the people's money to relieve the "stringency," and to furnish those men with money enough to continue their process of spoliation. Where is the country drifting when our public men stand ready to dip out of the Treasury the people's earnings and hand it over to be traded in by men of this class, who have piled up fabulous fortunes out of the crystalized sweat of toil? While the Secretary of the Treasury, the trusted custodian of the people's treasure, is dealing it out by millions in the purchase of bonds not yet due, and in the advancing of a year's interest, amounting to twelve million dollars, all to relieve what he is pleased to believe a "stringency in the money market" in New York city, while millions of people scattered all over the country are famishing for money. In the Western States farms are being sold by thousands and thousands every year under the sheriff's hammer, turning out a family from every one. Cruel as the process is, and dangerous as such a system must be in rapidly placing our land in the hands of landlords and making renters of our farmers, we find that most of our public men do not recognize the existence of the dreadful fact. We call the attention of our party leaders to these things, and they remind us that it is our business to do the voting, it is their business to do the thinking; it is their business to make the laws, and our business to obey them. When we call attention to the weight of our misfortunes, they tell us we are producing too much wheat, too much corn, we are raising too many cattle, too many horses, too many swine and sheep; that we are forcing upon the market too much cotton, too much tobacco, too much wool, and that we must change our methods of farming; that, being farmers and laborers, we know nothing about great matters of statecraft, and especially that we are endangering our interests and standing by meddling with financial affairs.

If the reader will now go back to the last paragraph quoted above from the Secretary's report, he shall have the remainder. "This," says the Secretary, "was followed by another" (another purchase of bonds and prepayment of interest upon the same terms as before), "dated September 6, inviting holders of the 4-per-cent bonds to accept prepayment of interest on those bonds to July 1, 1891, a privilege which was subsequently extended to the holders of currency sixes. Under this circular of August 30 there were redeemed $18,678,100 4½-per-cent bonds, and under that of September 6 there was prepaid on the 4-per-cent bonds and currency sixes interest amounting to $12,009,951.50." The reader will observe here one item, the last one, of $12,009,951.50 of interest prepaid to July 1, 1891, an advance of that much money to men who have no need of it. The purchases of outstanding bonds not due and payable might be excused upon the ground of paying a debt out of an overflowing treasury, but what excuse can be offered for the advance of a year's interest as a gratuity upon the part of the Government in order to assist men who are engaged in a business, as the Secretary very well knows, and as the rest of the world knows, not of providing the people with money, but of providing themselves with means of getting more money. It is a brazen outrage, utterly inexcusable from any point of view, a course of conduct which ought to be condemned in the strongest terms; and parties and policies which have originated such a system, and which maintain it and propose to continue it, ought to be utterly wiped out of American politics. It is time that labor should be emancipated, the money power dethroned, and the authority of the people restored. The farmer, the working man, the toiler in any and in every department of industry, may ask and plead until he grows hoarse and poor for relief from the "stringency in the money market" in his own case, while the men of Wall Street, at whose beck and call the Government of a great nation goes and comes, are living in luxury and ease at their expense.

Quoting again from the Secretary on the same page (page xxix): "The amount of public money set free within seventy-five days by these several disbursements was nearly $76,-660,000, and the net gain to circulation was not less than $45,-000,000, yet the financial conditions made further prompt disbursements imperatively necessary. A circular was, therefore, published September 13, 1890, inviting proposals, to be considered on the 17th, for the sale, to the Government, of $16,-000,000 of 4-per-cent bonds. The offerings under this circular amounted to $35,514,900, of which $17,071,150 were offered at 126¾, or less, and were accepted."

Here we have six different applications of the people's money, amounting to but little short of a hundred million dollars in less than three months to assist the financial operations of money changers in New York city, when farmers in every State in the Union are pleading for relief from an overpowering depression. Property values are depressed, farmers are scarcely able to pay their necessary expenses, including taxes and interest on their mortgages; wages among working men are being reduced continually, and it is probably safe to say that two million men, besides an army of women, are out of employment, the number of idle people steadily increasing. The writer desires to urge this important matter upon the attention of the people, so that they may see it and study it in all its enormity. The consequence of such a system long continued is inevitably the absorption of all the wealth of the country in the hands of a very few persons. It is going that way now with unprecedented speed. Wealth is accumulating in the large cities, more especially in those of the East, and those accumulations are continually fed by drains flowing away from the country people and working forces in the towns. Dark, deep lines are already visible between wealth and poverty, and they are becoming more and more conspicuous from year to year. It is time that this gigantic system of spoliation be stopped.

[Peffer contends that the power to regulate commerce, as well as the prerogatives of sovereignty, give the federal government the right to provide money at low rates to the laboring classes. What follows is perhaps the most distinctive theme found in his other writings, where he continues the discussion.]

. . . This brings us to where we can understand what the real function of money is—namely, *to serve a public use.* What the highway and its moving vehicles laden with produce do in the movement of commodities, money in circulation does in the exchange of values; as it is with the highway, so it is with money—the function of both is to serve a public use.

Before discussing further the philosophy of money and illustrating its uses and functions, let it be understood, to begin with, that the underlying proposition involved is that *money is a necessary instrument of commerce.* This proposition is not a new one. It has been suggested many times by economists, by statesmen, by lawyers in their briefs, and by courts in judicial decisions. Daniel Webster, in some of his most memorable speeches, asserted the doctrine. The Supreme Court of the United States has affirmed it, and it probably will not be disputed by any person claiming to have thought upon the subject. It is well that this be kept in mind. Money is a *necessary* instrument of commerce—not simply an instrument, but a NECESSARY instrument. Let it be inquired at this point why the people empowered Congress to regulate commerce among the several States? What is it to have such a thing as a regulation of commerce? Why is Congress authorized to levy duties upon imports? Why is Congress authorized to levy taxes upon the people? There is but one answer. All of these things are public functions, and besides being public functions they are classed among the prerogatives of sovereignty. The people of the United States constitute a nation. Congress represents our legislative power, courts represent our judicial power, the President and his subordinate officers represent our executive power. All of them combined are called the "Government." Acting in harmony they are an agent of the people for the purpose of executing the popular will. The reason why Congress was authorized to take charge of the commerce of the people is that when the people of the several States undertook to regulate commercial affairs among themselves it was found to be utterly impracticable. One of the principal reasons for adopting the Constitution and organizing a new government under it was that there might be a central authority somewhere to exercise the sovereign power of the people. Commerce means simply trading among the people, selling and buying, buying and selling, carrying property, exchanging values, moving things from place to place. The people are all alike interested in this matter, and for that reason chiefly the Government is empowered to take charge of it and to regulate it—not to please the Government, but in the interest of the people. From that comes the power to open and maintain thoroughfares; from that comes the power to take away lands belonging to the people; to move their houses and their fixed improvements in order that a highway may be opened there, that a canal may be cut through, or a railway constructed. These things are done in the public interest, for the common good. The land is taken because the public demands it; the property is used because the public wants it; it is all done to promote the general welfare. The railroad is as much a need of commerce as the common highway—indeed, it is much more important now, if such a thing could be, than the common highway, because producer and consumer are many miles apart. Wheat and corn grown upon a Kansas farm are used in Philadelphia, in New York, in Boston, in Liverpool, in London; it is carried to all parts of the world. Wool produced among the mountains of Montana is carried to Boston, manufactured there, and scattered all over the world. The internal trade of the United States, measured either in tons or in dollars, exceeds the aggregate foreign commerce of any half-dozen other nations. Its value is almost beyond computation. One of the essential parts of this vast system of trade, absolutely necessary for transacting it, is money. Without money commerce would cease; without money all movement of trade would stop; without money there would be no business; all exchange would be barter, and that would take us back to barbarism.

CONGRESS MAY REGULATE INSTRUMENTS OF COMMERCE.

If, then, Congress is authorized to regulate *commerce* among the several States, it is also authorized to regulate the *instruments of* commerce. It may prescribe what kinds of roads and ways shall be opened; what kinds of vehicles shall be run on them; what shall be the rate of toll; whether, indeed, any person other than authorized agents of the Government shall be permitted to manage and to control the ways. The same power which authorizes the Government to open and maintain highways, post roads, and the like authorizes it to build roads for the people without the intervention of any corporation whatever; to build the roads, to own them, to manage them in the interest of the people; and this right to regulate commerce includes necessarily—not only impliedly, but *necessarily*—every function essential to the work. That makes it plain that it is not only within the province and power of the people through their agent, the Government, to regulate money as an instrument of commerce, but to regulate its quantity, to regulate the manner of its issuance, to dictate the materia¹ out of which it shall be made, to prescribe the form, the inscriptions, and devices which shall appear upon it, to prescribe the amount which shall be issued, the channels through which it shall reach the people, and to regulate the charges for its use. If, then, the Government may not only make the money as it is doing now—that is to say, performing the mechanical work—and dictate the material out of which it shall be made and regulate its value, but also regulate the manner of its issuance and provide the ways and means by which it shall reach the people, and may also regulate the rate of charges to be exacted for its use among the people, there is no reason why the Government should not do for the people directly what it is now doing for them indirectly through banking institutions, and permitting the banks to charge a very high percentage for their services. If the Government may issue a hundred million dollars in bank notes to banking corporations upon the deposit of Government bonds as security and then permit the banks to lend that money to the people at 10 per cent interest, what is to hinder the Government from lending the money directly to the people and taking their property as security, just as the banks do?

. . . So, we see, we now have all the necessary machinery ready for the inauguration and management of a system by which the people can control their own financial affairs in their own way.

28. A Call to Action

The history of midwestern reform currents in the generation after the Civil War could be written through the person of James Baird Weaver of Iowa. Weaver was the presidential candidate of the Greenback party in 1880, and of the People's party in 1892, and three-time congressman, as a Greenbacker with Democratic support, in the years between 1878 and 1887. He spoke out consistently and strongly on the major issues during this period, sometimes alone among national figures, and in the election of 1880, when he received slightly over three hundred thousand votes, his canvass was so extensive as to crystallize these issues for subsequent movements of protest. Thus, politics became for him, as for other independents, a means of educating the people. There was no hope of winning elections on the national level, at least not until the phrase "educate, agitate, organize" bore more fruit, but this did not prevent Weaver from taking his case to the country at large. In 1892 he received over one million popular votes, and twenty-two votes in the electoral college.

In Congress, Weaver attacked the existing financial legislation, opposed speculation in the public lands, warned that the Interstate Commerce Bill was wholly innocuous and that it was consciously rendered so in order to create the fiction without the substance of actual regulation, and finally, called attention to the construction of armories in the late 1880's as being a not too subtle attempt to coerce the working class. Although he was considered moderate within the Populist spectrum, having called for a narrowing of the

Reprinted from James B. Weaver, *A Call to Action* (Des Moines: Iowa Printing Company, 1892), pp. 5-6, 27-36, 78-94, 185, 202-203, 206, 212-225, 247-253, 266-267, 280-298, 333-335, 439-440, 445.

platform and an endorsement of William Jennings Bryan in 1896, Weaver's policy of fusion cannot be interpreted as a hunger for office and a sellout on principles. That he could have secured a seat in the United States Senate long before, if only he were to sacrifice principles and work within the Republican party, is a well-known aspect of Iowa history. He turned that offer down on more than one occasion. His strategy in the 1896 campaign may have been mistaken, but it did not signify a repudiation of his twenty years of fighting for social reforms.

In these selections from *A Call to Action*, a book containing 445 closely packed pages, one cannot hope to bring out more than the outlines of Weaver's thinking.

The author's object in publishing this book is to call attention to some of the more serious evils which now disturb the repose of American society and threaten the overthrow of free institutions.

We are nearing a serious crisis. If the present strained relations between wealth owners and wealth producers continue much longer they will ripen into frightful disaster. This universal discontent must be quickly interpreted and its causes removed. It is the country's imperative Call to Action, and can not be longer disregarded with impunity.

The sovereign right to regulate commerce among our magnificent union of States, and to control the instruments of commerce, the right to issue the currency and to determine the money supply for sixty-three million people and their posterity, have been leased to associated speculators. The brightest lights of the legal profession have been lured from their honorable relation to the people in the administration of justice, and through evolution in crime the corporation has taken the place of the pirate; and finally a bold and aggressive plutocracy has usurped the Government and is using it as a policeman to enforce its insolent decrees. It has filled the Senate with its adherents, it controls the popular branch of the National Legislature by cunningly filling the Speaker's chair with its representatives, and it has not hesitated to tamper with our Court of last resort. The public domain has been squandered, our coal fields bartered away, our forests denuded, our people impoverished, and we are attempting to build a prosperous commonwealth among people who are being robbed of their homes—a task as futile and impossible as it would be to attempt to cultivate a thrifty forest without soil to sustain it. The corporation has been placed above the individual and an armed body of cruel mercenaries permitted, in times of public peril, to discharge police duties which clearly belong to the State.

"LET US ALONE."

. . . The corporations and special interests of every class created during the past twenty-five years by various species of class legislation and favoritism, have grown rich and powerful. They are now pleading to be let alone. They cry out, "You will disturb the peace, unsettle business and violate our vested constitutional rights." The world has heard similar lamentations before. The same spirit has lurked in the pathway of progress and hissed its sinister protests from behind the Constitution and from beneath the very altars of our holy religion, from the beginning until now. The same argument was urged against the introduction of the gospel in the early days of Christianity.

. . . This old plea is now urged, however, in behalf of corporation usurpers and tyrants. They have nothing to gain by change. On the contrary everything to lose. Their Juggernaut must move and the car of progress stand still. They would not have the situation otherwise than it is, and as the most effectual method of enforcing this policy they have quietly filled the Senate with their friends. The punishment meted out by the corporations to Judge Thurman, of Ohio, for the faithful discharge of his duty concerning the Pacific railroads, while a member of the Senate, and the defeat of General Van Wyck, in Nebraska, after the people had expressed a desire for his re-election—these and a score of similar instances—attest only too accurately the extent and the deadly character of corporate influence in this body.

[In an earlier portion, Weaver analyzes the powers of the Senate and how some of these have been taken away from other branches, and also makes relevant comparisons with English institutional history. What follows is an indictment of the Senate reminiscent of, but clearly antedating, the muckraking literature.]

The Senate, as we have seen, was incorporated into our legislative system as a check upon the rashness and apprehended extremes of the popular branch of Congress. But it was not contemplated, even by Dickinson and Hamilton, that it should become the stronghold of monopoly, nor that it should hedge up the way to all reform and make impossible the peaceful overthrow of conceded abuses. In fact no tendency in this direction was observable until within the past thirty years. But of late this body has come to represent both the evil and the inertia of government. When you visit the Senate chamber you are at once reminded of antiquity. You feel that you are not far removed from that period when the changeless laws of the Medes and Persians were in force. If, without diverting your attention, you could be suddenly transported to an Egyptian charnel-house filled with mummies, you would be likely to mistake it for a Senate cloak-room. The very foot-falls of the Senators, as they walk across the tessellated floors, sound like a constant iteration of statu quo! statu quo! statu quo!

THE SILVER EPISODE.

Recent occurances have caused many persons to doubt the correctness of public sentiment concerning the Senate. The whole country was taken aback and the majority of the people agreeably surprised, during the session of the Fifty-first Congress, by the passage through the Senate of a bill providing for the free coinage of silver. It was strangled in the House of Representatives and the people were amazed. Many thought that this called at least for a suspension, if not for a revision of public sentiment concerning the upper house of our Congress. A moment's reflection will explain it all. The Republican majority in the Senate is not large. There are a few Republican Senators like Mr. Jones and Mr. Stewart of Nevada, Mr. Teller of Colorado, and Mr. Stanford of California, who really favor free coinage; and so of a few Democratic Senators, like Mr. Daniels of Virginia, Mr. Vorhees, of Indiana, and others. But the great body of Democratic Senators voted for free coinage with no higher motive than to embarrass the Republican speaker, the leaders of the House and the administration, who were known to be hostile to such legislation. For example, Senator Carlisle voted for the bill in the Senate, and yet while he was Speaker of the House in the preceding Congress, he was known to be uncompromisingly hostile to the free coinage of silver; and although he always appointed Mr. Bland chairman of the Committee on Coinage, Weights and Measures, he invariably filled the committee with anti-silver men, and thus made legislation in that direction impossible. No, with a sort of feline cruelty they were only playing with the free coinage mouse. It could be allowed to escape from the Senate, but they felt certain that the presiding officer at the other end of the Capitol could be relied upon to slay it at first sight. And if, unhappily, it should run successfully the gauntlet of the House, there was a trap at the other end of the avenue already waiting for the intruder, and it could be relied upon to do its work—an Executive veto was in waiting. Had there been the slightest probability, or even possibility, that the bill would become law it could never have been reported for consideration. This view of the silver episode is in strict accord with the history of the Senate for fully a quarter of a century, and it is in harmony with the personal biography of a large majority of its members regardless of party.

INFLUENCE OF WEALTHY SENATORS.

The opinion expressed by Mr. Dickinson, in the constitutional convention, that men of wealth would be more likely to be selected for the Senate by State legislatures than by the people themselves, has been justified by the experience of the last thirty years. A large number of Senators are men of great wealth. Many of them have been the beneficiaries of class legislation which of late years has marked our history, and have acquired fabulous fortunes. A few have grown rich by superior energy and enterprise. A small number inherited their riches. But without regard to the methods by which their wealth was acquired, the over-shadowing influence of the wealthy members over their less fortunate colleagues is a fact beyond dispute. It is still true that knowledge is power, but its processes are often tedious and its rewards tardy. Accumulated wealth is also power and it can exercise its strength at a moment's notice and often, for the time being, drives knowledge ignominiously from the field. But the latter generally returns re-enforced by experience. Ready cash is the storage battery of social and business influence. When directed in legitimate channels its energies are helpful and safe; but it also possesses a death-dealing current and the world is full of its victims. Under our present method of electing Senators it is an easy matter for an unscrupulous man of wealth to secure the position. When elected it is extremely difficult to displace him. Length of service affords opportunity to become established socially and officially. When a new Senator makes his appearance he is duly estimated and every courtesy and clever attention is extended to him. If the new member is a man of wealth, his status is fixed at once. If he is poor, it will not be long, unless he be unusually alert, before he is likely to find himself under some obligation to his wealthy colleagues which tends to greatly circumscribe his power and limit his independence. If wealthy Senators were few in number they would still wield a dangerous influence over legislation. But when you add numbers to wealth, the danger is frightfully increased. At least a score of our Senators are millionaires. Another score are worth each a hundred thousand or more. Half a score are men of very considerable wealth. The remainder range from twenty thousand down to near the value of their salaries.

CORPORATION ATTORNEYS IN THE SENATE.

The immense volume of legislation relating to land grants, internal and external commerce, railway subsidies, excise taxes and import duties, contracts for carrying the mails, purchase of Indian lands, private land grants, steam ship subsidies, and a thousand and one other matters, have given rise to a flood tide of litigation unequaled in any age or clime. A large number of the contentions rising out of this legislation involve the construction of acts of congress, and not unfrequently their constitutionality also. In many cases the collection and proper disbursement of public moneys are called directly in question, and as long as Senators stand in the relation of law makers to the public, a proper appreciation of their high office should restrain them from appearing as attorneys, either for corporations or individuals, in cases involving the proper interpretation of statutes which they themselves have made. The practice, however, is just the reverse. When the Supreme Court is in session it is a common thing to see the leading Senators leave their seats and pass into the court room, there to act as counsel for the leading corporations. Many Senators are annually retained by corporations and other moneyed interests. Such things are incompatible with the faithful discharge of public duty. It is true that the salaries and lawful emoluments of Senatorial life are meagre and uninviting; but no one is compelled to accept them. When once accepted, however, the privileges of the lawyer should cease just where the duties of the public servant begin. At this point his relation to the public changes entirely. The Nation then becomes his client and he should appear in his place and plead the cause of the whole people without mental reservation or self-evasion. No other rule is compatible with public duty or private honor. Public sentiment which will knowingly tolerate the infraction of such rule is utterly demoralized, and law makers who insist upon such indulgence should at once be permitted to return to the practice of their profession and to private life.

THE DECLINE OF THE SENATE.

There is not a single great leader in the Senate of to-day, not one who is abreast of the times, or who can be truthfully said to be the exponent of American civilization or the active champion of the reforms made necessary by the growth and changed relations of a century, and which are now struggling for recognition.

. . . They are stifled by their surroundings and dwarfed by their parties. One and all, they stand dumb and aimless in the presence of the mighty problems of the age. The situation reminds one of the era in the history of our planet mentioned in the book of Genesis, when it is said: "There was not a man to till the ground."

This august body is literally filled with splendid specimens of a by-gone epoch—men whose only mission is to preserve the old order of things—to guard the embalmed corpse of the past from the touch of the profane reformer. They are the lineal descendents of the fellows who skulked in the camp of Israel when Joshua insisted on crossing the Jordan into the promised land. They are as much out of place in this pulsating age of reform as a mastodon or a megatherium would be among a herd of our modern well-bred domestic animals. They are fit only to adorn museums and musty cabinets. If their commissions could be recalled to-day and the question of their return referred to an open vote of their constituents, there is not one in ten who would stand a ghost of a show for re-election. They are not in touch with the people. Their strength lies in their entrenched position—not in their achievements nor the principles which they represent. If dislodged, they would be powerless to make another stand. We, of course, do not include in this criticism the two or three prophets of the new order of things, who have but recently been commissioned to go unto Ninevah, that great city, and to preach unto it the preaching whereunto they have been called. It will be time enough to speak of them when they shall have had opportunity to obey those who sent them.

Every great movement and struggle of the race develops its own leaders, who are forced to assault fortified positions and fight against great odds. Some positions have to be carried by storm, while others can only be taken by regular approaches which sorely try the endurance and resources of the besieging columns. Such were the characteristics of the great struggle of the 60's. Their storming parties were hurled forward with dash and power, and their sieges were stubborn and successful. To change the figure, the pioneers in the movement doubtless had a clear vision of the land to be ultimately possessed, but they quickly passed away and were succeeded by an inferior order of leaders who felt that they had done their whole duty when they had driven out the wild beasts, cleared away the forest and prepared the ground for the reception of good seed. They then rested upon their laurels and allowed the enemy to sow the field with taxes. The seed has grown, the harvest has ripened, and the reapers are under orders to burn the tares.

The moral, intellectual and political leaders during the twenty years immediately following the war, with the single

exception of Wendell Phillips, failed to comprehend the problems which confronted them. They stopped with the overthrow of the outward form of slavery. Through the strength
and suffering of the great army of the people they succeeded
in breaking the chains of chattel slavery and prepared the
way for the complete triumph of man over those who lived by
the enslavement of labor. All that was necessary was one
more forward movement of the column, and the victory would
have been complete. But they failed to make it and surrendered to a handful of task masters of another type, whose
triumphs in the slave trade have never, in all the ages, been
limited by distinctions of race or complexions of skin. This
class of slave drivers have never yet been routed or permanently crippled. They have plied their cruel vocation among
all the families of men. To overthrow them is the grand work
of the new crusade. Confederated labor has proclaimed the
new emancipation. Now let the great army of toilers move on
the enemy's works and enforce the decree.

[In his chapter on the House of Representatives, Weaver argues
the need for more ideological politics, so that congressmen will not
merely be slaves to party labels. More important, he anticipates the
necessity for democratizing House rules by taking away the absolute powers of the Speaker. He calls for the creation of a committee,
made up of members from the House, to determine committee
assignments.

Turning to the discussion on the Supreme Court, one can see the
richness of Weaver's background. In these remarks, at this point on
the policy of recruitment, he anticipates Veblen on certain aspects.]

. . . Let us now proceed to other important considerations
connected with this Tribunal. The members of this Court, as
a rule, must necessarily be selected from among eminent
members of the legal profession, actively engaged in practice,
or chosen from among those who have been elevated to the
District or Circuit bench or to judicial positions in the States.

The number from whom the selections might be made is reduced one-half from party considerations to begin with. Hence
the President, with whom the nominating power resides, is
confined within very narrow limits when he makes his selections, and he is still further restricted by other considerations,
which may hinder or accelerate confirmation by the Senate.

For nearly a century two kindred inspirations held control
of the legal profession in America. These baptisms of fire ante-
dated our present structure of Government and filled the
whole bar with an exalted ambition—first, to be eminent in
the profession ordained to aid in the proper administration of
justice; and second, to enter the halls of legislation where they
might serve the people and assist in the construction of a real
Republic, wherein the chief solicitude of all ages, liberty,
fraternity and justice among men, should be both practicable
and real.

At last, however, there came a falling away, and the relation
of the legal profession to the public began to show signs of
change. We shall not undertake to trace the decline, for both
its cause and its history are within the recollection of most of
the present generation. The unholy and lawless determination
to acquire wealth and personal comfort at the expense of a
weaker and less fortunate race, was the underlying spirit of
slavery. The commercial and political importance of this institution soon became apparent and prominent. To be secure, its
adherents contended that all branches of the Government
should be controlled by the friends of that institution. Who
will say that the contention was not logical? In fact such result
was inevitable. It requires but a slight acquaintance with the
history of our Federal judiciary to enable one to understand
that when a given influence dominates the Legislative and
Executive branches of the Government for any considerable
period, the judiciary, even when free from external intrigue,
is always brought into harmony with the influences which
dominate the other co-ordinate branches. If the Legislative

and Executive departments are held by a virile and rugged condition of public sentiment to a faithful discharge of their duties, the danger of the abuse of power by our autocratic Court becomes remote. But all history shows that when evil and despotic influences control the former, the tyranny of the court suddenly becomes intolerable; and the more so, for the reason that the judges are not subject to popular control. The slave oligarchy intrenched itself in the Supreme Court. In 1860, five out of the eight occupants of that bench were from slave holding States, namely: Wayne, of Georgia; Taney, of Maryland; Catron, of Tennessee; Daniel, of Virginia, and Campbell, of Alabama; and that fact had as much influence, if not more, than any other in precipitating the tremendous crisis which followed. The slave interest sought to make the Dred Scott decision the rule of political action for the people and all departments of the Government. We need but glance at the great debates between Abraham Lincoln and Stephen A. Douglass, in 1858, and to recall the fierce political combats which took place in every part of the land between that date and the election of 1860, to understand the truth of the above statement. The people suddenly awoke to the fact that slavery had debauched the whole Government, including the Court of Last resort. In his great speech, delivered in reply to Mr. Douglass, at Springfield, Illinois, on the evening of July 17, 1858, Mr. Lincoln declared, "That one-half of Mr. Douglass' onslaught, and one-third of the entire plan of the campaign" grew out of the attitude of the Supreme Court.

In fine this tribunal had completely blocked the way to freedom and enjoined the further march of civilization in the new world. Legislation could not reach the difficulty. Popular elections could not, for the reason that the Court was nonelective and held by the life tenure; amendment of the Constitution was out of the question, because of the attitude of the slave-holding states. There was no alternative but the sword. We shall not lift the curtain which hides that bloody drama from the gaze of the present generation. Let us hope that the atrocities connected with it may fade entirely from the memory of men and that the good evolved may flourish and bloom and fill the earth with blessing.

We shall now proceed to show that in the very midst of the struggle for the overthrow of the slave oligarchy, our institutions were assailed by another foe mightier than the former, equally cruel, wider in its field of operation, infinitely greater in wealth, and immeasurably more difficult to control. It will be readily understood that we allude to the sudden growth of corporate power and its attendant consequences.

ALARMING CHANGE IN THE SITUATION.

Consequent upon the growth of this power, the relation of the legal profession to the people and to the administration of public justice has undergone a frightful change within the past twenty years. The phenomenal growth and extension of corporate life, followed by the rapid concentration of wealth into a few hands, has lured the profession from its ancient paths, dampened its patriotic ardor, frozen the fountains of its eloquence, and diverted its attention from the ordinary emoluments of a laborious life and the meagre salaries of public positions, to the large and seductive rewards to be obtained in the service of monopolies, corporations, trusts, syndicates and combines. The strong men and great lights of the profession are, to a large extent, captured by these influences as fast as they rise above the dead level of mediocrity, and thus the public service, the profession and the people are degraded, while corporate influence is exalted. It is well known also that very many universities, law colleges and other educational institutions of note have prominent railroad attorneys employed to instruct the youth of the country on corporation law, while many of our Chancellors and Regents are chosen from among the same class of minds. The dangers arising from this state of affairs are of the most serious character, and may well fill the public mind with gravest apprehension. The bench, both

State and National, must be supplied from eminent members
of the bar, and practically all the so-called distinguished members of the profession are in the service of the corporations.
It does not necessarily follow that they are entitled to stand at
the head by natural endowment, or mental and forensic train-
ing. They are given that position and hold it securely by the
power of their clientage. The names of this class of attorneys
are of course kept constantly before the appointing power.
They are the Levites of the profession, set apart and conse-
crated expressly for service upon the Federal Bench, and are
ever looking forward and yearning for promotion. How can
we construct a safe building from unsound timber? When we
shall most need it as a refuge from the storm, it will prove to
be our greatest point of danger, and fall upon and crush us.
The corporations are not only able to employ the ablest talent,
but to back their attorneys with unlimited resources. They can
enable them to travel at trifling expense, open to them the
columns of the press, and grant them the free use of the telegraph to summon assistance at the critical moment. That these,
and kindred influences, have thus been enabled for a score of
years, to exercise almost unlimited control over the Legislative
and Executive branches of the Government is too well established to be denied by intelligent and candid men. That they
have made serious inroads upon every branch of our Judiciary,
and are now stealthily making still further and greater efforts
to obtain complete and, as far as this generation is concerned,
permanent control of our Court of Last resort, is a truth well
known to all whose eyes and ears are open to what is going
on about them. Indeed, it is believed that they have already
practically accomplished their purpose.

A TALK WITH DAVID DAVIS.

Early in the month of June, 1880, and only a few days prior
to the assembling of the nominating convention of the Na-

tional party at Chicago, the Hon. David Davis, Hon. E. H. Gillette, and the writer, had a protracted conversation at Washington, concerning the political situation. Mr. Davis was then a member of the United States Senate from Illinois. Previous to entering that body he had served upon the Supreme Bench for a period of fifteen years. He was a conservative man of great ability, extensive experience and wide range of information. His opinions on all questions were judicially formed and cautiously expressed. In former years he had enjoyed the companionship of Mr. Lincoln, had been his law partner, was appointed by him in 1862 to the Supreme Bench, and was finally the executor of the martyred President's estate.

. . . It was hoped that Judge Davis would consent to become the candidate of the third party for the Presidency, and such was the earnest desire of Mr. Gillette and the writer. Mr. Davis was aware of our preference for him, and the conference above alluded to was concerning that matter. It occurred in one of the Committee rooms of the House of Representatives and lasted for about three hours. The Republican convention was then in session at Chicago, and the ballotting was in progress. Judge Davis opened the conversation by stating that he felt grateful for the mention of his name as the candidate of the industrial people, and was in accord with most of their purposes; but that he was not in a situation to accept the nomination and must decline, and we were instructed to see that his name was not placed before the convention. We plead with him to yield, but without avail. The matter of his candidacy being disposed of, the Judge proceeded to state his views of the situation. He said the people did not know, nor were they in a situation to understand the extreme perils which were impending over the Republic. "The rapid growth of corporate power, of all classes and grades," said he, "and their corrupting influence at the Seat of Government; their overshadowing influence among party managers, from county primaries to National Conventions, fill me with apprehension.

No man is wise enough to foretell what the end will be." He then alluded to his long service upon the Supreme Bench, and said it was evident that the corporations were maturing their plans to gain complete control of the Supreme Court; that his extensive acquaintance with the great corporation lawyers and his daily contact with public men gave him a thorough knowledge of what was going on, and he remarked, "If I were blind I could still hear enough to alarm me. It is not lawful for me to utter many things which I have heard, because I get them in my private and confidential relations every day; but this is my chief concern. If we lose the Courts, we lose all." The Judge further stated that it evidently was the purpose in certain circles to overthrow the Legal Tender decision, the Thurman Act concerning the Pacific Railroads, and the Grange decisions of 1876, and that he felt deeply concerned in consequence. These were not the words of an alarmist; on the contrary, they expressed the sober judgment of an eminent statesman and jurist, who had been upon the Supreme Bench himself for half a generation.

Let us now inquire whether the fears of Judge Davis were well founded. It will be remembered that the conversation which is substantially given above, occurred in June, 1880. Since that time the following changes in the *personnel* of the court have taken place: Nathan Clifford, of Maine, died in 1881, and was succeeded by Horace Gray, of Massachusetts. Noah H. Swayne, of Ohio, retired in 1881, and was succeeded by Stanley Matthews, of Ohio. Ward Hunt, of New York, retired in 1882, and was succeeded by Samuel Blatchford, of New York. William Strong, of Pennsylvania, resigned in 1880, and was succeeded by W. B. Woods, of Georgia, who died in 1887, and was succeeded by L. Q. C. Lamar, of Mississippi. Chief Justice Waite, of Ohio, died in 1888, and was succeeded by Chief Justice Fuller, of Illinois. Stanley Matthews, of Ohio, died in 1889, and was succeeded by David Brewer, of Kansas. Justice Miller, of Iowa, died in 1890, and was succeeded by

Mr. Justice Brown, of Michigan. We wish it clearly understood that we do not call in question, in the slightest degree, either the personal or official integrity of the members of this important tribunal. In its *personnel,* the old court of *ante-bellum* days was beyond reproach. No one has ever seriously questioned that fact. And yet we all now know that they were as clay in the hands of the potter, and were moulded at will by the slave power. The professional life of the members of that court had budded, grown and ripened under the transforming but baleful influence of slavery. When they reached their exalted position upon the bench their perverted judgment and misguided conscience united to impel them to block the way of freedom. The sword came and emancipated both the slave and the Court. The American people are now passing through a similar experience. The patronage, influence and power of the slave oligarchy were mere trifles compared with the corporate dominion of the present day. The social, political and financial strength of the corporations unite to make their influence infinitely greater in American society than that of the slave power ever was, even in the days of its greatest ascendency. The corporation has submerged the whole country and swept everything before it. In the glacial period, geologists tell us, the icebergs lifted the solid granite boulders from their resting places in the north, bore them southward and dropped them upon what are now our western prairies, where they will forever remain as monuments of the elemental conflicts of that far-off age. The deep lines and scratches across their faces tell us the course of the current which submerged and carried them away. They were borne along by superior force. They were finally released when the ice melted beneath the genial rays of the sun. The corporation glacier is now sweeping over this country and lifting out of place the solid granite of our Judiciary and threatening to carry away the very pillars of the Republic. But the light of unclouded public opinion is shining full orbed upon the situation, and ere long, it is hoped, the

iceberg will melt under the fervent heat of well directed investigation and our great Court be permitted to settle back
upon the pedestal of the Constitution, to remain forever as the
hope and refuge of the people.

The election of Mr. Garfield took place in November, 1880.
On the 26th day of January following President Hayes sent to
the Senate the name of Stanley Matthews, of Ohio, for Associate Justice, to succeed Noah H. Swayne, retired. As Mr.
Matthews was known to be a prominent corporation lawyer,
the appointment was a sudden surprise to the country, and
met with strong opposition in the Senate and very damaging
criticism elsewhere. Many of the leading anti-monopoly journals openly characterized the appointment as a shameful disregard of public opinion and a gross betrayal of the people.
Mr. Matthews, while filling the unexpired term of Mr. Sherman in the Senate had, with great skill and adroitness, opposed
the passage of the Thurman act, touching the Pacific railroad
indebtedness, on the ground, as he claimed, of its repugnance
to the Constitution. The opposition to this appointment was
led in the Senate by David Davis, Allen G. Thurman, Mr. Edmunds, and General Logan. It is understood, however, that
Mr. Edmunds' opposition was caused by his desire to secure
the appointment for a friend in his own State. The friends of
Mr. Matthews were not strong enough to force confirmation.
Senators Ingalls and Lamar were the only members of the
Judiciary Committee who favored it. The nomination lapsed.
Then came the inauguration of Mr. Garfield, followed by the
usual extraordinary session of the Senate. On the 12th of
March the newly installed President again sent to the Senate
the name of Mr. Matthews. Senators Davis, Thurman and
Logan were still firm in their opposition. Protracted delay followed, and confirmation seemed for a while decidedly doubtful. Finally, after much delay, on the 12th day of May, just
sixty days after the name of Mr. Matthews had been sent in
for the second time, he was confirmed by a vote of 22 yeas,

21 nays. The public prints were full of uncomplimentary statements concerning methods made use of to secure confirmation, but it is foreign to our purpose to reproduce them here. We shall not stop to question either the motives of the two Presidents or the integrity of the appointee. The point we insist upon is this: the nomination of Mr. Matthews was in defiance of public opinion. This was clearly shown by the protest which followed and by the fact that it was at first practically rejected by the Senate. And we submit in all candor, that after the nomination had once lapsed in the face of the great popular opposition which it had evoked, proper deference to the well defined state of public opinion should have prevented the incoming President from again forcing the nomination upon the Senate and the country. This is a representative case, and it affords the reader a clear view of the influences which shape and control the most important affairs of our Republic. It is clear that there is some power in this country which is above the Government and more authoritative than public opinion, and which can exert itself successfully at critical moments in high places. A child can tell what that power is. It is the omnipresent, omnipotent corporation. It is the same old malevolent, insidious influence of organized oligarchy—of plutocratic power—and it is now asserting itself for the second time within the memory of the present generation. The pirate plunders by violence. The burglar enters your house prepared to take life if he cannot otherwise escape. But the corporation plunders by the permission or through the agency of the State, and to cut off all hope of redress they seize upon the courts, which constitute the only hope and refuge of an oppressed people this side of revolution. Organized wrong understands well the value of the courts of a country, and particularly of the Courts of last resort. Hence they look well to the appointing power. On the other hand, the people seem to be unmindful of everything pertaining to their welfare, and they suffer uncomplainingly until peaceful redress becomes well nigh

impossible. The old Court, under the influence of the oligarchy of that day, went to the extreme of deciding, in effect, that the Constitution was a skillfully constructed web of clanking slave chains, rather than a bristling panoply of freedom. But an obsequious Judiciary and a perverted Constitution could not, at that time, stay the onward march of freedom, nor hold even a weak and disfranchised race in bondage. And should the new Court encounter the storm center of public opinion, now rapidly forming, it will be as chaff before the gale.

A DECISION REVERSED.

On the 22d day of March, 1887, Mr. Lamar, then Secretary of the Interior, directed the Commissioner of the General Land Office, Gen. Sparks, to cause a grant of land in Wisconsin, made to the Chicago, St. Paul, Minneapolis & Omaha Railway, and its branch line, to be adjusted; and further directed the Commissioner to transmit to the Secretary for approval, proper lists of lands selected by said Company as indemnity lands, in lieu of lands which had been granted to them, but of which they had been deprived by the act of the Government. This was provided for in the grant.

The original act granting lands to this Company was passed in 1856, and granted six alternate sections to the mile on each side of the road. The act of May 5, 1864, increased the grant to ten sections per mile. The acts provided in substance, that if the Government had, prior to the passage of this grant to the railroads, disposed of any of the lands embraced within the limits of this grant, said lands were to be excluded from the operation of the act except as to right of way, and should not be affected by it, but remain as though no grant had ever been made. The task before the Commissioner of the General Land Office seemed easy enough. For all lands of which the railroad had been deprived by act of the Government, between the date of the grant and the definite location of the line of the road, they were to be allowed to select other lands. For lands which the Government had disposed of before Congress made the grant, they could not have other lands. The Supreme Court, in an able opinion delivered by David Davis, in the Leavenworth, Lawrence & Galveston, R. R. 92 U. S., 733, had held in 1875, that the road could not have indemnity for lands which had been disposed of prior to the date of the grant, and which were excluded from the grant by the terms thereof. With this decision and the granting act before him, Gen. Sparks proceeded to adjust this Wisconsin grant. He found that the Government had, prior to the date of the grant to the railroad company, appropriated about seventy-four thousand acres embraced within the limits of the grant. He very properly held that inasmuch as these seventy-four thousand acres had never been given to the corporation, but on the contrary, had at a prior date been set apart for other purposes, the corporation was not entitled to indemnity. Having never been granted, there had been no loss; and having been no loss there could be no indemnity. The adjustment and list were duly certified to Secretary Lamar for his approval. The Secretary promptly reversed the decision of the Commissioner and held that the corporation was entitled to select indemnity lands, in lieu of the seventy-four thousand acres with which the Government had parted prior to the passage of the act, and in his decision he stated that the opinion of the Supreme Court, before referred to, as delivered by David Davis, in the L. L. & G, case, had been overruled, and that if it had not been overruled it was dictum. A subsequent decision in what is known as the Barney case, 113 U. S., 618, was referred to as authority for his ruling.

The two cases were radically different as to the questions of law and fact involved. It is a notable fact that Field, Swayne and Strong had dissented from the opinion of the Court in the L. L. & G. case, and that Field delivered the opinion in the Barney case. It is evident therefore that Secretary Lamar regarded Judge Davis' majority opinion as unsound, and the dissenting opinion of Justice Field as the correct statement of the law.

This difference of opinion concerning the proper construc-tion of the law applicable to the Wisconsin case led to a mis-understanding between Secretary Lamar and Mr. Sparks, Commissioner of the General Land Office, which caused the latter to resign. Their respective views of the law were irrec-oncilable.

Shortly after Congress convened in December, 1887, the President nominated Mr. Lamar as Justice of the Supreme Court to succeed Justice Woods, of Georgia, deceased, and he was accordingly, after considerable delay, confirmed by the Senate. Mr. Lamar, during the pendency of his nomination in the Senate, resigned as Secretary of the Interior. But before doing so removed from office Mr. J. W. LeBarnes, the Law Clerk of the Department, who concurred in General Sparks' opinion of the law in the case above named. We do not call in question the good faith of Mr. Lamar, nor the motives of the President in making the appointment. But here was a grave public question, concerning which the members of the Supreme Court were themselves at variance. The land grant companies were interested in securing the appointment of a member of the Court whose construction of the law would give them the largest amount of land. The people were inter-ested in having Judge Davis' decision, which construed the grants strictly, sustained.

Let us notice for a moment the magnitude of this single victory over the people. First, the railroad company secured seventy-four thousand acres of land more than the Commis-sioner thought they were entitled to; second, they secured the removal of the Commissioner of the General Land Office, whose brusk honesty brought him into conflict with their ne-farious schemes; third, they secured the removal of Law Clerk, LeBarnes, who was a serious obstacle in their way; fourth, they overthrew the David Davis decision in the L. L. & G.

case, and secured the adoption of a rule, which, when applied to all other grants, as it has since steadily been, gives them probably ten million acres more than they could have obtained under the old rule. These ten million acres are worth to them at least one hundred million dollars.

While the confirmation of the ex-Secretary was hanging fire in the Senate, as we are informed by Gen. Sparks, the force in the railroad division of the General Land Office was kept busy almost day and night, issuing patents for the lands covered by this decision; and the lady who signs the President's name to the patents was sent for after night to affix the Executive signature to the patents which conveyed this land to the railroads. This episode illustrates with tremendous force the danger inherent in the method of selecting the members of this great Court.

. . . Slavery was restricted within narrow geographical limits and the visible manifestations of the evil were repulsive and hateful to all who were removed from its immediate influence. Not so with the present foe of justice and social order. It assails the rights of man under the most seductive guise. You meet it in every walk of life. It speaks through the press, gives zeal and eloquence to the bar, engrosses the constant attention of the bench, organizes the influences which surround our legislative bodies and courts of justice, designates who shall be the Regents and Chancellors in our leading Universities, determines who shall be our Senators, how our legislatures shall be organized, who shall preside over them and who constitute the important committees. It is imperial in political caucases, without a rival in social circles, endows institutions of learning, disburses monthly large sums of money to an army of employés, has unlimited resources of ready cash, is expert in political intrigue and pervades every community from the center to the circumference of the Republic.

[In Weaver's discussion of financial contraction in England and the United States, it is important to note his use of authorities, and his explanation for the coalescence of financial groups in both societies —not only common interests, but also similar backgrounds and world views.]

FINANCE IN WAR AND PEACE.

. . . Labor can create wealth but it cannot create money. It requires a statute to speak money into existence. It is the creature of law, not the product of nature. It can neither be made by the march of battalions nor by plowing in the field, but it can be made to change hands by both.

The beneficial effects of the bountiful issue of money in times of public peril, verify in the strongest possible manner the necessity for an adequate circulating medium at all times; and they bring out in strong light the duty of a great and powerful Government to furnish its citizens with a constant non-fluctuating money supply.

The history of modern nations is trumpet-tongued with warnings against all attempts to return to ante-bellum fiscal methods and financial policies after the perils of war have passed.

THE TWO WITNESSES.

It is our purpose in this chapter to introduce for the consideration of the reader the most important events, in war and peace, connected with the financial history of Great Britain and the United States, the two leading nations of modern times.

[This is followed by an intensive analysis of England in the periods 1793 to 1796, 1797 to 1815, and from 1819 onward. Weaver quotes at length from Sir Archibald Alison, *England in 1815 and 1845, or a Sufficient and a Contracted Currency.*]

. . . It is interesting to note that the English people passed through the same stages of controversy which have characterized the American situation during the past twenty-five years. British resumption was preceded, as before stated, with the demonetization of silver and the limitation of its legal tender quality, and also followed by an immense contraction of the currency which amounted to nearly one-half of the paper in circulation. Distress among the agricultural classes and among all branches of labor ensued, as a matter of course, and Parliament was petitioned by every class of industry for relief.

THE TARIFF DOCTOR.

At this point the tariff empiric made his appearance and the people were told that public distress was neither caused by a contraction of the currency nor by a deficiency of the circulating medium, but was caused by the sudden transition from war to peace and by the burdens of taxation. That as soon as the nation would be relieved from this burden and when again settled into its accustomed state of tranquility, things would go on as before and all classes of society would be prosperous.

They were told that the thing which afflicted English industries most was their system of indirect taxation—tariff duties. If these could be repealed all classes would at once emerge into an era of unparalleled prosperity.

The farmers were skeptical, however, and petitioned for loans from the Government at a low rate of interest—loans based on staple agricultural products and upon land. (See Ricardo's Works, p. 456.) But they were told this would never do as it would lead to an inflation of the currency which would certainly prove detrimental to all classes. Diminished burdens was the remedy. This would relieve them of their distresses. Nothing else was necessary. Constant use of cathartics and total abstinence from tonics was the sum total of the political therapeutics of the period. Ricardo published his work upon political economy; learned speeches were made in Parliament; reports of parliamentary committees filled the journals of both houses; and finally the concensus of opinion approved of the plan of repealing gradually the indirect taxes with a view to reaching ultimate free trade and to secure the relief so sorely needed. Accordingly the plan was entered upon, and between 1819 and 1845, there were 30,000,000£ of indirect taxes repealed and England reached a condition of trade which is characterized by the economists of our day as being practically free from the abomination of protective laws. Has British labor been emancipated in consequence? In spite of the relief which came to labor and agriculture from a repeal of the so-called protective duties, the condition of the laboring classes of Great Britain has grown worse from year to year, and the number of land-owners has constantly diminished. The reflective mind will find in this ample proof that labor needs something more than mere relief from its pack-saddle. The pittance saved by the repeal of taxes will not alone afford relief. He must have rest, food, and opportunity for intellectual and moral culture. To secure these essential comforts the income from his toil must be materially increased. Without money his wants can only be appeased at the hand of charity. If his money has been filched from him it should be restored. If withheld it should be granted him at once.

But let our enlightened historian, Mr. Alison, point out to us the real cause of distress among the British laboring people. After showing that the repeal of tariff duties did not relieve them, he says: [followed by a discussion of the contraction of the currency.]

. . . The evils which followed the passage of the resumption act threw British society into confusion, and distrust seized generally upon the public mind. In the autumn of 1817 the terrified Government induced the banks to raise the circulation to something near the amount that was flowing in the channels of trade prior to the commencement of contraction. We quote from an English work written and published by Jonathan Duncan, in 1857, to show the magical effect which this reissue of paper had on the commerce of the empire: [again, a long quotation.] . . .

. . . Having acquainted ourselves with the practical operation and effects of the liberal system of finance adopted by Great Britain during the protracted struggle for the overthrow of Napoleon, and having been made familiar with the disastrous and merciless consequence which followed the return of the mother country to the gold basis after the close of that struggle, let us now recall our own experience under like circumstances and policy of legislation. The duplication of history will become strikingly apparent as we advance.

AMERICA FROM 1857 TO 1861.

In the year 1857 the people of the United States were precipitated into financial revulsion. The crisis was brought on by an unhealthy extension of all forms of bank and commercial credit. This expansion occurred while the business of the country was on a specie basis. In the month of October of that year the banks universally suspended cash payments, and the importers of dutiable merchandise stored their wares without payment of duty, as the law permitted them to do, for a period of three years. The foundation upon which the business of the country rested suddenly gave way and of course the whole super-structure tumbled into ruins. The people were deluged with debt and stood empty handed amid the wreckage of existing disaster facing an impending crisis of prodigious magnitude which was destined to burst upon them before they could possibly have time to rebuild their fortunes. On December 22, Congress, following the recommendation of Secretary Cobb, passed an act authorizing the issue of $20,000,000 of interest-bearing treasury notes, which were made receivable in payment of all dues to the United States. This enabled the Government to meet current expenses, but relief was not extensively felt in the ordinary channels of trade as there were no notes issued of less denomination than fifty dollars. Business recuperated at snail's pace and the crippled fortunes of those who suffered disaster dwindled away or were largely consumed by costs incurred in legal proceedings brought for the collection of debt. The people staggered along as best they could for a couple of years and were slowly recovering from the panic, when they were suddenly confronted with the portentious political contest of 1860 which ushered in the protracted and bloody drama that followed.

When Mr. Lincoln was inaugurated he found an empty Treasury, and it soon became apparent that the accumulated resources of the country were wholly inadequate to meet the unprecedented emergencies of the situation.

The initial epoch in the struggle of Great Britain for the overthrow of Napoleon was of four years' duration—from 1793 to 1796, inclusive—and it was, as we have seen, a period of widespread financial depression. It is a remarkable fact that our Government was scourged and chastened in almost exactly the same way for a like period of four years prior to the breaking out of the rebellion. Our financial troubles began with the panic of 1857 and the early months of 1861 plunged us into the vortex of civil war.

FROM 1861 TO 1865.

Fort Sumter surrendered April 14. President Lincoln immediately called for seventy-five thousand men. By June most of the Southern States had seceded, and in that month General Butler, being insufficiently supported, was sorely pressed at Big Bethel. The disastrous battle of Bull Run followed in July and the Union forces fell back upon Washington. Within two days a call was issued for a half million volunteers to serve for three years. Congress met in extra session July 4. The meagre amount of specie in the country soon became apparent and the total inadequacy of our circulating media was plainly seen by all. The Secretary, Mr. Chase, submitted to Congress his plans for raising funds, which consisted of a resort to the issue of Treasury notes. By the acts of July 17 and August 5, 1861, the Secretary was authorized to issue two hundred and forty millions of twenty-year Treasury notes, bearing not to exceed seven per cent, or 7 3-10 per cent Treasury notes, and he was also authorized to issue a limited quantity of Demand notes, bearing no interest but receivable for dues. In August, 1861, Demand notes were issued, the total amount finally aggregating $60,000,000. The New York banks refused to receive them except on special deposit, and the railroads refused them in payment of fares and freight. The Secretary and subordinate treasury officials signed an agreement in writing to receive them in payment of their salaries! General Scott, in September, 1861, issued a general order, which was read to the army, stating that "The Treasury Department, to meet future payments to the troops, is about to supply, besides coin, Treasury notes in five, ten and twenty dollars, as good as gold."

These notes were made a legal tender by the act approved March 17, 1862.

Specie payments were suspended December 28, 1861, and as these demand notes were receivable for customs duties they speedily rose to par with gold and there remained, substantially, through all the vicissitudes of the war until they were retired.

Following the issue of Demand notes came the vast issues of Government paper of various kinds and descriptions. When this mine of wealth and power was opened up, the spirit and matchless courage of the army, the devotion and enthusiasm of the people, and the resolute unfaltering purpose of the administration united to astonish and dazzle the world by their achievements. As the sinews of war were supplied agriculture bounded into prosperity, labor found ample employment at remunerative wages, mercantile pursuits became lucrative, artisans flourished and unprecedented prosperity abounded in country, village and city—and all this despite the terrible strain of the war. The purse of Fortunatus had been found.

A vast mine of power, a great store-house—filled with almost limitless wealth, had been opened to the astonished gaze of the people, and from that moment the strength of the Republic became irresistable. The area of cultivated land rapidly increased, immense lines of transportation were projected and completed, and the revenues, which were so meagre at the commencement of hostilities as to render the Government an object of contempt, under the improved systems of taxation, public loans and the enhanced ability of the people to pay, suddenly became ample to meet the unprecedented emergencies and demands incident to that gigantic struggle. The power of the Government and the strength of its finances increased as the war advanced. Each succeeding call for additional troops was rapidly filled, and confidence in the value of public securities increased as the calls for the sinews of war multiplied. The capitalists who rejected the paltry sixty millions of Demand notes in 1861, were eager to invest in the almost illimitable issues of 1864–5. The Nation had been lifted out of the narrow and sordid ruts of bigoted economists and had emerged into the broad realm which recognized the omnipotence of the people.

The war closed in a blaze of glory after four years of bloody sacrifice. The soldiers of the victorious army returned to their sections of the Union and were amazed to find the country in a state of unexampled prosperity. About two billions of dollars of various kinds of money had been poured into the channels of trade resulting in a flood tide of opulence which reached to every village and hamlet in the North.

Secretary McCulloch, in his report to Congress, December 4, 1865, publicly recognized the improved condition of the country and said: "The country, as a whole, notwithstanding the ravages of the war, and the draught which had been made upon labor, is, by its greatly developed resources, far in advance of real wealth of what it was in 1857 when the last severe financial crisis occurred. The people are now compara-

tively free from debt." * * * * "There is an immense volume
of paper money in circulation."

Speaking of the advance in the prices of those articles which
were in demand by the Government, the secretary said:

"On a basis of paper money, for which there is no outlet, all
articles needed for immediate use, of which it became the measure
of value, felt and responded to the daily increase of the currency;
so that rents and the prices of most articles for which there has
been a demand have been, with slight fluctuations, constantly advancing from the commencement of the war, and are higher now,
with gold at forty-seven per cent premium, than they were when
it was one hundred and eighty-five. Even those which were affected
by the fall of gold upon the surrender of the confederate armies,
or by the increased supply or diminished demand, are advancing
again to the former if not higher rates."

The Secretary further says:

"It is undoubtedly true that trade is carried on much more largely
for cash than was ever the case previous to 1861, and that there is
a much greater proper demand for money than there would be if
sales were made, as heretofore, on credit. It is also true that there
is a larger demand than formerly for money on the part of manufacturers for the payment of operatives."

Both white slaves and black had been emancipated at one
and the same time.

THE GRAVE RESPONSIBILITY OF
THE SECRETARY.

The country, under the encouragement afforded by a sufficient
volume of non-exportable domestic currency, well distributed,
had grown and expanded into proportions which were but
feebly comprehended by the astute head of the Treasury department. It is evident, also, that both he and the speculative
and sinister coterie which surrounded him, were either unable

to comprehend the great economic lessons which had been
evolved by the war, or they were unwilling to accept the truth
which had been thrust upon them by the logic of events. In
the same report to which we have already alluded the Secretary further expressed himself as follows:

"The expansion has now reached such a point as to be absolutely
oppressive to a large portion of the people while at the same time
it is diminishing labor, and is becoming subversive of good morals.
* * * There is no fact more manifest than that the plethora of paper
money is not only undermining the morals of the people by encouraging waste and extravagance, but is striking at the root of our
national prosperity by diminishing labor. * * * The remedy, and
the only remedy within the control of Congress is, in the opinion
of the secretary, to be found in the reduction of the currency."

FROM 1866 TO 1875.

Congress responded to the fervent appeals of this high official
and passed an act approved April 12, 1866, which authorized
the Secretary of the Treasury, at his discretion, to receive
Treasury notes or other obligations issued under any act of
Congress, whether bearing interest or not, in exchange for
Government bonds. This inaugurated the policy of contraction,
set the cremation furnace ablaze for the cineration of our currency, and started the vast majority of persons possessed of
limited means and who were engaged in legitimate business,
across lots to inevitable bankruptcy. On the 31st day of August,
1865, the public debt reached its maximum and amounted to
$2,845,907,626.65. Of this only $1,109,568,191 was bonded
debt. (See Knox's work on U. S. Notes, page 85.) The remainder consisted of treasury notes and currency obligations of
various kinds in circulation as money. By June 30, 1869—a
period of three years and ten months, the bonded debt had
increased, under the currency contraction policy, to $2,166,-

568,920. (See statement of the bonded debt, at various periods, made by the Comptroller, in his report of 1889, page 35.)

In other words, the funded debt had increased over one billion dollars, while various kinds of obligations in use among the people as currency had decreased in like amount.

This tremendous contraction, coupled with the fact that more than ten millions of people residing in the south had, by the close of the war, been suddenly added to our money-using population, compelled the people to substitute credit for money. They ceased to pay cash and plunged into debt wholly oblivious to the fact that the money kings had decreed a universal and disastrous fall in prices. The ten millions of people in the South were now competitors for the residue of currency which has escaped the cremation furnace, and this fact alone would have produced a stringency if there had not been a dollar destroyed. But the vast body of business people, being entirely ignorant of what was going on at the Treasury and unadvised both as to the fact of contraction and the effect which was doomed to follow, plunged ahead as though nothing had happened, confidently expecting money to be as plentiful in the future as it had been in the past. Disappointment was of course inevitable; and then began the process of binding burdens upon the shoulders and backs of the people. The load was carried through the first year and then renewed and increased. At the end of the second, mortgage security was largely called for and prices continued to fall; but the people were assured that their sufferings were only the result of the over-production and transition from war to peace. Wages began to decline, manufacturers and the whole range of industries reduced their employes to the minimum, extra farm hands were discharged, domestic help dispensed with and incidental expenses curtailed throughout the entire country. But nothing could avert the impending calamity. The people staggered along as best they could from 1867 to 1873 and then fell down beneath the weight of accumulated burdens. Crash followed crash until it seemed doubtful whether there were any business establishments strong enough to resist the current of disaster. Mercantile and bank failures became so common as scarcely to attract attention and despondency took the place of hope and activity. Consumption of the necessities of life diminished in proportion as the ability to purchase was taken away. Meantime, as if to mock the short sighted and vicious economists and legislators of the period, Providence threw annually into the laps of the people such a succession of bountiful harvests as had never before been known since man began to cultivate the soil of the New World. And yet, notwithstanding it all, hunger stalked the streets of our cities, filled our manufacturing districts with gloom, and the lack of consumption at the centers of population left the crops to rot in the fields, mould in the bins or to be exported for what could be obtained on an over-supplied European market. Manufactures were sparingly called for and under-consumption became the forced economy of every household. The army of the unemployed increased as the bounties of nature multiplied, until every highway, every village, every city was thronged with tramps. They besieged every train and sometimes in such numbers as to force their passage from one locality to another. They slept upon the ground and begged for work and bread during the summer, and sued for lodging and a crust in the lockups and prisons in the winter.

But those who inaugurated the malevolent policy which precipitated these results were unrelenting and pursued their plan with cruel persistency. Like military chieftains who sit safely in the rear and cooly calculate the loss of life likely to take place in a contemplated battle, so these self-constituted economists had counted the losses and cost likely to follow the execution of their schemes and hence were not disturbed when they were brought face to face with them. Indeed they had the great precedent of modern times before them when they mapped out their plans, and knew approximately the calamities which were to follow.

THE ANGLO-AMERICAN COMBINE.

The influence of British wealth and British institutions have always been potential in financial circles in the United States. The confidential relations and sympathies which always exist between great financial houses and fiscal managers of neighboring nations, tend in the very nature of things to bring about mutual understanding and accommodation of ideas. Such persons are not likely to be deeply in love with the doctrine of human equality or to be especially interested in systems of political economy which are designed to build up the power and the independence of the industrial classes. The usurers of the world know what they want and they ask for it without hesitation. At the very first session of Congress under the Constitution an act was passed to charter a United States bank carefully patterned after the bank of England—an institution which has been the chief solace of the aristocracy and nobility of that realm since Patterson, the buccaneer, and Montague the courtier founded and fashioned it for their special benefit.

One of the chief reasons urged by General Jackson for his determined fight against the United States bank was the fact that British and other foreign capitalists were shareholders in it, and hence could undermine the prosperity of our people and endanger the stability of the Republic. The old hero understood that a Democratic government had no use for an aristocratic or monarchial system of finance. He knew that the two could not flourish together. But the times were not auspicious for the British system of finance in Jackson's day. There was no public debt upon which it could be founded. The last obligation was called in and paid during his admirable administration, and a large surplus was divided among the States and thus returned to the people.

Extensive and intimate Commercial relations between the two countries as well as the social and business courtesies constantly exchanged between the financial magnates of the old world and the new, served to impress upon the moneyed men of this country the superiority and excellence of the English system; and all that was needed was an opportunity and a plausible pretext for its introduction into our fiscal polity. Both were furnished by the late civil war, and they were eagerly improved. The promoters of the plot not only secured the adoption of the system, but they induced the Government to levy tribute upon the people to furnish the means necessary to its establishment. They monetized the credit of the whole people and bestowed it gratuitously upon men who had schemed throughout that perilous struggle to embarrass the Treasury and hence to discourage our arms.

The foundation of the English system was laid in this country when the various acts were passed to authorize the issue of the different classes of war bonds. This was a tremendous stride towards a perpetual National debt. Then followed in train the exception clause in the Legal Tender act, the law authorizing the exchange of United States notes at their face value for Five-twenty bonds. The whole scheme was finally consummated by the passage of the National Bank acts of 1863–4, and the contemporaneous act making the banks the fiscal agents and depositories of Government funds.

Next in order came the act pledging the payment of all Government obligations in coin. In due time (1873–4) came the acts prohibiting the further coinage of silver dollars and restricting their legal tender quality to sums of five dollars. In this they exceeded the British act of 1819 from which the American law was copied. The English act made silver a legal tender for forty shillings, about ten dollars in United States money.

The battle of Waterloo which terminated the long struggle for the overthrow of Napoleon, took place in June, 1815, and within a brief period thereafter preparations began for the resumption of cash payments. Peel's bill for this purpose passed in 1819, but preliminary legislation, such as the act to demonetize silver and others, were passed prior to that date. They were about four years in inaugurating the cruel and relentless policy. A like period was occupied in this country. Our so-called Resumption Act was passed in 1875, and it provided for resumption of cash payments January 1, 1879. The result in England is graphically described by Sir Archibald Alison, in the quotations above given. The reader will note how completely the afflictions following resumption in this country correspond with the dire calamities which befell Great Britain under like fatal contraction.

When the financial crisis of 1873 was precipitated upon this country, who, as a general rule, were first to suffer? It was the industrious poor and those engaged in business with small capital. The first were cast adrift without labor and the latter driven into helpless bankruptcy. The gloom of despair settled over whole communities of laboring people and labor centers became the centers of want and destitution.

The next disheartening manifestation was among the tillers of the soil. The price of agricultural products fell far below remunerative prices, and with but short exceptional periods, the same discouraging situation has continued until the present day. The great majority of those who were in debt when the panic came, have been unable to extricate themselves. They lost their homes and were driven into the towns and cities to find a precarious subsistence in localities already congested and overcrowded. Gradually, those possessed of large capital which had been doubled by the fall in prices, began to loan their money at high rates of interest, taking agricultural lands for security. This seemed to promise relief to this important branch of industry, and as the distress was universal, the borrowing became general. It reached every community in every state. But the prices of all kinds of farm produce continued to rule so low that it was soon ascertained that after taxes and a bare living were deducted from the income of the farm, there was barely enough, and in thousands of instances, not enough left to pay the interest due on the mortgage. It was found that in every instance where the farm was mortgaged, there were two families to be supported from its products—that of the mortgagor and that of the mortgagee, and the latter's family had to be supplied first. New England had become to the agricultural West and South a veritable Old England. Our wealth was drained into her coffers as certainly as that of Ireland was drained into the pockets of the landed aristocracy of Great Britain.

Population continued to increase and money became proportionately scarce. The song of over-production was sung, the convenient theory that our distresses were caused by the sudden transition from war to peace was urged from every stump and filled the pages of every magazine, Executive message, and financial report, but still the blight and mildew remained.

The next noteworthy manifestation of the abnormal condition of our economy was the rapid multification of incorporated companies. Finding money scarce and hard to get, combinations, incorporated and clothed with special privileges, not enjoyed by individuals, were formed to crush out personal enterprise and control trade. These have multiplied by tens of thousands in every state and territory in the Union. Thus rivalry sprang up between corporations and the warfare gave rise to the trust, which is an association of corporations formed to limit production and arbitrarily fix prices. This form of association controls almost every branch of manufactured products and casts its baleful power into every community. It has grown so strong as to defy the Government and proudly challenge organized labor to open combat.

These were exactly the phenomena which accompanied contraction and specie resumption in England. The depression among the agricultural classes there produced great distress and the farmers organized and petitioned for Government loans. But they were hampered by ballot restriction and could not make their petitions effective. And now the same old tariff quack is abroad in the United States. He is prescribing the same medicine for the American patient. Take, he says, the same treatment that was prescribed for England under like conditions and all will be well.

Such is the story, briefly and imperfectly told, of the lamentable situation among our industrial people. The picture falls far short of an adequate representation of our alarming condition. But the testimony of the two witnesses, England and America, covering the whole page of the century, cannot be disregarded. If properly studied and honestly applied, the two great examples will transform the political economy of the world. We respectfully commend it to the thoughtful consideration of all who honestly long for the perpetuity of Republican institutions.

[Weaver then returns to the discussion of corporations, this time in the context of piracy.]

. . . For a full quarter of a century the individual, as such, has been lost sight of in a mad rush for corporate adventure. The corporation and the wealth which it brings have become the chief concern of society and the State. The man and the family have been driven to the wall, the weak trampled under foot and the choicest opportunities of the century showered upon chartered combinations. Wealth, already possessing great advantages, is not satisfied, and incorporates in order that it may have still greater power. Every class of business, every calling, everything except poverty, operates under a charter. The poor must defend themselves as best they can, single-handed and alone. Competition and personal responsibility, except with the remaining multitude of the poor, are literally and absolutely annihilated by these monstrous combinations.

They exist in every State in the Union, by thousands. They control the business of every city, thrust their paid lobbyists within the corridors and onto the floor of every legislative assembly, and importune every city council for exemptions, concession and privilege.

The picture which opens to our view as we lift the curtain upon the scene of corporate rapacity, is so vast and so terrible as to cause us to shrink back aghast. One scarcely knows where to begin the story, and having once begun, it seems like mis-prison of a felony to withhold a single fact from an outraged public. But the field is illimitable and the desolation indescribable. We can only pause in the presence of the picture for a few moments—barely long enough to call the attention of the reader to the outlines of the situation.

We have already, in our chapter on Rome and the United States, spoken of the Anthracite Coal Association controlled by the great railroad and mine owners of Pennsylvania. We wish here to point out some of its acts of spoliation and piracy.

The annual consumption of anthracite is now not far from 35,000,000 tons, of which the West consumes about 8,000,000 tons. In July, 1883, the combination put the miners upon half work for three months in order to limit the production and increase the price. This is their settled method of business and is repeated from year to year. In 1871, the legislature of Pennsylvania entered upon an investigation of the combine. The testimony showed that a number of private companies desired to terminate a strike then pending among the miners in the locality, by accepting the terms of the working men. But the six great companies, controlling all the railroads leading to and from the field of this industry, immediately increased their rates to three times the previous figures and thus made it impossible for the small companies to operate their mines. The price of coal immediately advanced to $12.00 per ton. The small owners were bankrupted while the miners and their families were turned out to starve and to die.

The New York legislature investigated the same combination in 1878. The investigation was caused by the sudden rise in the price of coal to double what it had formerly brought. The legislature found that a number of private mine owners were willing to supply the market at prices much below those asked by the combine and "would do so if they could get transportation from the mines to the market." This was denied them by the six great companies. The committee found that "the combination can limit the supply and thereby create such demand and prices as they may deem advisable." They also found that the companies had advanced the price of coal seventy-five cents and one dollar per ton. An advance of only fifty cents per ton, would, on 35,000,000 tons, amount to $17,500,000 in a single year! Can the annals of piracy on all the seas, for any period of ten years in its history, equal the rapacity of this single transaction? This crime is repeated from year to year, while 64,000,000 people stand helpless and aghast at the audacious spectacle!

In this manner the vast fortunes of the six companies and their share-holders have been accumulated. Their wealth is the result of the murder of hard-working men, the starvation of innocent and helpless women and children and the open and periodic plunder of the inhabitants of a continent.

The Congressional investigation in 1887–8, concerning the strike at the Redding Collieries, found that the Operators intentionally provoked the miners to violence in order to give opportunity to shoot the "rioters."

Take the report of the Ohio Legislative Committee concerning the horrors of the Hocking Valley strike in 1885, the assassinations by the Pinkertons, and the heart-rending appeals of women and children for mercy, shelter and bread. Look again at the gaunt starvation at Braidwood. A whole city full of industrious people groaned in the agonies of want—babes dying of hunger in their mothers' arms, and mothers and off-spring perishing together on pallets of straw without food and without mercy. Let the reader take a glance at the horrors of Punxsatawney, of the suffering at Brazil, Ind., and at the starvation, carnage and heartless evictions taking place as we write in the Coke regions of Pennsylvania—each and every instance being the result of corporate rapacity, and then tell us candidly what he thinks of the relative cruelty of the two systems of piracy—the old-fashioned sea-roving, with its black flags and bloody decks, and the modern amphibious method resulting from the union of the pirate and the brigand, represented by the corporation with its organized systems of pillage, reinforced by the agency of hunger and the Pinkerton thugs.

Take one other instance from among the coal fields, Spring Valley, Illinois. This mining town was started in 1885, under the auspices of three gigantic corporations and a newly incorporated town site company, composed of the principal men in the three corporations, namely: the Chicago & North-western Railroad, the Spring Valley Coal Company, the Spring Valley Town Site Company and the Northwest Fuel Company, of St. Paul. It is estimated that the capitalists associated in these enterprises represent at least $500,000,000. Great inducements had been held out to the people and particularly to miners, to locate in the town and invest their small savings in homes and town property. Hundreds, and even thousands of men rushed to the new field from Streator, La Salle, Braidwood, Peru, and in fact from almost every mining locality in the Northwest, and went to work. The results were not as fortunate as had been anticipated, but upon the whole were re-assuring and promised well for the future. The mining population soon became large and the community was prospering and being rapidly built up. In December, 1888, without a word of warning, with no differences of opinion or known conflict of interest existing between the mine owners and the men, seven hundred miners were suddenly told to take away their tools at the close of the day and not return, as that part of the mine was to be closed. No explanation whatever was given. And this in the face of winter! But a considerable force of men in other parts of the mine were allowed to remain and they aided, as best they could, their unfortunate brethren and their families.

In April following, the balance of the force was dismissed in the same unceremonious manner. Previous to this lock-out on the part of these millionaires, they had been paying out monthly to the miners of this district about $250,000, and the miners had been investing their small savings in the purchase of homes under the promise of steady employment. The committee appointed by the Governor to investigate the facts in this dreadful case, reported in September, that the loss to the miners in consequence of the lock-out amounted at that time to $800,000. Every effort was made by the outside world to relieve the distress, but the corporations were relentless. Sickness and death ensued. The committee already named, say in their report: "There have been no actual cases of starvation as the miners freely divide with each other. * * * There has been suffering in sickness for want of medicines and proper medical attendance. * * * They do not parade their suffering; they conceal it rather, especially from their employers, knowing that the operators rely upon this suffering to bring them sooner or later to terms."

On August 11, 1889, a car load of provisions was sent down from the good people of Peoria. A press account of its arrival stated that "One thousand men and women tramped down from Spring Valley to the Rock Island depot at midnight, and waited for hours for the arrival of the car. The crowd went wild with delight when the car arrived. The *Spring Valley Sentinel*, of August 31, declared "That the wives and children of miners were dying of starvation right in the garden of the world." A correspondent of the *New York World,* sent to the locality especially to investigate the situation at Spring Valley, reported that "From a cursory examination, it is a low estimate to say that seven out of every ten families are sick—seriously so. Malarial fevers, diphtheria, cholera-morbus, ague and pneumonia form the bulk of the ailments. * * * * Scores of men, women and children have found a last resting place in the cemetery since the lock-out." This account further says that 1,200 heads of families had been out of employment from May to August, and that half of these families had been without food, except that which had been given them by charity. But why pursue further the sickening story? Henry D. Lloyd, in his work entitled "A Strike of Millionaires Against the Miners," has portrayed the infamy in all of its tragic details. This book is the Iliad of the battle now raging between man and the corporation in America. Works of far less merit have convulsed empires and revolutionized society. It is an alarm bell at midnight to startle those who slumber and should be read by the million.

. . . It is not by any means claimed that all corporations for pecuniary profit are vicious, either in design, management or consequences. We simply affirm that the power to do wrong is conferred without the possibility of accompanying restraint. The children of men acting under the repression of moral and legal accountability, evolve about all the evil that humanity can bear, and the supplimentary harvest of injustice and wrong doing which results from the creation of a horde of artificial persons, who are void of the feelings of pity and the compunctions of conscience, inflames the situation to a degree which threatens the destruction of social order.

[In comparing Rome, Britain, and the United States—relying for example for the first on Sismondi, Michelet, and Gibbon—Weaver develops the notion that the concentration of wealth and landownership will bring about tenantry, poverty, and ultimately a crisis. For Weaver, America has the resources and productive potential to absorb large numbers, and to eliminate want. Concerning England, he stated:]

. . . The situation of the human race in that part of the world, under present systems, seems well-nigh hopeless. Impoverished, disarmed, helpless, held in subjection by enormous standing armies, even the power to rebel is taken away. The state is armed and the citizen disarmed. The only alternative left is the possibility of escaping to some other country where the laws and conditions are more humane. This accounts for the restless tide of immigration constantly rising on our shores—a tide that ever flows but never ebbs.

But what is the situation in our own beloved

AMERICA?

The Roman Empire had been in its tomb more than fourteen hundred years when our nation was born. But it should ever be remembered that man cannot get away from his own type, and that like causes will produce like effects in all ages and among all peoples.

Does the young but great Republic hold out any hope to mankind? Are we still a beacon light, or has our lamp so soon grown dim? Are we still an asylum for the oppressed of all nations, or are we about to become a policeman for the monarchs and despots of the old world—a despicable, international slave-catcher, under a world-wide fugitive slave law—engaged in the business of arresting and returning to their cruel task-masters the poor slaves who are fleeing hither to become citizens and to escape from hopeless conditions? We blush to think that the events of a single century under our own unobstructed administration, have relieved the reign of George III. from at least one aspersion contained in our Declaration of Independence, namely: the charge of "obstructing the laws for the naturalization of foreigners; refusing to pass others to encourage their migration hither."

We are but an infant among the nations, but we have inherited a large estate. Our country is sparsely populated;

we have hundreds of millions of acres of fertile soil which have never felt the energy of the plowshare nor yielded a single grain for the sustenance of man, and yet we are complaining of immigration!

England has 420 inhabitants to the square mile, New York has about 130, Massachusetts, exceptionally populous, has about 220, Belgium has 450 to the square mile. Her territory is about the size of the state of Maryland, but her population outnumbers the latter nearly five to one. If Ohio were peopled as densely as Belgium, she would contain 20,000,000 people and Illinois would contain 24,000,000. Iowa would contain over 21,000,000. If our whole country were peopled like Belgium, we would number more than 1,400,000,000 souls, or a greater population than now lives upon the whole globe!

PRODUCTIVE POWER OF OUR COUNTRY.

We find the following astonishing, yet nevertheless reliable, statements in a speech delivered by the late Samuel S. Cox, in the Fiftieth Congress, upon the bill providing for taking the eleventh census:

"The land in actual use for growing maize or Indian corn, wheat, hay, oats, and cotton in the whole country now consists of 272,500 square miles, or a little more than the area of the single state of Texas.

"The entire wheat crop of the United States could be grown on wheat land of the best quality selected from that part of the area of the state of Texas by which that single State exceeds the present area of the German Empire.

"The cotton factories of the world now require about 12,000,000 bales of cotton of American weight. Good land in Texas produces one bale to an acre. The world's supply of cotton could therefore be grown on less than 19,000 square miles, or upon an area equal to only 7 per cent of the area of Texas."

How completely do these statements and figures demonstrate the truth that our economic troubles are the results of puereile and vicious systems—systems born of avarice and upheld for plunder.

What has become of our Christianity? There is certainly room and to spare, at our table. The laws which govern the reproduction of our race are not at fault. The world is impatient for an explanation and our dilemma must be quickly interpreted.

A century of experiment has shown that our economic system is utterly unsuited to an increasing population, to the unerring laws of nature and to the fundamental wants of the human race. Think of the barbaric savagery of a system which permits a single generation to appropriate to itself the whole planet upon which it lives, in defraud of all who are to come after them! Is it any wonder that we hear of conflicts between capital and labor? Of conflicts between those who have appropriated the earth and those who have been excluded from its occupancy and its blessings? We may be mistaken, but if we know anything of the laws which govern human nature and which must at last find vent and expression, the difficulties which now exist in our country and which are daily manifesting themselves in strikes, lock-outs and incipient riots, are simply the picket firing which precedes the general conflict, if the people of America refuse much longer to listen to the voice of reason. If the troubles of to-day are serious, what will be our peril twenty years from now with our population grown to a hundred millions? Society calls aloud for readjustment and it must come speedily. The promptings of duty, the voice of justice and the ties of consanguinity unite in a three-fold persuasion to urge us to enter at once upon the work before it shall be unalterably too late.

The child, who is born while we are penning these thoughts, comes into this world clothed with all the natural rights which Adam possessed when he was the sole inhabitant of the earth. Liberty to occupy the soil in his own right, to till it unmolested as soon as he has the strength to do so and to live upon the fruits of his toil without paying tribute to any other creature, are among the most sacred and essential of these rights; and any state of society which deprives men of these natural and inalienable safeguards, is an organized rebellion against the providence of God, a conspiracy against human life and a menace to the peace of the community. When complete readjustment shall come, as come it must quickly, it will proceed in accordance with this fundamental truth. The stone which the builders rejected will then become the head of the corner.

But let us see if we are not traveling with frightful velocity along the same road which led Rome to the grave. It is true that our chief magistracy has never yet been sold at public auction; but does any one doubt that it has frequently, of late years, been purchased at private sale? The enormous campaign assessments, personal contributions and wholesale disbursements which have characterized the presidential contests of late years leave little room for either doubt or apology, and they do not fall far short of open and avowed purchase. A seat in the United States Senate is now rarely secured except by the corrupt use of money and none but the wealthy need apply. It is an open secret that official positions, from the highest to the lowest in all the states and municipalities are often captured by an expenditure of money largely in excess of the stated emoluments of the office. It is well-known to all who are familiar with public life that there has not been a single session of Congress within a quarter of a century which has been free from formidable schemes of jobbery—schemes looking either to the inauguration of new systems of plunder or the consummation of old ones. Our state legislatures are universally beset by formidable lobbies which either represent those who are seeking some new grant of power, or the beneficiaries of former vicious legislation who are now anxious that "vested rights" shall not be disturbed.

A prominent Pennsylvania gentleman, long familiar with public affairs in that State, says: Inside of seven years the Standard Oil Trust spent $325,000 at Harrisburg. In five years it spent over $60,000 in Columbus; at Albany, but covering different years, $35,000—for what? Has the reader any doubt? Not a single legislative session passes in any of the states where this crime is not substantially committed over and over again, from year to year, by the various classes of corporations and their agents

[Weaver next turns to the question of land monopoly.]

. . . But the curse of land monopoly is increasing in our own country in an alarming ratio.

The Committee on the Judiciary in the House of Representatives, for the Fifty-first Congress, was charged with the duty of investigating the extent of alien land ownership in the United States. They made a report (No. 2388) during the first session of that Congress. They say:

"Your committee have ascertained, with reasonable certainty, that certain noblemen of Europe—principally Englishmen—have acquired and now own in the aggregate about 21,000,000 acres of land within the United States. We have not sufficient information to state the quantity owned by untitled aliens, nor is it so important, as it is generally held in smaller bodies. This alien non-resident ownership will, in the course of time, lead to a system of landlordism incompatible with the best interests and free institutions of the United States. The foundation of such a system is being laid broadly in the Western States and Territories. A considerable number of the immigrants annually arriving in this country are to become tenants and herdsmen on the vast possessions of these foreign lords, under contracts made and entered into before they sail for our shores."

. . . The committee further report that Mr. Sculley, who resides in England and is a subject of the Queen, owns ninety thousand acres of land in the State of Illinois, occupied by hundreds of tenants, mostly ignorant foreigners, from whom he receives, as rent, $200,000 per annum, and expends it in Europe. The Scheuley estate, consisting of about two thousand acres within the city limits of Pittsburgh and Alleghany, from the rents of which the Scheuleys, who are subject to the British Queen, draw annually not less than $100,000, is another remarkable instance. The committee then very pertinently remark that "No other Nation in the world allows the subjects of other Governments to acquire such possessions within its jurisdiction."

The committee also state that "The tenth census shows that the United States have 570,000 tenant farmers, (it will doubtless reach 800,000 at the present time) the largest number possessed by any nation in the world, notwithstanding our policy of giving homes to all natives and foreigners who have declared their intention to become citizens if they will but reside upon the land for five years."

BAD EXAMPLE OF ONE CITIZEN.

. . . Ex-Governor Coburn, of Maine, in 1877, owned in his own State, forty-five thousand acres, eighteen thousand in Michigan, thirty-five thousand in Wisconsin, eighteen thousand in Minnesota, thirty-five thousand in Dakota and one hundred and thirty-five thousand in Canada. His last purchase was thirty-five thousand acres from the Northern Pacific Railroad corporation, and Mr. Whipple, his land agent in Dakota, declared it was among the most fertile land in all the West. This is only one instance among hundreds of like enormity.

ANTHRACITE COAL LANDS.

The total amount of anthracite coal land in Pennsylvania is between two hundred and sixty thousand and two hundred and seventy thousand acres. Of this the Reading Coal and

Iron Company owns ninety-five thousand acres; Central Railroad of New Jersey, fourteen thousand acres; Lehigh Valley Railroad, twenty-five thousand acres; Delaware, Lackawanna & Western, twenty thousand acres; Delaware & Hudson, twenty thousand acres; Pennsylvania Coal Company, ten thousand acres; and the Pennsylvania Railroad, ten thousand acres. The remainder is held by parties who are forced by transportation exactions to follow the lead of their more powerful neighbors and rivals.

The capitalization of these companies and their allies is $500,000,000. Even the New York Legislature thought it was excessive.

IN THE RING.

The anthracite combination consists of the Philadelphia & Reading Railroad Company, the Lehigh Valley Railroad Company and the Lehigh Coal & Navigation Company, the Delaware, Lackawanna & Western Railroad Company, the Pennsylvania Railroad Company, the Delaware & Hudson Canal Company, the Pennsylvania Coal Company and the New York, Lake Erie & Western Railroad Company. The companies are named in the order of their importance as coal miners and carriers.

Two great combinations control the output of soft coal in Western Pennsylvania and Ohio.

One of these pools is called the Buffalo Pool. It consists of the railroads which control all the products which come by way of Buffalo for a market—the Rochester and Pittsburg, the Buffalo, New York and Philadelphia and the Erie Railroad. They are named in the order of their importance as coal carriers. They bring the yield from the Western Pennsylvania coal fields.

The other pool is known as the Ohio Pool, and it controls, as its name implies, the output from the Ohio fields. The syndicate consists of the four coal carrying roads which control the transportation from that section—the Hocking Valley, the Wheeling and Lake Erie, the Toledo and Ohio Central and the Panhandle division of the Pennsylvania system, naming them in the order of importance.

These combinations in the soft coal regions are rapidly extending over all the known coal and iron fields of the country, and they are largely controlled by those who are prominent in Eastern pools. They extend also into the coal and iron fields of the South and West. In short, the curse is everywhere.

The great coke industries are also controlled by powerful combinations which have imported Hungarians and Poles in great numbers to compete with American labor. These cruel and barbarous combinations are responsible for the bloodshed, rioting and merciless evictions which are in progress as we pen these lines. (May, 1891.)

THE CONCENTRATION OF WEALTH.

About one-thirtieth part of the English people own two-thirds of the wealth of that nation. But the wealth of her mightiest citizens fall greatly below the average wealth of a score of Americans. Mr. Thomas G. Shearman has rendered the cause of liberty the world over, a most patriotic service, by his startling contributions to the Forum Magazine for November, 1889, and January 1891, upon the distribution or rather concentration of wealth in England and America.

The richest of the Rothchilds, and the great banker, Baron Overstone, each left an estate of $17,000,000. Earl Dudley, the great iron manufacturer, $20,000,000; the Duke of Baccleuch, $30,000,000; the Marquis of Bute, not to exceed $40,000,000; the Duke of Norfolk, $40,000,000; the Duke of Westminster, $50,000,000.

After but a partial examination of the field, mostly within

the range of his personal observation, Mr. Shearman, in the papers named, gives a list of seventy names, none of whom possess less than $20,000,000; many of whom possess above $100,000,000 and as high as $150,000,000, and their average wealth is $35,000,000. The total wealth of the seventy reaches the startling sum of $2,700,000,000. Mr. Shearman finds sixty-seven millionaires in Pittsburgh, sixty-three in Cleveland, whose wealth aggregate $300,000,000; sixty in three villages of New York, whose wealth sums up $500,000,000. One of the estimated parties declares that the calculation is too low and that $750,000,000 would not be beyond the truth. Fifty families in Boston pay taxes on $1,000,000 each. And finally Mr. Shearman says that the annual income of one hundred of the richest Americans cannot fall short of $1,500,000 each; while the annual income of one hundred of the wealthiest Englishmen will not exceed $450,000 each. He finds that 250,000 persons own three-fourths of the wealth of this country and that out of this number less than 40,000 families own fully one-half of the entire wealth, or $31,000,000,000. Upon careful examination of the field he is convinced that the number who own the $31,000,000,000 can safely be reduced to 25,000 families.

That born aristocrat, the Duke of Marlborough, in a recent paper contributed to the *Fortnightly Review,* notes the bold and aggressive power of the American plutocracy and speaks of "An irresponsible railway aristocracy far more dangerous in its ways than any aristocratic class that ever existed in England."

Let us endeavor to grasp something of the significance of the above figures. The late war commenced in April, 1861, and closed April, 1865, a period of four years, or 1,460 days. The cost was about $3,000,000 per day, or $4,380,000,000 in the aggregate. A great part of this expenditure was due to the depreciation of our currency which was inflicted upon the people by the statutory exception touching its legal tender quality and which was inserted for the benefit of speculators. At the present price of supplies of all kinds, the seventy millionaires referred to by Mr. Shearman, with their $2,700,000,-000 of wealth could maintain an army in the field equal to the Union forces in the late war, for a period of four years and then emerge from the conflict out of debt and entirely solvent! The 250,000 persons who own the $17,000,000,000, could equip and support an army equal to the Union and Confederate forces in the late war combined, and for a period of four years, with an expenditure of less than one-fifth of their present accumulated wealth! We should bear in mind that these colossal fortunes have been accumulated since 1861, by men who started in moderate circumstances at the beginning of that period. With their immense accumulations of wealth and class laws still operating in their favor, what may they not accomplish within the next ten years? These colossal fortunes have no parallel in the annals of the world. Unless the causes which have produced them be speedily removed they foreshadow the utter destruction of republican institutions and the inauguration of another tragic era in the history of civilization.

. . . According to the census reports of 1880, there were five hundred and thirty-nine million acres of cultivated land in the States and Territories of the United States. Let us estimate it as seven hundred millions at the present time. After careful inquiry and investigation we deem it a low estimate to say that two-thirds of these lands are under mortgage, paying such excessive tribute to the usurer, that after keeping up repairs, paying taxes and defraying the current expenses of families, there are no profits left. Usury has swallowed them up and in many cases leaves each year a deficit against the proprietor. Each farm is supporting two sets of proprietors, the nominal land owner and the mortgage owner. The man who holds the mortgage really owns the land; only the equity of redemption and the right of occupancy remain with the mortgager.

Now two-thirds of seven hundred million acres are 466,-666,666⅔ acres, and this is precisely 729,166⅔ square miles, or an area of 142,666⅔ square miles greater, as we have seen, than the total tillable land in Italy, Spain, Portugal, France, Germany, Great Britain and Ireland. This analysis shows that we are drifting toward ancient Roman and modern British conditions as a rudderless ship would drift before a howling hurricane. We are amazed and appalled as we contemplate the velocity at which we are traveling toward perilous times. Like a meteor falling through space we will ignite by sheer friction. And when we consider that our unhappy condition has been reached in a single century, and practically during the last quarter of a century, it does not require the gift of prophecy to foretell what the end will be. If such results are normal and flow from legitimate and healthful influences, it becomes pertinent to ask what are the peculiar advantages and safeguards of republican institutions over monarchy or an aristocracy?

Providence has been bountiful with us. We have a fertile country blessed with a mild climate. We are eighteen times greater in area than the republic of France, while we have at present less than double her population. Our supply of raw material is abundant, and our facilities for manufacturing without a parallel. We have every variety of climate with fruits and cereals ample to supply the wants of the world. By what evil genius are we controlled? Is there some fell spirit at the helm determined to drive our bark upon the rocks? We submit that it is the duty of the American people to immediately search out the causes of these conceded evils and this growing discontent; and we must apply, and apply quickly, the amplest remedies which good hearts and wise heads can devise.

THE SILVER PROBLEM.

This whole book could be devoted to the silver question—the history and use of silver among nations, ancient and modern, the relation which it bears to the commerce of our day and to the circulating media throughout christendom; but such treatment of the subject is beyond the scope of this chapter and, as we think, unnecessary at the present stage of practical inquiry. We shall restrict ourselves to thoughts concerning the necessity and importance of its full reinstatement as money in our own country, the motives and influences which led to demonitization in England, Germany and the United States, and shall endeavor to answer some of the arguments, or to speak more accurately, the fallacies and sophistries now interposed to prevent the unrestricted coinage of the white metal. The remarkable stability which has always characterized the ratio between gold and silver will also be alluded to, and tables will be appended for the information of the reader, covering a period of nearly four thousand years.

The Government of the United States is in its youth. Our resources of every description necessary to human comfort and advancement, are without a parallel. Our population, when compared with our inhabitable area and generous resources of soil, climate and products, is but meagre. With such surroundings as these it is right that we should look for happiness and contentment among the people. Instead, however, we find that discontent, debt and destitution exist throughout every state and territory in the Union. It is true that this condition of affairs does not extend to the whole population. But it is beyond dispute that it includes a very considerable portion of those who earn their living by manual labor. We find millions of people homeless and out of employment; millions more in danger of losing their homes, and still more millions working for wages scarcely sufficient to sustain life and respectability and so meager as to shut out hope for the future. These things result neither from pestilence nor famine. The situation is full of the most aggravating contradictions. This destitution, low condition of wages, idleness, debt, and this homeless condition among so many people —all of these distressing things—exist along side of abundant crops, within sight of millions of acres of unoccupied land and in spite of the fact that three-fourths of our country is still in the rough, new, unfinished and sadly in need of labor. In spite of the fact that our products of food and raiment are ample to feed and clothe the world, the whole country is startled with the cry of destitution and poverty! It is certainly the duty of statesmen, philosophers, philanthropists and christian people to search out the real causes of these distressing evils. And having ascertained the cause or causes, it is their duty to remove the sources of irritation if within the range of human power.

[Finally, writing on the national debt, Weaver discusses the notion of sovereignty.]

NATIONAL DEBTS.

. . . When misfortune befalls an individual and he is forced to make expenditures which exceed both his store of money and available resources, he is likely to become the victim of avarice and fall into the clutches of those who possess that which he does not—ready cash. Few men under such circumstances are strong enough to avoid this common fate. An individual can simply direct his own actions and is only partially Sovereign over himself. As to all other persons he must control them, if at all, by contract or persuasion. But an independent and powerful Nation, if wisely governed, is not subject to such limitations and vicissitudes. The Nation is supreme and rules over the whole body as an individual controls his own person. It commands and every member, the head, the eye, the ear, the tongue, the hands, the feet—the whole organic structure must obey. No member of the body politic can become so great as to rise above, none so insignificant as to fall below the control of the Sovereign will. If circumstances warrant, the Sovereign hand can be laid upon the persons, the property, the commerce, and even the lives of its subjects. That power so vast should be exercised with prudence and caution none will gainsay. But Government was created to meet and master emergencies with which individual powers and capacities are inadequate to cope. Each individual member of society consented to the full exercise of this power when his citizenship began, and this consent can neither be withdrawn nor ignored; neither can the primal functions of Government ever be rightfully surrendered. What moral right have the rulers and lawmakers of a Sovereign and Independent Nation to refuse to exercise the legitimate powers entrusted to their care? What right have they to dethrone their Sovereign and send him forth into the market as an individual to beg where he should command, or to borrow where he should create? It is worse than the sale of the purple to the highest bidder; it is equivalent to advertising for a despot, an offer in advance to present him with the purple gratis when he shall appear, and finally to put the people under tribute to him and his successors forever.

The policy of public borrowing is subversive of sovereignty and is as illogical as it is full of evil consequences. No other system could possibly be devised that is so well calculated to enthrone the capitalistic classes among the nations of the earth. If a Nation becomes involved in war when its current revenues and available resources, as ordinarily understood, are inadequate to meet the strain, it must, nevertheless, have money or perish from the face of the earth. Resort is generally had to borrowing, either from its own citizens or from foreign capitalists. This implies a contract into which the capitalist, of his own volition, may or may not enter. It implies the right on his part to prescribe the terms on which the loan shall be made and the right to refuse the loan altogether. It places the life of the Nation at his mercy and the relation of Sovereign and subject is lost sight of completely. In fact, the Sovereign becomes the subject, and the subject the Sovereign. They exchange places and a new *regime* follows as certainly as if one king should abdicate and another be enthroned. When the sovereignty of the people is thus displaced, either by voluntary surrender or by the gradual and cunning usurpation of capital, it is rarely ever regained—never except by upheavals which convulse society from center to circumference.

[The book concludes on this note of affirmation.]

. . . Truth is a marvelous weapon; it transforms itself into a thousand shapes, but it is always the truth.

Sometimes it is keen and lithe like a Damascus blade and again heavy, blunt and jagged like a savage battle-ax of the medieval age. This wonderful agency has done its work during the nineteen years just passed. The farmers through their Grange movement led the way. Then followed the Peter Cooper movement led by the purest philanthropist of the times, and represented upon the hustings by one of the most brilliant, powerful and persuasive orators which this country has ever produced, Gen. Samuel F. Cary, of Ohio. Succeeding this came the Union Labor party, and now the united movement of all the industrial forces of the continent. Through all this period those who have administered public affairs—presidents and cabinets, law-makers and parties— have unwittingly wrought in unison with the patient efforts of self-sacrificing philanthropists to unerringly demonstrate, in a variety of ways, that all of the accusations which had been made against them and against existing leadership, were absolutely true and that no good thing could be expected of them.

We have also had the contrasts of bountiful harvests accompanied by ever-existing destitution; of penury following close upon the track of industry; of vast armies of homeless tramps ever wandering alongside of vacant land held for speculation; of employers building palaces in foreign lands out of profits filched from toil, and labor forced into the maelstrom of strikes, riots and lock-outs; of armed mercenaries usurping the place of regular police; of corporations crowding the individual to the wall and trampling the poor into the dust; of one-half of every city set apart for the abode of Lazzaroni and the other for the sumptuous palaces of the rich and powerful. Such things—such aggravating contrasts have aided to convince the judgment and ripen the convictions of millions of honest men and women dwelling in every section of the Union. Of one accord they have risen up, pledged fidelity to one another and sworn that these things shall cease. Nor is this the result of the hasty ebullition of passion. It is the outcome of sober conviction based upon thorough investigation and verified by personal experience. It is sanctified by the conviction of justice and the promptings of charity. It has passed the point of experimental endeavor and reached the plane of lofty resolve where the Golden Rule becomes the law of the conscience and where personal sacrifice is welcomed as a boon.

STRIKE NOW!

. . . We have challenged the adversary to battle and our bugles have sounded the march. If we now seek to evade or shrink from the conflict it will amount to a confession of cowardice and a renunciation of the faith. Let us make the year 1892 memorable for all time to come as the period when the great battle for industrial emancipation was fought and won in the United States. It is glorious to live in this age, and to be permitted to take part in this heroic combat is the greatest honor that can be conferred upon mortals. It is an opportunity for every man, however humble, to strike a blow that will permanently benefit his race and make the world better for his having lived. Throughout all history we have had ample evidence that the new world is the theater upon which the great struggle for the rights of man is to be made, and the righteous movement now in progress should again forcibly remind us of our enviable mission, under Providence, among the nations of the earth.

29. The People's Party Campaign Book

These selections from Thomas E. Watson's campaign book serve a two-fold purpose: to illustrate the kinds of issues—income tax, strikes and Pinkertons, financial legislation, public ownership of the railroads—which Populists considered important, and to reveal more about how Watson himself felt concerning these issues. Since this book was a campaign document, tailored to provide ammunition for the lesser lights in the movement, the writing has a terse, sledgehammer quality, and the arguments are reduced, in some cases too much so, to their simplest form. One sees in these pages an aspect of Watson which made him a devastating orator on the stump; his combination of wit and ridicule, here directed primarily at the Democratic party.

[In this political handbook, the following chapter is typical of Watson's succinct instructions for the stump speaker.]

Reprinted from Thomas E. Watson, *The People's Party Campaign Book* (Author's edition: n.p., n.d.), pp. 40-45, 52-56, 103-109, 127-131, 178-180, 186-188, 210-221.

CONTENTS:—VICIOUS LEGISLATION REPEAL OF
THE INCOME TAX. WHO DID IT? WHO IS
RESPONSIBLE FOR NOT
RE-ENACTING IT?

SECTION 1.   A Tax upon Profits is surely the easiest of all
to pay.

If a citizen is compelled to pay a heavy tax upon a stock of
goods when there is no net income from those goods, it is a
hardship.

If he has to pay upon a tract of land at a time when he is
actually losing money, farming on that land—such payment
is a burden which he most keenly feels to be unjust.

When he has to pay tax upon cotton or corn or wheat, which
cost him more than it will bring, it is an addition to his
misfortune which necessity alone can induce him to tolerate.

How much more bitterly must these burdens be resented
when the citizens who pay such taxes are aware of the fact
that those who are making the profits are exempted from tax.

The great Bondholders pay no tax.

The great National Bankers pay one per cent. and are
allowed to salve their wounded feelings by making the people
pay from eight to twenty-five per cent.

The great Tariff Barons, as will be shown hereafter, not
only lose nothing by taxation, but gain by it immensely.

The Rail Road Kings pay no Federal Taxes whatsoever, but
upon the other hand compel a four per cent tax from the
people upon $4,500,000,000 watered stock.

These are the men whose astonishing wealth has been so
rapidly accumulated.

Practically, they reap all the profits of all the industrial
classes of America.

Practically, they are the moneyed class, numbering a few
thousand for whom sixty millions of people toil.

The Income Tax would reach them—therefore they oppose it.

Under their dictation, the Income Tax Law was repealed in 1871.

The Repeal Act passed the Senate January 26, 1871; by a close vote, Yeas, 26, Nays, 25.

Seven Democrats voted for Repeal. *Only Two voted against it!*

[The list of those voting for repeal is given.]

. . . So, it will be seen that both Democrats and Republicans are guilty of this crime.

This Income Tax Law passed Congress July 1, 1862. It did not go into effect till 1863.

By its terms all incomes in excess of $600 and under $10,000 were taxed at 3 per cent; over $10,000, at 5 per cent.

This was surely very moderate.

The Tax was collected under the Internal Revenue System.

From this source the Government collected $2,741,857 in 1863.

For the Fiscal Year, ending June 30, 1864, it collected $20,-294,733.

On the 3rd day of March, 1865, the Act was amended so as to substitute 5 per cent. for the 3 per cent. on the smaller incomes and 10 per cent. for the 5 per cent. upon the larger ones, commencing with an income of $5,000.

Under these acts the Government collected $32,050,017.

In 1866 this tax yielded $72,982,395. In 1867, it yielded $66,014,429.

In 1867 the Law was amended. The tax was diminished in effect one-half. The Amendment also provided that the Act was to expire with the year 1870.

In 1868, $41,455,599 was the sum collected. In 1870 it was $34,791,857. On July 14, 1870, the Tax was extended one year, and reduced to 2½ per cent.

This was repealed, as before stated, by an Act which passed the Senate January 26, 1871, and the house on March 3, 1871. The Yeas and Nays were not taken in the House.

Taxes already due before the Repeal of the Act continued to be collected in 1871 and 1872 and 1873. The last were not in till 1877.

The total amount collected under this very moderate Income Tax was $346,906,738.

Does anyone doubt that it would now be practicable to collect enough revenue from this source to run the Government?

Fortunes have so amazingly increased in the hands of the millionaires; profits so stupendous have accumulated in the hands of Standard Oil Magnates, Coal Barons, Rail Road Kings, Sugar Trust Operators, Steel and Iron Combiners, that a good, heavy tax on incomes above $10,000—the tax growing heavier as the income was larger would be phenominal in its yield.

The reasons why such a tax would be better than any we now have are sufficiently obvious.

1.   It would put the burden on the class most able to bear it.

2.   It would put the support of the Administration upon those who derive the greatest benefits under the Laws.

3.   It would interest the most powerful class in the cause of Economy. Rich men get particular when they know they must foot the bills.

4.   It would put the Pension debt on the men who got rich off the victories of the soldiers.

5.   It would discourage the accumulation of enormous fortunes and would afford a legal method of checking the growth of concentrated wealth.

6.   It would abolish the Tariff, which, as a system of collecting taxes is the most costly, one-sided and monstrous the world ever saw.

7.   It would supplant Internal Revenue Taxes upon Whiskey and Tobacco—which subjects of taxation should be relegated to the States.

8. It would give to tax-oppressed people all over the land a relief from the crushing burden of indirect, cowardly and illegal taxes which are wrung from them in the name of the Law for the benefit of privileged classes.

The nations of Europe recognize the justice of the Income Tax.

In England it yields about $60,000,000 annually; in Austria, $12,000,000; in Italy, $45,000,000; in Prussia, $30,000,000.

SECTION 2.   On June 15, 1878, an attempt was made to reenact the Income Tax.

It was proposed to commence with a Tax of *One Per Cent.* on Incomes exceeding $2,000, and to gradually increase it as the Income grew larger. On Incomes exceeding $100,000 the tax was to be 10 per cent.

This was defeated. Yeas, 94, Nays, 139.

Of the Yeas, 66 were Democrats and 31 Republicans.

Of the Nays, 58 were Democrats and the balance Republicans.

It will be seen that this Act would have been passed if the Democrats or the Republicans voting No, had cast their votes the other way.

Hence it is perfectly clear that both the Old Parties are responsible for the failure to reimpose this Tax just as they were both responsible for its repeal.

Among the Democrats voting No, were Messrs. Blount, of Georgia; Carlisle, of Kentucky; A. S. Hewitt, of New York; Hooker, of Mississippi; W. M. Robbins, of North Carolina; W. M. Springer, of Illinois; Tucker of Virginia; Fernando Wood, of New York.

Among the Republicans voting No, were Cannon, of Illinois; Keifer, of Ohio; Kelly, of Pennsylvania; Garfield, of Ohio; Blair, of New Hampshire, and Jay Hubbell, of Michigan.

It should be stated that this Bill came up while the Internal Revenue Bill was under discussion, and that Mr. Tucker, of Virginia, who was endeavoring to secure a reduction of the

Tobacco Tax from 20 cents per pound to 16 cents per pound, requested all the friends of his Amendment to vote against the Income Tax. In other words, his Amendment of four cents a pound on Tobacco was bigger, in his eyes, than an Income Tax on millionaires which might have yielded sufficient revenue to run the Government, and thus not only have removed all the taxes from Tobacco but also from the 3,000 articles loaded down with Tariff duties.

Of such short-sightedness has our statesmanship since the War been composed. An immediate and pressing local want is allowed to override and subordinate questions of the greatest magnitude—full of promise of the most beneficent general results.

No Democratic National Platform has demanded the Income Tax. No National Convention of that Party has denounced its repeal.

The same is true of the Republican Party.

The Greenback Party was the first to denounce the Repeal and to demand its re-enactment.

The People's Party is the only political organization which to-day declares in its favor.

As long as the Old Parties are dominated by the influences which now control them, the Income Tax will remain a dead issue—a monument to the servile party spirit which makes laws in the interest of plutocracy.

[In a later chapter Watson discusses the surplus and national banks.]

CONTENTS—HOW THE SURPLUS WAS
SQUANDERED. PET BANKS.
SPECIAL PRIVILEGES.

... SECTION 1.   By the operation of the Federal Tax Laws the Revenues of the Government during Cleveland's Administration largely exceeded its Expenditures.

Not that the Expenditures were small. By no means. They were some Three Hundred and Fifty Millions of Dollars. But the Taxes were so heavy, the Tariff burden so great, that the people were compelled to pay into the Treasury upwards of One Hundred Millions of Dollars over and above its needs.

In other words, vicious legislation forced this annual excess out of the pockets of the people and put it where the Politicians, the Boodlers and the Privileged Classes would have full swing with it.

As I have already stated, a similar condition had once before existed but on a much smaller scale.

Under Jackson's Administration in 1837, the Surplus had been fairly divided among the States as a Loan.

But under Cleveland, the Wall Street influence was supreme and the idea of putting out the surplus among the States was not thought of. Some $59,000,000 of it was put in the National Banks so that they could enjoy the benefit of lending the Tax-money to the Tax-payers to whom it belonged at a high rate of interest.

The Banks paid the Government nothing.

I doubt if the history of the world furnishes a parallel to this as a matter of Government Favoritism. Some $60,000,000 of this Surplus was paid away in Premiums to the Bondholders in the purchase of Bonds not due.

These Bonds were drawing a low rate of interest, 4 and 4½ per cent.; they still had a long term to run; yet the Administration could find no better way of disposing of a fund which belonged to all the people than to adopt a policy which resulted in paying off National obligations before they were due and giving the National Creditors a bonus of $60,000,000 for being kind enough to accept payment in advance of pay-day.

What brilliant Democratic Finance!

At the time this policy was put into practice under the lead of Mr. Mills, of Texas, the Taxpayers of the Country were in a distressed condition; were groaning under a Mortgage Debt of stupendous size, and were paying exhorbitant rates of interest.

They began, most respectfully, to ask the Government to consider the proposition that in the distribution of the National Currency, Bonds alone should not be regarded as the only respectable collateral, but that Lands, and non-perishable Produce be treated as fairly as that species of Mercantile Paper called Bonds.

With a howl of derision they were put aside.

They were told by Roswell Flower, the Democratic National Banker of New York, to "go home, attend to their business, work harder and talk less."

Almost the same language was held on the floor of the House yesterday, by Hon. Joseph D. Taylor, of Ohio, a Republican National Banker.

"Work harder and talk less"—and the National Banker will consider you a more valuable slave than he even now does.

In Premiums on Bonds, as I have stated, the Democrats managed to donate some $60,000,000 of the People's money to a Privileged Class.

When the Republicans took hold, their plan was different, but it got there just the same.

They voted it away in Appropriations to Sugar Bounties, Ship Subsidies, Navy Enlargements, River and Harbor Bills, etc.

The people to whom the money belonged got none of it.

However much the Old Parties might differ upon other matters, on this they were agreed;—that the Tax-payer himself was the last man who had a right to seek the benefit of that money.

It was constitutional to donate part of it to the Chicago Fair and to the Bondholders; legal to lend part of it to National Banks free of Interest.

But to talk of donating a part of it to the Drought-stricken Farmers in Texas and Nebraska to buy seeds to plant their lands was all bosh and nonsense. No decent man, anxious to be called a "Statesman" would countenance such a scheme.

To lend part of it to these Farmers on lands or produce was even more criminal in its demoralizing tendencies.

Such suggestions were promptly squelched.

How much of that Surplus of Tax-money had the Bond-holders paid into the Treasury?

Not a cent.

How much of it had these Farmers paid in?

Precious near all of it. Yet the men who paid it in could get none of it as a Loan, while those who had paid none of it got it as a Gift.

The man who gives away money to a class who have no right to it is a "Statesman."

The man who would lend that money to the class to whom it belongs, is a Demagogue.

Such is life.

John Sherman, of Ohio, is a recognized Leader of the Republican Party.

In the Democratic Campaign Book of 1880, it is charged that while he was Secretary of the Treasury he was Partner in the First National Bank of New York; that he gave this Bank the inside track on the refunding of the Ten-Forty Bonds into Four-per-cents; that he and his Partners made $115,000,000 off the Government by the operation; and that to prevent further exposures he issued an order that the employees of the Treasury Department should give no news to the Press.

Thus it goes: Democrats making out the case on the Republicans and the latter making it out on the former.

Pot and kettle all around.   Mr. Sherman has been in Federal Office many years; could not possibly have become a millionaire on his legitimate earnings as a salaried official; and the very fact that he is so enormously wealthy shows that he has used his official advantages to fill his pockets.

As an illustration of the Class Legislation prevalent in both Political Parties, consider the favors shown the Great Western Whiskey Ring.

They have unlimited capital and deal in a Product which no one claims makes this country happier or more prosperous. It would be easy to charge up to them a heavy proportion of poverty, disease, wretchedness and crime.

It would seem they might be modest enough to take their places among other Tax-payers and fare as they do.

Not so: They obtain from Congress a Loan of many millions of dollars annually at 5 per cent. interest at the expense of the other Taxpayers. The Tax on Distilled Spirits is 90 cents per gallon. The production is so great that the annual revenue aggregates $65,000,000.

Under the Bonded Warehouse Law the Whiskey Ring has the privilege of borrowing this neat sum of money for three years by paying 5 per cent. interest on it for two years. They get the Loan one year free of charge. The result of this is to hold back $65,000,000 of Taxes for three years.

Does any other Tax-payer have that privilege?

Not much.   Suppose a farmer or a merchant should ask to have his Tariff Taxes or his Tobacco Taxes loaned to him for three years—would he get them?

Not much.   In the mad whirl of Class Legislation which has grown to such shameless proportions since the war, it is hard to point out a more glaring example than this.

The law simply allows the Whiskey Ring to say to the Tax Collector:

"I don't feel like paying you to-day;—call again, three years from now."

The Collector bows humbly and walks off—rejoiced to have escaped without being kicked in the rear.

[This general theme is developed in a different context farther on in the book.]

. . . SECTION 2.   In an Editorial in "The People's Party Paper, of Atlanta, Ga., I have made the following comments upon this—"Squandering of the Surplus!"

What was the surplus?

It was cruel, excessive taxation which brought into the Treasury more money than the Government needed.

Who did the Surplus belong to?

All the Tax-Payers. All the People.

What did the Democrats do with it?

They gave $60,000,000 of it to the Bondholders as premiums upon Bonds not due.

Did the Bondholders pay any of that tax into the Treasury?

Not a cent.

Their property was exempt.

Yet the Democrats gave $60,000,000 of our tax money to the class which pays no tax.

How much did they give to the Farmers, Laborers, Merchants, Mechanics etc., who had paid that money into the Treasury?

Not a cent.

This Democratic policy was carried out under Cleveland. Mr. Mills, of Texas, led the Democratic forces in the House.

The Surplus could have been divided among the States; could have been devoted to the schools; could have been distributed among the people in loans upon good security at fair interest.

About the time this $60,000,000 gift to the Bondholders was being originated, the Farmers of Texas were knocking at the doors of Congress and asking for loans upon lands.

They were kicked out. Loans on lands were communistic, unconstitutional and undemocratic. Nobody but a demagogue would advocate a law to lend Farmers money on land—said our Democratic Silver-plated Statesmen.

So, having a surplus on hand they refused to lend it to the Farmers at reasonable interest. They preferred to give it to Bondholders as premiums on Bonds not due. $59,000,000 of the Surplus was being used at that time by Cleveland's "Pet Banks" as a loan without interest.

To allow this favoritism was "Broadminded Statesmanship."

To do this was not communistic; not unconstitutional; not undemocratic.

To do this was not class legislation; was not giving special privilege; was not giving bounties on wealth at the expense of Labor.

Oh no! it was "Broadminded Statesmanship" of the Tammany Hall, Silver-plated, silk undershirt sort.

Gifts of countless millions to the Plutocrats! Gifts of abuse and ridicule to the Laborers.

Yes, Democrats did it and the Record is there to condemn them in the eyes of Posterity forever.

Many an honest old Democratic Farmer will read these names with amazement, and will rub his eyes and look again to see if indeed his interests were so neglected by the men he trusted.

The citizens who paid that money into the Treasury were laughed at when they asked the poor privilege of borrowing some of their own hard-earned cash. They were denounced as Socialists, Demagogues and Fools.

The Bondholders who had paid none of that money into the Treasury asked it as a gift—and they got it.

Yet at that very time the men who were refused the loans were almost on the brink of starvation while those who were granted the gift had riches beyond the dreams of Aladdin!

By Act of Congress approved July 12, 1882, the Banks were authorized to extend their charters twenty years. "Unless sooner dissolved by act of the shareholders owing two-thirds of the stock, or unless its franchise becomes forfeited by some violation of Law or unless hereafter modified or repealed." Many people believe that the National Bank Law was a War Measure and that the Government passed it as a necessity.

This is not true. The first issue of National Bank Notes took place on January 1, 1864.

On July 1, 1864, only $26,000,000 were out. On April 22, 1865, $147,000,000.

Not a dollar of all the immense issues of these notes helped

the Union during the War. The truth is that the Law as first
enacted did not please the Capitalists. State Banks were left
to compete with them. It was only when Congress in 1864
taxed State Banks out of existence that the greater shylocks
of National Banks supplanted the lesser Shylocks of State Banks.

On July 1, 1867, the National Banks had some $300,000,000
of their notes in circulation. By 1874, $350,000,000. When it is
remembered that the Bankers were drawing interest upon the
Bonds deposited as collateral in the same manner as if they
were not so deposited; when it is remembered that for every
One Hundred Dollars in Bonds, they could circulate Ninety
Dollars in Money; that this money only cost them 1 per cent.
(about enough to cover the expenses of printing it) while they
loaned it out at high rates of interest compound—at convenient intervals; that they paid no Tax on the Bonds; that the
people paid the interest on the Bonds to the Government
which the Government turned over to the Banks and at the
same time paid the high compound interest on the circulating
notes which the Bankers put in their pockets, it will be readily
seen that as a system of commercial spoliation of the masses
for the benefit of the Money Class, its like was never seen
since the morning stars sang together.

The Masses bore *all* the burden. They shared *none* of the
profits.

The money issued to the Banks was virtually Legal Tender
Government money.

The Guaranty of the Government was behind every dollar
and kept it at par.

The Bonds held as collateral were Government Issues—
valuable only because of the Government's power to Tax all
the Land, all the Cotton, all the Corn, all the Wheat, all the
Cattle, all the Merchandise and thus raise funds to pay the
interest and finally the principle.

In other words, the Bonds were good because the people
had the spondulix, and because the Government of the people
had the power to take enough of the people's property, by way

of Taxation to meet the obligation contained in the Bonds. But these Bonds were not the only basis upon which this Bank Money rested.

It will be seen from my analysis of the Law that the Government undertook to make good to the holders of the Bank Notes any deficiency between the value of the Bonds and the amount of the notes.

In plain English, the Government of all the people became endorser of the Promissory Notes of a Class of the people in order that the Class might plunder the Mass.

If bankers were dishonest as frequently happens, the Tax money of the people was taken to make good the fraud which the Bankers had perpetrated upon them.

This was nice:—for the Bankers!

But this was not all. As a still further basis of credit the Government made these Notes of the Bankers Legal Tender, *to the same extent as its own Notes.*

Now let us sum up the beauties of the situation:

1.   The Government furnished a Warehouse or Sub-Treasury in which the Bondholders could store their property and furnished costly vaults, safes, etc.

2.   It furnished a Manager of the Warehouse and a large number of assistants at good salaries.

3.   It entered into a written contract showing how it received the property of the Bankers and for what purpose.

4.   It allowed the Bankers to come into the Warehouse once a year and take a look around and see if their property was all right.

5.   It made a loan of 90 cents on the dollar to the Bankers on the Bonds held at the Warehouse. *It guaranteed the payment of the Loan,* and charged a duty of one per cent.—or about enough to cover expenses of paper, ink and printing. It not only guaranteed the re-payment of the Loan but compelled every citizen in America to accept a Banker's Promissory Note as money, EXCEPTING THOSE BANKERS THEMSELVES!

Consider it a moment and then collapse and go to bed.

The Promissory Notes of those Bankers were to be good pay for everything except interest on Public Debts.

What were the Public Debts?

The Bonds which those bankers held!

Some one will say that Duties on Imports were also excepted.

True; but the Government demanded Gold of the Importer for a certain express purpose.

What was it?

To pay the Public Debt.

What was the Public Debt?

Those Bonds of the Bankers!

Now reflect;—the Government compelled every citizen in the land to cancel his debt and part with his produce in exchange for a Promissory Note of the Banker and allowed the Banker to repudiate and refuse to accept his own note and to demand that the people (out of what was left of their hard earnings) should pay him Gold.

A greater Infamy never had the Sanction of the Statute Law!

No wonder that National Bankers grow marvelously rich.

No wonder that the People grow marvelously poor.

It is estimated that the average net profits of the Banks off the people, on the circulating notes alone, have aggregated Twenty Millions of Dollars annually for the last twenty-five years.

This does not include the profits they made out of the Bonds, nor out of Deposits, nor out of Contraction of the Currency.

For it must not be forgotten that perhaps the worst feature of the Law was that the Bankers got control of the volume of the Currency.

They struck down the Greenback which they could not control and in its place put their own Notes which they could control and thus acquired unlimited power over all the productions of Labor.

To what extent this has wronged the Producer, God, only knows.

[In the following discussion of Pinkertons, it should be noted that Watson accords considerable space in a Populist handbook to the problems of industrial labor, only a portion of which is reprinted here. Beaumont, whose statement appears first, was both an official of the Knights of Labor and a prominent Kansas Populist.]

CONTENTS: THE STANDING ARMY OF THE

CORPORATIONS. MONEY vs. MEN.

WINCHESTERS vs. RIGHT.

. . . SECTION 1. Perhaps the best way for me to write this Chapter is to let the Record speak for itself.

I shall therefore present to the reader, page after page of actual history—very recent history at that.

I only regret that I have not the space to make an exposure of the Organized Hell which exists in Pennsylvania among Coal and Iron Mines.

From the Official Records of Congress; from Reports of its Committees (never acted on) a case could be presented which would fire the indignation of every just man in America.

With this brief introduction, I now present the Record.

RALPH BEAUMONT'S LETTER.

HISTORY OF THE NEW YORK CENTRAL.

THE PINKERTONS MUST BE ABOLISHED. NO

CORPORATION IN ITS CHARTER IS CLOTHED

WITH POWER TO DECLARE WAR ON

AMERICAN CITIZENS—THE DUTY

OF THE STATE.

The newspapers in the sections of the country through which I have passed during the last few days are all filled with telegraphic dispatches, of a more or less sensational character, relating the particulars of a strike of the employes on the New York Central Railroad. One report says that Vice-President Webb informed J. J. Holland of the General Executive Board that the company did not propose to tolerate any interference from outsiders. This, in plain English, meant that Mr. Webb could act as agent of the New York Central stockholders, but denied the right of Mr. Holland to pose as the agent of the employes of the corporation. After all, there seems to be some difference between "tweedle-dee" and "tweedle-dum." It is evident from this that Vanderbilt's son-in-law considers the workers a commodity which he places on a lower scale than any other commodity that he purchases. For instance, Mr. Webb purchases iron from Carnegie & Co., of Pittsburg, through an agent of that firm, but to allow the labor used by his company to be represented through an agent is a thing that he, in his exalted position, declines to tolerate.

Where did Vice-President Webb secure the power which he assumed when he told the accredited representative of the employes that he (Webb) would not listen to his statement or allow a stranger to interfere in the matter? This is a very appropriate question at this time. The corporation of which this man is the mouth-piece is the creature of the State of New York, and the workers are part of the State. This corporation receives its very life from the State. It could not exist for one moment if the wage-earners of the State of New York were to will it otherwise. When the New York Central received its charter from the State, it received its right to exist under the following conditions: That it should charge but 2 cents per mile per passenger, and that it should pay only 8 per cent. per annum to its stockholders upon their investment. So we see that the State, when it granted this franchise, limited the amount of wages that capital should receive, but it did not place any such restrictions upon the laborer who was a part of itself. It would seem that the creature has now become greater and larger than the creator. Even under the restrictions placed upon it, the surplus earnings of this corporation during the prosperous years of the war—from 1862 to 1869—accumulated in its treasury to about $35,000,000, or nearly the total cost of the road. Now to whom did this surplus rightfully belong? Certainly not to the stockholders, because they had the earnings on their stock fixed before the enterprise started. I will tell you what was done. During the administration of Boss Tweed the New York Central stockholders struck for higher wages. They secured the passage of a law which gave them power to declare a scrip dividend, and every one who held $100 in stock received another hundred, and the remaining surplus was spent in improving the road by laying two more tracks. Since then these stockholders have been receiving 16 per cent. on the original cost of the road, or double the wages that they agreed their capital should work for. They not only struck for higher wages, but they struck for back pay as well. I see that this aristocratic snob Webb has hired a gang of hessians called Pinkertons to do the fighting for his bantling. Here is where the corporation is greater than the State. What would have been the result if the employes of this railroad, when they stopped work, had hired a crowd of laborers, armed them with Winchester rifles and brought them on the ground where the trouble existed? Rebellion and treason would be charged against them most surely. I desire to ask Governor Hill this question: How is it that Webb and his brother officials can bring armed brigands and thugs into the State and put them in the field with orders to kill on sight, and completely ignore the power and authority of the lawful guardians of the peace, without such tyrannical conduct being characterized and chastised as it deserved? It is not treason or rebellion on the part of a greedy, grasping, grinding corporation, but it would be regarded as such on the part of organized labor. It seems to make a deal of difference whose ox is gored. The press dispatches report that several innocent citizens have been killed and wounded by Bob Pinkerton's hired assassins—one a woman who was engaged in her domestic duties in front of her house was shot down, and a boy was badly wounded. The so-called preservers of peace must be queer brutes when they cannot discriminate between a mob and a small party of sober citizens. The dispatches also state that Pinkerton complained to the Chief of Police at Albany that his men were hit with stones. What is he kicking about? The Chief of Police did not bring him or his hirelings there. It was Webb who hired him and others of his ilk—the same Webb who protested against Mr. Holland's interference, but engages hundreds of Pinkerton's sleuth-hounds and pays them to interfere. And did not Webb urge the Governor to call out the State troops to interfere also? He said he wanted the military to protect his property. Is that what the militia is for? What is the matter with calling out the troops to protect life? When Mr. Webb discharged many of his best and most faithful workmen and threw them and their families out to starve, where was the military then? Where is our Mother, the State? Where is this great Mother, who, in times of war, says to these workingmen: "Leave your wives and little ones; risk your lives in my defence so that I may live?" Why does she not now come to the front and say to this corporation: "These are my children, my bone and sinew; thou shalt not turn them out to starve?" Why is it that in strikes and lockouts the military is always called out to protect the interest of capital, but never to protect the toilers? I say to the employes of this corporation: We must strike the State and see that she does her duty by us. We must also declare that it is treason for capitalistic combinations to hire armies and equip them with muskets and revolvers for the purpose of slaughtering our citizens. No candidate must be elected to office who is not pledged to vote for a law that will make it treason for any corporation to arm free-booters and murderers. The Civil Government of the State is abundantly able to protect public and private property, and when the civil guardians are powerless we have the militia to fall back upon. There is only one Government in this country that must and should be respected. The Pinkerton Government must be abolished and outlawed. It has no status under the Constitution of the United States. No corporation in its charter is clothed with power to declare war and raise armies. That power is vested in the President and Congress, and they cannot and have not delegated that authority to Bob Pinkerton.

Atchinson, Kan.   RALPH BEAUMONT

[This is followed by some fifty pages of evidence, including long extracts from the proceedings of the New York State Board of Arbitration and Mediation investigating the New York Central strike. Watson then states his own views in a letter to a St. Louis newspaper.]

To the Editor of the Republic.

House of Representatives U. S., Washington, D. C., February 11, 1892.—Your editorial notices in connection with the Pinkerton resolution introduced by me show that you are friendly to the movement to correct the "hired bravo" nuisance.

You say, however, that the Bill I have offered is clumsy and will not stand the fire of the Courts.

In the utmost good faith I invite any corrections or suggestions. By to-day's mail I sent you a copy of the bill.

You will see that the first section requires that the persons employed shall be residents of the State where the duty is to be performed.

Again, that the employer and the owner of the property shall be responsible for the conduct of those employed.

The second section provides, substantially, that no private citizen shall employ others (also private citizens) to discharge the duties that devolve on police, State and Federal officers by law.

The third section provides, substantially, that no private

citizen or association shall organize or maintain a body of armed men for the purpose of hiring them out to perform the duties, which, under the law, devolve upon police, State and Federal officers.

If these sections are leaky I shall gladly calk them into greater tightness.

What I am after is the correction of a national evil, and help from any quarter will be more than welcome.

I claim that the Federal Government should deal with this question because there are certain phases of it that the States cannot deal with.

Every Railroad is, by Law, a Post Road. Therefore wherever the Pinkerton question relates to the interference with Railroads Congress has jurisdiction.

Nearly every Railroad crosses State lines. Hence Interstate Commerce is involved, and the Federal Government, and not the States, has jurisdiction over the policing of the trains and the regulations that may be necessary to apply thereto.

Again, if a State grants the right to any private citizen or Corporation to maintain what is really a band of mercenary troops, the Federal Government has Constitutional power to suppress it.

Really, however, I think your editorial some days ago took the soundest view of the whole question, viz: That it was a matter of public policy.

The Federal Government is to maintain public tranquility, suppress insurrections and compel all citizens to obey the law. The purpose of such organizations as "the Coal and Iron Police" of Pennsylvania, the Pinkertons of Chicago and others of like character is to usurp a Governmental function; relegate the maintenance of the peace to private and irresponsible persons; put the power of life and death into the hands of the hirelings of one side to the dispute instead of leaving it all to the responsible, impartial and legally constituted authorities of the cities, the States and the Republic.

The one course is bound to bring about law and order. The other is anarchy.

Very respectfully,
Thos. E. Watson

[A very brief period was allotted in Congress for debate on Watson's anti-Pinkerton resolution. What follows—delivered on May 12, 1892—is his own contribution to the discussion.]

... Mr. Watson.   Mr. Speaker, I simply desire to say to the House that this resolution of mine contemplates a fair legal investigation and a fair and legal settlement of this question. It is believed by a great number of people that the Pinkerton Detective Agency is really a standing body of armed militia which Corporations can hire to do the work of militia forces in troubles with their striking laborers.

I went before the committee and produced what I thought was as complete evidence as could be furnished outside of the use of sworn witnesses. For instance, I showed that in the New York Central Railroad strike a year or so ago, Mr. Webb, who was in control of the New York Central in the absence of Mr. Depew, hired a large force of Pinkerton detectives, and hired them before the strike was even inaugurated—hired them before he appealed to the City authorities, the State authorities, or the Federal authorities for the protection of the property of the Company; that those men were brought into Albany. N. Y.; that they were under the control of the Railroad authorities, paid by the railroad authorities, and that during this strike, these men shot down in the streets of Albany men, women and children, who were non-combatants, who were violating no law, and not disturbing the peace. The Governor of New York said that the State authorities could have preserved the peace. The Mayor of Albany said that the city authorities could have preserved the peace. The Chief of Police said that the very first disturbance was caused by these Pinkerton men.

Afterwards all the facts were investigated before the State

Board of Arbitration of New York. Mr. Webb was a witness on the stand. He was asked by Gen. Roger A. Pryor, who represented the workingmen, what were the instructions that he gave those Pinkerton men when he employed them and sent them forth with Winchesters in their hands; and Mr. Webb refused to answer the question, treated the Board with contempt, and left that tribunal without ever having answered the question.

Now, Mr. Speaker, we say that this is a country with law and order or it is a country of anarchy. If the regularly constituted authorities can administer the law and preserve the peace, we want to know it; if they cannot, we want to know it, that we may strengthen their hands.

I am as much opposed to laborers having a standing army as I am to capitalists having it. I believe in law; I believe in order; I believe that when there is civil disturbance the peace should be preserved by an impartial magistracy, not by the armed belligerents on either side. [Applause.]

Now, Mr. Speaker, a word as to the law of the case. By means of the Interstate Commerce law the United States Government undertakes to regulate to running of engines and trains; it undertakes to prescribe appliances for the safety of passengers and employes; it undertakes to require that special means of coupling or other life-saving apparatus shall be used. More than that, every railroad is a post-road, and the Government surely has the right to say how its mail trains shall be operated. Therefore I thought that by some amendment to our Interstate Commerce law or by some statute independent of it this great Government could say that in this immense domain of Interstate Commerce, where the States are powerless —in this immense domain of the postal communications, in which the States are powerless, the Government has the right to say these roads shall not operate their trains by means of dangerous bands of irresponsible men who take life without authority of law.

Further than that, Mr. Speaker, I believe that when the

Constitution declares that a State shall not maintain a band of armed men, no State has a right to charter a corporation which may do it. For these reasons, sir, I thought this a legitimate subject of investigation. Let us see what this thing really is. Let us see whether there is not an evil which deserves to be restrained or corrected in the interest, not of the laborer, merely as a laborer, not of the striker, merely as a striker, but in the interest of the citizen, whether he is a laborer or a capitalist—in the interest of the good order, the peace, and the dignity of society. [Applause.]

[Turning in the handbook to the question of government ownership of the railroads, Watson provides this rapid-fire series of replies.]

OBJECTIONS TO GOVERNMENT OWNERSHIP CONSIDERED.

. . . First.   That there is no law for it.

The answer to this is that Railroads are Public Highways and necessarily under the control of the Government. The law of eminent domain condemned the land when the Roads were built. Surely what the law took from the people it can restore. We propose to pay a fair price for the property, to be assessed according to law.

Second.   That they would cost too much.

No man loses anything by purchasing good property; especially if that property is injuring him. No tax would have to be laid on the people to pay for the Roads. Legal Tender Treasury Notes can be issued direct from the Treasury to pay for them; thus adding to our circulation without taxing anybody. By operating the Roads upon a basis which would yield 4 per cent. upon their actual value, we would save $250,000,000 per year in freights and yet accumulate a fund in the Treasury which would soon pay the price of the property.

Third.   That it is Paternalism.

No more so than the Post Office is. No more so than coining money is. When a power becomes dangerous to the life of the Republic, the Republic must subordinate that power or die. That is the situation to-day.

Fourth. That persons injured by the trains will have no redress.

The jurisdiction of the Court of Claims can be extended to embrace such issues. There is no trouble whatever on that point.

Fifth. That it will put the Roads "in Politics."

Where are they now? Would to God we could say they are not in politics:—controlling, corrupting and enslaving. By substituting Government ownership, we take away the motive for plundering the people and the crime will die with the death of the motive. If the people are capable of Self Government, they can be trusted with the Railroads. Civil Service Reform is an assured fact of the near future and this will prevent indiscriminate use of Railway appointments for Political purposes. Certainly the isolated, moderately paid, closely watched Railway official, whether Republican or Democrat cannot do anything like the harm that is now done by closely organized, lavishly paid Railroad Kings who defy watching and control elections, and legislative issues, by shameless use of the Corporate funds. This could not be done under Government ownership.

ADVANTAGES CONSIDERED.

First. It would give a death blow to the "Reign of the Corporation." The people would be boss again.

Second. It would stop corrupt Legislation in their behalf. The motive would be gone.

Third. It would unshackle Trade and Commerce from "the Trust" and "the Ring." They cannot operate without the aid of the Railroad.

Fourth.   It would stop discriminations against certain persons and certain places. The motive would be gone. The Post Office treats all alike. So would the Government Railway.

Fifth.   It would stop speculative Railroad Buildings. The Government would lay out a new Road where needed and nowhere else.

Sixth.   It would to a great extent destroy the tyranny of Capital over Labor and render strikes well nigh obsolete.

Seventh.   It would enable the Cotton Planter to exchange products with the Corn Planter on fair terms which would leave a profit to both. At present the Railroads impoverish them both.

Eighth.   It would remove the causes of the hatred of the people to the Roads and harmonize all interests.

Ninth.   It would equalize all avocations and shippers; and would take away the power the Roads now have to destroy a business, a section or an individual.

Tenth.   It would put into the hands of the people a weapon with which they could destroy any Combine among Capitalists in any Article of Commerce.

Eleventh.   It would save enormous sums now paid in fancy salaries.

Twelfth.   It would save the 30,000 lives lost every year for lack of safety appliances.

Thirteenth.   It would bring about absolute Free Trade and cheap traffic between all sections of this great Country; destroy "the pool:" knock the pins from under the Stock broker: put an end to the insolence with which so many officials treat the Public: remove the leverage which English Capital has on our Labor and its Products: give a death-blow to this infernal "booming" of towns and cities at the expense of the country and for the benefit of a few Capitalists over many Laborers. It would be a giant strike in the direction of equality and manhood rights and to the destruction of our Class System of Special Privilege, Shoddy Aristocracy based on Commercial

Spoils and advancing through the dirty lanes and perils of bribery and corruption.

. . . No wonder Jay Gould despises the people. He thinks that if they possessed either sense or spirit they would not submit. Some day the limit of patience will be reached. Possibly, it has already been reached. For myself I believe it has not only been reached but passed. I believe that the storm clouds have already been evolved from the angry elements and that the end of the Modern Feudal System is approaching with the accelerated speed of a cyclone. Let no man forget Gould's insolent admission before the New York Legislature that his Railroad had controlled the elections with money. Let no man forget the Credit Mobilier exposure of the Pacific Railroad robbery. Let no man forget how Huntington got away with his booty from the same roads by methods fully explained in the Colton Correspondence. Let no man forget how Joe Brown bribed the four leading daily newspapers of Georgia to aid him in his spoliation of the taxpayers of Georgia to the extent of $1,200,000. Half the money was stolen at the expense of the poor little ragged, bare-footed, school children of Georgia. Those newspapers are to-day fighting the Reform movement bitterly. Of course. Joe Brown is fighting it. Of course. Joe Brown is a millionaire. Of course. He is a convict lessee. Of course. He is a rigidly correct member of the church. Of course.

[In concluding, Watson develops his notions on the "great middle class" of the future social order.]

FINAL CHAPTER.

. . . In the foregoing pages I have briefly sketched the Legislation, the abuses, the villianies against which the people some years ago began to organize a revolt. The leaders of the people were strong men, fearless and true, and under their guidance the movement grew with startling rapidity. The bosses of the Old Parties, the officials in high places, the money king's in royal palaces paid little heed to the mutterings of the gathering storm. They laughed it aside as did the profligate nobles of the Old Regime in France. Carlyle is quoted as saying that they sneered contemptuously at Rousseau's Book on the social contract wherein was taught the doctrine of Liberty, Equality and Fraternity, but that the second edition of the work was bound in their skins. So rapid was the growth of the revolt against ages of tyranny, crime and impoverishment.

In this country we have appealed to reason. We have stated the grievances, their causes and their remedies. We have been met by both the Old Parties with ridicule, with slanders, with abuse, with mere mule-headed opposition. We have never owed an advance to the generosity of our adversaries. Each time they have given away when their fears were aroused. Not until then. It is so always. We might as well recognize the fact that human cupidity is always the same and never surrenders till the necessity is plain. There never was a breaking of the lines of plutocracy at any epoch of Reform till some Stonewall Jackson sternly said "we must give them the bayonet."

No concession was ever made to Ireland till England dared not withhold it longer. The fear of Civil War produced remedial laws which justice had in vain appealed for. Even in England itself, Parliamentary Reform, Ballot Reform, Corn Law Repeal never stood a ghost of a chance till the aggressiveness of the movement put the Rulers in fear. When the Duke of Wellington had seen his windows smashed; when the Duke of New Castle had seen his castle burnt; when Bristol broke out in a flame of riot; when the King and the stubborn Peers were hissed and mobbed in the streets, then and not till then, did the Throne heed the people. Fear conceded what justice had denied. On one Continent the great French Leader hurls his defiance at the Crown and cries out "we are here by the will of the people and no power save the bayonet shall drive us hence." On the other Continent, the great American Leader peals forth the battle cry "We must fight. I repeat it, sir, We must fight!"

It is always the same. Petitions are rejected: remonstrances spurned: complaints laughed aside: protests silenced: resistance stamped out with iron heel. All these things are done as long as it is supposed they can be safely done. It is only when Tyranny sees danger that it hears reason. It is a sad lesson, but as true a one as humanity ever had need to learn.

There is nothing more singular than the infatuation of a system which has been weighed and found wanting and over which hangs the sentence of doom. Belshazzar is repeated at every epoch and wherever the mad King reaches his last evening on earth his feast is certain to be had. Revelry and wine and music within: the tread of Cyrus and his Persians without. The pampered Aristocrats will listen to no warning, until Daniel strides into the Hall and the laugh of the voluptuary freezes on the lips of the quaking coward.

The Congress now sitting is one illustration. Pledged to Reform, they have not reformed. Pledged to Economy, they have not economized. Pledged to Legislate, they have not legislated. Extravagance has been the order of the day. Absenteeism was never so pronounced. Lack of purpose was never so clear. Lack of common business prudence never more glaring. Drunken members have reeled about the aisles—a disgrace to the Republic. Drunken speakers have debated grave issues on the Floor and in the midst of maudlin ramblings have been heard to ask "*Mr. Speaker, where was I at?*" Useless employes crowd every corridor. Useless expenditures pervade every Department.

Honorable members made strenuous efforts for a Relief Expedition to the starving Russians. They hooted at the idea of relieving the starving Americans. Honorable members grew white in the face denouncing the wrong we put on "the poor

Chinaman" when we passed a Law requesting him to "Stay at home and board at the same place." But they grabbed their able hats and went to lunch when "the poor American" was mentioned. Distance lends enchantment to the Congressional view—on the poverty question. They can see a case of distress on the other side of the ocean—not on this side. That's the kind of eyes they have. The grievances of the Laborers and Producers of America have nothing to hope from these men. A general turning out of this old mossback crowd is the first preparation for real information.

In the business world another illustration is found. The Capitalists will not see; will not hear. They offer no conciliation. They not only claim all the advantages they illegally hold, but demand more. They denounce the Reform movement, abuse its Leaders, ridicule its Platform. Mr. Taylor of Illinois (a National Banker) taunts the Farmers on the Floor of the House and says to them "What you want is to talk less and work more." Mr. Boutelle of Maine shouts defiantly during the same debate this insult: "Quit howling and go to work"—an insult which comes with peculiar cruelty from those who say in the next breath, we have become poor by working too much and producing too much.

Bankers do nothing to relieve the distress. They combine to speculate on it. The Corporations do not lessen their exactions. The actual Railroad returns show fat profits all around. Profits they must and will have. Their labor force is reduced; the streets are full of their discharged employes; those who remain do so with reduced salaries. All this is done that Dividends may be paid on Fraudulent Stock. The Money Kings were never in higher feather. They feel good. The money is on their side; the Law is on their side: the Government is on their side. No wonder they rest cosily in their high places and say "the people be damned." Jay Gould says the McKinley Tariff may produce higher prices for clothes; but the only effect will be that the workingman, who bought two coats before, will now buy one. All right Mr. Gould. But how about the fellow who could only buy one coat before?

The young Emperor of Germany said last year "I alone am Master:"—the most insolent assertion of despotism since Louis XIV said "I am the State." Later on, the young Emperor administered the oath of Allegiance to his Army Recruits. He told them that their oath bound them to obey him alone; and that if he should order them to shoot down their own parents in the streets they must obey. This was last spring. Before the leaves had fallen and grown green again, the order was given and was obeyed. The streets of Berlin ran red with the blood of laborers whose grievances are as soundly based on justice as were those of O'Connell or Kossuth or Patrick Henry. This spirit of repression has a strong hold in this country. Strengthening of our Navy; building Forts, Arsenals, and Dock Yards has a deep meaning lurking underneath. Let the people keep their eyes open and their vigilance unrelaxed.

With this spirit above, and with intense suffering beneath, is it any wonder the revolt grew? Millions were wasted on feasts while gaunt starvation walked the streets. Music, dancing, revelry sounded at midnight in the palace of Vanderbilt, and money flowed like water to gratify every whim. Within a few blocks, there were other houses filled with sickness, suffering, premature decay and untimely death. Men, women and children famishing for want of work, food, raiment, shelter. Vanderbilt's ball rooms were lit by the spoils he had wrung from those poor laborers under the forms of law; and at the very moment when brilliant couples waltzed to voluptuous music beneath the thirty thousand dollars worth of flowers which festooned the walls, his superintendent, Mr. Webb, had in his employ a regiment of paid assassins to insult, overawe, and shoot down the employes who were struggling for their plain rights under the law. They earned their money; the wage or the murderer. Innocent men, helpless women, sweet little children were shot down like so many dogs in the streets of Albany.

Carnegie cuts his wages and robs his workmen of a million dollars. He gives ten per cent. of it to Charity; and the Pharisees all cry out, "blessed be Carnegie." Rockefeller plunders the people to the neat extent of Ten Millions per year on the Oil Monopoly. He puts little dabs of the booty here and there among Colleges and Schools and they all flap their wings and crow; while the press says, "blessed be Rockefeller." The pity of it is that humbuggery is so victorious. Nearly every scheme of the Corporations obtains popular favor under the specious pretext of "developing the country." Every real estate job in the cities is sanctified under the name of "building up the city." Labor is robbed under the baptismal designation of Protection and it is very seldom that the Laborers themselves do not assist. They are entrapped, misled, deluded, defrauded, rifled and jugulated in the name of Arcadian Friendship. A millionaire is never so plausible as when he explains why he loves the laborer; how their interests are identical with his; how they must work together. He never explains why the operation leaves all the money in his hands and none in the hands of his laborers.

Seventy-five thousand men have just been made tramps by the Reading Combine. A clearer violation of law never existed. It will go unpunished. The Corporation is more powerful than the law. The infamous sweating system is driving women and children to poverty and crime. Dire necessity is hurling thousands of girls into vice; boys into crime. The red flag of the auctioneer is in every street. The Sheriff's hammer is never idle, and with every minute which passes the light of some home goes out forever.

Where will it stop? How can human nature stand it always! Let no man dream that it can last. The sword of Damocles never hung by a slenderer thread than does the false system of to-day. When men suffer for food it is hard. When their wives and children so suffer it is harder. But when that suffering is felt to be undeserved, then it is hardest. And when to this undeserved distress is added the belief that some other man is withholding just dues, honest wages, fair reward of toil, then revolt is at hand. And when, to this condition, is added the fact that the man who withholds those just dues is feasting on them, reveling on them in riotous excess of gathered spoils, while, in the wretched hut of the man to whom they rightfully belong lies the worn and faded wife, dying of hunger,—lies the frail and withered child, gasping for God's pure air, then revolution is as inevitable as the laws of the universe. The prophecy of Alex. Stephens is coming home. The warning of Abraham Lincoln rings in the ear. Woe unto the system which robs the people and then mocks them in their agony! These and conditions like these, produced the revolt. Accumulated provocation, increasing burdens, official imbecility and lack of patriotism, has widened the scope of the work and the numbers of the workers. As the Nobleman said to the King, the night the Bastille fell, "No sire, it is not a Revolt, it is a Revolution."

So it is. Peaceful, bloodless, unstained by crime, but as resistless as destiny. It is no longer the fretting of the waves; it is the roar of the rushing tide. It is no longer the brush of the picket lines; it is the burst of flame all along the advancing front of battle.

To restore the liberties of the people, the rule of the people, the equal rights of the people is our purpose; and to do it, the revolution in the old systems must be complete. We do not blindly seek to tear down. We offer the good Law for each bad Law; the sound rail for every rotten rail. We work in no spirit of hate to individuals. We hate only the wrongs and the abuses, and the special privileges which oppress us. We call on good men and good women everywhere to aid us. We call on God above to aid us. For in the revolution we seek to accomplish, there shall be Law and order preserved in-violate. But the Law shall be founded on right and the order shall silence no man's cry of distress. We do not assert that poverty will disappear. We do not assert that the Law itself shall make no more of it. We do not assert that there will be no more crime; we do say that vicious Legislation shall cease to produce it. We do not say that there will be no more suffering; but we do aver that hereafter and forever the statutes shall not empty the homes of the people, turn their children into the streets and fill the hospitals and the alleys and the gutters with the distracted victims of the Law. We do not say that the strong man will cease to have the advantage of the weak one. But we do say that the infernal shame of the Law in aiding the strong man to pilfer the weak one can be stopped and must be!

The hot-beds of crime and vice to-day are at the two extremes of Society. One is among the class who will have all the work and no money; the other is with the class who have all the money and no work. The one class is driven to crime and vice by hardships, despair, desperation. The other class chooses crime and vice because of their surplus of money, their lack of purpose, their capacity to live in idleness and gratify sensual pleasures. The great Middle Class is the main-stay of life. It is the judicious mixture of work and leisure which makes the complete man; the useful man; the happy man; the God-fearing, law-abiding man.

Any system which increases the Moneyed Class where there is all money and no work, debauches Society. Any System which increases the class where there is all work and no money debauches and endangers Society. Any system which will add to the great Middle Class where there is reasonable work and fair reward, secures to Society the best results of which humanity is capable. Every principle advocated by the People's Party seeks that end and logically leads to it.

When this System comes, (and it is bound to come) the

Revolution will be complete. The dens of vice will loose their feeders. The supply-trains of crime will be cut off. The Barroom will disappear and the gambling hell sink to its larger namesake. The attendant train of evils which the present system carries with it will vanish with the system itself.

Manhood will count for more than money. Character will outweigh the dollar. The Laborer whether he work with brawn or brain, with thought or speech, will be the monarch of the new order of things.

30. A Political Revelation

James H. Davis, who has already appeared in these pages, was the center of no little controversy in Texas Populism. That he was an able orator, that he introduced many to Populist doctrine, that he mesmerized large numbers with his theatrical flair (mounting the platform oftentimes with ten large volumes of the works of Jefferson) cannot be doubted. Yet these gains were offset by the dissension created when Davis led the fusion forces in the state party against the more orthodox wing under Milton Park. More relevant for present purposes, it can be said that Davis was neither a profound nor an original thinker. He reflected rather than initiated further advances in Populist thinking, and to that extent, provides interesting light on the way the movement made use of Jeffersonian doctrine. It is the editor's impression that southern, more so than midwestern, Populism was infused with this doctrine and hence was somewhat less inclined to place heavy reliance on the national government. Still, one should note that Jefferson has been broadly interpreted. Populists could speak of "strict" construction to deny special privileges to business groups, while at the very same time

Reprinted from James H. Davis, *A Political Revelation* (Dallas: The Advance Publishing Company, 1894), pp. 13-15, 70-75, 81-86, 92-93, 95-101, 112-114, 168-170, 199-200, 230-233, 264-265.

find in Jefferson ample justification for government ownership of the railroads. In sum, even in this selection, the most avowed strand of Jeffersonianism the editor has detected in Populism, one can see the selective borrowing noted in the Introduction.

The principles of the Declaration of Independence, the Constitution of the United States, and the National Demands of the Populists or People's party, being the objects of discussion in this work, we think it proper to state in the outset that we believe these three documents contain all the requisite provisions for the grandest and most perfect civilization. If put into action there could be no monopoly in our landed interests. There could be no corporate or foreign control or influence over our finances, neither in coinage volume, distribution, or rate of interest. These would all be under government service, and exercised for the good of the whole people. There could be no foreign or corporate control or interference in the management of our highways. Thus the people, through their national government would coin money for their own use, and would coin enough to transact the business of the country with ease, security and safety. Having coined the money for their own use, they would see that it got into the channels of trade without foreign interference or franchised bank toll gates, charging them toll on the money they, through their government, had coined. There being no monopoly of lands, no aliens allowed to own lands, no corporations allowed to own land; banking, railway and telegraph companies being no longer in existence, could not extort tolls and usury from the public, and buy up and absorb our lands with the money thus wrenched from the people. The government would exercise its full sovereign power to coin money, would coin enough money for the needs of the people, and they would not be forced to borrow foreign money and mortgage their lands, and with a reasonable limit of individual ownership and possession, each industrious individual would have the privilege of a home where he could produce and enjoy the comforts of life. The government being in charge of the great highways, all men would be on an equal footing in the distribution of their wares, products or merchandise. The government by virtue of its constitutional power would coin money for the people at cost of coinage. The government, through a natural operation of the national and state government, would carry traffic and mails, transmit telegraphic news, and transport the people themselves over the country at actual cost, or if above cost the excess over cost would go into the treasury and relieve taxation that much. Then there would be no monopoly in lands; all persons would have to rely on their own industry for support and comforts; one could not go to the government and ask it to aid him by giving a charter on some avenue of industry or public necessity, hence there could be no monopoly in the production of wealth. There being no monopoly in transportation there would be no monopoly in the distribution of wealth. No monopoly in the coinage and distribution of money being possible all men would be in a manner equal before the law in the privilege to secure a home as well as in production and distribution of wealth.

[Contending that the government can act directly on the people and has the full power to satisfy their needs, Davis turns for support to revolutionary history, the Declaration of Independence and the Constitution as providing the foundation for the Populist principles. In the chapter on the Constitution, he continues:]

. . . The "caption, preamble or enacting clause" is as old as the history of law and civilization itself. We are told by ancient writers that it became so by custom of the kings, whose proclamations were law, and were posted in conspicuous places and read to the king's armies, and, in order to enable the people to better understand the meaning, purposes and intentions of the law, captions were put over it to explain it. This principle is sacred today in most, if not all, our States, and if omitted violates the law. Now we must conclude that our forefathers in forming our Constitution fully understood this application, and put that caption or preamble over the Constitution to explain it. Let us transpose the preamble thus: "We, the people of the United States, do ordain and establish this Constitution for the United States of America in order to form a more perfect union, establish justice, insure domestic tranquility, provide for the common defence, promote the general welfare and secure the blessings of liberty to ourselves and our posterity." Now we must admit that from the above every power in the Constitution was given for those purposes, and were expected to be carried out so as to secure the benefits therein named. We are not to presume that Congress can do anything and everything it chooses to think would secure the purposes named in the preamble, but it can and must do everything named in the Constitution. And in every one of these powers we contend that it is the duty of Congress *to act directly on the people and for the people,* and not through the States, counties or any other subdivisions of government, *much less through corporations or syndicates.* Where a power of legislation is given Congress it is by the "Rules of Nations" and the common law complete within itself, and carries with it the logical right to make all laws necessary for carrying it into effect. Without it constitutional governments of all kinds would be failures. Again, we must consider that this Constitution was formed by the representation of sovereign States, and they conveyed their own rights of sovereignty to the United States in every one of the powers they gave. But the framers of that instrument were not disposed to leave this matter to rest on general inference, so, after naming the general powers as found in section 8, they gave one more power that settles the question and covers the powers in relation to all matters in the Constitution. The last clause in this section reads thus: "To make all laws which shall be necessary and proper for carrying into execution the foregoing powers and all other powers vested by this Constitution in the government of the United States or in any department or offices thereof." Now let us examine some of the powers and the manner in which they are applied.

First. Congress has power to lay and collect tax duties, imposts and excises. In all these matters she acts directly on the people; her impost or tariff duties are collected by her own officers direct from the shippers. Her excises (internal revenue as we call them) are collected direct from the people by her own officers, etc.

Second. To borrow money on the credit of the United States. Under this provision she issues bonds and does a thousand things not mentioned in the Constitution. The fact is, in all the powers above Congress does what it considers "necessary and proper" to carry them into effect.

The next power is: "To regulate commerce with foreign nations, and among the several States and with the Indian tribes."

Reader, please inform me what Congress is doing to carry this power into effect, or what has ever been done? Will you answer that she has a tariff law that regulates trade between the States and foreign nations? Certainly she has tariff laws, and rules following in volumes, but that is all in answer to the power to "lay and collect imposts." Now why not apply the same reasoning to this clause that is applied to the others? Why not declare the government to be in possession of this power for the same purposes that she possesses the others, with equal power to carry it into effect? Certainly our forefathers intended this should be done; they intended that the government should act direct on and for the people in this matter just the same as in every power; yea, ten thousand times more urgent is this power, for it was this power that served as a mainspring to build up our government; it was a violation of this power that led us to war with King George;

it was a disregard for rights of shippers by the States and a want of some power that could act *on the people to protect the trade,* that gave birth to this Constitution, and do you for one moment suppose that they intended it should lie dormant for a hundred years? Why not put this power into execution by owning the railways and operating them, by sworn officers, for the good of the people? It is the only reasonable and logical manner of carrying the power into execution.

Next: "To establish a uniform rule of naturalization and uniform laws on the subject of bankruptcy throughout the United States." The above powers are carried out the first in a very reasonable manner; the last, by "federal receivership" to the great corporations which becomes a source of oppression and of fraud, entailing millions of debt to pay judges, juries and court expenses, and millions more as lawyers' fees, that would be saved if the government owned the roads.

Next: "To coin money regulate the value thereof, and of foreign coin, and fix the standard of weights and measures." Here is another sovereign power, unconditional and absolute. There might be some excuse for Congress refusing to coin enough money for the business of the people if the States were free to coin, but in another section they are prohibited. To make the matter short, this is one of the most important powers in the Constitution. In this Congress should act directly on, and for the people as in other matters. In the exercise of this power, like the power to regulate commerce, Congress allows, yea even charters, licenses a lot of cold, faithless, soulless, heartless, merciless corporations, to stand between the government and the people, and usurp the blessings conferred by this power, forcing the people to look to these conscienceless beings for money and transportation to carry on their commerce.

Next: "To provide for the punishment of counterfeiting the securities and current coin of the United States." In this power they act directly on the people, pass all laws necessary to carry it into effect.

Next: "To establish postoffices and postroads." This power they carry into effect about as reason and justice would demand in most cases. The word "establish" is used to give them the right to build and own postoffices in the name of the government, and under the same they can build and own railroads. A double purpose would be served and two objects of the Constitution met, for here is a specific grant given to establish a road and when established it can be used as a means of regulating commerce also.

Next: "To promote the progress of science and useful arts, by securing for a limited time to authors and inventors the exclusive right to their respective writings and discoveries." In the exercise of this power they have passed all reasonable laws necessary to carry it into effect. Under this grant of power they have, as in the postoffice department and many other instances, created separate branches of the executive department, with all necessary rules, laws, buildings, etc. Under this clause they have a mammoth building called the Patent Office, where millions of models and records are stored and kept. They act directly on, and for the people, as should be in all cases. All we ask is that all the power shall be treated with the same reason and judgment in its application.

We boldly affirm that the power to regulate commerce and coin money are the most important powers, so far as the masses of the people are concerned, and were so considered by the framers of our Constitution. It was for these purposes that the National government was formed. And as James Madison and Thomas Jefferson tell us, the old Federal government was insufficient for that purpose, and when a National convention met, under their Articles of Confederation, *to regulate trade* among themselves and foreign countries, they found it impossible to do so and carry it into effect without giving the government more power, a power, as Jefferson said, to act directly on the people and not through the States, and to make the system that might be adopted uniform and just throughout, and to give the States off the coast the rights

and benefits of trade without discrimination in favor of coast
States required a change of government.

. . . We believe in State rights, but only such rights as do
not conflict with the rights of the United States as named
in the Constitution. Like James Madison, in his letter to
Edmund Randolph, just before they were to start to the
convention to form the Constitution, we "hold it for a fundamental truth that an individual independence of the States is
utterly irreconcilable with an aggregate sovereignty," hence
we believe the Constitution means what it says when it declared that the laws of the United States, made in pursuance
of the Constitution, shall be the supreme law of the land,
and we boldly announce that in every power it is a Nation
and is expected to act through its own officers, and must so
act, and act directly on the people. To "farm out" or delegate
its powers to anyone is to betray the trust of the people. The
States were first sovereign. They surrendered their sovereignty
in certain matters to the general government, and all matters
not therein mentioned are left to the States. Hence agreeing
with the Supreme Court, that the United States is an indis-
soluble Union of indestructible States, we still contend that
the United States is supreme, absolute and sovereign in every
power named in the Constitution. All we, as Populists, ask, is
that each power in the Constitution shall be treated with the
same regard and respect that is given to others. Our forefathers did not mean that the Constitution should be difficult
to understand, and it is not. It names in plain language what
powers Congress shall have; then it names in plain terms
certain things that neither Congress or the States shall do;
then it tells how the different branches of government shall
be organized and continued, and then gives Congress a right
to make all laws necessary and proper for carrying these into
execution, and then declares that all such laws shall be the
supreme law of the land. But in order to assist you in this
matter of understanding the Constitution, let us here take

an extract from Thomas Jefferson. Certainly no patriot can refuse to listen to Jefferson; all men of all countries acknowledge his wisdom, patriotism and love of universal liberty. When he was first elected President, the legislature of the State of Rhode Island wrote him a letter of congratulation, and being greatly interested in the then young but growing commerce of the country, they asked some questions relative to what course he would pursue, and in answering them, giving his views of the then comparatively new Constitution, he writes as follows (Jefferson's Works, vol. 4—398): "To the United Nation belongs our Eternal and Mutual Relations. To each State severally the care of our persons, our property, our reputation and religious freedom." Then, according to Jefferson, all mutual relations between the citizens of different States is under Congress. Certainly that is proper, and we do not have near as much mutual relations in the mail service as we do in the railroad service, and the same reasoning that gives Congress charge over one should give it charge of both, even if the Constitution did not require it. Then again, while Jefferson was President, in 1807, in writing to Governor Cabell, of Virginia, officially, in passing on some questions that arose in some military laws and regulations, in Jefferson's Works, vol. 5—259, we find that he says, "In the construction of law, even in judiciary cases, where the opposite parties have a right and counter right in the words of the law, the judge considers the intention of the law given as his guide and gives to all the parts and expressions of the law, that meaning which effects instead of defeating its intentions. But laws, merely executive, and where no private right stands in the way, and the public object is the interest of all, a much more free scope of construction in favor of the intention of the law ought to be taken, and ingenuity should be exercised in devising constructions which may save to the public the benefits of the law. Constructions must not be favored which go to defeat instead of furthering the principal object of the law." This theory of construction is elementary in every treatise of law we ever read, but Jefferson is grand authority and he also expresses it so plainly that we quote him in preference to others. Now read the clause of the Constitution which says that Congress shall have power to regulate commerce among the several States, apply Jefferson's manner of constructions to it. Remember its objects are to establish justice, insure domestic tranquility, provide for the common defence, promote the general welfare and secure the blessings of liberty to ourselves and our posterity. Now if the government owned and operated the railroads and telegraph lines it would certainly establish justice, for then all would have to pay the same price for freight and travel. The poor could ship and travel just as cheaply as the rich. The government would serve the pay-roll and the workers would be paid more and the officers less, about as in other services of the government. There would be no such thing as the roads being three or four months behind on pay-rolls, or roads becoming insolvent and defeating claims and "work hands." No such thing as turning off fifty or seventy-five thousand men as was done this summer in the West and South, because the company could not make money, pay princely salaries to officers and keep them employed. The government would keep a sufficient number of men at all times to keep the roads in good fix and operate them well. The operatives would have a term of service and regular work under civil service laws. Headquarters would be fixed and permanent at state capitals and county seats, and then griping corporations could not bleed and boycott towns in locating depots, round-houses and headquarters, and every dollar that they collected in excess of the operating expenses would go into the treasury and not into the pockets of arrogant and lordly millionaires. Surely you do not have to "exercise your ingenuity" to see that all these would follow a proper construction and application of the principle, and justice be established throughout the Union. Remember, too,

that Jefferson said: "To the United Nation belongs our external
and mutual relations" and all must admit that a line of railroad and telegraph extending from New York to Galveston,
which comes in business contact with thousands of persons in
each State each day, must be construed to be our "mutual
relations."

Another object is to "insure domestic tranquility." Well
there would be no such thing as strikes on railroad and telegraph lines if the government had charge of them, for the
employes would all be well paid and get their pay regularly,
and the eight-hour law now prevails in government service,
and would, so far as practical, in that service also. So it surely
insures a great deal more domestic tranquility than now prevails in such service. Certainly every unbiased person must
confess that it would provide greatly for the common defence,
for all roads could then be used as military roads, etc., free
by the government.

Now without schooling you further in this line, we ask
you to apply Jefferson's rules of construction to all our propo-
sitions, every one of which must rest on the Constitution, and
in passing on their constitutionality consider first the objects
of the Constitution, and remember that constructions "must
not be favored which go to defeating instead of furthering
the object" of the Constitution. With this request we close
this chapter.

[Thus Davis uses Jefferson to suggest that the Constitution supports the government ownership of railroads. This is followed by
the reprinting of the Omaha Platform. He then adds:]

. . . Our demands may be classified into three parts, viz:
Land, Highways and Money.

The object of our platform is to set down ways and means
by which a monopoly of either of these great blessings so
necessary to civilization can be abolished and prohibited,
and to establish a system of laws and regulations that will

prevent all kinds of monopoly and all kinds of aristocracy of wealth, and at the same time encourage individual industry in the acquisition of property and the enjoyment of the same; establishing an aristocracy of industry, merit and honor, instead of an aristocracy of wealth, arrogance and idleness.

. . . Now the reader will see from the foregoing that basing our principles upon undisputed grounds of justice, the object of our platform is to prevent monopolies or government powers being used in the acquirement of property for individual gain. Here let us lay down a text which must serve as the key to this book, the line of demarkation that divides a Democratic or Republican government from a socialism. A Democratic government recognizes the rights of the individual to own, use, produce and enjoy property. While socialism recognizes no private right to property, but forms the government into one vast partnership, all labor and all property being public, held in trust for public good. All civilized governments are more or less a socialism. The courthouses are all owned and held in trust for the public, the poor and the rich being alike interested. Our public schools are owned and held in trust for the public. Our public school systems contain many extreme features of socialism and paternalism. Our roadways, rivers, lakes, streets and commons are held in trust and owned by the public. Hence the dividing line between socialism and Democracy is the right and recognition of private property. We favor a Democracy and stand by the principal that governments are organized to perform for the whole people at cost, that service which the citizen and family in their own right cannot best perform for themselves. Upon this principle rests all our public affairs. Thus we have civil courts to settle the business matters between persons who fail or refuse to settle among themselves. And we have criminal courts holding censorship or paternal care over society, naming certain things the individual shall and shall not do, a violation of which is pronounced criminal. Thus running through all our public affairs, National, State, county or municipal, we are paternalistic, socialistic or communistic; therefore these terms need not alarm you. There is a proper limit at which government should stop. But in a government which is organized as ours, by the people for their own good, there need be no fear so long as the power is kept in the hands of the people and a constitutional limit recognized. But when the power is taken from the people and placed in the hands of a few, and those few chartered into corporations with almost unlimited power over lands, highways, and money, and under no oath of office, obligation or bond to the people, who toll without conscience the tillers of the soil for the use of the earth, either for home or tillage; assessing a rent roll from the laborers of our cities with more greed and avarice than ever an English lord or duke manifested towards his vassals; laying a tariff on the distribution of life's comforts that pass over our highways which prostrates and impoverishes the producer on the one hand and the consumer on the other; and with the Bible-cursed, but government-chartered hand of the usurer, taxing every element of labor, industry and enterprise throughout our country by demanding tribute for the use of every dollar that passes from the mints of our government into the commerce of our people, we find today a "communism of capital," a despotism of aristocracy unknown to our Constitution, foreign to our theory of government, repulsive to our ideas of justice, and which, if not arrested in its devastating sway, must soon result in the complete vassalage of the masses and the aristocracy of the classes.

Now, before we go further, let us agree that the government of the United States is not a separate thing from the people, geared up and held in the hands of a royal family or aristocracy. The people here constitute their royal family; every man is just as much a sovereign, or is just as much a king as any other man. The government is the organized agency through which the people rule themselves, and in all governmental affairs we are a great partnership, every person's rights being equal. The people are the masters, and the office-holders are the servants or agents of the people. There are no titles of nobility by birth in this land; our Declaration of Independence affirms "that all men are created equal, endowed by their Creator with certain inalienable rights, among which are life, liberty and the pursuit of happiness; that to secure these rights governments are instituted among men, deriving their just powers from the consent of the governed." Every word in the above means volumes. It was the separating point between kingdoms and republics. It was the decree that took away from King George and his royal family and retinue of nobility the right to rule us, and asserted our right under God's law to rule ourselves. It meant a new theory of government in which there should be no royalty, no nobility, no special classes, either born as nobility or titled by law. That Declaration, which was the pillar of fire that led our hungry, suffering sires through that dark night of revolution, tells us that "all just powers are derived from the consent of the governed" and the caption of the Constitution tells us that the Constitution was formed "in order to establish justice." Hence we must infer that the framers of our Constitution did not mean to contradict the principle that all power of government is derived from the people who are to be governed. Hence, when a traffic association consisting of railway managers meet and issue orders, tariff or tax rates that control the commerce of eight or ten States (sometimes the whole United States), they are governing the people, and under this government they have thousands of officers with more power over the people than the President of the United States. Many of these officers appoint more officers under his government, and distribute more patronage and more money than the governors of half a dozen States. Yet his power is not derived from the people; it is a usurpation, a species of royalty, because he exercises a power independent of and without the consent of the people. And when a bankers' congress meets, which occurs almost every year in the United States, they, representing the same kind of a government that the traffic association does, issue their orders, rules, regulations and decrees with the same potency and with more direful effect on the people than the traffic association. In both cases it is a collection of officers drawing immense salaries under no oath or bond to the people, whose orders or decrees can make or break any town or citizen in the Union, and they can tax the citizen of the United States or issue bonds enslaving us and our children to build roads in Mexico, South America and Africa.

The United States government was instituted to secure the rights of life, liberty and pursuit of happiness. To secure physical life, liberty and happiness there are three great fundamental principles necessary. First, that all men's rights to the earth (the unborn as well as the present) should be protected and secured in every way consistent with the common rights of all. And as the commerce of civilized society consists in the production and distribution of what is known as wealth, and as the earth is known to be the source of all wealth, we hold that there should be no monopoly of land. That vast tracts of land held either by individuals or corporations, without being occupied either as a home or used in the production of wealth, is contrary to divine law, in violation of every principle of civil liberty and justice known to Republican or Democratic government, and retards the advancement of civilization, disinherits posterity and creates an aristocracy of its holders and their offspring. A home and some portion of the earth from which to produce comforts, and upon which to rest our weary limbs after a day's toil in production; a home around which lingers a halo of endearment to every human being; a home, the absence of which tends to make man an alien to his God, an alien to his country, and to convert him into a vagabond, a wanderer and an outcast; is so essential to human happiness that the decay of liberty, the downfall of society and the wreck of happiness in every age and every country have been measured by the homeless numbers within her borders. Our platform contemplates a civilization in which the sacred rights of home in reasonable amount of acres, and the production and enjoyments of comforts are held inviolable, and when you have produced more of any kind of wealth than you wish to consume, and you wish to send over some highway to consumers elsewhere, instead of chartering a soulless, heartless corporation to take your goods in transit and rob you and consumer both for his own gain, the government will take your goods as it does your letters, and distribute them at actual cost. Allow no monopoly in land, no monopoly in highways and no monopoly in money, and all men would be equal in production and distribution of wealth and there would be neither monopoly nor scarcity of money, for there would be no railways to draw it away from the people in extortion, and no bank monopolies to draw it out of the country in usury. Then the man who produced the most would be the most prosperous, and each individual would have to depend on his own industry or energy to make or secure his comforts and blessings.

[Relying on Jefferson's statement that one generation cannot bind the next, Davis turns to a discussion of specific planks in the platform.]

. . . Now, reader, remember that governments are organized to protect man's natural rights, to encourage industry, and that each man's rights to the use of the earth, free and unencumbered, is a decree of God. And we, as Populists, contend that a sovereign nation, with full power to coin money enough for its own needs and the needs of its people, need never borrow a dollar. That money is a decree of law, naming some particular substance which shall serve in all official and legal transactions as a measure of value, to adjust business,

that the idea of a government with sovereign power to make, coin, imprint or manufacture money, having to borrow money is a relic of barbarism. Hence our idea is to pay off all national and State debts, just as rapidly as can be safely done, then allow no bank monopolies, land monopolies, highway monopolies or other monopolies to be chartered or formed. The power to borrow money to be paid by posterity, and legally bind posterity to pay the same, we deny as a matter of right, and think it wrong in government to force such laws and systems on posterity. And in the present age the government does not only violate this sacred right of man, but it allows great corporations to issue bonds, binding whole States as it were, for a half and even a full century, not for any purpose of public good, but simply to enrich their own families, and build up colossal fortunes for themselves. Binding posterity by forms of law, to pay these debts, gives these corporations a chartered power to tax the entire commerce and travel of the country, in a sum sufficient to pay interest on all they have borrowed; no matter how much that may have been; and no matter for what purpose the corporation may have borrowed. Railway managers may issue bonds, mortgaging one of their lines for four millions of dollars and spend one-fourth in building mansions for themselves, another fourth in luxurious living at health resorts and traveling, then charter banking companies, loan the remainder out and live off the income; elect themselves officers of both the railroads and the banks, set their own salaries at twice the salary of the governor of the State who signed their charter, and yet under the laws of this country lay a tax, tariff, toll or freight rate sufficient to pay a reasonable interest on the money they have borrowed and squandered in revelry and ribaldry, together with all running expense, and the immense salaries of their political lawyers, who attend conventions, go to Congress, the legislature, and otherwise look after their interests. Can it be that this is American liberty such as our fathers intended?

On this question let us turn to vol. 3, page 103, Jefferson's Works, and read what he says, viz: "The question whether one generation of men has a right to bind another, seems never to have been started, yet it is a question of such consequence as not only to merit decision, but place among the fundamental principles of every government. That no such obligation can be transmitted, I think capable of proof. I set out on this ground, that the earth belongs in usufruct to the living; that the dead have neither powers nor rights over it. No man can by natural right oblige the lands he occupied to the payment of debts contracted by him, for if he could he might eat up the usufruct of the earth for several generations to come, and then the earth would belong to the dead. The conclusion then is, that neither the representatives of a nation, nor the whole nation itself assembled, can validly engage debts beyond what they may pay in their own time." Thus spoke the immortal Jefferson, and yet today our States, nation, counties and cities, are not only violating that sacred law, but they allow corporations, led by private greed alone, to violate by issuing bonds in boundless millions, put the money and goods thus borrowed into their own pockets, and tax the unborn generations to pay these bonds.

[Davis then moves from a discussion of land to that of transportation, with extensive quotations from Jefferson.]

. . . Yes, Mr. Jefferson, your presentment was true. Banking institutions and moneyed incorporations have charge of all our highways by steam, control all our labor, own all our coal, iron and mineral lands, all our best city property, issue bonds and tax our people millions, yes billions, each year. They have done what you said nothing on earth could induce you to give your consent to the government to do. They have bonded and enslaved our posterity to the full value of our lands for two generations to come; yes, they have plundered our plowman and beggared our yeoman. When General Jackson was leaving the Presidency, after a hard fought battle with the banks and money power, he saw the coming evils of corporate greed. He foresaw that evil which is so plainly visible today, and in his farewell address warned his countrymen against banks, corporations and monopolies, and in speaking of the evils then present and the vastly greater evils to come, he says: "The mischief springs from a power which the moneyed interests derive from a paper currency, which they are able to control. From the multitude of corporations, with exclusive privileges, which they have succeeded in obtaining in the different States, and which are employed altogether for their benefit, and unless you become more watchful in your States and check this spirit of monopoly and thirst for exclusive privileges, you will find in the end that the most important powers of the government have been given or bartered away and the control over your dearest interests has passed into the hands of these corporations."

General Jackson! beloved and revered hero and statesman, the spirit of monopoly and thirst for exclusive privileges of government was not checked, and now these men, who claim to be following you, are among the most clamorous for its perpetuation and they boldly affirm that we who seek to check it are anarchists. And, General, you were correct; our dearest interests have been bartered away and are now in the hands of the corporations. They hold under exclusive government rights, franchised control over all our highways, our money, most of our lands and property, and hold millions of bonds issued by themselves without our consent, sold in Europe or America, pledging the entire wealth of whole States to pay the same. They hold over five thousand of the best paying offices in our land, to which they have elected themselves, and then tax us to pay exorbitant salaries of the same. In other words, they are our "lords and masters;" we are their slaves and peons.

One thing is quite plain to everyone who reads history, and that is, that whatever power over commerce was given to Congress was intended to be used by and through government officers and not through corporations, for the thought of an "incorporation" or "a bank" created a tremor in the mind of our early statesmen who opposed Hamilton, and the "moneyed incorporations and the banks were always opposed to the people," and this class of people during the revolution were generally tories, and the people did not think that a man was sound or a good Whig if he was interested in these things. During the presidential terms of Washington and Jefferson, a man was not considered a sound man to fill a government office if he was a banker or "stock broker" or corporation man. Certainly our forefathers never intended to leave the regulation of commerce to corporations.

. . . It is a well-known fact that the people are taxed to pay interest and dividends on about three times the cost of the railroads of the country, or, in other words, three times as much as it would cost to build them today. What we mean by a tax is that the managers and so-called owners of the roads set a freight and passenger tariff to cover about three times as much as the roads would cost to build them.

Turn to page 15, Report of Interstate Commerce Commission for 1888, and we find some light on this subject. They there give it as their opinion that the roads are bonded for what they are really worth, showing that the so-called owners have not a dollar of cash in the road; that through their corporate capacity they issued bonds just as a county or city; sold the bonds for money to build the road, and levy rates on the people to pay interest on these bonds, just as the county or city officers do in such cases. When the road is built, then they say it is worth twice as much as it cost, and issue "stock certificates" in shares of ten, one hundred or one thousand dollar blocks to the amount of the other half.

These stock certificates bear interest, or, as a basis of so-called ownership, the company must levy a rate sufficient to pay a profit on them also. If the road is bonded for what it cost, or what it is worth, then whatever amount of stock is issued is called watered stock, and when they certify that this road cost more than was actually spent, and collect money off the public on the basis of that falsehood, they are getting money under false pretenses, in the spirit and meaning of the law, but instead of sending them to prison, as we generally do the common person who thus falsely and fraudulently obtains money, we have been charitable enough in many cases to condone their offense and let them off by punishing them with a few terms in the Legislatures, on the bench, or in Congress.

[Davis next discusses money and the sub-treasury plan.]

. . . Coin all the gold and silver that can be had, repeal every law allowing an issue of promises to pay or bills of any kind to supplement the volume of gold and silver, coin some other metal or paper into absolute unconditional money, with equal money functions with gold and silver, circulate it by paying out on government expense, or issuing to the States instead of to banks; allow no banks of issue to continue in this line until we have at least $50 per capita in circulation. Then when the other parts of our platform is in operation and the corporate leeches are abolished, the money will remain in circulation and not to drift and congest in money centres.

There would then be no such thing as a money centre, except in a productive centre.

In this way we would have a regular stable and sound money, in regular volume. Then to meet the increased demand for money to move the crop each year, and to make us independent of Europe and other countries, in the price of the same, we should have an automatic volume of money each year, which should be gauged by, and issued on the wealth of the country instead of the debts, as is now done through the banks. The issue should be gauged by the productive industry of the country and distributed so as to prevent a depression in the price of the crop and product it was intended to relieve. This may be done through the warehouse plan of the Farmers' Alliance, or through fiscal agencies or by a reparation to the State, based on the annual product of each State, to be by them distributed, and returned in automatic recurrence, as the movement of the crop required. This is the principal involved in what is known as the sub-treasury plan.

It is a grand conception indeed, and will forever prevent a panic, stringency or plethora of money matters, for it gives the people, and not the speculator, control over the actual commodity to be handled by it. It contemplates the issue of money on the product of the country instead of the debts, and sets a premium on industry, because the more there is produced the more money will be issued. The more money issued, the more commodities will be consumed, for when the producer gets more money for his product, he buys and consumes more, and thus the scale grades up, each increased output of commodities will call for the money to exchange itself, and yet never interfere with the regular stable current volume. Whereas, now, the greater portion of our money is a money unknown to the Constitution, and is issued on the debts, giving the creditor class absolute control over the money issued, and also making them in a measure, fiscal agents for the government, and the people in the distribution of that money, with almost unlimited power to speculate upon the misfortunes of the country; and hence their interest is to run prices down, so as to make a greater margin for speculation in the fall and by leaving the country stranded, it gives them a greater demand for the loan of money in the spring. So the producer is at their mercy, in the fall in the sale of his commodities, and the whole country at their mercy in the spring, and must put up any security, and make any terms, that the banker demands. The workings of our present financial system are a curse to civilization, a blight on industry, a burthen on legitimate business. It famishes the laborer and feasts the usurer, pauperizes the many and pamperizes the few, but the overshadowing depravity and injustice of the measure is found in the principles upon which it is based. Any system that issues money on the debts of a country is vile and cruel. It gives the debt holders a monopoly over the money. It gives them power to draw interest both on the debts and the money issued on the debts. To increase the money you must increase the debt; the interest on the debts, and on the money thus issued, absorbs the benefits of the money so issued, hence it is like a man sucking his own blood to get water. As this volume contains an appendix by Mr. Harry Tracy, on the details of the sub-treasury plan, we shall be brief upon this question, viewing mainly the principles involved.

We affirm that the principles of the plan are not only salutary as an economic measure, but they are the true principles upon which the sovereign power to coin money should rest for the following reasons:

First. The money is issued on the wealth and product, thereby furnishing adequate means for its own consumption.

Second. When the product increases the volume of money increases, holding all values, and labor, stable and regular.

Third. It would prevent all power to contract or inflate the circulation except as the business required.

Fourth. It would abolish the business of money loaning as a means of gain, and money would be used to produce wealth and consume it, instead of taxing both producer and consumer for its use as now.

The following three questions which must be answered affirmatively by all reasonable men will settle the matter in our favor under our constitution:

First. Does the Constitution place the exclusive power to coin money in Congress? Yes.

Second. Does that carry with it the logical constitutional duty of Congress to coin enough money to transact the reasonable business of the country? Yes.

Third. Does that make it a constitutional duty of Congress to devise some plan, process or system to get that money into the channels of trade, and to the use of the people without fraud, favoritism or monopolies? Yes.

We invite all persons who believe in the above to join with us and help us. If the warehouse plan is not the best plan to invoke the use of the above principles, then let us find some other plan. The principles are eternal, the methods are immaterial if they carry the objects.

[After discussing corporations (reprinted above in this volume), Davis concludes by stressing the Jeffersonian elements in Populism.]

. . . The Populists are the defenders of the people and the Constitution, the upholders of liberty in its broader grander sense, consistent with our form of government, and we believe our forefathers formed our government with these things in view. Populists are the true Democrats, the true Republicans; the opposition are the real tories and aristocrats.

Public thought and discussion was divided between two general ideas of government in the beginning. One idea was to risk the people—give them all power and management of the interests of society or government through agents or officers elected by themselves. The leading advocates of this idea were Jefferson, Madison, Randolph, Mason *et al.*

The other idea was that the people were unsafe; that they were not educated, were not competent; that they should have as little to do with government as possible; that the rich, who had better opportunities and were better educated, should have all the powers of government in their hands; that the wealthy classes should rule the masses; that an aristocracy should hold the offices and rule the people. The advocates of this idea were led by Hamilton, Morris *et al.* And as they could not teach the people to submit to royalty, they usurped the same power in the government through the banking system and corporations, all of which confer every benefit, so far as salaried officers are concerned, and other privileges that royalty enjoys in Europe, and thus having power to create offices for themselves by creating corporations, their power to create officers is only limited by the power to create corporations. Hence their power to create officers for their own benefit and to tax the people for the payment of the salary is far superior to the European royalty, which must depend upon the accident of birth. In 1824 Mr. Jefferson wrote a letter to Mr. H. Lee which is found in vol. 7, page 376, in which he says: "Men are naturally divided into classes.

First. Those who fear and distrust the people and wish to draw all power from them into the hands of the higher classes.

Second. Those who identify themselves with the people have confidence in them, cherish and consider them as the most honest and safe, if not the most wise depository of the public interest.

Call them, therefore, Liberals and Serviles, Jacobins and Ultras, Whigs and Tories, Republicans and Federalists, Aristocrats and Democrats, or by whatever name you please, they are the same parties still, and pursue the same objects.

The last appellation of Aristocrats and Democrats is the true one, expressing the essence of all."

We thank you profoundly, Mr. Jefferson, for this definition; by it we affirm all our opponents to be Aristocrats; they are pretendingly afraid for the people to have power; they want the corporations to have charge of our highways and control over our money. We Populists are willing to trust the people, and they are not. They are the enemies to free government; we the friends of freedom.

31. The American Plutocracy

Milford W. Howard was a Populist congressman from Alabama with something of a literary bent. In addition to the present work,

Reprinted from Milford W. Howard, *The American Plutocracy* (New York: Holland Publishing Company, 1895), pp. 24-32, 35-36, 42-44, 46–48, 51–56, 100–103, 106–107, 141–144, 147, 150.

he also wrote *If Christ Came to Congress* (1894), a sensational novel about immorality and intemperance in government circles, no doubt prompted by W. T. Stead's more famous book with a similar title and by Tom Watson's charges of "Congressional jags," both of which appeared two years earlier. Howard continues his theme of the general corruption found in existing society by showing, in *The American Plutocracy,* the disparities of wealth and ways of life between the rich and the poor, and attributes these to the functioning of the economic system. Howard was born and reared in Floyd County, Georgia, and he moved to Fort Payne, Alabama, in 1891, where he was admitted to the bar the following year. He subsequently became a leading Democrat there, as well as the county solicitor, until he joined the reform movement in the early 1890's. With this southern background, it is interesting to note his concern for, and familiarity with, the conditions of the urban poor in northern cities.

THE GREAT ISSUE—PLUTOCRACY v. DEMOCRACY.

In placing the above title at the head of this chapter I do not mean Democracy as represented by the so-called Democratic party of the present day, but real, genuine Democracy. The Democracy that contends for a government of the people, for the people, and by the people.

I do not mean the Democracy of Grover Cleveland, for it is only plutocracy masquerading in a stolen costume. I mean the Democracy of Thomas Jefferson, Andrew Jackson and Abraham Lincoln.

The issue is now clearly defined and it is to be the greatest, the most stupendous struggle of all the ages. It is the uprising of the people against the money power.

It is quite the fad among certain large daily papers representing the money power to say there is no plutocracy, that it is all a mere hallucination. They scoff at the idea that this question is to enter into the politics of the future; but while they thus scoff and pretend to feel no alarm, there is no question but what they hear the mutterings of the approaching storm. But the more imminent the danger, the more arrogant and insolent the plutocrats and the Wall Street subsidized press become. It was so before the French Revolution. It was so with Charles the First, it was so with England when our Revolutionary fathers were compelled to declare for freedom. It was so with the slave-holding South when it would accept no terms of compromise; and so to-day the money aristocracy, intoxicated by power, reveling in an excess of wealth, surfeited with a redundancy of money, has grown bold and arrogant in its demands, and asks that the toilers of the nation, those who work with brawn and brain, be made slaves to this libidinous plutocracy.

. . . The greatest tools of plutocracy in this country to-day are Grover Cleveland, President of the United States, and his trust champion, Attorney-General Richard Olney.

Time was, in the days of our fathers, when a man holding a high office who willfully refused to discharge the duties which he had taken an oath to faithfully perform, would have been impeached. Upon what degenerate times have we now fallen that the Attorney-General of the United States persistently refuses to enforce the anti-trust law, and is upheld in his nefarious course by the President.

And yet these men call themselves Democrats. Shades of Andrew Jackson, what a misnomer!

But these tools of plutocracy are hastening the ruin which is coming upon the heads of the masters whom they serve. Their open defiance and disregard of the law has aroused a perfect storm of indignation throughout the land, and the people who have long been blinded by the sophistries of the money power, are now beginning to understand what the issue is to be. It is the rule of wealth against the rule of the people. If wealth is to rule, our great nation must perish; if the people once regain the reins of government and rule wisely, we will have the happiest people and most prosperous country of all the ages.

. . . Laborers of America, whether you work with brawn or brain, will you longer close your eyes to the great issue? You owe it to yourselves, to your wives and children and to posterity to face this great issue like men, to throw off party shackles, lay aside partisan prejudice, and get out from under the party lash; and, as did our fathers at Bunker Hill and Yorktown, let us fight for freedom.

It is a battle, yea, a terrible battle. Plutocracy is thoroughly organized and equipped for the conflict. Let the people rally round the Stars and Stripes, shouting the battle-cry of freedom. On the side of the money power will be the hired tools and minions of plutocracy, who sell themselves for gold. On the other side, free men who are willing to sacrifice much to still maintain equal rights for all and special privileges for none.

Men of America, let us win the battle while we can do so by constitutional methods. Now it need be only a battle of ballots. But if we prove recreant to our duty and betray the trust which our fathers have reposed in us, then constitutional methods will not avail, and this continent will be shaken by a mighty revolution.

The signs of the times are so plain that they may be read by all. A wayfaring man, though a fool, cannot mistake them. Let us be wise to-day.

[In this book, Howard concluded each chapter with an endnote, sometimes humorous in tone, designed to illustrate the concentration of wealth. The one below follows the preceding passages.]

To accumulate one million dollars, a man would have to earn and save $100 a day (Sundays excepted) for thirty years.

To earn the fortune of John D. Rockefeller would therefore require the saving of $100 a day for 3,750 years.

Suppose the working man could save ten cents a day, then to accumulate $1,000,000 would require 30,000 years.

To accumulate Rockefeller's fortune, at a saving of ten cents a day, would therefore require 3,750,000 years. It would require 10,000 men, each saving ten cents per day, 375 years to accumulate his fortune, and saving a dollar per day it would take 10,000 men 37½ years.

What working man can save even ten cents per day above the support of his family? Yet these are the men who have earned Rockefeller's fortune for him as well as the fortunes of all the other members of the American plutocracy.

THE TRAIL OF THE SERPENT.

. . . Plutocracy should be called the great national crime. It is certainly a sad reflection on our patriotism that we have allowed it to so intrench itself in power, that the people are wellnigh helpless.

. . . While the curse rests most heavily upon the masses of the people, it does not fail to visit all classes. The stubborn fight of the poor for bread finds its counterpart in the frantic efforts of the rich to acquire more money. There is misery in the hovel and a feverish unrest in the palace. There is hunger gnawing at the crust of bread in the alley and the fierce craving of the heart in the mansion. We meet the beggar in the street and look into the sunken, downcast, furtive eye; we go into the busy marts of the world's commerce, and the burning, restless, eager eye of the speculator pierces with eagle-like scrutiny. Truly can it be said that the trail of the serpent is over them all.

The spirit of avarice is devouring the great heart of this nation. The greed for gain gets such possession of men's souls that they become demons. They rush into the maelstrom of money-getting, and soon lose all fear of God and love for their fellow-men, and before they realize it, they have become slaves to a passion which is as cruel as fate and as remorseless and unrelenting as death.

[Contending that materialism corrodes all aspects of American society, he turns to a discussion of the stock exchange.]

. . . In every large city we have these gambling hells. In this business, which plutocracy has made a most honorable one, thousands of men are engaged. They never earned an honest dollar in their lives, yet many of them are worth millions. How have they made it? In gambling on the prices of corn and wheat which they never grew, but which has been produced and sold by the honest old farmer at a price so small that he is hardly able to pay his taxes and the annual interest on his mortgaged farm. They have made it speculating on the cotton which they never saw and never will see, while the poor farmer in the South, who sells it for four or five cents per pound, is unable to send his little children to school even for three months in a year, and must see them go barefoot in winter, and look with pity on their tatters and rags.

Every dollar gained by one of these gamblers is taken from some honest toiler. Every million they accumulate means a multitude of wretched homes and desolate firesides. While money rules the country, there is no help for it. There can be no hope for the people. But the curse of plutocracy, as already said, is not confined to any class. It is a vulture which will eventually destroy those upon whom it preys, and then it will turn and rend those whom it enriched.

[After pointing out instances of extreme poverty, Howard next comments on trusts.]

. . . Trusts are the outgrowth of plutocratic rule. Almost everything we eat or wear is controlled by some trust. The Standard Oil trust is, perhaps, the most powerful and absolute trust in the country. It not only controls the oil traffic in the United States, but is now reaching out its grasping fingers to control the whole world, and there is but little doubt but what it will succeed.

Then come the sugar trust, the beef trust, the whiskey trust and trusts galore, until we are dumbfounded with the list. Write the history of the Standard Oil trust and the whiskey trust, and you will have pages blackened by the blasts of Hell and stained with human blood. From every page would stare the eyes of hunger, the gaunt, pinched faces of suffering humanity. Between every line you would see the bright nails upon the coffin lid. Outlined on every page there would stand a hideous gallows. And at the turn of every leaf you would hear the creaking of prison doors and the rattle of felons' chains. These trusts have been guilty of bribery, lying, perjury, high-handed robbery, midnight assassinations and cold-blooded murders. They have crushed competition, bankrupted thousands of honest men, oppressed the poor, robbed and plundered the helpless, until to-day they are absolute and supreme masters of the situation, able to regulate production, control prices, grind the faces of the poor, build up enormous fortunes for the trust fiends, elect Governors and Presidents, own the Attorney-General of the United States, purchase Legislatures and Congresses, and hold high carnival while the dance of death goes merrily on, and people starve, and rot, and die all over the land.

The trust first crushes all competitors by selling the "trusted" product for less than the cost of production, and when the small dealers or producers can no longer hold out, they are paid a small sum of money and go out of business, and then the great trust, which has swallowed up all competitors, raises prices, according to the promptings of its cupidity.

Another form of the trust is the combining of all the small trusts or corporations under one head and "pooling" the commodity to be handled.

The profits accruing to the trusts are enormous. The Standard Oil trust had an investment originally of not more than

six million dollars. It issued ninety million dollars in trust certificates. These are worth to-day about three hundred million
dollars, and are nearly all owned by a few men. This trust has
paid millions of dollars already to its organizers.

The sugar trust has a capital of seventy-five million dollars,
the actual value being about seven million seven hundred and
forty thousand dollars. In 1893 it paid in dividends ten million
eight hundred and seventy-five thousand dollars, put aside a
surplus of five million dollars, in addition to the enormous
sums paid as salaries and the vast amounts spent in bribing
legislators, corrupting officials and contributing to campaign
funds.

In addition to the trusts already enumerated, there are a
beer trust, a leather trust, a salt trust, a match trust, a coal
trust, a bread trust, a railroad trust and hundreds of others;
and last, but not least, an undertakers' National Burial Case
Association trust.

We must serve the trusts while we live, and when we die
our relatives or friends, if they are able, and if not, then some
charitable organization, must pay some trust two prices to
bury us.

These trusts are often formed by very pious and very religious men. The class of men whom Robert Burns calls the
"unco guid." The richest man in this country is John D. Rockefeller, who is worth one hundred and twenty-five million dollars. He made it out of the oil trust. He is a member of the
Church, and has given large sums of money to religious, educational and benevolent societies. I suppose he has some great,
charitable scheme working in his benevolent heart at the present time, and that he needs some more money to carry it out,
for the price of oil has been advanced, and the poor are now
paying more than twice as much for it as they did a short
time ago.

. . . When the pious Mr. Rockefeller makes his offerings to
the Lord, does he ever think of the drops of blood from broken
hearts, the groans from squalid misery, the tears from human

agony, which have been coined into each shining dollar? Does he realize that he is offering the Lord blood money? But the trust of which he is the leading spirit has so long been accustomed to bribe officials and legislators that Mr. Rockefeller actually has the impudence and assurance to try to bribe the Lord.

Jesus Christ did not say to the rich young man, "Go, rob the poor of all they have, and bring the thousandth part to me as a bribe, a sort of sin offering, and then follow me." But he said: "Go, sell all thou hast and give it to the poor, and then follow me."

When the Judgment Day comes, and the men whom Mr. Rockefeller has driven to suicide, the wretched creatures he has hounded into insane asylums, the women who have been forced into poverty the most abject, the children whom he has stripped of clothing, deprived of food and turned barefooted into the street to leave foot-prints on the cutting ice and snow, all rise up as a cloud of witnesses against him, and in answer to all the terrible accusations he says, "Lord, Lord, did I not give large sums of this money unto thee?" what think you the God of Justice will answer? Will it be, "Well done, good and faithful servant," or "Depart from Me; I never knew you." I have not the space in this work to treat fully of trusts, and can only touch upon the subject.

. . . Let us overthrow plutocracy, and we will destroy the trusts. There can be no halfway measures. No compromise between monopoly and the American people. Liberty and trusts cannot long exist together. One or the other will soon be destroyed. Let us rise up and crush them before they bind us hand and foot and make of our children abject slaves.

THE HERITAGE OF DEATH.

. . . The author is aware that he will be called a "calamity howler" for attempting to describe the want, woe and misery which is so widespread in our country. He is conscious of the

fact that every newspaper which is in sympathy with plutocracy will attempt to discount the pictures of desolation and
impending peril by sneers and sarcasm. But the burdens the
people are now compelled to bear are so great that he would
be untrue to himself and to those who bear them if he did not
"cry aloud and spare not."

Plutocracy has cursed the land with a thousand ills, but if
we can believe the signs of the times it has not done its worst.
It yet has in store for the American people many more woes.
Already it has given us a great army of unemployed. There are
in the United States almost four million men who cannot find
work enough to do to obtain their daily bread. This means
four million tramps, for when a man is out of employment and
starts to seek work, he is at once classed by the plutocratic
press as a tramp.

While these four million men are idle, there are almost four
million homes desolate—homes where mothers sit by hearth-
stones which do not have the ruddy glow of burning coals,
around which hover and shiver little children, hungry,
wretched, ragged. There is no hope in the faces of the mothers;
there is no light, no childish happiness in the eyes of the
children. There are no papers or periodicals on the table, no
books in the libraries; there is no carpet on the floor, no music
in the home, no joy in the heavy hearts of the inmates; there
are no new shoes for winter, no nice clothes for Sundays and
holidays; there is nothing to live for in the present, and nothing to hope for in the future. Each day the wolf comes nearer
to the door; each hour the poor wretches are nearer to suicide,
shame and death. Piece by piece the scant furniture is sold,
and soon there is nothing left but a pallet of straw. The days
drag slowly by into weeks, and the weeks lengthen into
months, and one by one the wretched victims of plutocratic
rule fall by the wayside and find an unmarked grave in the
potter's field.

The almshouses are filled to overflowing, the jails and penitentiaries have a plethora of prisoners, the madhouses are packed, the streets are full of homeless wanderers, the morgue has each year a larger number of suicides. The sweat shops resound to the groans of helpless children and frail women; the brothels are daily replenished from the ranks of our fair American girls. Thousands are driven to a life of shame each year. It cannot be questioned that all these things are the outgrowth of plutocracy.

A few greedy, grasping plutocrats and the wealthy trusts and corporations have gotten possession of all the wealth, so there is nothing left for those who labored early and late to produce it. The daily papers are full of accounts of suffering, poverty, wretchedness, starvation and death, and even then the one-hundredth case is not reported.

Here is the account of a young married man who was driven to robbery by starvation. It takes but a few lines to tell the story, yet it speaks volumes of human suffering:

"New York, Jan. 29.—Driven apparently by lack of food and inability to support his wife and child, James Flower, 28 years old, an engineer, committed highway robbery last night. When captured he killed himself by swallowing some prussic acid which he carried on his person."

Here is the story of another unfortunate, and the number is rapidly increasing:

"James Mohar died of starvation yesterday noon at the Brooklyn City Hospital. A native American, he had walked the streets of New York without food for eight days looking for work, and late Saturday afternoon fell exhausted and unconscious at the Brooklyn tower of the great bridge. At the hospital all that science and unremitting attention could do was done. A special nurse gave her undivided attention to him. A nutriment was administered at frequent intervals, but the patient relapsed into insensibility. Said Dr. Molin, the house surgeon, as Mohar drew his last breath: 'It is a clear case of starvation, nothing else. There are indications of

Bright's disease, due directly to exposure and lack of nourishment; but otherwise he has no ailments save exhaustion. In most cases it is impossible to save a patient when he is as far gone as this one, although we pull them through sometimes. After being entirely without food for eight days, the organs are unable to assimilate even milk and whiskey, which we generally use.' "

From the New York "World" of April 18 I clipped the following account of the suffering caused by the high-handed operations of the oil trust in advancing the price of oil to more than twice what it was worth:

"Isaac Beck and his daughters, Sarah and Sophie, work as clothing finishers. They begin at 5 o'clock in the morning and work until long after midnight.

" 'And all we manage to earn within that time,' said Sarah, the elder daughter, 'is not quite a dollar. My poor mother went crazy over the work.

" 'I mustn't cry,' she said. 'The tears will interfere with my work. We must be quick and deft now as long as the daylight lasts, because the 15 cents that we pay for oil eats up a good deal of our profits.'

"Aaron Kleber occupies a room adjoining that of the Becks. His wife is stone-blind and sickly. They have a fifteen-year-old daughter, Sadie, and a baby boy, Benjamin. Sadie's whole time is devoted to the baby. Food and shelter and clothes are got by the hard toil of the father.

" 'All I can earn is 25 cents a day," he said. 'Light at night is a luxury beyond my reach. If it were not for the kindness of Mr. Beck, who allows me to sew by his light, I couldn't make more than 10 cents a day.'

"While Kleber was talking his daughter and wife came in. The wife was holding her baby clasped to her bosom.

" 'Papa,' said Sadie, 'please get us some bread. It is getting late, and we haven't had a morsel all day. Mamma is faint, and Benjamin——'

"Well, it wasn't necessary to utter any words. It was evident that Benjamin was starving. His face was no larger than a fist, the ghastly white cheeks sunken as if they would meet, and the black-encircled eyes were set deep in the sockets.

"Kleber looked appealingly at his neighbors. A groan broke from his lips.

"'We, too,' said Beck, 'have eaten nothing to-day.'"

Only the other day a boy was found under a cart, gnawing the putrid flesh off of a bone with all the avidity of a hungry dog. He was ragged, dirty, unkempt—a miserable specimen of humanity. Indeed, he looked more the wild beast than he did one of God's children. When asked where he lived and who he was, he replied that he was nobody and lived nowhere.

[After still more contrasts between the rich and the poor, Howard turns to an indictment of the political system for taking people's minds off the real issues. In what follows it should be recalled that Howard is a southerner, and that his remarks have relevance for a discussion of the relation between the Negro and Populism.]

BLIND FOLLOWERS.

. . . In 1864 President Lincoln made the following prediction:

"The money power will endeavor to prolong its reign by working upon the prejudices of the people until all wealth is aggregated in a few hands."

Could he live to-day he would see the fulfillment of his prophecy. Nearly all the wealth has been aggregated in a few hands, and the money power is now industriously engaged in working upon the prejudices of the people and using every artifice to delude and deceive them.

So far it has been quite successful, and how much longer these tactics will be availing remains to be seen.

The cunning of plutocracy equals the ingenuity of the devil. For thirty years it has kept aflame the sectional bitterness engendered by the War.

In the North there has been a vigorous and persistent waving of the bloody shirt, while in the South it has been the race problem, "nigger supremacy," as we call it down there.

In the North the shibboleth has been, "vote as you shot." In the South it has been, "down with the carpet-bagger and Yankee."

All these years the people of the two sections have been ready to fly at each other's throats politically, while the money power has urged them on.

There is one discovery which I have recently made, that is perhaps worth mentioning. All the plutocrats have a perfect understanding among themselves. They have no sectional bitterness, no political prejudice. Politics with them is a matter of business. They support political parties for the return they expect to get in dollars and cents. They care not whether the Democratic or Republican party wins, so long as both parties favor the money power.

No one in this country really cares anything about politics, except the politicians who are seeking the boodle, which is supplied by plutocracy, and the people, the toilers, the wealth-producers of the nation, who are all the time voting just as the money power wants them to.

At every election they vote for men who will rivet more closely upon them the fetters of slavery.

The plutocrats, the class for whom all laws are enacted, care not a whit for politics.

Every four years there is a great commotion throughout the country, and the Democrats nominate a candidate for President, and the Republicans nominate a candidate, and then both parties go to plutocracy and say, "We must have campaign funds with which to make this fight." They get the money, and then the loud-mouthed campaign orators go out to harangue the people, and each abuses the other's party, and says the leaders are the meanest men on earth, and that the members of the party are all too corrupt to occupy even a humble place in one corner of His Satanic Majesty's Kingdom, and they proceed to wave the bloody shirt on the one side in the wildest alarm, while the followers on the other side shout at the top of their voices, "Nigger, nigger!" and when the people are all worked up, almost to a frenzy, the wily old plutocrats get together and determine which candidate must be elected, and at once go to manipulating and wire-pulling, so that they can accomplish their purpose.

They arrange with the leaders for certain financial legislation in the interest of capital, and then dine at Delmonico's, and over their costly wine and cigars they chuckle about what fools they are making of the people.

All this time the poor, deluded voters are howling themselves hoarse, carrying torch-lights, beating tin-pans, blowing horns and making fools of themselves in general, thinking that they are patriotic and are doing great things for their country. They are blind followers.

The leaders make all the noise and flurry they can, and the voters fall into the procession. They allow themselves to be misled by false issues and blinded by foolish prejudices.

Year after year they have gone on voting the old party tickets, never thinking, never caring, saying, "The nominee of my party is good enough for me." Until now they look around in a dazed sort of way and ask stupidly, "Where are we at?"

It is clear to any thinking mind that both of the old parties are the friends of plutocracy. The leaders—a great many of them—are under plutocratic influence. Both of the old parties go to the money power for campaign funds, and put themselves under obligations to plutocracy at the very outset.

But a great tidal wave of reform is sweeping over the land, and the people are not quite such blind followers as they have been. They are beginning to think for themselves, and understand that the great beating of drums, sounding of tom-toms, blast of trumpets and blazing of torches are a ruse to lead them away from the real issue and make them become the celebrants of plutocracy's triumph over labor's downfall, and the laboring man has been the chief rejoicer at his own funeral, not realizing what it all meant.

. . . If the workingmen band together, they are called anarchists; if they strike for living wages, it is called mob violence.

When has the military been sent out to compel greedy, grasping plutocracy to do its duty by labor. Never. How often have soldiers been sent to shoot down and maltreat strikers and compel them to submit to the demands of capital. Always when plutocracy asked for it.

So far have we departed from the principles above declared by Lincoln that a daily paper, published in a great city largely populated by workingmen, recently gave utterance to the following remarkable sentiment:

"When the communistic cry of bread or blood comes up from the laborer, we should administer a decoction of strychnine in quantities amply sufficient to meet the emergency in every case that neither bread nor blood will disturb them hereafter."

And the pity of it is that such sentiments as these can be expressed here in this land of the free and home of the brave, without causing one word of comment among the workingmen. But the time is coming when such red-mouthed minions of plutocracy as the man who wrote these anarchistic utterances, as well as the arrogant monsters whom they serve, will cringe and bow before the workingmen of America.

Labor is prior to and above capital. It possesses a dignity which capital does not.

Let us no longer crawl upon our bellies and lick the dust at the feet of capital, but let us rise up like men and make capital our servant.

Labor created capital, therefore labor is the rightful master, and capital should be the obedient servant.

Workingmen of America, be no longer blind followers, but be the flower and chivalry of the land.

[Howard then turns to a criticism of charity.]

NOT CHARITY, BUT JUSTICE.

. . . In every great city there are charity organizations, and good men and pious women devote much of their time to the collection and distribution of money among the poor and helpless. The Churches give away large sums in charitable work. Individuals contribute a great deal of money to the starving poor.

It would be impossible to even approximate the amounts thus spent each year. It takes a small army of employees to carry on the work of charity.

Thousands of families are now subsisting partially or wholly on charity. The number is not decreasing, but is ever on the increase.

As our country grows and develops, as we build more magnificent homes and costlier churches, as railroads and telegraph lines keep reaching out and exploring new fields, as our commerce grows, it seems that we would have fewer objects of charity, until by and by there would be little use for charity at all. Such, however, is not the case, for within the shadows of the costly homes, the splendid churches, the abjectly poor are multiplying at a frightful rate. Thousands of people have starved in America within the past twelve months; tens of thousands are now suffering for want of bread; millions have not the ordinary comforts of life.

Yet there is no famine in the land. We have no pestilence, which has prevented the farmers from producing their usual crops.

We have had no universal drought, which has burned up all the cotton, the corn, and other cereal products.

We have had no murrain which has killed all the cattle.

We have had no cholera to destroy the hogs.

We have had no pestilential disease to take away all the sheep, yet the people are starving, and must be fed out of charity's spoon.

The granaries are bursting with wheat; the bins are filled with corn; the stock-yards are overflowing with cattle, hogs and sheep; the fields of the South have been white with cotton—an abundance everywhere throughout the entire country. Of it we can say, as was said of the Promised Land of Canaan, "It flows with milk and honey." Notwithstanding all this, the people are starving.

Soup houses have been established for the poor. Cheap lodging houses have been provided. Parks have been opened up, filled with trees, birds and flowers, where the poor can go and carry their scrawny, sickly little children. Free bathhouses have been provided for the poor, and now free places of amusement are being talked of.

Millions are annually spent to provide food to keep them from starving, and yet they are famishing, falling by the wayside, and dying all around us.

It seems that charity has not been a success. Would it not be wise to study the causes of its failures and seek a remedy?

I do not believe that we need or want all this so-called charity. Indeed, I do not think it is charity at all. It is simply the price which plutocracy annually pays to maintain itself in power. It is the very small pittance it doles out to the people it has robbed.

If the money had not been taken away from the people they would not be reduced to such a pitiable state, and it would not be necessary for the rich to contribute to their support. There is plenty and to spare in this great country of all that goes to make up human happiness; then why should it be necessary for such a large portion of the human family to subsist on the crumbs which fall from Dives' table?

It is not charity we want, it is not charity we need. What we want, what we need, what we ought to demand and what we must have is JUSTICE. Yea, the justice which guarantees to every man the fruits of his honest toil, justice which protects the weak against the strong, and prevents the powerful robber from appropriating that which the laboring man has accumulated through years of toil.

Justice, which will give to every man employment and reasonable compensation for what he does, and after his day's work is done and he lies down to sleep, a justice that will guard the day's earnings, however scant they may be, and prevent the thief, who will not work, from coming at the hour of midnight and robbing him.

Under the reign of plutocracy a few robbers steal the earnings of the people, take all they have, and leave them penniless, and when they are starving they give back a few pence in charity to buy crusts of bread to keep life in their poor, miserable bodies.

Such charity as this is the charity of the devil, which would keep his victims alive, so they could endure torture for a while longer.

. . . Take away your charity and give us justice.

Justice! Justice! The cry goes up from thousands of crushed, broken hearts.

[Howard concludes by drawing the distinction between plutocracy as men and as products of the legislative system.]

. . . Those who belong to the plutocratic class are not so much to be censured as our unjust, unwholesome and pernicious laws, which make plutocracy possible.

32. On Agrarian Discontent

As a young man in Hardy, Arkansas, W. Scott Morgan was a farmer, a journalist, and an active member of the Agricultural Wheel. In 1889, he published the book, *History of the Wheel and Alliance, and The Impending Revolution,* from which the following selection is taken. This massive (774 pages), verbose work seeks, as its title indicates, to present a history of the organizations that merged to form the National Farmers' Alliance and Industrial Union, and to document the conditions against which southern farmers protested.

[Morgan begins with a statement in support of a labor theory of value: the producer is the most important factor in the productive system, and should derive the benefit from the wealth he creates. He then turns to the abuses of the railroads, and the business system in general.]

The natural law of labor is, that the laborer is entitled to all the fruits of his toil. There is no variation to this rule. It is fixed upon the universal law of nature, and any infringement upon it is not only repugnant to the laborer but is dangerous to the welfare of the State. There is, however, a difficulty arising in the application of the rule where labor becomes mixed with other forms of capital, such as material, machinery, etc. To properly and equitably eliminate it and fix a just reward for the laborer, is a problem that should commend itself to all who would reach the bottom of the "labor question."

The true principle, and one that would forever settle strikes, riots and all differences between labor and capital, is, that the

Reprinted from W. Scott Morgan, *History of the Wheel and Alliance, and The Impending Revolution* (Fort Scott, Kansas: J. H. Rice and Sons, 1889), pp. 21-32, 41-42, 52-54, 56-61, 122-125, 208, 210-211, 215-218, 222-223, 560, 598-608, 687, 714-715, 717-718, 756-757, 774.

laborer should be rewarded according to that that he does, and not according to what the employer can get the labor performed for. We are aware of the fact that when we make this remark we are treading on debatable ground, but if it is necessary, in order to sustain our position, we can fall back upon that universal natural law, "The laborer is entitled to all the fruits of his toil." A universal violation of this rule would culminate in the adoption of the barbaric one that "might makes right," and the weak would be compelled to succumb to the strong. For certain reasons which we have neither time nor space to discuss here, men are better than the laws they live under. If we are asked why, we simply reply it has always been, and for certain physiological and moral reasons, will ever be so. Were it not a fact, the selfishness of those who have unjustly, though legally, acquired capital in our own country, coming in contact with the interests of, and robbing labor of its profits, would have ere this produced a revolution. But a spirit of forbearance born of the fathers of the Revolution, and an instinctive dread of the horrors of war have often averted such a catastrophe. But he who closes his eyes to the fact that the world is approaching a crisis without a parallel, in some respects, in all its past history, must be either influenced by a spirit of selfishness which has characterized tyrants of all ages, or densely ignorant of the ominous import of such widespread dissatisfaction among the producing classes throughout the world. The fires of discontent are burning on both continents. Where the freedom of speech is denied the foundation of governments are honey-combed with secret societies. Where freedom of speech is permitted labor organizations under various names, but all having the same object—self-protection—in view, are springing into existence. The rapidity of growth and the number of these organizations is absolutely without a parallel. To assume that there is no just cause for all this uprising on the part of labor would be equivalent to courting national suicide. Some will contend that competition will correct all inequalities arising in the various conditions of labor. Adam Smith says, "it is the great regulator of industrial action. It is beneficent, just and equalizing. In the market of the world it is what gravitation is in the mechanism of the heavens, an all-combining and balancing and beneficent law. Any invasion of this principle is contrary to the law of nature and of sound political economy." This might perhaps be true if we had, or it were possible to have, like competition in all things; and while it will apply to the markets of the world in the sale of the products of labor there are various conditions in the sphere of expenditure of wages which it cannot affect; and as to the things which might be affected by it, it is injurious or has a trick of failing at the moment something is expected of it. Taxes, to which every man owning property is liable, is not affected by competition; and, when we speak of taxes we mean both direct and indirect. Rents are practically unaffected by it, as also a number of other things to which the laborer is subject and over which competition exerts no influence. Competition in wages, when based upon necessity, is decidedly injurious and signifies an unhealthy condition of the industrial interests of the country. Competition in commerce, trade and transportation fails "at the moment something is expected of it," because it leads to combination. In proof of this theory we have only to point to the numerous trusts that have sprung up in our country within the past ten years, and to the consolidation of numerous railroad companies. In the latter part of Dr. Smith's proposition, however, we most heartily concur; "Any invasion of this principle (competition) is contrary to the law of nature and of sound political economy." And right here we might as well add, that the violation of this principle is one among the many causes which are responsible for the present condition of American labor. Competition is killed by combination, and the laws of trade are perverted to the end that the few are enabled to enrich themselves at the expense of the many. Having briefly considered some of the elementary principles relating to labor we are enabled to make the following general deductions.

First.—Man is naturally disposed to take pleasure in remunerative employment.

Second.—He is justly entitled to the fruits of his own labor.

Third.—Any violation of this natural law will breed social disorder, and an universal violation will bring national calamity. Add to this that labor creates all wealth and provides not only the necessities of life, but all the comforts and luxuries; that wealth is only past labor—power over nature—crystalized into tokens of value, called money, and controlled in many cases by those who have performed but little labor themselves. The wealth of the Vanderbilts, Rothchilds and Goulds is but the accumulated labor of millions who have received but a part of a just reward for their services. The individual laborer is not the master of his own actions. He must work or suffer and is therefore compelled to submit to the exactions of his employer who is also his master. He is but an integral part of the society or community which "fixes the condition of his life." Society is the State or government in which he lives. He must therefore appeal to the State for that relief which he has tried in vain to reach through the instrumentality of strikes. An associated effort on the part of the community—or State—of which the laborer is a part may go far towards correcting the evils to which he is subject. A community may be a force tending to a better or worse order of life, as it may happen; or its power may be wielded for evil by the more perfect association of a large and influential portion of its members. It is no longer a matter of doubt but that the American laborer has just grounds of complaint against the assisted importation of cheap labor from foreign countries. In its encouragement, and our "haste to become rich and mighty," we find ourselves confronted with a question that threatens the very foundations of our social and political structures. The community is a sick man suffering from the anti-social disorders of ignorance,

selfishness and unlimited competition. The hypocritical philanthropists have thought it a good practice to give the patient
fresh doses of ignorance and barbarism. They seem to be
charmed with the near dollar to be made out of cheap labor,
but utterly ignore the inevitable degradation of the community, and its peril to the estate of those who are fortunate
enough to accumulate anything, and to the future of the
Republic.

LABOR'S WRONGS.

It is not proposed in this chapter to enter into a detailed discussion of the many ills to which the laborer, and more especially the farmer, has been subjected for many years. The
more important among these have received due attention in
the second part of this volume. To deny that these evils exist—
and to an alarming extent—is to commit a folly that is nothing
less than criminal; and to universally ignore, is a national
crime. Whatever may be said of trade and commerce and the
professions, it has long been evident to earnest thinkers that
the farmers were the most cruelly oppressed class of our community. It is certainly a very unfortunate and unnatural condition of society that dooms the principal and the most useful
portion of the producing class to the greatest amount of oppression; but such is the evil that is upon us. For many years
the country has been suffering from evils of which all have
been conscious, but which it would seem none have had the
courage or wisdom to correct. Prominent among these are the
burdens that have been fastened upon the people by the
reckless and unscrupulous course of the great railroad monopolies that have sprung up in our midst. These vast and powerful corporations have established a series of abuses which
have gradually and almost effectually undermined the solid
basis upon which our internal commerce was supposed to rest.
They have debauched and demoralized our Courts and Legis-

latures; have bribed and taken into their pay the high public officials charged with the making and execution of our laws; have robbed the nation of a domain sufficient to constitute an empire; have flooded the land with worthless stocks and other so-called securities; have established a system of gambling at our financial centres that has resulted in a financial crisis which covered the whole land with ruin and suffering; have set at defiance the laws of the land and have trampled upon individual and public rights and liberties, openly boasting that they are too powerful to be made amenable to the law; and not content with all this, not satisfied with the ruin they have wrought, they continue to petition the law making power to give them still greater means of robbing and oppressing the people. It is useless to deny the facts. The issue has got to be met. We have had bountiful seasons and our crops have been abundant. Indeed the abundance of the crops has been one of the alleged causes of the present hard times. The farmers have been economical and industrious. They have had the use of improved machinery. Yet in the face of all this, the cold stern fact confronts us that the condition of the American farmer is growing gloomier with each succeeding year. In fact, as has been remarked by the Governor of one of our Western States, and as a matter capable of proof, the railroads have to a considerable extent ceased to figure on rates at which they can afford to carry freight, but have made a calculation of what a thing can be produced at and a bare subsistence obtained by the producers, and they take the difference between this figure and the market price of the article at the point of delivery, for freight charges. Nor is the great railway corporations the only means of oppression with which the farmer has to contend. From the time that his produce leaves him until it reaches the consumer, whether domestic or foreign, it does not move nor go through a single transition that some relentless, grasping and powerful corporation does not lay a tribute thereon. And this is true, not only for what he sells, but on everything he buys these same exacting corporate monopolies, trusts and combinations which are protected by legal enactment, and their property guarded by armed detectives, have levied their contributions. A few men combine and make the price of beef and pork; of steel and iron; of sugar and salt, nails, earthenware, cotton bagging, binder twine, and of almost every other article of necessity to the farmer. A combination will "bear" the price of wheat down to-day and the "bulls" will toss it up to-morrow. The dealer or producer ships for the high price and his grain reaches the market after the "bulls" have unloaded and the bottom has gone out of prices. Another serious drawback and heavy tax upon the farmer is the exorbitant prices he is compelled to pay for supplies while raising his crop, and this is more especially true if he buys on a credit, as most farmers do, especially in the Southern States. We do not mean to say that the town or country merchant is making too much money; it is the system that is at fault more than the men.

. . . It is hardly worth while to dwell upon the evils of giving a mortgage on a crop yet to be raised, or upon the farm animals and implements with which it is made, a practice that is very common among Southern farmers. The idea is so repugnant to common sense, and the practice fraught with such far-reaching evils, that the only wonder is that such a law is permitted to remain upon the statute book among a civilized people. We do not wish to convey the idea that we are making a wholesale onslaught on the means of transportation and the persons engaged therein, and in the trades of various kinds.

As public benefactors the railroads take their place first among the great discoveries of the nineteenth century; but they should not be used as a means of oppression. Against Jay Gould, Russell Sage and other great railroad men, who, by the force of their genius have acquired control of thousands of miles of railroad and accumulated millions of dollars of wealth, we have no personal fight to make. They were perhaps only actuated by the instinctive desire possessed by most men —to become rich and powerful. They are perhaps no worse than other men would be occupying the same position. But they are the representatives of the worst system of despotism in existence, and they are shrewd enough to regard the interest of their roads as paramount to that of the public. The constitution gives to Congress the power to regulate commerce between the States, but for years the presidents of the trunk lines between the East and West have been exercising that power, and fixing the price that the farmer shall have for the products of his farm. It is certainly inconsistent with free institutions to lodge such power in the hands of a few men who have every incentive to abuse it, and it remains for the people to say how long such a state of affairs shall continue. This power is used against the interests of the people. This despotism in common with that of other monopolies threatens them in every relation of their national life.

. . . The burden of excessive rates is perhaps more keenly felt by the Western and Southern farmers than their brethren in the East. This becomes more apparent when we take into consideration the fact that the entire corn crop of the United States for the year 1887 was 1,456,000,000 bushels; and of wheat 456,000,000 bushels. Of this the States of Arkansas, Illinois, Iowa, Indiana, Kansas, Kentucky, Michigan, Mississippi, Missouri, Nebraska, Ohio, Tennessee, Texas, Minnesota, Wisconsin and Dakota raised 1,145,000,000 bushels of corn, and 339,000,000 bushels of wheat; or more than three-fourths of the entire product of the United States. All the surplus of this vast area must pass over the railroads to find a market. The cost of transportation to the East consumes one-half, and in some instances three-fourths of the value of the grain products of the farm, and the farmer's profits are made small in order that heavy freights might be paid and large profits gained by the companies. But an unjust tariff rate is not the only evil which the railroad companies impose upon the farmer. They frequently by iniquitous combination dictate the dealer to whom he shall sell the products of his farm.

Said an Iowa farmer recently: "The railroads of this State discriminate unjustly against the farmers in the transportation of crops; that is, give other men advantages which they deny to farmers. Let me explain: here is a wheat or corn buyer who makes a living by purchasing grain of the farmers and shipping it to Chicago. Of course he makes a profit on it—grows rich in fact. Now the farmers think that if they ship their own grain directly to Chicago they might save the profit that this middle-man makes. They engage a lot of cars, load them, and send them forward, but they find when they have paid the freight and the other expenses which the middle-man must necessarily also incur, they don't have as much left for their grain as he offered them. Now, how is that explained? The railroad company gives the grain trader a drawback on the grain he ships, which it refuses to the farmers; and in some instances, at least, these traders are in partnership with railway officials. I thought when the idea of co-operative shipments was first proposed, that these favors were given solely on account of the amount of business that these men brought to the railroads. I supposed that the deductions were simply those that would be naturally made to wholesale trade, and in speeches to farmers I told them so. But we have learned differently, for when our farmers have combined and offered freight in large quantities to the railroad companies, they have refused to give us the advantages which they give the favorites. The terms of these contracts are secret. But we know that they must be considerable, or these men who have them could not make so much money. You see what this kind of railroad management amounts to. The company comes in and says: 'You shall sell your grain to a certain man and for a certain price, which we will fix.' That's one thing we complain of, and we will not long submit to it. But I have not told you all. In certain cases the roads have fixed the rates of freight very high, and then men have appeared among farmers, offering to buy our produce at prices just a shade higher than it would net us to ship it ourselves, but at rates much below what it ought to bring us. We have often supposed that these men were the agents of the railroad companies or of the railroad managers. If our suspicions were correct, you see what an outrage on the farmers it was.

"The railroad people knowing our necessities, and that many of us are obliged to sell, even at a loss, for the purpose of obtaining money, first arbitrarily fix the price of our produce and then force us to sell to them."

[After continuing on the plight of the farmer, Morgan turns to the conditions in the sweatshops.]

. . . Nor, are the farmers the only sufferers among the great army of laborers. The greed of capital dominates every class of laborers, and women and children are the victims of this relentless car of juggernaut. The *New York Sun,* referring to the deplorable condition of the working women of that city, says: "Ann Fullmon lives at 618 East Ninth street, New York City. She finishes pantaloons for a living; sews on buttons, makes buttonholes, puts on straps, buckles and presses them for 13 cents a pair; averages $2 a week for self and family.

"Kate Crowley makes men's drawers at 10 cents for a dozen pairs. She can finish two dozen pairs in a day by working from 6 a. m. to 9 p. m., and gets 20 cents for her day's labor."

The recent developments of the condition of the working girls of Chicago made by a brave young lady correspondent of the *Times* of that city is thus briefly told by the *Industrial West.* "Nothing has been said or printed this year which has caused a more profound sensation, and aroused the indignation of the people more than the series of articles published in the *Chicago Daily Times,* entitled "City Slave Girls." The *Times'* lady reporter, Miss Nell Nelson, took upon herself the embarrassing duties of dressing herself in the attire of a factory girl, and visited, each day, one or more factories where women are employed, where she secured employment and worked a few hours or managed to stay long enough to learn the condition of the employees, and the *Times* contained the story of misery as seen by Miss Nelson.

"On July 10, she visited the Western Lane factory, 218 State street. There she found the most wretched conditions of poverty and serfdom. As she entered the office she was followed by a young lady who had been crocheting mats, and as she had come to draw her pay and quit the company's service, it gave the reporter an opportunity to make a note of her earnings, and when the clerk opened the books, it was found the poor girl had worked from the first of last January to July 10, for the princely sum of fifteen dollars, and instead of paying her she was put off in a dark room to wait until the proprietor came in. Miss Nelson then applied for work and learned that for making mats of the size and style made by the poor girl, the company had paid 60 cents per dozen; that a dozen was an ordinary week's work, and that all the other grades of work given out by that company were correspondingly the same price. That company lets its work out by the piece and the employees carry it to their homes. The *Times* reporter found that to get work one must pay two dollars for the privilege, and deposit one dollar to secure the return of the material."

. . . But it is useless to continue to multiply evidence of the sad and deplorable condition of the American laborer. It might be continued indefinitely, but it seems so apparent and "plain that a wayfaring man, though a fool, cannot err therein." In vain has the farmer pleaded; in vain has he sought that relief which his common sense convinces him he is justly entitled to. He has been put off, on one pretense and another until "forbearance has ceased to be a virtue;" and having learned, to his sorrow, that in combination there is strength, he is seeking through a counter combination of his fellow laborers to consummate that which he knows can never be accomplished in any other manner. Their appeals to the Legislatures and to the Courts have been met with the corrupt use of the money of corporations. The farmers are calling a halt. . . .

. . . The farmer and the laborer are marching on to victory. A great general was once asked why he did not at once move upon the enemy. He answered: "I am organizing for victory." The farmers and laborers of the United States are "organizing for victory." They are preparing to move upon the enemy. Not in the gaudy trappings of war, with flying banners and martial music, and amid the boom of artillery, the rattle of musketry and the clash of swords, accompanied with all the horrors of physical contest; but silently, peaceably, and by force of reason and the potent influence of the ballot do they expect to accomplish this mighty revolution in behalf of oppressed labor.

It is useless for men to call attention to the many railroads that have passed into the hands of receivers, or been sold under mortgages, as evidence that the railroads do not pay good dividends on the capital invested. If it proves anything, it is the utter recklessness and incapacity of some of those who engage in railroad enterprises, and the criminal profligacy of their management. If a wildcat railroad scheme is conceived and a road built through a country where it is evident the traffic will not support it, a business blunder has been committed or a swindle perpetrated; either of which is no evidence that railroads do not pay. The same failure might, and does occur in all kinds of business. It would be unfair to take such failures as evidence that the railroads of the United States do not pay. A much graver question, however, is the inevitable tendency of these grasping monopolies that are springing up around and among us, and the inexorable law which punishes corporate greed with confiscation. No student of history, especially of the history of the great corporations of the century, can fail to discern the fate of many of our great railway companies. One set of men after another growls and submits. One

Legislature after another threatens and is cajoled or bought off. But the intolerable oppression continues to grow worse, and year by year the instinct of rebellion grows stronger and stronger, and it is to be hoped that the day is not far distant, when it will have coherence enough to make its demands with an emphasis that will brook no delay. Then no man can stem the tide of popular indignation or set a limit to party fury or the popular will.

The mutterings of the coming storm are already heard in the many labor organizations that have sprang up in our midst within the past few years. It is worse than idle to talk about measures being unconstitutional. Constitutions may be changed as well as laws, and if the policy of the gigantic corporations is to utterly ignore the popular will, setting every principle of justice at defiance, until the indignation of the people is wrought to such a pitch that the day of spoliation of railways will come, and neither vested rights nor common honesty is likely to obtain a hearing, they may console themselves with the reflection that they were the transgressors.

[Morgan next includes a history of the Agricultural Wheel written by W. W. Tedford, a farmer in Prairie County, Arkansas, who was one of the seven original members. Here one sees the conditions which promoted the growth of that organization.]

CAUSES WHICH LED TO THE MOVEMENT.

The question has often been asked, what gave rise to the Wheel? This question is as easily answered as asked, *Monopoly!* This is the answer in a nutshell. A monopoly that wants to buy the earth, and with it the souls and bodies of the people who inhabit it. A spirit instigated by Satan, the head of the firm and proprietor-in-chief of the entire concern, who has inaugurated the infamous system, sent forth his agents, instructed to use every means possible to reduce the world to hellish slavery. . . .

. . . It recognizes no rights, makes no compromises. Like other sins, it comes to us in disguise, draped in broad-cloth and silk, with a smile of seeming innocence playing over its countenance as bright as the sunshine after an April shower, but inwardly it is as black as midnight, and the home of the devil himself.

God hates monopoly, and so do we, and heartily endorse his condemnation of it. To all whose hands and souls are stained with this vile sin we say kick as you may, your conduct has given rise to the Agricultural Wheel, and wherever it rolls it will be a perpetual monument of your wickedness, and a witness against you.

If in struggles to submit all things touching the interest of the laborer to a crucial test, all the existing parties are torn into tatters, and their banners made to trail in the dust of humiliation, it can truthfully be written as an epitaph, *Monopoly*. But to get nearer the subject: What led to the Wheel movement? Monopoly is the true cancer, but like other cancers its roots penetrate the entire body on which it subsists. In consequence of which we challenge the world to produce the equal of some Arkansas monopolists on a small scale. We know of a certain mercantile firm who twenty-five years ago owned nothing comparatively, but to-day owns 18,000 acres of land, a great part of which is in cultivation; also several mules, horses, cattle, and several stores. Perhaps one person would be more correct than a firm, for one person owns the greater part of the property.

The inquiry arises, how did this man, who had no capital to start with, amass that amount of property in twenty-five years, while farmers who had capital grew poorer every year? The answer is, monopoly and extortion! These, in the instance named, were managed through the "anaconda" mortgage, which he succeded in obtaining on crops and stock, and often on lands. Then began the wholesale robbery by charging two and three prices for the goods furnished, thereby reducing his victims to extreme poverty, yea, to financial skeletons. The poor victims, unable to comply with the enormous demands, were "sold out" at shamefully low prices, the mortgagee being the purchaser, at two-thirds the cash value placed on the property by appraisers chosen to put the lowest valuation that decency would permit. In the name of reason and justice, why should not the property bring its full value or no sale, or better, that there be no mortgage.

[Tedford then describes the crop-lien system, in which the farmer must mortgage his crop in advance to the merchant to secure necessary supplies for the coming year.]

. . . At the time the Agricultural Wheel was organized flour was selling under mortgages at $10 per barrel; meat at 20 cents per pound; coffee from four to six pounds to the dollar, and other things in proportion. I am stating what I know, for as the Irishman said, "me, himself, was one of the victims;" the merchant who was careful to charge $2.50 for recording the mortgage, to his customer, did all the weighing, measuring and pricing of both goods and produce. With these advantages he accumulated almost unconsciously great wealth, causing the property of the country to come into the hands of the few to the impoverishment of producers. The nature of a mortgage is well known in our state, but a quotation from a well-known writer on it will not be out of place here. "The instant one of these anaconda mortgages is executed the maker becomes practically the slave of the mortgagee; he is deprived of all means of obtaining credit elsewhere; he is compelled to trade with the holder of the mortgage; he cannot object to the quality or quantity of the goods offered him, nor to the prices charged. If he wants a pair of No. 8 shoes and the trade has a pair of No. 12 unsalable boots, he must take the latter; if he wants a bushel of corn meal, and the trade has a barrel of sour flour he must take it at a price double that of the sound barrel. If the season is favorable and the industry of the tenant is likely to be rewarded with a bountiful crop, so much the worse for him; commodities at still higher prices are forced on him until the limit of the value of his crop is reached.

" . . . As originally enacted, this law made it a felony, punishable by imprisonment at hard labor in the penitentiary for not less than one nor more than two years, for the mortgagor to remove beyond the limits of the county, or sell, barter, exchange or otherwise dispose of any part of the mortgaged property."

The same writer says by way of illustration, "Samuel N. Beard executed an anaconda mortgage on his stock and crop to be grown; he drew $43 worth of supplies at the usual prices in such cases. His stock and crop were worth more than that amount. His wife languished on a bed of sickness during the summer, and at last was too weak to digest any longer the strong and coarse food which her husband had, and her doctor ordered beef tea. The door of the cabin in which he lived had no shutter; the chill November winds were sweeping through it, imperiling his wife's life. In this extremity he bartered seventy pounds of his cotton for lean beef to make soup for his wife and for a shutter to the door. For this, Beard was indicted and sent to the penitentiary one year. He offered to show that the property covered by the mortgage exceeded in value the mortgage debt, and that he could have no intention to defraud; but the Court said that the statute said nothing about the intention with which the act was done, and that it was also immaterial whether the remaining property was worth more or less than the mortgage debt, that the offense by the words of the act was complete by the simple act of selling or trading any part of the mortgaged property, without regard to motive or any other facts, and the Supreme Court of the State affirmed the judgment. (Beard vs. State, 43 Ark., p. 284.) But the judges of that Court were so shocked at the inhumanity of the law (and should have been none the less shocked at the merchant) that they urged upon the Legislature its repeal or modification, and under pressure of that recommendation it was modified; but in the meantime Beard was sent to the penitentiary. He was pardoned by the Governor."

At the time the Wheel was started this abominable instrument held with an iron grasp the purse-strings of Arkansas farmers, owing to a severe drouth that made it almost a desert. The merchants, doctors and others, instead of offering to sustain a part of the loss of crops, only drew the reins tighter and harder. In this extremity the doctors, whom the farmers had made, met in Lonoke county and resolved that after a specified time that they would not practice in any family indebted to them, unless the head of the family would give a mortgage. All that we could hear in Prairie county was mortgages! *mortgages!* MORTGAGES!

. . . It is sometimes asked, why do farmers mortgage? This is a question asked by monopolists with evident pride, if farmers give us a mortgage the right to dictate prices goes with it. The answer is, to secure the debt, and the fact that they are willing to make the merchant safe and pay an additional per cent.; yea! double the lawful interest on money, besides granting them the privilege of weighing, measuring and pricing both goods and produce, would seem to be inducement enough to make even the dishonest act justly, but such is not the case, or found to be true in dealing with the average middle-man, who in actions, says, Sir, you are obliging enough not only to patronize my house but to mortgage, and for this kindness I am mean enough to take every advantage; yea, every piece of bread out of the mouths of your children, and then let you "root hog or die." The Wheelers of Arkansas are determined to revolutionize this entire old monopolous system of trade, and inaugurate on the wreck a co-operative plan, owned and run by Wheelers; and more, we demand the right to weigh, measure and price our own commodities. If it were necessary, a great many other causes could be named that led to the organization of the Wheel which will be referred to in another place.

[What policies did the Wheel favor? Morgan reprints the following early expression (from 1887) of agrarian protest. Since the Wheel became one of the constituent parts of the Southern Alliance, this program is of more than passing interest in studying the currents feeding into Populism.]

. . . We, the members of the National Agricultural Wheel, in convention assembled, at McKenzie, Tennessee, November, 1887, do hereby demand of our National government such legislation as shall secure to our people freedom from the shameful abuses that the farmers and mechanics are now suffering at the hands of the arrogant capitalists, powerful corporations, and the seemingly insatiable greed of Shylock. We demand:

1. That the public land, the heritage of the people, be reserved for actual settlers only—not another acre to railroads or speculators, and that all lands now held for speculative purposes shall be taxed at their full value.

2. That measures be taken to prevent aliens from acquiring title to lands in the United States and Territories of America, and to force titles already acquired by aliens to be relinquished to the National government by purchase and retain said right of eminent domain for the use of actual settlers and citizens of the National States, and that the law be rigidly enforced against all railroad corporations which have not complied with the terms of their contract by which they have received large grants of lands.

3. That we demand the rapid payment of the public debt of the United States by operating the mints of the government to their full capacity in coining silver and gold, and the

264 *The Populist Mind*

tendering the same without discrimination to the public creditors of the nation according to contract, thus saving the interest on the public debt to the industrial masses.

4. That we demand the abolition of national banks, the substitution of legal tender treasury notes in lieu of national bank notes, issued in sufficient volume to do the business of the country on a cash system; regulating the amount needed on a per capita basis as the business interests of the country expands, and that all money issued by the government shall be a legal tender in payment of all debts, both public and private.

5. That we demand that Congress shall pass such laws as shall effectually prevent the dealing in future of all agricultural and mechanical productions, preserving a stringent system of procedure in trial as shall secure prompt conviction, and imposing such penalties as shall secure the most perfect compliance with the law.

6. That we demand a graduated income tax, and as we believe it is the most equitable system of taxation, placing the burden of government on those who can best afford to pay, instead of laying it on the farmers and mechanics, exempting millionaires, bondholders and corporations.

7. That we demand the strict enforcement of all laws prohibiting the importation of foreign labor under the contract system, and that all convicts be confined within the prison walls, and that all contract systems be abolished.

8. That we demand that all means of public communication and transportation shall be owned and controlled by the people, and equitable rates everywhere be established, on the same basis as is the United States postal system.

9. That we demand the election of all officers of the National government by a direct vote of the people, and that all willful violations of the election laws be declared a felony, and a part of the punishment be, the prohibition of the party convicted, from voting in all future elections.

10. That we demand the repeal of all laws that do not bear equally upon capital and labor, the strict enforcement of all laws, the removal of all unjust technicalities, delays and discriminations in the administration of justice.

11. That we demand the tariff laws be so amended as to remove all import duties, on articles entering into our manufactures, and that the duties be levied upon articles of luxuries not above the importing point.

12. That we demand that the government shall protect the Chickasaws and Choctaws, and other civilized Indians of the Indian Territory, in all of their inalienable rights, and shall prevent railroads, and other wealthy syndicates, from over-riding the law and treaties now in existence for their protection.

13. That we are unqualifiedly in favor of the education of the masses, by a well regulated system of free schools.

14. That we demand that no patents shall be renewed, after the expiration of the time for which they were originally patented.

15. *Resolved,* That this body will not support any man for Congress, of any political party, who will not pledge himself in writing, to use all his influence for the formation of these demands into laws.

[Morgan next shows that the organization was expressly nonpartisan, but that this did not preclude an interest in political activity. His remarks, which can be applied to the other farmer groups in the late 1880's, illustrate how the movement toward independency in the South was more or less compelling, despite the traditions of white supremacy and a one-party system.]

IS THE WHEEL A POLITICAL ORGANIZATION?

. . . The fact is too frequently lost sight of that there is a wide difference between the terms partisanship and politics. If we were asked the question, "Is the Wheel a partisan organization?" we should answer, No. But if asked, "Is it a political organization?" we should answer, Yes.

. . . It [the Wheel] is made up principally of farmers. They propose to think and act for themselves. If the laboring man was to remain silent on questions of political economy, take what was given them and ask for no more, there would be none of this hue and cry against them which the ring bosses and a subsidized press raise at each election.

So long as the professional politician was allowed to do the thinking for the laboring masses everything went along smoothly. But when they assert their right to think and act for themselves without consulting the political bosses, the English language is incapable of furnishing epithets strong enough, and mean enough, to apply to those who thus assert their rights. If the farmers and others in the country see fit to withdraw their support from a party which they have long trusted in the vain hope that it would do something to relieve them, whose business is it to question their act? Must they go to the boss of some court house ring to apply for this privilege? Have the farmers any independence, intelligence and manhood of their own? Who is to look after their rights if *they* do not? Of what use is the right of suffrage if they must vote as dictated to by machine politicians? Is it not to secure these rights that we are organized? What rights are we demanding? What wrongs are we suffering? What is the nature of the evils with which we are afflicted? How are we to act intelligently unless we discuss these matters among ourselves? The preamble to our constitution says that "all monopolies are dangerous to the best interests of the people," and "calculated to enslave them." The National banking system is a monopoly. A trust is a monopoly. These things are chartered by law. They are fostered by the government. To discuss them and a remedy against the evils which they impose, would be intrenching upon the domain of politics. It would be the discussion of politics in the Wheel. Dare we do it? Are we willing and ready to surrender our rights as American citizens the moment we enter the sacred precincts of our Order, for fear that the mere mention of these evils will hurt some poor brother's feelings? Away with such nonsense. The men who, for years, have been suffering from the evils of vicious class legislation, are strong enough to "eat meat." We have never yet seen the man who was opposed to the Wheel going into politics, provided it was his politics, or the politics of his party, they were about to embrace. This "milk and cider" and "sugar-teat" way of breaking the ice must be abandoned. Tell the truth. Tell it like a man, boldly, bravely, resolutely. If it is bad, tell it. If it is good, tell it. "Hew to the line, let the chips fall where they may." Is it any harm for a member to say that National "banks are more dangerous than standing armies?" "Yes," says one. "Why?" "Because history records the fact that the Republican party instituted the system, and our Republican brethren will think you are making war upon their party." 'Fudge! Then history records that other fact that Democrats have taken kindly to the system, fostered it, and loaned them more free money than the Republicans ever dreamed of.' But that is not the question. Is the statement true? If so, then National banks ought to be abolished. To accomplish this requires a plan. To discover these remedies, and apply them, requires something to do with politics. Without discussing these questions and the proper remedies, we could not proceed intelligently.

. . . There are three things which we are bound to consider if we arrive at a proper understanding of the real situation, and a correct remedy for the evils with which we are burdened:

First. Our Condition.
Second. The Cause.
Third. The Remedy.

. . . With regard to the condition of the country we are all agreed. Upon the cause there is but little difference of opinion. If we can agree upon the remedy the battle is already half won. If we fail to agree our effort will have been in vain. If we delay the application of the proper remedy, the evils of which we complain will assume a more aggravated nature, and the bonds of slavery be more securely fastened. We have already clear and well defined views of our wrongs and their cause. We are aware that we must have some legislation to remedy them. How are we to secure this without going into politics?

. . . What did we mean by making those demands? Was it mere child's play? Did we mean business? Did we consider them to be just? If so, there is only one of three things to do. "We must fight, run or surrender." We have the power of numbers, the force of intelligence and the means at hand to carry our demands to a successful termination. Do we lack the manhood? Are we wanting in courage? If parties have left the highways of statesmanship, of honesty and justice, are we compelled to follow them for fear some imaginary foe will set upon them and rob them of a success which they have forfeited by their neglect of the rights of the people? Must we condone their wrongs? Is party success so dear to the American farmer, as to be purchased at the price of hard labor for life, and perpetual financial bondage to his children? Is the success of the demagogue more desirable than the overthrow of monopolies? Can the siren songs of the wily politician be harmoniously blended with the groans of the hungry, naked and distressed? Does allegiance to a party fostering a system that robs the poor, ignores the cries of the oppressed, and laughs at crime, harmonize with the teachings of Christianity, and render sweeter to the ear the songs of Heaven? What is the matter with the people? They have all got pitch-forks and want to pitch the blame on some one else. For shame! Be men, at least long enough to compare the platforms of your party with the demands of labor. Read the speeches of your Senators and Congressmen. Not the speeches they send out to you, but the ones they don't send out; the ones which they prefer you should not read.

"Oh, our party has not had a chance," says one. Hasn't it? Did it have a chance to make its own platform, and define its policy? Did it have a chance to embody your demands therein? Did it have a chance to leave the old nominating political machine in the closet for once, and allow a representation of farmers in the legislative halls in proportion to their numbers and interests? Did it have a chance to say to old-time convention manipulators, "stand back and let the laboring man have a fair show?" No. What *did* it say? "Stick to the grand old party. Don't bolt the convention, or scratch a ticket. Don't act independent, you'll be one of the other fellows if you do. Vote 'er straight. Don't kick. Help us this time. If you don't see what you want in our platform, ask for it. Wait till we get there, and we'll show you how 'tis done. Whoop 'em up down in your neighborhood. Use dynamite and lay it on the other party. Use whisky. Vote 'em wherever you find 'em, niggers and all. Cry negro domination; low tariff; high tariff; radical; reconstruction; Powell Clayton; rebel; liar; thief; scoundrel; anarchist; bloody shirt; war; rebellion; blood and thunder. Anything to get up an excitement, and rouse men's passions. If you can't carry your point that way, buy voters, bribe judges, stuff, steal and burn ballot boxes. It's all right. The other fellows do it, and we must get there this time or the country will go to the dogs." . . . A story is told that in the canton of Berne, in Switzerland, the people had grown up under the system of keeping a bear at the public expense; and had been taught that if the bear died there would be some great national calamity fall upon them. So they kept the bear notwithstanding the expense and the fact that he would frequently inflict fatal injuries on the children, and make raids on the pigs and lambs that came within his jurisdiction. But one day he sickened and died. Great efforts were made in vain to secure another bear.

"During the interim the people were amazed and delighted to see that the sun continued to shine, the corn to grow and the vintage to flourish, and everything went on the same as before, saving the danger and expense of the bear, so they came to the sensible conclusion not to keep any more bears." There are those in this country who insist that it is necessary to keep two bears, and maintain that if either dies the country will go to wreck and ruin. And not only that, but they still further insist that one portion of the farmers and laborers shall worship one bear and the balance the other. We may be dull of comprehension, but we have been studying the color, size, weight and habits of these two animals for fifteen years and hope we may be excused if we can not discover any material difference in the two, except that at times one gets more to eat than the other and appears fat, sleek and contented, while the other keeps up a continuous growling, and acts "worse than a bear with a sore head." We can not see how the death of either one or both of these—provided some other useful animal could be substituted in its place— would be a great calamity. For our part we are in favor of either compelling them to work in the harness or giving place to some useful animal that will work, and not stand and growl at one of its own species.

[Some 340 pages later Morgan voices skepticism over the Interstate Commerce Commission, and condemns the practices of railroads.]

. . . Do we believe what we say in the preamble to our constitution and the declaration of our principles? Then we are threatened with a multiplicity of monopolies that menace our liberties. No country in the history of the world has ever been cursed with so many and such gigantic monopolies as free (?) America. Free, only in name. Free, only in the fact that we still have a glimmering hope of crushing this monstrous system of robbery by an intelligent use of the ballot; that failing, all hope is lost, except that last fearful resort— revolution. May the God of our fathers prevent it.

What are the natural results of railroad monopolies? Like all other soulless corporations, their only ambition is gain; and that gain must come from the producer. With this sole object in view, they are blind to the true principles of government, and, like all other tyrannical powers, regard not the rights of the people. They do not hesitate to buy our executive officers, corrupt our courts and prostitute our legislators to the attainment of their nefarious schemes.

MONOPOLY OF TRANSPORTATION—RAILROAD RATES—EXTORTION.

. . . We have remarked in another chapter, that the rate on the railroad traffic of the United States might be reduced 18 per cent., and the companies still pay a fair dividend on the capital actually invested. We will now proceed to further test the truth of the statement, in the light of the facts at hand. Relative to the cost of the construction of roads and the amount of capital actually invested therein, one of our most distinguished bankers and financiers says:

"The mischief, financially, socially, and politically, has not yet been reached. In a large number of cases—nearly all— there has been financial reconstruction. Of our 125,000 miles, with stock and debt of $7,500,000,000, at least 60 per cent. has gone through the debt scaling process."

Here is the plan pursued: Bonds are issued and sold for proceeds with which to build and equip the road; the stockholders who furnished the money to build the road got nothing; mortgage is foreclosed, the road sold for what it will bring under the hammer, and the debt wiped out.

The stockholders purchase the road at a nominal price; reconstruct and reorganize it under a new name. The bondholders who furnished the money to build the road get nothing; while the stockholders, whose stock represents water, get all. The Cotton Belt Route of our own State (Arkansas) which recently wiped out a million dollars of debt, is a fair illustration.

An eminent writer says: "Two billion dollars represents fully the real cost of the roads."

The *Chicago Grocer* says: "The president of one of our longest trunk lines believes that fares from New York to Chicago might be reduced to $2. He says: 'We often carry hogs from Chicago to New York, for $1 apiece, and feed them on the way, too. Yes, we have to unload them twice and feed them, and transport their keepers from Chicago to New York, at $1 apiece. Now, men load and unload themselves. Fifty men can get into a car. So, I tell you that we can carry passengers from New York to Chicago for $2 apiece and make money—and for $1 apiece, provided we can carry a full train.'"

If we take these figures as a just rate for passenger transportation, we have the fare reduced to $\frac{1}{4}$ cent per mile. The average rate on all the roads in the United States is a fraction less than $2\frac{1}{4}$ cents per mile. The aggregate receipts on all the roads for passenger traffic, for the year 1886, was $212,-000,000. This would indicate an extortion of $187,000,000 on passenger traffic alone, for one year. If, however, we calculate the fare at four times what this railroad president said he could afford to carry them at, or 1 cent per mile, we still have an overcharge on passenger fares for the year above indicated, of over $100,000,000.

"On page 652, Vol. 2, 'Transportation to the Seaboard,' we find: 'Taking the figures of the quotations of the 28th as our standard, and we may say it costs 39 cents to send a bushel of wheat from St. Louis to New York. This is 12.4 mills per ton, per mile, for 1,043 miles, on the cheapest kind of freight (except coal), known to commerce, hauled the maximum distance, with the greatest profit to the company.'"

"The average rate on all the roads of the United States, according to Poor's Manual of American Railways, on all classes of freight, is 1.04 per ton per mile; while the report of the Pennsylvania company show that on all kinds of freight on a great number of more or less profitable lines, the average rate of freight was only 8.98 mills per ton per mile. The above figures would indicate a fair and possible reduction of 16 per cent. But we have seen that the railroads were charging 39¢ for carrying a bushel of wheat from St. Louis to New York.

"This is 12.4 mills per ton per mile for the 1,043 miles of road. If we take the Pennsylvania rate to be fair and just, there is an over charge of 3.42 mills per ton. This is not taking into consideration the fact that wheat is below the average class of freight, as they are rated. Taking the Pennsylvania road as a basis, the above figures indicate a possible, fair reduction of 38 per cent. A ton of wheat at 39 cents per bushel from St. Louis to New York, will cost $14; but twelve men, weighing a ton (or about 170 pounds each), are charged $20 apiece, or at the rate of $240 per ton.

"We must take all the factors to arrive at a just basis of rates. Coal has been carried in England, on roads costing nearly three times as much as our American railways, for 3.2 mills per ton per mile."

Assuming that the difference in the cost of the roads would offset the difference in the class of freight, our own roads could transport wheat for 3.2 mills per ton per mile. At this rate the cost of transporting a bushel of wheat from St. Louis to the seaboard, would be a fraction less than 11 cents, or a net saving to the farmers of the West and Northwest of 28 cents per bushel. It is safe to say that there is an extortion on the rates of corn and wheat shipped to the seaboard of 20 cents per bushel. In 1886 we exported 180,000,000 bushels of wheat, for which the farmers should have received 20 cents a bushel more than they got, or the sum of $36,000,000. Of corn we exported 187,000,000 bushels, on which the extortion amounted to $37,000,000, or a total of $73,000,000 on these two cereals. But the mischief does not stop here, as the shipping price governs the local markets, the farmer is compelled to sell to the feeder, the miller and others, at the reduction caused by extortionate freight charges.

Jeremiah S. Black, ex-judge of the supreme court and ex-attorney-general of the United States, in speaking of the extortions of the railroad companies of the United States, says: "They express their determination to charge as much as the traffic will bear; that is to say, they will take from the profits of every man's business as much as can be taken without compelling him to quit it. In the aggregate, this amounts to the most enormous, oppressive and unjust tax that ever was laid on the industry of any people under the sun. The irregularity with which this tax is laid, makes it still harder to bear. Men go into business which may thrive at present rates, and will find themselves crushed by the burdens unexpectedly thrown upon them after they get started. It is the habit of railroad companies to change their rates of transportation often and suddenly, and, in particular, to make their charges ruinously high without any notice at all. The farmers of the Great West have made a large crop of grain, which they may sell at fair prices if they can have it carried to eastern ports, even at the unreasonably high rates of last summer. But just now it is said that the railway companies have agreed among themselves to raise the freight 5¢ per hundred weight, which is equal to an export tax upon the whole crop of probably $75,000,000. The farmers must submit to this highway robbery or else keep the products of their land to rot on their hands."

"A committee of the United States Senate reported, six years ago, that even at that time the men who controlled the four great trunk lines between New York and Chicago, could, 'by a single stroke of the pen, reduce the value of property in this country by hundreds of millions of dollars. An additional charge of five cents per bushel on the transportation of cereals would,' they said, 'have been equivalent to a tax of $45,000,000 on the crop of 1873.' No Congress would dare to exercise so vast a power, except upon a necessity of the most imperative nature."

At the rate coal is carried, 3.2 mills per ton per mile, railroad cross ties could be shipped from Hardy, Arkansas, to Kansas City, for 11 cents apiece, and from Jonesboro for 13 cents; the present rate is 29 cents. Within the past five years there has been 3,000,000 ties taken from the line of the Kansas City, Springfield and Memphis railroad, between the Missouri State Line and Big Bay.

There was an average overcharge of, at least, 10 cents per tie, indicating a loss to the people along the line of $300,000 on the single item of railroad ties, and on a territory of less than 100 miles in extent. A Philadelphia merchant stated, that a car load of corn had been shipped to him from Iowa; the freight and commission charges were $233.70; and the grain brought only $233.07; leaving a deficit to the shipper of 63 cents.

Another man went out to Iowa and bought a lot of corn for 13 cents a bushel, shipped it to Springfield, Mass., where he sold it for 69 cents, and made just 1 cent a bushel. The writer remembers having once shipped a car load of flour from St. Louis, a distance of 226 miles, for which he paid only $22, but at this point it was transferred to another road, that charged $28 for hauling it twenty-three miles. At another time he paid $16 for a car load of hogs a distance of seventeen miles, and at another $10 for a car load of wood nine miles. By unjust and inconsistent charges and discriminations, railroad corporations have created a prejudice against themselves on the part of the public that bodes them no good in the near future. As a means of developing the resources of the country, to lighten labor and add to the happiness of the human family, when used legitimately, railroads stand at the head of the column in the benefactions to the human race.

But the avarice, the greed, the corruption and the tyranny which has characterized the American railroad corporations has known no bounds nor respected any rights of either persons or property. . . .

. . . By a system of rebates they have violated and set aside the operation of the law. In this way they have assisted in the formation and growth of the giant monopolies of trade that have become an incubus upon labor. In this way has the Standard Oil company grown and prospered, its rebates amounting to $10,000,000 in eighteen months. Under the shadow of the protection of railroad monopoly exists the greatest coal combination in the world, who have it in their power to fix the limit of production and set a price upon every ton of coal used in the cities of the Eastern States.

It is nonsense to talk about competition regulating transportation and insuring a just schedule of charges. Whatever effect competition might have had in the early days of railroads, it is no longer a factor in adjusting a schedule of rates. Besides the most atrocious system of stock watering and exaggerating of the real capital invested, various other pretexts are resorted to, for the purpose of absorbing and covering up the enormous profits wrung from the industries of the people. Exorbitant salaries are paid the officials, and frequently the most reckless extravagance indulged in in the management of the road. Many attempts have been made by the Legislatures of States to control the traffic within their borders; but so far their efforts have met with such limited success that it might almost be said to be a failure. An open defiance of the law has frequently characterized the railroad corporations, and having such a total disregard for the rights of the people that an issue in court depends, not so much upon the justice of the cause, as the patience and persistence of the people to hold out against the money of the corporation.

The *Chicago Daily News* statistician says: "The railways collect what the traffic will bear. The liabilities of the roads

in Illinois at the beginning of 1886 were $730,093,003, repre-
senting an actual value of one-third this sum. In other words,
it is endeavored to collect a high rate of interest on property
at three times its actual cost. By what right does a public
highway, deriving a franchise and right of domain from the
State for the public good, to be exercised for reasonable compensation, go on piling up capital account, adding in deferred
dividends, equipments, floating debts, surplus, increasing
yearly the total, and collecting on this fictitious total an exorbitant rate of interest? We pay to the railways of this State
each year nearly twice the interest on the national debt.
The tax affects all classes indirectly, but the producer—the
farmer—the most. The middle man and the trader shift the
burden; the consumer may curtail his consumption, but the
farmer must sell."

Just where and how the matter will end is hard to foretell.
The farmers demand protection, and it seems as though the
State Legislatures and Courts are either unable or unwilling
to grant it. Congress, yielding to the popular clamor, passed
the Inter-State Commerce law. But the provisions of the
law are worded so intricately, and its operations are so
inadequate to the demands of the existing evils, that it is a
question whether the bill was got up and passed in the
interests of the people or the railroad corporations. The only
clause in the law that could benefit the people to any extent
is the one referring to the long and short haul, and it reads
as follows: "That they shall not charge more for a short
haul than a long haul under substantially similar circumstances and conditions, over the same line running in the
same direction."

Gen. J. B. Weaver, in a speech at Lima, Ohio, referring
to this law, said:

"I do not wish to omit the statement that Congress, at its
last session did undertake to regulate commerce among the
states and they passed a law known as the Inter-State Com-

merce Law,—and I can't be accused of making a partisan statement here, because all parties supported this measure. But they passed a law, and having been a pretty close student of the Bible, I will state before this audience here to-night that it will be no harm for you to worship it, for it is not like anything in the heavens above, or the earth beneath. That law says, speaking of the long and short haul,—and that is about all there is in the law,—that they shall not charge more for a short haul than for a long one. Well, this is remarkable, is it not? But, if it stopped there, it would be a very good law, notwithstanding some contradictions of terms. It says they shall not charge more for a short haul than a long one under substantially similar circumstances over the same line in the same direction. What does that mean? You know the Knights of Labor believe in having laws so plain that the people can understand them when the children read them. I defy all the lawyers in Lima to tell me; there is no one under the sun that can tell what it means. 'Shall not charge more for a short haul than a long one under substantially similar circumstances and conditions over the same line running in the same direction.' Why, it was drawn so nobody could understand it.

"Just imagine the Great Law-Giver, when he gave the ten commandments: Thou shalt not kill; Thou shalt not steal, under substantially similar circumstances and conditions over the same line in the same direction. (Loud and tumultuous applause.) No, that was put in that law for the purpose of deceiving the people. The people clamored for a law regulating inter-state commerce, claiming that commerce was put into the hands of these great corporations and controlled by them. And they answered you by giving you a law which was declared, in the face of its promoters in the House, to mean simply to leave the question to the railroads to decide what was the similar circumstances and conditions. They passed it, and last week the five commissioners decided it to mean exactly what we told them it meant—that the railroads must determine what was substantially similar circumstances and conditions, and then, if the people didn't like it they could go—where? The law tells them where, and only where. Either in the federal court, away off from their homes, or before the five commissioners at Washington City."

Section eight of Article first of our Constitution says: Congress shall have power "to regulate commerce with foreign nations, *and among the several States,* and with the Indian tribes."

Congress has exercised this right with regard to "foreign nations" and "Indian tribes," but who has been regulating commerce among the "several States?"

. . . For years the managers of railway systems have been controlling the greater part of commerce between the States; for years the people have been robbed by these modern uncrowned but no less powerful kings.

There seems to be but one remedy for the evils growing out of our present railroad system. It is for the government to take absolute supervisory control of the roads, or, by right of eminent domain to become the owner of the roads by gradual purchase. In advocating this remedy we are not unaware of the fact that it is stoutly opposed by the adherents of the two great political parties in the country, and by the subsidized press. But for many reasons which it is not our purpose to discuss here we believe it to be the only correct solution of the transportation problem. The roads are public highways and of right ought only to be operated for the public good. Any system that is not for the public good—that is detrimental to the public welfare—is and of right ought to be subject to public control. Men talk about "Chartered Privileges" and "Vested Rights." If a "vested right" becomes a nuisance—a public wrong—it is no longer a "right," vested or otherwise; for a right can not exist in a wrong. If such was a fact a man's right to carry on a slaughter house within the confines of a densely populated city could not be questioned, provided he held a deed to the property. No man has a right to operate against the public welfare and against their expressed will.

[After pointing out the vituperative attacks reformers are subjected to at the hands of the press, Morgan turns to the whole problem of a new party. Writing in 1889, he reflects a sense of groping, and yet the determination to rectify grievances which many reformers felt.]

. . . All reform movements have met with like opposition, but here in free America it would seem that the voter is only free to do, peaceably, what some self-appointed political boss tells him to do. If he exercises his own free will and does something that is not consistent with the political bosses' plan, he subjects himself to be called anything which said political boss or his satellites see fit to call him; and every political boss has his organ to aid him in this commendable work. We merely mention these things to call attention to the fact that if the reader ever expects to assume any independence of his own and protest against the domination of pothouse politicians and "potato lawyers," he may expect to have to bear a vast amount of abuse and ridicule.

The power of an epithet and ridicule to turn men away from reform movements is very great, and none know this better than the monopolist and his efficient servants, the professional politicians. When Christ was being scourged and mocked, the great and good Peter denied him. It is still within the memory of old men how the placards on Democratic parade wagons, "Fathers and brothers, save us from negro husbands," and the epithets, "Black Abolitionist" and "Northern Gorillas," retarded the growth of the Republican party. All men who are now pressing for industrial reform must expect nothing but kicks, cuffs and hard words. The work of reform is neither a pleasant or a profitable business, and the men who want an easy, lucrative employment had better not enter upon it—it is better for themselves and for the party of reform that they stay with the boodlers. . . .

Not only unity of *purpose*, but unity of *action* "is imperatively demanded," if we expect to be successful in obtaining recognition of our demands. Then the logical result of this would be the formation of a new party? No, it does not necessarily follow. As far as the new party is concerned, it already exists. Parties are not formed; they form themselves. The millions in this country who are demanding political reform already constitute a new party, inasmuch as they are a new factor in politics. The only thing wanting to make them a new party, in fact, is coherence. And this will not be wanting when there is occasion, apparent to all, that the needed reforms cannot be accomplished in any other way.

. . . Parties seldom, if ever, do as much as they promise in their platforms, it is folly to expect them to do more. This is eminently true, and history records no great reform or revolution accomplished through the agency of an old existing organization. We had as well set out our old corn-stalks in the Spring and expect them to yield a bountiful supply of ears because they had done so the year before. The present policy of the two great political parties is similar to the action of a conceited old maid, who admires herself for what she once was and the conquests she had made. The history of the nations of the world teaches us, that, while principles never die, the lives of parties are of short duration. In the ever-changing circumstances of life, new issues are rising, which give vitality to new organizations.

. . . Let us look for a moment and see what we are ready to do. Are we united? No, only in purpose. What, then, is in the way? Prejudice; selfishness; cowardice; sentimental politics. Too much sentiment and not enough sense. The first thing to do is to remove all these obstacles. How is it to be done? By education. Suppose a man, driving along the road with a loaded wagon, should get into a mud-hole, and his team be unable to pull it out. Directly another man comes along, and is requested to help pull the wagon out. Now, suppose they differ as to the best method of getting the wagon out, one wanting to pull it out backwards, and the other forwards. Would it not be foolishness for each one to undertake to carry out his plan? Common sense would teach that they must both pull the same way. Yet the farmers and laborers of America have been pulling against each other for years. The politicians and "bosses" have them hitched up to different ends of the wagon, and continue to apply the party lash whenever they undertake to unite and pull the same way. This is what we call party prejudice. A better name would be tomfoolishness.

. . . It is quite natural that the most violent protests come from those whose interests have been so well protected of late years by the representatives of the people—that is, the capitalists. If a new party is formed it will be by the people. Thomas Jefferson said:

"I am not among those who fear the people. They, and not the rich, are our dependence for continued freedom." The great masses of the people are demanding either a new policy of the old parties or a new party which shall receive its vitality from the vital issues of the hour. The men who control the policies of the old parties are opposed to either a change of policies or the formation of a new party. Thus the contest widens and deepens.

There are only two sides to the question, and both the two great political parties, by their policies and their acts, occupy one side. Look at their platforms and their records! What have they done for the people? They have simply boasted of their records and sought to perpetuate their power on the glory of the past. On every vital issue of the day they occupy a position with the capitalist. This condition must be changed. These policies must be dropped or the masses of the people will be forced into poverty. It is for the people to determine which is easier, to "turn the rascals out," who control the policies of the parties, or to organize a new party upon the vital principles which effect the interests of labor.

[Morgan closes with these words.]

. . . Laboring men of America! The voice of Patrick Henry and the fathers of American Independence rings down through the corridors of time and tells you to strike. Not with glittering musket, flaming sword and deadly cannon; but with the silent, potent and all-powerful ballot, the only vestige of liberty left. Strike from yourselves the shackles of party slavery, and exercise independent manhood.

Strike at the foundation of the evils which are threatening the existence of the Republic.

Strike for yourselves, your families, your fellow man, your country and your God.

Strike from the face of the land the monopolies and combinations that are eating out the heart of the Nation.

Let the manhood of the Nation rise up in defense of liberty, justice and equality. Let the battle go on until all the people, from North to South and East to West, shall join in one loud acclaim, "Victory is ours, and the people are free!"

33. The Proper Distribution of Wealth

Thomas L. Nugent was the People's party nominee for governor of Texas in 1892 and 1894, and would probably have been the candidate again in 1896 had he not died in December 1895. Nugent was something of a legend in his own time. He was not necessarily

Reprinted from Catherine Nugent (ed.), *Life Work of Thomas L. Nugent* (Catherine Nugent: Stephenville, Texas, 1896), pp. 126–127, 146-157, 159-163, 165-169, 176-177, 182-187, 195-196, 204-205, 207-208, 211-218, 221-223, 227-229, 235-236.

the best-known Populist in the state, and was by no means the most popular orator in the movement. Yet, there was never any doubt that Nugent stood out in Texas Populism as its most qualified and respected political figure. Not only were his credentials of a high order—a college education, and a distinguished record on the bench as district judge for two terms—but more important to an understanding of his hold on the movement's rank and file, Nugent both articulated and personified the moral principles infusing Populist doctrine. His whole cast of mind bore the imprint of a well-defined moral outlook, one which governed his view of economics just as it did his ideas on the conduct between man and man.

Nugent was deeply religious but a member of no organized religion. There is a striking fusion of rationality and mysticism in his outlook. He offered a rational proof for the existence of God, and yet saw God as life and as the essence of all things. Nugent was impressed by Swedenborgian doctrine, but went even further in searching for a satisfactory statement of his own convictions. The key to his position, and why he was prompted to support the Populist movement, and why in turn he was revered by the people, can be seen in the comment of a friend, written shortly after Nugent died. "He looked upon the whole human race as being conjoined to the Lord—and this conjunction he called the Divine Humanity. All things were to him a One. Each a part of an organic whole whose soul God is, and whose body is man." For Nugent, the nobility of the masses was a living reality, and he waged his campaigns with this thought in mind. As his speeches will show, Nugent did not talk down to the people. Indeed, he posed for them a standard which they could only hope to work toward without perhaps ever achieving—a standard of selfless devotion to human betterment.

Nugent, born in 1841, had all of the advantages which came with membership in the Louisiana planter class, and some of the prejudices as well. He did not repudiate slavery until after the Civil War. In later life, Nugent urged that Negroes should assume positions of responsibility on the basis of merit, but by and large thought in terms of a separate but equal framework on matters pertaining to education and welfare. Thus, his conception of the all-embracing oneness of mankind was limited in this one crucial respect. As for his economic stand, Nugent's speeches in the 1890's point to an essentially moderate position. He was clearly more radical than the major party leaders, but throughout his speeches one can find scattered references in opposition to full-scale socialism, and in favor of property rights so long as property was not used for speculative purposes. Selections from four speeches delivered by Nugent in the period from 1892 to 1895 are presented here.

I

[This speech, part of Nugent's first campaign for governor, was made in the late summer of 1892.]

. . . A great thinker has said that "as institutions grow larger, men grow small." It is so. The "rule of the ring" has been supreme in this republic of ours for the past thirty years and he who can manipulate most skillfully the political machine secures the prizes of public life, the offices and spoils. Great men no longer lead the old parties because great men are men of soul, of humanity, of genius, of inspiration. They are never machine men. Fitted by nature to soar amid the stars, they cannot sprawl in the gutter or court companionship with slime. Capable men are no doubt working the party machines for the usual rewards, but the times demand great men to mould the elements of reform into proper shape, and they will come as the inspiration finds them amid the ranks of the common folk. The farmer of to-day is a reasoning and thinking man, rejoicing in a new-found intellectual strength of which but lately he did not dream. Moreover, he has developed into an orator as well, and his rude and touching eloquence flaming forth from heart and brain burning with a sense of injustice and wrong, stirring the hearts of plain people as they were never stirred before. Behold the leaders of that new crusade against conditions that make virtue impossible and against inequalities that stamp labor with the curse of all the ages!

Meanwhile leaders of democracy, who have inherited from Jefferson nothing but a few well-worn formulas of speech, and leaders of republicanism, to whom the humanity and unique greatness of Lincoln have value only in firing the hearts of the faithful and impelling them to renewed efforts for party success, marshall their political hosts on the two sides of the sectional line where every four years they stand in solid array, glaring at each other with the old-time hate gleaming in their eyes. This has been the unhappy political status for thirty years. The South can always be trusted for her votes by Wall street democracy, but never for a place on the national ticket. Contributing the funds, Wall street has always claimed the right to dictate the candidates and the financial policy of the country, and thus, from Seymour to Cleveland, so-called sound finances and the business interests of the country have, on the election of candidates, been matters of chief concern to the party leaders. Wall street must, at any cost, be appeased. The big bankers and money lenders, the stock jobbers, the men who bull and bear the market, must be kept in good humor, must, indeed, be satisfied that their special privileges are not to be taken from them, otherwise campaign funds must dwindle and party success be jeopardized.

Thus both parties have tacitly agreed to ignore the silver issue and leave the gold standard intact. What does Wall street care for the tariff question, so long as she controls the finances? With even free trade, control of the money of the country would give her control of the prices, control of wages, of usury, of the property and the labor of the country. What more could she have under protection? But parties must have issues, and the tariff and bloody shirt issues are, of all issues, least of all hurtful to Wall street. Hence it is that

the old quarrel over the tariff and the force bill is to be renewed, while the money kings rub their hands gleefully and
watch with delight the "sham battle" whose "clamor" drowns
the cry of distress that comes from the farm, the workshop
and the factory. Labor is in chains, while the politicians are
skurrying over the country repeating political platitudes,
holding up tariff schedules in one hand and the "bloody shirt"
in the other, vainly endeavoring to head off the moving column
of reform as it advances to victory. It will not win.

[Then, after a long discussion of the contraction of the currency,
in which he presents tables on per capita circulation and on business
failures, statistics on the concentration of wealth, and a review of
the debates on silver coinage, Nugent turns to the question of the
tariff.]

. . . But the question of remedies should be considered in
relation to the problem of the proper distribution of wealth.
The production of wealth would doubtless be largely increased
by free trade, but it could not secure an equitable distribution of wealth products. Tariff for revenue only, if practicable
at all with half a billion dollars revenue to raise annually,
would doubtless afford some relief, as would any reduction
in import duties, but it would have no effect to distribute the
wealth of the country more equitably than the system of
high protection. In so-called free trade England the rich
still grow richer and the poor, poorer—millionaires and paupers
are the joint products of their economical and industrial
system. There, as here, the hovel rests in the shadow of the
palace, starvation overtakes thousands, and a large section
of the humanity of the United Kingdom is literally rotting
down in poverty and crime, in the very presence of the
palaces which shelter the chiefs of finance, trade and the
factory.

Besides, if the tariff for revenue is the single and only
remedy, how was it that immediately after the war, with an

abundant circulation and a war tariff enormously protective, the country prospered as it never prospered before? The Democratic platform demands tariff for revenue only, but it does not specify what rate of duty would constitute such a tariff, nor does it show what rate would be necessary to maintain our national revenues as now fixed, nor does it propose any reduction in the pension charges or in any other expenditures, so as to bring the annual revenues within the limits of a strictly revenue tariff. To be sure, the free list may be somewhat enlarged, but if the Springer bills at the late session, or the Mills bill of 1888 are to furnish the rule, then the free list under Democratic policy must be understood to include free raw material with high protective duties on the manufactured product. How will all this effect a proper distribution of wealth? Besides, are we to presume that the protected industries of the country, and particularly the protection Democrats of the east, will not successfully oppose any radical reduction of the tariff? It seems idle to assume any such thing. The Cleveland platform of 1884 makes this declaration: "From the foundation of this government, taxes collected at the custom house have been the chief source of federal revenue. Such they must continue to be."

With this distinct committal to the tariff as the chief source of federal revenue and our annual appropriation "justly growing," (as Senator Gorman declares), how are the Democrats going to get the country down to a strict revenue tariff—one not involving the principles of protection? A lower tariff will doubtless increase the revenues, but this, with $500,000,000 of revenue to raise, must be protective. Why, the Democratic house at the last session passed a river and harbor bill appropriating, if I am correctly informed, $48,000,000. This does not justify the expectation that public expenditures will run down materially under Democratic rule. But listen to what Henry George, the most philosophical and accurate thinker on the question of free trade in this country, says, in the book which Democrats published in the *Congressional Record* as a campaign document: "The abolition of protection would tend to increase the production of wealth—that is sure. But under the conditions that exist, increase in the production of wealth may itself become a curse—first, to laboring people, and ultimately to society at large." Again: "In countries like Great Britain there is still a large class living on the verge of starvation, and constantly slipping over it—a class who have not derived the slightest benefit from the immense productive power, since their condition never could have been worse than it is—a class whose habitual condition in times of peace and plenty is lower, harder and more precarious than that of savages." Again: "This fact (that the laborer finds it harder and harder to get a living in the United States) destroys the assumption that our protective tariff raises and maintains wages; but it also makes it impossible to assume that the abolition of protection would in any way alter the tendency which, as wealth increases, makes the struggle for existence harder and harder. This tendency shows itself throughout the civilized world, and arises from the more unequal distribution which everywhere accompanies the increase of wealth. In England the same tendency has continued to manifest itself since the abolition of protection. . . . The depths of poverty are as dark as ever, and the contrast between want and wealth more glaring." Again: "The entire abolition of protection—the mere substitution of a revenue tariff for a protective tariff—is such a lame and timorous application of the free trade principle that it is a misnomer to speak of it as free trade. A revenue tariff is a somewhat milder restriction on trade than a protective tariff." Again: "The problem we must solve, to explain why free trade or labor saving invention or any similar cause fails to produce the general benefits we naturally expect, is a problem of the distribution of wealth."

Indeed all history and the commonest dictates of reason

teach us that as conditions now are in the United States, no mere increase in the production of wealth could bring adequate relief to the toiling and over-burdened masses. Free trade would enhance production and while, as Mr. George shows, it might benefit the laborer by increasing his wages, such benefit would be temporary only—the concentration of wealth would still go on as in England, and all of the evils resulting from an unequal distribution of wealth might appear in even an aggravated form. Tariff for revenue only, under present conditions is only a question of schedules of greater or less protection. The democratic party with its national leadership composed of such men as Gorman, Brice, Whitney and others, not only opposed to silver but to greenbacks as well, friendly to national banks and identified by social and pecuniary interest with the classes who live and thrive on monopoly and legislative favoritism, has a herculean task before it. Senator Mills, with his fervid and highly imaginative nature, full of southern chivalry and eloquence, no doubt has persuaded himself that a revenue tariff will create and distribute wealth, destroy monopoly, open the vaults of the banks and bond holders and send the money so long hoarded there, in vitalizing streams, to every nook and corner of the country; but the difficulty of impressing such views upon the cold-blooded national leaders referred to stamps his undertaking as the task of the century.

But I submit that the platform of the people's party does present a far more comprehensive and reasonable plan of relief than that offered by the democracy. We propose, in the first place, to set ourselves in undying opposition to land monopoly—to so shape the policy of the government that the public land shall be used only by the actual settler, and to reclaim it from corporations, as far as practicable. This will prevent any monopolization of the public lands in the future for speculative purposes.

In the next place, we place in our platform a declaration

of principle which lies at the foundation of any real reform on questions of taxation. "Every dollar taken from industry without an equivalent is robbery." A protective tariff violates this principle, and we stand pledged to remove protection from our tariff as soon as it can be safely and properly done; and in order that this may be accomplished, we favor a graduated income tax which will enable us to greatly reduce the amount of revenue to be raised by duties on imports. By means of this supplementary tax, there is no doubt that we can raise largely more than one-half the revenue now derived from import duties, and thus be able to reduce tariff taxation and afford relief to farmer and laborer. By availing ourselves of the income tax and resolutely applying ourselves to the task of limiting "all state and national revenues to the necessary expenses of government, economically and honestly administered," we shall be able to enter upon the policy of "progressive free trade"— thus conforming our political action to the declaration of the old democracy as contained in the national democratic platform of 1856—the memorable declaration in favor of "free seas and progressive free trade throughout the world." But knowing that reform must be as comprehensive as the evils to be corrected, and that a mere reformation of tax systems cannot remedy evils growing out of false systems of finance and transportation, we propose: 1st. A currency "safe, sound and flexible," issued directly to the people by the government, without the intervention of the banks. 2d, Free coinage of silver. 3d, Increase of the circulating medium to $50 per capita; and 4th, Government ownership of railroads. In advocating the free coinage of silver, we put ourselves in line with the traditions and teachings of the "old democracy," all of whose great leaders, from Jefferson down, believed in bi-metalism.

. . . It will be seen that our opposition to national banks is supported by the teachings of Jefferson, Calhoun and the other great leaders of democratic thought, as well as by the platforms, the traditions and history of the old democracy. Who can fail to admire the fight of the old party under the leadership of Jackson and his successors, in favor of free trade and against national banks? Complete separation of the government and its revenues from banking institutions was the old slogan of democracy until the civil war and the vicious conditions produced by it induced forgetfulness of the warnings of the fathers. Since the war, look at the leaders of democracy—August Belmont, Manton Marble, W. H. English, Calvin Brice, Senator Gorman, Samuel Tilden, Samuel Randall, Grover Cleveland, W. C. Whitney, Daniel Manning and others of like kind. All of these men have favored national banks and a protective tariff. Some of them are interested in national banks, and are in favor of maintaining the present financial system—all have opposed greenbacks and free silver coinage, all favored the national banks and the gold standard. The democratic platforms since the war have never expressed any opposition whatever to national banks and have three times favored tariff for revenue with incidental protection. The platform of 1876, upon which Tilden was elected, denounced the republicans for not having paid off and retired the greenbacks, the non-payment of which it declared to be a "disregard of the plighted faith of the nation." This was the great reform platform which, in addition to avowed hostility to the greenbacks, proposed a system or plan of resumption which would at no time alarm "the public mind into a withdrawal of that vaster machinery of credit by which 95 per cent of all business transactions are performed," thus plainly referring to and endorsing the national bank system.

Mr. Bayard, Cleveland's secretary of state and a pronounced anti-free coinage man, in a public speech during the campaign of 1880, in New York, used this language: "I have seen it charged that the Democratic party were foes to the national banks, but I am at a loss to know the authority for this. The platforms of the party contain no such suggestion and admit of no such construction, in that for the second place on our ticket we have named Mr. William English of Indiana, one of the ablest financiers and business men in the whole country, whose management of the affairs of a national bank, of which he was president, was conspicuous for success." The heads of the treasury department under Mr. Cleveland recommended and urged the cessation of silver coinage and the retirement of the greenback circulation—advising that the greenbacks be funded in bonds to be "issued only to national banks presenting greenbacks" to be funded, the bonds to be "available only as a deposit to secure national bank circulation and to entitle the bank depositing them to receive circulation notes to the amount of their face." In addition to this manifestation of extreme regard for the national banks, Cleveland caused $60,000,000 to be deposited without interest with certain favored national banks, taking their bonds only for the return of the principal. Thus in violation of the principles of the old Democracy, the money of the government was mingled with the funds of banking institutions, to be by them loaned at enormous rates of interest to the people. Of course the banks love and support Cleveland.

But it will be observed we propose the government shall issue directly to the people paper currency, not in unlimited quantities but enough to bring the aggregate circulating medium up to $50 per capita, such currency to be full legal tender. Mr. Whitney, the national banker of Los Angeles, California, who has carefully investigated the subject and written most learnedly upon it, says that this is a safe limit, and it is well known that France, with less capacity than the United States to absorb currency, has in circulation more than $50 per capita and it is prospering by its use.

[After citing Ricardo and others on how the government can determine the value and supply of money, Nugent continues:]

. . . The means of getting this money to the people must be determined by the government. We favor the sub-treasury plan of the Farmers' Alliance, unless some better scheme

should be presented. Thus we hold ourselves free to co-operate upon this line with the old parties upon any feasible plan
of relief which may commend itself to our mind as superior
to the sub-treasury. So far no remedy has been suggested
looking to an increase in the circulating medium, except
"wild-cat bank paper," for which we could hardly be expected
to exchange the sub-treasury plan.

With respect to the railway question, we favor a commission, with power to fix and maintain rates—looking to government ownership as the only final and adequate solution of
the problem. For myself, I believe in a strong commission
law conferring full power upon a commission to regulate and
control railroads and to fix and maintain rates. I believe,
however, that a commission, organized under such a law,
should proceed with great caution, seeking always to do
"equal and exact justice" to the people and all interests involved. In the nature of things, however, the commission can
not take from production the burden which our system of
railway transportation puts upon it. It concedes that railroads
are the private property of the corporations and must necessarily leave to the latter to determine the number and kind of
officers, agents and employes, their duties and compensation.
Hence, in adjusting rates, so long as these roads remain private
property the commission must concede to the owners the
right to fix the amount of operating expenses, the amount to
be expended in betterments, etc. Hence the burden of the
present rates must very largely remain; and when, in fixing
rates, the commission drops to a point at which the roads cease
to produce a reasonable income, as viewed from the standpoint of the owners, litigation must inevitably result, or a
struggle in some form with the commission—all calculated
to weaken and impair this form of regulation, possibly to
destroy its usefulness. At best, in my judgment, the remedy
is a partial one, liable to great abuse, and if thrust into politics,
likely to engender periodical bitterness and strife—to bring

on, in fact, a war between the railroads and the people not favorable to a just and reasonable settlement of the great question of regulation. Government ownership, I verily believe, will obviate all of these troubles. The cost of the roads need not be more than $5,000,000,000. Mr. C. Wood Davis, himself a practical railroad man of large experience and especially learned on this subject, says, in the Arena for June, 1892, that, estimating the cost of the roads at $30,000 per mile, the total value of the 160,000 miles of roads in the United States will be $4,800,000,000; but adding 25 per cent. to this and assuming that $6,000,000,000 of 3 per cent. bonds are issued to pay for the roads, he finds the annual showing, under government ownership, to be about as follows:

EXPENSES.

Interest on bonds..................	$180,000,000
Cost of maintenance and operation....	670,000,000
Sinking fund	50,000,000
Total annual expenses........	$900,000,000

The present cost per annum of operating the system is $1,050,000,000—balance saved by government ownership, $150,000,000. He further in the same paper shows various other savings amounting in the aggregate to $160,000,000, and makes this remark: "It would appear that after yearly setting aside $50,000,000 as a sinking fund, there are the best of reasons for believing that the cost of the railway service would be some $310,000,000 less than under corporate management." It will be seen that there is no suggestion here of issuing $10,000,000,000 of paper money to pay for the railroads, neither is there any such suggestion in our platform. The newspapers represent Senator Mills with charging us with such a design. Possibly the wish is father to the thought; possibly the distinguished senator would be glad, for the sake of the Democratic party, if we had proposed to issue nine billion promises to pay, as in the case of the French assignats, predicated, as John Law's bank issues were, upon unsettled lands in some distant country. Possibly Col. Mills would be glad if he could place to our account the $150,000,000 annual appropriation made necessary to pay pensions under a bill largely supported by good Democrats—an appropriation which the Chicago convention failed to include in its otherwise comprehensive and frantic denunciations. The senator should not fight an imaginary twelfth plank in the People's party platform. He was present at Chicago when his party platform was constructed, and justly received from his party friends distinguished recognitions of his presence. Pity his great influence was not used to induce his party to levy a thunderbolt at the law that has run our pension bill up to the enormous sum mentioned. Pity he permitted his party to avert its virtuous face from this enormous expenditure and that provided for the river and harbor bill, and to content itself with furious denunciations of the corrupt head of the pension bureau. But political life is full of such inconsistencies.

Nearly 1900 years ago a wonderful man, well known to history, but not much talked of in political parties, made his appearance in an oriental country. He was an embodiment of truth. Plain people gathered around him and heard him speak with delight. I presume because he spoke and lived the truth the emanations from the truth of his life and words charmed and attracted such folk. It is not written that he drew to him those in authority, the wealthy or the elite of society. How could he do so, seeing that he was but an humble man and was clothed in the coarse garb of a mechanic? But on one occasion he went up "into a mountain" away from the multitude and when a few simple-hearted men (his disciples) gathered around him, history records it that he preached a sermon which has come down through all ages, and by common consent contains more truth than can be found in all the sermons of all the great divines who ever occupied the sacred desk.

One remarkable thing he said: "Whatsoever ye would that men should do unto you, do ye even so unto them." This sublime utterance has so impressed the human mind that men in Christendom, without exception, call it the "golden rule." So it is; but the author earned by its utterance the crown of thorns and death on the cross. Social and industrial justice has since that time been denied to the toiling and suffering classes, because truth has been on the cross wearing the crown of thorns. But truth is abroad once again among the common people, as of old; it is calling its own and its own is hearing the call. They are crowding to the front as in that olden time and thank God that times are now more auspicious than they were then. The inspiration leads them. They do not threaten, but they demand justice. All the vituperation that can be hurled at them, all the derision, all the denunciation known to the political vocabulary cannot turn them to the right or left. Thirty odd years ago many of them stood before the blazing cannon's mouth in defense of an abstraction. The burden of all the ages is now upon them—the heaped and piled up burden of injustice and wrong. To the idle thunderbolts of politicians, such men can only answer with a smile. The banner of right waves above them; they are moving to victory.

II

[The second speech was delivered in San Marcos. From the context it is not clear whether the date was 1892 or 1894. In addition to the generally voiced economic demands, there will be found here Nugent's own particular contribution: a discussion of the role of the reformer in history, and an enlarged conception of the conduct appropriate to the reform forces. Nugent emphasizes that the reformer must transcend his immediate historical context and look for more universal values of justice.]

There have been reformers in every age of the world. History is full of their schemes, their successes and defeats, their heroic lives and martyr deaths. In the temples of religion and the halls of legislation, in the forum and on the hustings, they have thundered denunciations at wrong and pleaded the cause of right. Political wrongs, social wrongs, religious wrongs— wrongs that destroyed liberty and created despotism; wrongs that have blighted innocence and extinguished hopes; wrongs that have aggrandized the few at the expense of the many, and brought conflict and disaster to the human race; wrongs sustained and supported by superstition, by tradition, by misguided affection; wrongs recent and old, in church and state; in the social system and family circle; wrongs of every kind and description have been in every age and among every people, the subject of their indignant protests; and in labor'ng for the suppression of these wrongs they have relinquished worldly honors, surrendered fortune and sacrificed life itself.

The darkest shadows upon human history have been cast by the persecution they have suffered, the defeats which have attended their efforts, and the cruel injustice they have received from those whom they have sought to protect and defend. But persecution and defeat have failed to entirely suppress them or destroy their work. Seemingly driven from his field of labor at times, whenever and wherever evil conditions have brought suffering and distress to earth's despairing multitudes, then and there the reformer has reappeared with the same devotion to the cause of humanity, the same self-abnegation, the same boundless confidence in his schemes of relief; and his reappearance has ever been signalized by the same outpouring of derision and contempt, the same misconstruction and opposition. To the man whose interests and prejudices were involved in the existing order of things, he has always appeared as the enemy of his kind, the disturber of the public peace, the fomenter of discontent among the people. Yes, he has been smitten to death by the hands whose shackles he unbound, and innocent women and children, the beneficiaries of his unselfish labors, have been taught to sing praises over the shedding of his blood. Unfortunately, he has not always been richly endowed with worldly wisdom—his knowledge of practical affairs, of the methods by which a selfish world does its business, has been limited. He has often times been "as harmless as doves," but, alas! how seldom "as wise as serpents." He is not always a man of insight. He sees the external wrong—the dark shadow upon the world's life. The injustice and suffering which evil conditions bring to the toiling multitude, the undeserved power and prestige which these same conditions bring to the favored few—poverty for the millions, vast, unearned wealth for the very few. All of this he sees and his very soul flames up in honest indignation at the awful and apparently hopeless inequality which has been the one universal product of all human efforts to organize and administer government. His schemes of relief have, for the most part, been directed against superficial evils—evils of administration or policy which reappear in spite of all palliatives. Now and then, indeed, noble men in whom the forces of evolution have in some mysterious way been focalized have arisen, and by pure weight of character have wrought changes of a more or less radical character in existing institutions, and thus have, so to speak, drawn the race to higher levels of political and social life. But even such exalted characters have never pierced to the core and uncovered the hidden causes of social evils. They have changed governments and policies and preserved to society its capacity to exist, to maintain its organic life and to receive and hold, through its crude and broken forms, the divine ideals which throughout the ages have been slowly but surely evolving to the surface of human life. Men as a rule, even those of the exceptionally gifted and nobler classes, have not, in thought or action, been able to transcend their external environments. The reformations started by them have run in grooves worn by existing social and political systems. Heredity and habits of thought and life have determined the scope and character of their efforts, hence social abuses have, in spite of those efforts, been transmitted from age to age, and the lines in which men now think are very much those which shaped human thought hundreds of years ago.

Men, from habit, become conservative. We learn to love what we are accustomed to, and misguided affection makes us cling with death-like tenacity to social and political institutions long after they have ceased to be useful or serviceable to the human race—yes, long after they have become the instruments of injustice and oppression. Luther's reformation corrected many abuses in the Romish church, but the Protestantism which he left to the world carries in its bosom the tyranny of opinion which, while greatly mitigating the severity of former church discipline, is quite effective in deterring men from too liberal indulgence of independent thought in the construction of doctrinal standards. The church does not compel a recantation on bended knees of obnoxious scientific opinions, but it puts a quietus on advanced thought by a resolution of its general assembly, lest the vulgar world, the laity, may be set to thinking outside of established theological lines. The methods of silencing Briggs is no doubt to be preferred to that applied to the tongue of poor Galileo, but both methods answered the purpose and both illustrate the tendency of institutions to perpetuate themselves by means of the veneration in which they are held and the dread which they inspire. Institutions represent public opinion, and public opinion is as potent as thumbscrews to repress independence and enslave thought. As long as the system remains we permit non-essential modifications, changes in methods, but revolt at radical innovations that would sweep away the system itself even for something better. Romanism reappears in Protestantism in a less severe form with apparently a larger tolerance and a more benignant spirit —but is still carrying in its bosom all of the possibilities of old Romanism as it existed in Luther's day.

There is this difference, as a writer suggests, modern civilization has too many material interests at stake to permit an extreme indulgence of the propensity to persecute. It puts its staying hand, therefore, upon the tendency to ecclesiastical domination, and thus unconsciously enables the liberal and humane sentiment to more fully assert itself in all the churches. But then this staying hand does not press against the system itself. This would be to shock and outrage inherited prejudices and affections which civilization finds it convenient and useful to foster, and civilization may be always depended upon to take care of its own. What is said here of churches may be also said of political parties. The latter may not be as pure and clean as the former, but in both, though by different modes and with different ends and motives, the spirit of domination asserts itself and is made effective by means of an imperious public opinion. In both there is rulership that will not brook opposition. Of course it is admitted that in both alike the resort to discipline is justified, though in different degrees, by conscience and what men regard as their highest duty to their fellows. But I speak of the fact as one to be considered in testing the quality and possible effects of any reform movement.

Take the great and wonderful religious movement begun by Wesley in the last century, or that started by Alexander Campbell some fifty years or more ago. Each of these movements resulted in the establishment of distinctly organized ecclesiastical bodies. No one can doubt the zeal, the philanthropy, or the good conscience of the membership of these religious organizations, but every dispassionate mind must see that so deeply involved in the affections of its members is each of these churches that any effort to change its simple customs or formulas would excite alarm and apprehension throughout the entire body. Some hardy reformer might, however, after years of toil and misconstruction, effect useful changes in these, but it would only be by leaving the essential features of the system untouched. Thus, in the course of time, even vital doctrines of the creed might vanish, while the system itself would remain to circumscribe and dominate human thought and effort for many generations. And this for the reason that affection, social custom, and the inexorable demands of conventional life would combine to prevent its displacement.

[After reviewing the record of the Democratic party in recent times, he states:]

. . . These men, with few exceptions, belong to the class of reformers who in all preceding ages have failed because of an inherited incapacity to think outside of or against the existing order. Broken gleams of truth reflected upon the dark surface of social life have thrown a grateful radiance over their minds and they have felt themselves warmed and thrilled with strange sympathy for the suffering and stricken multitude, but they have been overborne and trodden under foot by the sordid and selfish horde who bear the standards of the parties, dictate their policies and control the offices which they dispense as the spoils of victory. A political party thus marshalled and led is as relentless as an invading army, and the men who control its policy and run its campaigns would as readily as Caesar, Alexander or Bonaparte, convert the world into a human slaughter pen, if that were necessary to the gratification of their lust for dominion.

Reform from such source! Never, unless right is to be confounded with wrong and truth with fiction. But is there no hope of reform—no hope for the downtrodden and oppressed? Yes, there is hope; not "hope deferred that maketh the heart sick," but hope brightening and glowing with ever-increasing effulgence. Great, humane, cultured men have toiled through weary years of investigation, vainly endeavoring to solve the problems of human life, but few of them have ever penetrated beyond the mere physical basis of existence. Truth, lying within and above the existing order of things, only comes forth when conditions favor to stand in glorious transfiguration before men, and then only to men who win her as a bride. When the opportunity serves she reveals herself to those who reverently wait upon her coming—it may not be in full-orbed splendor, but it will always be in a vision of glory, although shadowed by human infirmities and circumscribed by human limitations. But truth is not found by mere searching; thinking alone does not disclose her. She is seen, loved, embraced as a bride, embodied in the spirit and the life. In all ages the wise and learned have sought her with longings unutterable, unquenchable; but it was given only to certain wise men to see her perfect star in the east; and that star led them to the babe in the manger, the "golden child" of promise. Since then men have been learning the law of human service. "He sleeps in God who wakes and toils with men," says the rarest of modern reformers. Here is the lesson—the rule—and he who works out the rule in practical life will know truth by an interior recognition far more convincing than any process of human reasoning. The Christ of history was not an ecclesiastic, nor a politician, nor a cultured theorist. He was a "man of the people." Little cared he for the petty differences among men—for their creeds and dogmas and beliefs. He came and taught and labored, not to inaugurate a system, but to reach and cure the world's ills which he clearly saw. . . .

. . . Yes, Christ saw the cause of human ills, and to reach and cure those ills he came, illustrating in his person and life the lowly condition of the multitude—those who chiefly bear the world's burdens, who feel the pressure of its hard conditions, and whose life longings are for relief that never comes until eternity brings light and hope to disperse the darkness and despair of time.

. . . I am not a theologian, nor even a member of any church, yet in this wonderful man and his work I see the ideal reformer, the one single, complete and symmetrical character of human history, giving his life to the work of arresting the evil tendencies inherent in the world's social and political institutions, upbearing the rule of absolute right in the face of an age given over to superstitious veneration for dead forms and

whose highest ideals never rose above the level of the merely
technical or legal.

. . . Here was the beginning of Christian socialism. A new
force was liberated into the world—vital, fundamental truths
thrown upon the currents of public thought, and thus sent
drifting down the ages. . . .

[With an analysis of the current situation, Nugent concludes:]

. . . But, as in the days when Christ preached reformation in
Judea, the common people are beginning to hear the truth
with gladness. The spirit of humanity which Christ left in the
world has not departed, although periodically subjected to
partial suppressions. It is here in this wonderful country of
ours and among our wonderful people. But it is kindling the
fires of reform, not among the socially or politically wise and
mighty, but among the untutored masses. In the popular heart
"deep is calling unto deep," and the social brotherhood is
slowly evolving and growing among the people as breast after
breast thrills responsively to the sound of that "calling." For
the present, so long as selfishness demands its law of competition, we can only hope to make a successful fight against monopoly—to give back to the people their ownership of public
utilities, to enact the "initiative and referendum" by which the
country's legislation shall be placed under the direct control
of the voters, to recognize the supremacy of the individual in
matters of private concern, to restore to the commercial and
social world the lost ideas of equity and justice, thus to un-
trammel legitimate industries and skill and leave them to
pursue in freedom the beneficent work of producing wealth;
and this reform movement necessarily must, upon humane and
economic grounds, include "free trade throughout the world"
within its scheme of remedies.

What may be beyond that which is here outlined, only He
can know who holds the destinies of the world in the hollow
of His hand. Human selfishness must, of necessity, place limi-

tations upon every social or political movement. If it shall ever be transcended, the glorified industries will arise in orderly unity and harmony like the "City of God," and the dream of Bellamy will be a realized fact in concrete social life. As yet, such a state can only, as the millenium, exist in hope. Already Jeffersonian simplicity is transcended—composite age is dawning upon the world with its quickening and uplifting power.

The transformations already effected and which yet impend are largely due to the fundamental, political truths taught by Jefferson. A crude generation appropriated them only to the demands of an extreme, selfish individualism, but the opening epoch will appropriate them to the demands of social and political justice.

III

[In his opening speech for the gubernatorial race in 1894 in Grandview, Texas, Nugent uses the Pullman strike as the point of departure for the following characterization of American society.]

. . . These industrial paroxysms are, however, object lessons, and they have in large measure disclosed to the masses what has been for some time apparent to the philosophical student of recent history, viz.; that the spirit of plutocratic capitalism is the dominating force in our organized social and industrial life. Yes, it gathers the fruits of industry and divides them at its will. It controls and manipulates with almost unbridled power and license, every function of trade and finance. Its speculative lust finds opportunities of gain in the tolls levied upon the right to occupy the earth. It denies to the people the heritage which the Creator gave them "without money and without price." It gathers into its storehouse the bounties which nature designed for the common use of all. The treasures of soil and forest, of water, and air, and sunshine, are poured at its feet. The subtle forces that run their mysterious circuits in invisible realms are chained to its chariot wheels. It robs genius of its glory, makes of intellect a drudge and a slave, and utilizes the achievements of science to raid the stock markets and enlarge the margin of profits. Thus it wipes out as with a sponge the distinction between right and wrong, makes merchandise of the noblest ideals, sets gain before the world as the highest end of life, and converts men into predatory human animals. As another has said, it substitutes the "rule of gold for the golden rule;" and after devoting six days of the week to the prosecution of schemes for the exploitation of labor, on the seventh it invades the sanctuaries of religion, where its votaries may often be found close to the holy altar, joining with seeming reverence in services rendered to the incarnate spirit of truth and love. Fortunately, for our christian civilization, there are heroic men and women from whose minds the foul spirit of greed has not been able to drive the sweet ideals planted in the world's thought by the Son of the Galilean carpenter. But for these, spiritual hope would perish from the Earth. Capital could never have attained such ascendancy, but for the legislation which has given it unjust advantages and enabled it to monopolize both natural resources and public functions and utilities. Every person is entitled by the law of natural justice to possess and enjoy the fruits of his own skill and industry. Give to all equal opportunities, and under the operation of this law each would get his just share of the world's wealth; but give to any man the right to take not only the produce of his own labor but a portion of that which is derived from the labor of his neighbor, and you unjustly increase his opportunities of gain. Give to a few individuals organized into a corporation the right to dispense for a price services of a necessary and public character—services essential to the existence and well-being of organized society—and you arm them with the power to levy tribute upon the whole community, and acquire wealth almost without limit. You in other words provide for those consummate products of present economic conditions, the millionaire and the tramp.

By the telegraph, telephone and railway monopolies, the monopolies of money and land, it is easy to see that we have placed in the hands of individuals and corporations the power to levy toll upon all the productive industry of the country— to virtually place all the labor of the country under tribute to a mere fraction of the population. And when we consider the vast and all pervading power and influence acquired by means of industries thus brought under the dominion of the few, every intelligent mind must see at a glance, that we could not in any other way have provided conditions so favorable to the undue concentration of wealth. And let it be remembered, that it is not the excessive production of wealth, but its unequal distribution, which constitutes the menacing evil of the times. Under normal conditions, the greater the production of wealth, the more widely diffused would be its benefits. As population increases and society becomes more highly organized, so ought the means and facilities of civilized life to be more and more within the reach of the great body of the people, and the comforts and conveniences of life to more and more abound. The point ought to be thus reached at which poverty would disappear. Such a condition could only be brought about, however, in a community all of whose members were afforded fair opportunity for the exertion of their faculties; for thus only could each be enabled to produce a proportion of the common stock of wealth and participate in the general enrichment derived from the co-operating efforts of all. In such a community there could be no material waste, no check in production, no limitation to the aggregate wealth by means of monopoly or the possession of unjust advantages. To produce results of this kind, nothing is needed but to destroy monopoly in those things which productive industry must have for practical use. Protect these from the speculative greed of men, disembarrass trade of arbitrary legal interference, give free play to competition within the proper sphere of individual effort and investment, and steadily oppose those extreme socialistic schemes which seek by the outside pressure of mere enactments or systems, to accomplish what can only come from the free activities of men—do these things, and you will have achieved the real, genuine and lasting reforms which labor and capital equally need, and which in fact are the only practical reforms lying within the range of party action.

The social condition is now almost desperate, and it is not confined to our own country. Both its evils and its causes are world-wide. Senator Stewart, exceptionally well informed on such subjects, says that "the wages of 60,000,000 people now living upon the globe average from one cent to six cents a day," and we know that in this country statistics show that 91 per cent. of the population own only 29 per cent. of the aggregate wealth. Millionaires are so common and wealth accumulations so rapid, that it seems only a question of a few years when Billionaires will make their appearance. Inevitably, as the concentration of wealth goes on, pauperism must continue to grow and spread among the people. Already in Paris, France, one out of every eighteen, and in London, England, one out of every forty of the population are paupers; and yet in both cities the wealth of the few is fabulous. That the monopolization of land and transportation facilities is chiefly instrumental in producing the concentrations of wealth which all recognize and deplore is conspicuously shown in the case of the Astors, whose real estate values mount into the hundreds of millions of dollars, and that of the Vanderbilts, who have absorbed possibly even more of the national wealth. These are merely striking illustrations of what every man with open eyes may read in facts lying within the common reach of all.

Nor need we think that this vast concentration of wealth in the hands of the few is in this country without its unhappy effects on the balance of the population. In the larger cities and the more densely populated rural districts pauperism is increasing. Mr. Flower in his little book "Civilization's Inferno," has given unimpeachable evidence of the existence of poverty and wretchedness in Boston, the Athens of America, so utterly squalid and hopeless that one with the horrible picture before his mental vision is almost tempted to doubt whether justice has any place in the affairs of men. Yet such conditions exist in all the larger cities where wealth accumulations are greatest.

Wages have only been maintained by labor organizations; but recent events convey the warning, that the apprehension of strikes will soon have spent its force, and then corporate wealth, no longer under its spell, will boldly throw off the mask behind which it has been masquerading as the friend of labor, and freely cut wages to enhance the gains of capital. The example of the Pullman Company will not be without its legitimate fruit; but while it carries to corporate wealth throughout the country a suggestive illustration of how the workingman may be fleeced and robbed with impunity, it may serve to accentuate the evil of monopoly which now overshadows and darkens the world's productive labor. Pullman's monopoly from the standpoint of capital, is simply ideal. Here is a corporation owning a tract of land on which it has erected a great car-building plant, churches, schoolhouses, and dwelling houses in which to keep its thousands of employes. It waters its stock, until property representing $10,000,000 of invested capital is converted into a dividend paying investment of more than $36,000,000.00, without the addition of a dollar of real value. To enable it to continue its periodical dividend payments and so maintain the value of this watered stock, it cuts the wages of its employes in a period of depression and panic, but still remorselessly collects its exorbitant rent. Here the laborer is both tenant and employe—the victim at once of both usury and rent. He is dependent upon Pullman for work, for the opportunity to earn wages, to feed and clothe his family—he is dependent upon Pullman for standing-place on the earth. Thus Pullman holds a monopoly of the land which is nature's divinely given opportunity to work, and of the opportunity artificially created by the investment of capital. By the wages which Pullman pays to his employe, the employe is enabled to pay rent to Pullman. When wages cease, rent ceases; but eviction follows the cessation of rent. Thus the apprehension of eviction which means loss of home to the laborer and his family, hangs perpetually over the latter to enforce silence and submission, when wages are cut to make dividends for fictitious stock. If the situation suggests the impolicy of cutting wages, capital may still maintain its margin of profit by raising the scale of rent. In a big city land values are ever advancing, and the landlord finds in this fact an always present justification for increasing rent. Who will contend that the employe of Pullman, working under such conditions, is a free-man. Yet, the employes of every mining corporation in the country, except in the few instances in which the local laws have afforded some mitigation, are in a condition of servitude even worse, if possible, than that which prevails at Pullman. Extend the two-fold scheme of monopoly and spoliation so cunningly devised by the Pullman Company to all the corporations handling large investments in mining, manufacturing and mechanical pursuits, and the condition of the wage-worker and artisan would become utterly hopeless and helpless. And that our public policies must rapidly carry us in this direction has been made more evident by the recent injection of the element of force into the settlement of labor disputes. Heretofore, controversies between railroad companies and their employes, although accompanied by the incidental stoppage of the mails and the interruption of interstate commerce, have not been regarded as presenting conditions of violence justifying the use of the regular army.

[Nugent develops further his generally favorable view of property.]

. . . The power with which the corporations are now armed cannot be overcome by strikes, which at best are unwise and oftentimes unjustifiable. Besides, the conditions they leave behind are frequently worse than those which aroused and provoked them. In addition to all of this, it must be remembered, that corporations are but aggregations of individuals, and individuals are very much alike in whatever business or pursuit they may be engaged. Unfortunately the laboring man is not always unselfish, but, fortunately, the capitalist is not always sordid. It is a fact that calls for grateful recognition, that among all classes, in every trade, business, or calling, there are noble, humane, fair-minded men, whose sympathies quickly respond to the demands of justice, whose hearts are deeply affected by wrongful conditions, and who are not practical reformers battling for the people's rights because, involved in the general movement and organized social life of the times, the view-point from which they regard economic questions prevents them from recognizing fundamental truths which are now rapidly coming forth into the common thought of the people. Wealth acquired in legitimate ways, by the exercise of the industry and skill and the investment of capital, cannot hurt either its possessor or the community. It is the spirit of gain run to riot in monopolies, that poisons and corrupts the fountains of individual and social life: and against this spirit must the efforts of populists be directed. But in combatting monopoly, let us never forget that neither force nor infringement of individual liberty is justifiable or safe. Let us remember that we ought above all others to set ourselves against anarchy in every form, against every measure calculated to break down the security which the laws afford to private property, and in favor only of those lawful and orderly methods which can always be successfully defended, and the observance of which will never fail to enlist for the workingman the sympathies of the good and worthy people of every class. Let us cultivate the duty of submission to lawful authority, and in times of civil commotion, be first to give it support in its conflicts with the lawless. A good cause committed to violent methods inevitably finds in them its grave. An intelligent ballot is the only refuge of justice and liberty. . . .

[In closing, Nugent urges that a proper balance be struck between capital and labor.]

. . . Finally, fellow citizens, let me say that the great, vital, controlling question of the times is the "labor question." A thorough analysis of the situation discloses this "question of questions" lying at the center of the social difficulties into which our country has been led. Solve this question, so that the man who produces wealth shall own a just proportion of it, and those difficulties will vanish as mists before the rising sun. Labor, slowly rising from the dust of ages, stands at last erect upon its feet. Already it confronts capital, not to provoke strife, but for reconciliation and peace. It does not ask charity, it demands justice. It does not ask that capital be enslaved, but that it, the age-old burden-bearer be made free. It demands for itself, not superiority, but equality; and it knows by a wise instinct that, in the opening epoch now dawning upon the world, equality is coming to it in the sure unfoldings of God's providence. This it knows; and it rejoices that in that day of deliverance the doom of "special privileges" shall be pronounced, and "equal rights" shall come to all alike.

IV

[The fourth speech, where Nugent develops the notion of inconvertible paper, was given before the state meeting of the Farmers' Alliance, at Lampasas, in August 1895.]

Prior to the civil war there was no silver question in this country—that is, no question involving the proposition to permanently demonetize silver, or limit its coinage. If it existed in the mind of any public man of prominence, whose views could have had any serious effect on the public policies of the times, it was prudently kept from the masses. It is true, that to meet a contingency, Mr. Jefferson directed the mints to cease coining silver dollars; that to meet another contingency the ratio was changed in 1834, and that to meet still another supposed contingency, the act of 1853 reduced the weight of the minor coins and limited their legal tender qualities to payments not exceeding five dollars. Yet, during all these years, no leading public man ever suggested that the mints should be closed to either metal, or that either should have less of debt-paying capacity than the other. There must have been cogent reasons for this eighty years of failure to raise a question which is now agitating the popular mind throughout the length and breadth of the country. The period embraced between 1792 and 1860 was largely devoted to the study and discussion of the federal constitution. Almost every important question of public policy, which gave rise to political differences, and determined party alignments, was either settled upon constitutional grounds, or involved one or more questions of constitutional construction.

[From what follows it can be seen that Nugent's stress is not on free silver per se, but on the national banking system.]

. . . Daniel Webster had said, "I am clearly of the opinion that gold and silver, at rates fixed by congress, constitute the legal standard of value in this country, and that neither congress or any state has authority to establish any other standard or to displace this standard."

This was at the time the accepted doctrine, and it had worked its way into the popular apprehension, and had stood without question since the organization of our government. "The congress shall have the power to coin, and fix the standard of weights and measures." The constitutional duty of congress was fully discharged only when it provided for the coinage of silver and gold, the great money metals in use at the adoption of the constitution, at a ratio decreed by law.

This view prevailed among all classes of our people during the whole period antedating the civil war. The money power in view of this invincible public sentiment was discreet enough not to raise the question of demonetization with respect to the coinage of our own mints. It waited until the war had left its demoralizing effects upon public thought and morals, and the people were divided over sectional issues, and then proceeded to accomplish the work it feared to undertake in the fifties. It has succeeded in practically demonetizing silver, but its great undertaking is not yet achieved. The question now before the country is not whether gold shall constitute the actual circulating medium. The people who are now clamoring for the gold standard do not pretend, if they succeed, that the yellow metal will go into actual, bodily circulation, and do money duty in the channels of trade. They are wise enough to know that, if the world were forced to depend upon gold for its actual circulating money, it would be impossible to hold the masses down. For the overthrow of such a system, the world of despairing and suffering men would rise up in open revolt—with arms in their hands if need be. The question at the bottom of this great agitation is larger and more far reaching even than the question of what the redemption money of the country shall be. The real, vital and comprehensive question is what shall be the permanent financial system of the United States. Mr. Cleveland, and those who accept his views, in response to this question, are now proposing to establish a monetary system involving: 1st, the elimination of all forms of paper currency issued by the government; 2d, the use of bank paper as a circulating medium for the country; 3d, the use of gold only as a redemption fund or base for bank paper.

It will be seen at a glance that this system will virtually delegate to the banks the money-issuing power of the government, and compel the people to look to private corporations for their money supply. Now under such a system the gold coinage will do duty simply as reserves in the vaults of the banks as a fund kept hoarded and out of circulation, to serve as a basis to hold up bank credits. It will be remembered, that Mr. Cleveland's policy, during his two administrations, has been to discontinue silver coinage, and withdraw the greenbacks, funding them in interest-bearing bonds, to be used by the banks in floating their notes. Indeed, the policy, which he has with great consistency and courage persisted in since his first election, found appropriate expression in the plan submitted by Mr. Carlisle to the last session of Congress. This plan was simply that of the bankers, formulated at Baltimore, with a few modifications, and involved the elimination of the various forms of government paper from the circulation, and the issue of bank notes as the sole paper currency of the country. Let us submit this proposed system to the test of reason. Prof. Taussig, of Harvard University, a distinguished advocate of the gold standard, in an article in the *Popular Science Monthly,* after commenting on the extent to which paper substitutes for money are used, says: "It has been attempted to obviate the dangers arising from the use of paper substitutes by enlarging the basis of specie; and the wider use of silver is advocated as one method of broadening the base of the superstructure. But efforts in this direction are likely to have but temporary results. A broader basis of specie is likely, under the same forces which now lead to an extended use of credits, to bring about in due time an expansion of credit machinery in some way proportionate to the enlarged foundation on which it rests. The surer method, and that which is developing under the stress of need and the growth of experience, is to strengthen the foundation rather than to enlarge it. The specie which serves as the basis of the swelling volume of credit transactions is massed in fewer hands, and so is made more effective in sustaining the super-structure. The great public banks of European countries are guardians of the treasure which gives tone to their currency and serves as the standard for transactions in which it is used to less and less extent in bodily shape." The professor, in alluding to the possible increase or diminution of silver production concludes his article as follows: "In either case silver ceases to be the basis on which countries of advanced civilization rest their monetary system, not so much for physi-cal unfitness, as from the increasing use of a more refined and highly developed medium of exchange, needing for its founda-tion a moderate supply of specie, having a stable and uniform value." I have quoted from the writings of this accomplished man, for the purpose of disclosing more fully than can be gathered from our current political discussions, the plan or scheme of finance, which the administration is so actively promoting. There is consistency at least in this plan, and it can easily be comprehended. It recognizes the indisputable fact that civilization demands a more refined circulation than the coins, and virtually concedes, as Mr. Sherman some time ago declared, that paper is destined to be that circulation. Now, so far, populists can have no serious quarrel with the system. They have been for years saying what these gold advocates now admit, viz: that the world's business cannot be done with gold and silver alone, and that resort must be had to paper currency to supplement these metals. Indeed, populists recognize the utility of banks as business agencies. They know that they do an important and useful work in affording the trading world the means of rapid and effective exchange, and in keeping its financial books. They are willing that banks of discount and exchange shall, with proper safeguards, remain until the advance in social thought shall enable the government to take charge very largely of the country's banking.

But they will not consent that the purely public and social function of dispensing money to the people shall be turned over to private banking corporations, whose sole motive in discharging such a function can only be the ordinary human desire for gain. Here, therefore, they part company with the gold men. Narrow the base of circulation by limiting it to gold—strengthen the base by massing the gold in the vaults of the banks; then give to the bankers the monopoly of the business of supplying the country with paper money thus based! The policy implied in this scheme is to limit rather than inflate the currency; in fact, it proposes to provide against inflation except in so far as the bankers themselves may come to see the necessity of increasing the money supply. Note the language of Mr. Taussig, in stating his objection to the broadening of the base of circulation by adding silver: "A broader basis of specie is likely . . . . to bring about an expansion of credit machinery in some way proportioned to the enlarged foundation." Of course the "surer method" proposed by him inevitably narrows the base and reduces the volume of credit money so that it shall not be out of proportion to the diminished foundation. The "massing" of gold in the hands of the bankers will give "tone" to the credit circulation, and prevent the inflation that might result from the enlargement of the "foundation" by the addition of silver! This is the monetary system which we are promised by the gold people, at a time when the productive capacity of our population is growing as never before. Consider the fact that, by the invention and application of labor-saving machinery, the capacity of our seventy millions of people to produce wealth has been augmented tenfold over that of the same number of people a hundred years ago—that, to express it more plainly, these seventy millions of progressive, energetic and speculative people can, by means of their mastery of natural and mechanical forces, which the inventive genius of the age has given them, produce more wealth within a given time than could have been produced a hundred years ago by 700 millions of people similarly endowed with mental and physical capacity; consider that this immense productive capacity, under the spur of constantly improving facilities for intercommunication, and the exchange of wealth has developed a commensurate volume of trade, so that the annual commercial transactions of this country, in the judgment of competent men, now closely approximate, if they do not amount to, the inconceivable sum of $100,000,000,000; consider also, that we are adding to our population at the rate of more than a million souls per annum, many of whom are wealth producers from abroad, and that the volume of transactions is thereby greatly augmented year by year; consider also, that improvements in the means of transportation and the transmission of intelligence have practically brought widely separated communities and nations close together, thus enabling them to trade more easily and rapidly, and thus giving additional impulse to the constantly swelling volume of business; consider that the protection afforded by quarantine and improved scientific sanitation against the spread of infectious or contagious diseases, and the longer intervals between great wars resulting from the spread of humane, Christian thought, have practically fixed the enormous annual increase of population in this and other countries as permanent wealth producers in the world's industrial system, thus guaranteeing a steady, rapid and unbroken growth in production and trade; consider that by almost universal consent the supply of gold for monetary use is not likely (to use Prof. Taussig's language) to increase rapidly in the future; that the "use of gold in the arts is apparently increasing and is likely to continue to increase and that it absorbs a growing part of the annual supply," and consider finally that the highest authority concedes the necessity of a steady increase in the circulating medium to meet the demands of the rapidly increasing wealth and population and the constantly enlarging volume of trade.

Consider all this, and then endeavor to compass the awful significance and the possible effects of this world-wide movement to limit the world's primary money to gold alone, to turn over all this gold to a few people inspired and actuated only by the desire of gain, and give them in perpetuity a monopoly of the business of furnishing money to the balance of the population of the globe! The absolute atrocity of such a scheme, the depth of poverty and distress and the utter enslavement which it promises to millions, even hundreds of millions of human creatures, can scarcely be conceived by the average mind!

I have shown that the scheme of the gold men does not contemplate that gold shall ever be circulated; that it in fact proposes to drive gold out of circulation. In this the system cannot be an improvement upon the proposal of silver men to open the mints to the free coinage of silver. For if free silver will drive gold out of circulation (assuming it to be in fact in circulation) the country will no more have the benefit of gold circulation, if by Mr. Carlisle's system the gold is locked up in the vaults of the banks. In fact, however, gold is not in circulation at this time, the Treasury reports to the contrary notwithstanding. The *Dallas News* a few days ago published a statement of Mr. Kilpatrick, sub-treasurer of the United States at New Orleans, which purported, among other things, to give the "gold and silver coins" in circulation on August 1 of the present year. The gold circulation is put by this statement at $485,778,610, and the silver circulation at $51,746,706. One might well ask where all of this gold is circulating. I shall not risk anything if I say that it is not doing money duty among the masses. In Texas, at least, it rarely shows itself in actual transactions, while silver is apparently doing full duty, entering into almost every business transaction where money is used at all. If, therefore, silver is in such common use, and gold so rarely employed in actual transactions, seemingly a little less than $52,000,000 of silver is doing more effective work as a circulating medium than $485,000,000 of gold. The truth is, gold is now hoarded— piled up largely in the vaults of the banks—in anticipation of the success of the present gold propaganda. He who has gold in his clutches, when the Cleveland-Carlisle financial policy is enacted into law, will find himself equipped with power to gather spoils from labor, and put the burdens of slavery on the backs of toiling men. Bear this in mind; gold has practically already disappeared from the channels of trade; it cannot, therefore, be driven out by silver; but silver and other forms of currency are needed to take its place, and ultimately force it back into circulation, or drive it out permanently to the peace, prosperity and happiness of all honest, patriotic citizens.

But the scheme under discussion involves the continuance of the national banking system, with all the perils to the country which arise out of it. The experience of recent years has shown quite plainly that the bank classes are solidly welded together in the fixed determination to control the financial and currency legislation of the country. To do this they must necessarily act in unity, and this is effected by means of their national and state associations. It is folly to deny this. There are, indeed, individual bankers who dissent from the views of the majority of this class of citizens, but they exercise no influence whatever. Even the great banker St. John, who stands for popular rights on the great question of the coinage, and whose views are the result of years of philosophical and scientific study, is powerless to check, in the faintest degree, the movement, which the combined and organized plutocracy has set on foot in this country to force upon the government this stupendous scheme of spoliation and wrong. Backed as these people are by any amount of money, by the metropolitan press, by the shrewdest politicians and the ablest lawyers in the country, the amount of political influence they can bring to bear in effectuating their purpose must be seen to be perilous in the extreme to our free institutions. The fact that individual bankers are honest, upright gentlemen, is of small account. As a class they are inspired by the single selfish purpose of gain. Put them in control of the government and no man can measure the unhappy effects upon the masses of the people, which the policy they boldly advocate must inevitably bring about.

There is but one remedy. As Mr. Jefferson said with reference to banks of issue, "Carthago delenda est." The national banking system, like Carthage of old, must be destroyed, and the national government must no longer be permitted to farm out its credit to corporations to be used for private gain. In the monetary policy of the government we must demand equal rights for all, special privileges for none—a principle wholly ignored by the scheme of the gold man.

. . . Our population is spread over an immense, fertile territory, and notwithstanding the artificial scarcity of land produced by excessive holdings for speculative purposes,—they find access to it in some form, though to a constantly diminishing extent, as proprietors. So that, although distress and poverty exist in the dense centers of population in most aggravated and alarming forms, and in somewhat milder forms elsewhere, we present to people of other countries a seeming of general prosperity. Yet even here, as the general aggregate wealth of the nation increases, so the hungry mouths and ill clad bodies increase, so grow upon us poverty, insanity and crime. We are erecting, apparently, a splendid civilization, and yet its heart is being eaten out by the insatiate spirit of greed. The monster who stands over that civilization, ready in the very exhilaration of baleful success to suffocate and destroy it, is Shylock. Usury, land monopoly, these two stand before the growing public intelligence as the twin criminals of all the ages. They are responsible for all the want and misery, that mortal man or woman or child has suffered; their buried victims of bygone centuries in ghastly throngs rise up to condemn them, and as the sun of truth mounts to heaven, they must get themselves in readiness for the sure destruction which awaits them.

But, it is said that the laboring man's dollar will buy more than at any time in our history, and that this is due to the policy which has put us upon the gold standard. Why, then, are so many men struggling for the same dollar? Why the Pullman strike of last year, the outpourings of thousands of penniless working men, the marshaling of military forces, the declaration of martial law, the unseemly haste in resorting to courts for injunctions against the striking laborers, the quick condemnation and imprisonment of Debs, the labor leader? Why all these labor organizations—these combinations formed to keep up wages? Why does discontent pervade the ranks of laboring men throughout the whole country? If wages are high, if a dollar will buy more of the products of labor than ever before, and if this increased purchasing power of the dollar is such an inestimable boon to the laboring man, then surely men who work for wages ought to be contented and happy and prosperous. But on the contrary, the laboring classes live constantly under the apprehension both of wage reduction and the loss of jobs. The high wages paid skilled workmen in certain lines of production afford no test of the situation.

It is the fact, rather, that there are millions of laborers skilled and unskilled, who get no jobs and hence no wages at all. No financial or economic system can be good which tolerates such conditions of idleness and poverty as prevail in this country. The demand which labor makes is, not that it be fed by the charity of government or individuals, but that it be given fair opportunities to exert itself; that social and economic conditions be so adjusted that every laboring man will find, not a job artificially created for him by a makeshift of legislation, but employment freely coming to him from the liberated, enlarged and rivivified productive forces—coming to him in fact under such beneficent changes in our laws and public policies that he can hold in his firm and honest grasp all of the fruits of his labor. But again, an honest dollar that would bring benefits and blessings to the laboring man ought equally to benefit all other classes. Labor in its various forms produces the nation's wealth. This is the ultimate truth. The exchange of this wealth constitutes all of the diversified business of the country. The vast throng of busy thousands who produce this wealth also in large measure consume it. If they are now in possession of an ample supply of sound money, they must exchange it for this wealth.

How is it, then, that all men of all classes complain of hard times, and chiefly of the difficulty of obtaining money with which to gratify their wants or carry on business? Why is it that so much of this wealth cannot be exchanged at all? Why, to specialize a little, does the farmer find it so difficult to sell his horse, his corn, his hogs, his crops, in fact, any part of his personal property except at ruinously low prices? Why is it, when property enters into competition with money, it inevitably goes to the wall? Why is it that the money owner does not care to buy property and cannot be induced to invest his money in productive enterprises? Is it not that money is enormously valuable as compared with property and commodities? And, as money has value in proportion to the quantity of it out, do not such conditions show beyond question that the monetary circulation is insufficient, and that the dollar which buys so much of the products of labor, is dwarfing and stinting trade and preventing the free and rapid exchange of commodities?

[Nugent then goes on to explain how the Populists differ from the silver forces.]

. . . From every point of view, this system, to which the national administration is so wedded, can only be regarded as one in the interest of the people who aspire to control the world's money supply. To the millions it means slavery. But the silver democrats, seemingly more liberal in their financial views, propose to adhere to the use of paper money, but they want this to be issued by the government without the intervention of banks, and they want to broaden the base of this circulation by adding silver to it. In other words they want free coinage of gold and silver at the present ratio, and government treasury notes, or promises to pay, convertible into coin (gold and silver). Here is a recognition of the necessity of paper money. So far we have no quarrel with the silver democrats. But their kind of paper money does not suit populists. It creates a public debt to be paid off in some way and at some time. So long as it exists it will constantly invite attacks from the people who now so clamorously assert that the greenbacks constitute the weak element in our financial system. The money power of this country will not let go its hold upon the government so long as the financial legislation of this country affords it the opportunity to make gain by the manipulation of the public funds or money. So long as government notes redeemable in coin are in circulation, they will always find it practicable to deplete the national treasury of its coin reserve. The fact that they have done so in recent years makes it altogether certain that they will continue to do so in the future. The United States treasury is today dependent upon the Rothschild-Morgan syndicate for the preservation of the gold reserve against the attacks of combinations formed to deplete it.

When this protection is withdrawn the reserve will go, unless, to perpetuate the reign of honest money, Cleveland should again purchase a similar immunity by subsidizing the Rothschild-Morgan combine. If this is the condition now, what will it be if the silver democrats triumph? The banks and syndicates will not stand by them—on the contrary, will hold themselves aloof, watching for the opportunity to go in and gather the spoils. It is useless to say they cannot do this. Experience, if not common sense, warns us that they can. They will not let go so long as convertible paper exists to induce speculative raids on the metallic reserves, or invite efforts in favor of some funding schemes from which they may gain profit. But if this menace to the public funds should not exist, where will the government get its supply of gold and silver to serve as the base for its own credit money? It can only get it from its own revenues or by issuing coin bonds. Our silver democratic friends, equally with populists, scout the idea of selling bonds in time of peace. They must, therefore, depend upon such coin as may be derived from the current revenues. This, as may be easily seen, will afford but a meager sum—an insufficient "base" upon which to supply 70,000,000 of people with a circulating medium. Confessedly, this scheme must be kept within the limits of safe banking, and, therefore, the supply of treasury notes must be limited to a sum greatly below the wants of the country. If, however, it be supposed that the government can with impunity extend its credit beyond the limits of safe banking and therefore issue its notes to any amount, the answer is, money-getters care as little for the government as for individuals; they understand that as the volume of credit paper expands, the facilities for making raids upon the coin base will proportionately increase, and they will not be slow to avail themselves of such favorable opportunities for gain at the expense of the public funds. This will become clear when we reflect, that it is not proposed to put us on a paper basis, but to maintain specie payments. During the greenback period just after the war, specie payments were suspended, and there was no coin in circulation. As long as this condition continued, greenbacks circulated freely, and there was no fear of a corner on a redemption fund. Only since the resumption of specie payment, under the act of 1875, have withdrawals of gold from the treasury been possible by means of the control of government paper. This paper being payable on demand, how will the silver democrats be able to hold their silver and gold reserves intact, if they attempt to float an enormously disproportionate quantity of convertible notes? With a volume of credit money out of all just proportion to the metallic base, withdrawals of coin will become all the more easy, and the difficulty of maintaining the volume of paper circulation must be greatly enhanced. The fact is, that the small reserve of coin must either restrict the paper issues below the wants of trade, or imperil those issues if enlarged sufficiently to afford a just supply of circulation to the country. There is in fact no compromise between the paper system of the gold men and that of the populists. Populists favor the free and unlimited coinage of gold and silver at the present ratio, and the emission of inconvertible paper to supply any lack of circulation, thus to make the entire volume of money sufficient to supply the demands of trade. We cannot compromise on the perilous plan proposed by silver democrats.

[Nugent then draws the important distinction between the increased production of wealth and the actual distribution of wealth.]

. . . The aggregate wealth has increased, and will continue to increase, however small the compensation labor is permitted to receive. Reduce it to a bare living, and compel it to serve in rags and filth, and it will still produce wealth rather than starve. The rags and filth will not cast a shadow on the beautiful creations of industry, even though they come fresh from the hovels of poverty to minister to the taste and comfort of those who "neither toil nor spin." The structure of wealth must still rise, even if the prostrate and tortured form of labor lies beneath its gilded foundation. It is not that the world grows more wealthy as the years pass, which gives labor its cause of complaint—it is rather the fact, that labor can only, under its present conditions, have such a portion of that which it creates as suffices to forever keep it dependent and enslaved—that, in fact, it must sit like Lazarus beneath the tables of the world's robbers, to pick up the crumbs and have the sores upon its body licked by the dogs. There is wealth enough and to spare, but it goes to the pampered few. Let us not forget that the millions of toilers are in more pressing need of remedy that shall prevent the unjust concentration of wealth, than they are for one which only can insure the increased production of wealth.

PART THREE

JUSTICE FOR THE OUTCAST:

I

THE UNEMPLOYED

Populists stood almost alone in the 1890's in befriending the men who had been chewed up by the economic system and spewed out over the dark landscape of unemployment and hunger—the men derisively labeled tramps and vagabonds by a society unwilling to concede that the concentration of wealth was accompanied by widespread social misery. These were men who wanted to work but who could find no work to do and consequently wandered from town to town looking for jobs, then tasks, then meals, then bread—until there was nothing left but despair and jail. And these were men who filled the ranks of the large reserve army of labor, and who soon joined an even more pathetic army, the industrial armies of Coxey and others, who walked from all parts of America to Washington as a living petition to present their grievances to Congress. For Populists, the so-called tramp symbolized the increasing number who had been thrown off the land and displaced from the factory, and who now could not even find work at subsistence wages. But more, Populists felt the tramp was not only a symbol of hardship but that he personified the tendencies found in industrial capitalism. Through his person one could see the vicious circle of high profits, the introduction of labor-saving machinery, low wages as more and more men competed against each other for fewer and fewer openings, then still higher profits, still lower wages, still more men forcing the wage scale down, until finally one had the tramp as the logical outcome of the economic system. Populists maintained that capitalism created the superfluous man.

34. The Tramp Circular

In the first selection, Governor Lorenzo D. Lewelling of Kansas speaks out to the municipal police commissioners of the state against the punishment of those who are searching for work. Although his directive concerned the immediate situation in Kansas, Lewelling saw the problem in the larger context of how industrial societies in their formative stages seek to discipline the emerging labor force so that there will be a ready supply of workers at hand. To accomplish this, men must first be stripped of any vestiges of independence and transformed to a dependent, helpless condition. This executive proclamation, issued on December 4, 1893, was termed by contemporaries "The Tramp Circular."

In the reign of Elizabeth, the highways were filled with throngs of the unemployed poor, who were made to "move on," and were sometimes brutally whipped, sometimes summarily hanged, as "sturdy vagrants" or "incorrigible vaga-

Reprinted from *Daily Capital* (Topeka), Dec. 5, 1893. Kansas State Historical Society.

bonds." In France, just previous to the revolution, the punishment of being poor and out of work was, for the first offense, a term of years in the galleys, for the second offense the galleys for life. In this country, the monopoly of labor-saving machinery and its devotion to selfish instead of social use, have rendered more and more human beings superfluous, until we have a standing army of the unemployed numbering even in the most prosperous times not less than one million able-bodied men; yet, until recently it was the prevailing notion, as it is yet the notion of all but the work-people themselves and those of other classes given to thinking, that whosoever, being able-bodied and willing to work can always find work to do, and Section 571 of the General Statutes of 1889 is a disgraceful reminder how savage even in Kansas has been our treatment of the most unhappy of our human brothers.

The man out of work and penniless is, by this legislation, classed with "confidence men." Under this statute and city ordinances of similar import, thousands of men, guilty of no crime but poverty, intent upon no crime but that of seeking employment, have languished in the city prisons of Kansas or performed unrequited toil on "rock piles" as municipal slaves, because ignorance of economic conditions had made us cruel. The victims have been the poor and humble for whom police courts are courts of last resort—they cannot give bond and appeal. They have been unheeded and uncared for by the busy world which wastes no time visiting prisoners in jail. They have been too poor to litigate with their oppressors, and thus no voice from this underworld of human woe has ever reached the ear of the appellate court, because it was nobody's business to be his brother's keeper.

But those who sit in the seats of power are bound by the highest obligation to especially regard the cause of the oppressed and helpless poor. The first duty of the government is to the weak. Power becomes fiendish if it be not the protector and sure reliance of the friendless, to whose complaints all other ears are dull. It is my duty "to see that the laws are faithfully executed," and among those laws is the constitutional provision that no instrumentality of the state "shall deny to any person within its jurisdiction the equal protection of the laws." And who needs to be told that equal protection of the laws does not prevail where this inhuman vagrancy law is enforced? It separates men into two distinct classes, differentiated as those who are penniless and those who are not, and declares the former criminals. Only the latter are entitled to the liberty guaranteed by the constitution. To be found in a city "without some visible means of support or some legitimate business" is the involuntary condition of some millions at this moment, and we proceed to punish them for being victims of conditions which we, as a people, have forced upon them.

I have noticed in police court reports that "sleeping in a box car" is among the varieties of this heinous crime of being poor. Some police judges have usurped a sovereign power not permitted the highest functionaries of the states or of the nation, and victims of the industrial conditions have been peremptorily "ordered to leave town."

The right to go freely from place to place in search of employment, or even in obedience of a mere whim, is part of that personal liberty guaranteed by the Constitution of the United States to every human being on American soil. If voluntary idleness is not forbidden; if a Diogenes prefer poverty; if a Columbus choose hunger and the discovery of a new race, rather than seek personal comfort by engaging in "some legitimate business," I am aware of no power in the legislature or in city councils to deny him the right to seek happiness in his own way, so long as he harms no other, rich or poor; but let simple poverty cease to be a crime.

35. In Search of Work

What it meant to be refused work at every door, to be hounded from town to town by the local authorities, to spend one's days walking and one's nights sleeping in fields or in jail, can be scarcely understood by those who have not experienced the plight of the unemployed. There is, however, a letter written to Lewelling which captures some of the suffering of the men who wandered in search of work. R. L. Robinson had been a cook in Chicago until he was laid off earlier in the winter of 1893. He then began the long journey, along with another man, to look for employment. With all of their savings invested in household gadgets which they hoped to sell to tide themselves over, the two men arrived in Kansas with their money exhausted.

We managed to pay all expenses untill we arrived at *Sponset* but being unable to make a sale there, we became stranded, but at night a good hearted conductor allowed us to ride to Kewanee which he though[t] would be a good town, at the same time advising us to stay in the calaboose over night. after arriving at Kewanee we went to the calaboose and explained our circumstances and ask permission to stay over night, to which the officer in charge readily consented, so after being searched we were placed in a cell there being no covering but simply an iron bench to lay upon but we were thankfull for even that and tried to sleep. about one oclock we were comanded to get up and go into the office where we were subject to a cross-examanation as to where we had worked & after which we were told to get into the cell again and talking in a [tone] much worse than a man would talk to a

R. L. Robinson to Lorenzo D. Lewelling, Dec. 5, 1893. Lewelling Papers, Kansas State Historical Society.

dog he said we had come to town on the bridge and we would have to get out in the same manner the first thing in the morning. My friend explained that he wanted to see the Mayor in the morning and secure permit to sell or else look for work, but was told if we tried to sell or look for work, he would arrest us, at the same time calling my friend an impudent pup e[t]c.

. . . I think such treatment as that would soon make a criminal of me, and I realy believe that many criminals are made in this manner.

36. A Natural Product of Our Social System

The Topeka *Advocate* immediately commented on Governor Lewelling's proclamation in its editorial of December 6, and for the next eighteen months kept up a running analysis of tramps, industrial armies and labor-saving machinery. For the *Advocate,* the existence of the tramp was deemed a sufficiently strong indictment of the industrial system to warrant calling for a basic social transformation. To remove the conditions which produce tramps, maintained this newspaper, there must be greater reliance on what it termed paternalism. The three editorials which follow appeared in the three weeks after the "Tramp Circular" was announced.

I

We are confronted to-day with very peculiar conditions, peculiar, not because they are new, but because they are so entirely unnecessary. In a land of unlimited resources, and of most marvelous plenty, millions of honest and willing hands are idle and in consequence thereof, they and those dependent

---

Reprinted from *Advocate* (Topeka), Dec. 6, 27 (two editorials), 1893. Kansas State Historical Society.

upon them, are suffering from hunger and cold. These un-necessary conditions are the result of our vicious social and economic system. Idleness is enforced in consequence of vicious and discriminating laws, and to treat the helpless victims of these unnatural conditions as criminals is itself a crime against which every instinct of humanity revolts. . . .

Is poverty more tolerable in one age than in another? Are the poor of America poor from choice any more than were those in the reign of Queen Elizabeth, or in France under a "dissolute monarchy"? Is a dissolute monarchy any worse than a dissolute republic?

II

Hungry men are dangerous men always, just as hungry wild beasts are dangerous; and who can blame them, when surrounded by an abundance of everything they need, and which a false and vicious social and economic system has made it impossible for them to obtain by honest toil? . . . The system under which wealth is concentrating, and poverty extending, is creating a wide gulf between the rich and the poor not only in condition but in feeling. . . .

Shall the fear of "paternalism" prevent interference with the system which has caused these conditions? Can government only provide work and food for men after they become criminals?

III

Wither are we tending, anyway? We hear a great deal in these latter days about anarchy, but we hear very little about the unwarranted and lawless invasion of human liberty which is every day practiced under the garb of respectability by national, state and municipal governments. Let the reader remember that tramps are men, and that they are a natural product of our social system. There must be discovered some way to deal with them consistently with these facts. Can it be done without a revolution of our system? We think not.

37. A Defense of the Poor

Governor Lewelling received numerous letters supporting his stand on behalf of the unemployed. The unifying theme in these responses was the assertion that the tramp was destitute through no fault of his own. One correspondent, in fact, saw the growth of the unemployed as a warning signal that American society had reached the crossroads in its development. This was a crucial decade which would decide the fate of freedom in this nation for future generations. Several other writers also ascribed great significance to the growing number of tramps, and rooted the problem in the nature of the existing system. Of the ten letters which are presented here, the first comes from Lawrence; the second from an editor in Newton; the third from North Wichita; the fourth from Parsons; the fifth from the secretary of the People's party county central committee of Bourbon county; the sixth also from Lawrence; the seventh from a woman in the town of Ottawa; the eighth from a woman thrown off the land in Kansas who now resided in Arizona; the ninth from a Kansan living in California; and the last, and by far the most detailed, from Lawrence. Endorsements of the governor's position ranged from such letters as these to resolutions passed by county alliances and local organizations of the Knights of Labor in Kansas.

H. M. Greene to Lorenzo D. Lewelling, Dec. 5, 1893; Emmett Tiffany to Lewelling, Dec. 5, 1893; J. A. Huffman to Lewelling, Dec. 6, 1893; I. W. Canfield to Lewelling, Dec. 6, 1893; C. E. Shepard to Lewelling, Dec. 7, 1893; W. H. Sears to Lewelling, Dec. 7, 1893; Mrs. P. E. Emery to Lewelling, Dec. 7, 1893; Mrs. F. V. Curns to Lewelling, Dec. 20, 1893; Frank Dibert to Lewelling, Dec. 21, 1893; G. H. Fish to Lewelling, Dec. 9, 1893, all in Lewelling Papers, Kansas State Historical Society.

I

It is a terse and cogent statement of what every humane citizen has thought, since the iniquitious practice of "rock-piling" and "bull-penning" American citizens for the crime of hopeless and helpless poverty has been practiced. It is more —much more. It is a proclamation of justice in behalf of the poor outcasts, who are the target of heartless sneers and the slaves of the tyrants who rule our parties, our social circles, and—in shame be it spoken the churches of the Master, who himself "had not where to lay his head." . . . But above all it is an act of justice to recognize these poor wanderers as entitled to the right to liberty, for the exactions of our damnable system of misgovernment has left them nothing else safe life, and it is but a step to take that in the progress? of American autocricy.

Whatever may be the opinions of the plutocrats, the aristocrats and all the other rats, God and the people will bless you for this brave word.

II

Many of my friends in Kansas at this moment, honest, able-bodied men willing, yes, begging for work at any wages, are criminals under that statute, as they have no visible means of support or any legitimate business. The subsidized Press will go after you, and all the little "me too" fellows will shout "*arnicky*," but all honest thinking men will honor you for that letter.

III

The tendency of the times is to force the masses into a propertyless condition, then persecute them for vagabondage.

IV

The time has fully come when all good men should raise their voices against the growing tendency of our, so called, higher civilization to legislate in favor of making the rich richer, & which while closing up the channels of prosperity against the poor treats them, not only as the mere mudsills of civilization, but as criminals because of their poverty. . . . Your views are on the side of God & humanity. And good men generally throughout the State will approve your views, & desire the successful enforcement of them. What we want is legislation for the good of all, especially the poor. What we want is legislation tending, at least, toward "peace on Earth & good will among men," so that whether we succeed or not, we may not be classed among the enemies of God & of Mankind. I am not a politician, but an humble citizen observing, as I have opportunity, what is transpiring in our State & Country.

V

I voice the sentiment of the peoples party of bourbon Co. when I say—we heartily endorse the honest and humane sentiment expressed in your letter of the 5 *inst* in condemnation of methods employed in treating our unfortunate brothers who are guilty of no other crime than enforced idelness

one of our honest toilers may today be thrown out of employment—tomorrow he may be arrested for haveing no visible means of support—next day he may be released a fellon[.]

VI

Your bold, sturdy utterances come at a peculiarly opportune time, now that the country is flooded with the unemployed. Not a day passes but one or more of these unfortunates, call at our kitchen door for something to eat; and I have never

yet turned one away. I never look into one of their faces, but
my heart warms to them, and I think of my own unfortunate
experience.

The very people & party, that made the conditions that
gives us this army of unemployed, or "tramps," if you will,
are the first to denounce your courageous & manly words.
If this is anarchy, then I am an anarchist.

VII

Now *Govenor* those men have done nothing they are Some
Dear Mothers Sons—the unfortunate victims of circumstances
times are hard work Scarce at this Season of the year I am
a women with a very Strong belief in liberty when people
are doing no crime, it would be as just to arrest & put on
the rockpile the great army of girls and women who go about
Seeking work—if no work they *too must* beg God forbid that
poverty must be treated as crime in Kansas.

VIII

God only knows how the poor are being oppressed, all over
the United States and scarcely any one in power to help
them. . . . My story is the same as many thousands Mortgages with the fall in prices forced us out of Kansas to this
new country. And here it takes the united effort of the whole
family to make a bare living clothes is out of the question,
so I have to make over old ones. I am a Populist through &
through and think no other party will give us relief.

IX

Let Government first legislate in the interest of the people
so that it may be possible for all to have work. It will then be
time enough to talk about laws to confine men in their own baili-

wick who desire to seek labor elsewhere. These are certainly poor times to confine hungry men in bull-pens and on rock-piles, unless their families (or other dependant relatives) be confined and fed with them.

X

Allow me to congratulate you from my heart, and best thought and convictions, upon the ethical *practical* and *courageous* stand you have taken in your address to the boards of police commissioners. I know it brings upon you the trained shafts of ridicule from the bigoted, prejudiced, vindictive and malicious partizans. But for your encouragement may I not suggest as I believe you realize, that the necessities of each succeeding year are now proving that the pronounced "vagaries" of the past one should be enacted into the civic law. Whether we lead or not gov., fate or Providence is now *pushing* us by dire distresses and necessities, to rise to *the inauguration* of a humane and Christian system. Who that now looks, with unbigoted & unpartizan prejudice, can not see that, by the individualistic, monetary, *dollar* system, that the *class* that has sound means has the advantage over the one that has not. That the class that has more over them even, and that the class of vast individual wealth—by the perfected art of combination—the trust and its refined seductive, diabolical methods is rapidly absorbing and enslaving *all*. Supposing, by any especial act of congress, a vast amount of money *is* put into *circulation,* and business seems active in the scramble of each and all to get some, how long would it be before the men of wealth, and especially the trusts, by their superior, helishly enfranchised advantages, would have about all of it and the last state of the people be worse than the first by their (the wealthy few) increased wealth being tabulated in bonds and mortgages upon the people. In business is not the dollar, instead of humanity, by law and custom the object of supremest regard and protection. *Who* does *not* bear constantly with him the dark specter, that by another year perhaps he and his may be *vagrants,* and does not each succeeding year give to the word a deeper and more damning dye. Are not wrong principles and courses, if persisted in, cumulative in volume and results? Is not *now,* a pivotal time of the *ripening* forces of many centuries? Is it not a pivotal or turning point in time, by human necessity or *Divine* will, when every element for good or *evil* is *developed to a* ripened maturity of forces. Events, indicating progress or decadence, strike in rapidly and incisively, as the miner failures and successes of a long delayed but hard fought battle of great contending armies. Such as Homestead, Buffalo Cour-Dehllen and Tennesee, and at the capital last winter. Train roberis etc. How much longer will the farmers produce for *general sustenance* being still farther impoverished by roberies? When may not a little more universality of privation and hunger inaugurate a universal riot and there be a *positive* want of supply, instead of only want of unequal distribution? I believe governor you see the iminence of all this in the near future. Can it be stayed by efforts for education to the end of adapting specific measures of reform?

38. The Army of Destitute Unemployed

The *Farmers' Alliance* contended some twenty-one months earlier than Lewelling's proclamation that profit and poverty were inextricably linked under industrial capitalism. The former could be sustained only through the maintenance of a large reserve of unemployed workers, so that individual laborers would be compelled to work at whatever wages were offered to them. This newspaper

---

Reprinted from *Farmers' Alliance* (Lincoln), March 10, 1892. Nebraska Historical Society.

also pointed to an analogous situation concerning the nonindustrial sector: Returns from agriculture would be siphoned off through control of interest rates and transportation facilities. The result, according to the *Farmers' Alliance*, was an economic system promoting the concentration of wealth in comparatively few hands.

Capital is glad to see half a million poor emigrants land here yearly, because with more seeking work it can force down the price of labor and absorb a larger percentage of labor's product. The army of destitute unemployed is the source of its power, the misery of the unemployed is the club with which it enslaves all workers. The legalization of land monopoly, and interest, are the sources of its strength, the canals by which it turns wealth from the channels of natural and just distribution.

Again capital enslaves otherwise independent labor, that which is in possession of land, by monopolizing the means of transportation, so controlling commerce. Standing between producers and consumers and exacting an unjust price for its labor it makes itself a king, levying tribute upon all classes. Capital with its present legally conferred and popularly permitted kingly power, will rule despotically as long as it can make labor work for it upon its own terms, or collect tribute from those who need credit.

39. The Coxey Movement

To dramatize their grievances and call national attention to their predicament, groups of unemployed workers banded together in the late winter and early spring of 1894 to march to Washington

Reprinted from *Advocate* (Topeka), April 11, 25, 1894, May 2, 1894. Kansas State Historical Society.

and there petition Congress to alleviate their suffering. The best-known contingent in this movement was led by Jacob S. Coxey of Massillon, Ohio, who wanted to present his views on financial legislation and on a federally sponsored program of public works. Coxey did not receive a hearing, but was instead arrested as soon as he reached the Capitol. The charge was that he had been walking on the grass.

While the nation as a whole ridiculed Coxey and the industrial armies, Populists were among the very few who perceived the situation differently. Their views were not only an expression of sympathy; for they believed that here was one more instance signifying the oppressive tendencies of industrial capitalism, one more example of an economic system which was transforming men into tramps. In April and May 1894 the Topeka *Advocate* presented a series of editorials on the significance of Coxey's Army. Three of these are reprinted below.

I

In all the allusions of republican and democratic papers to this movement, all reference to the causes which have produced it is studiously avoided. The men engaged in it are contemptuously spoken of as cranks, tramps and vagabonds who deserve to be arrested and treated as criminals upon general principles. The causes which produce tramps and vagabonds are never alluded to. It is in this fact that the danger to the peace of the country really exists. Men do not become tramps and vagabonds from choice. When forced into idleness and compelled to take to the road in the fruitless effort to find employment it requires but a short time to make a vagabond of the man who under other and more favorable circumstances would be numbered among our best citizens. The causes which force people into idleness are therefore responsible, not only for this Coxey movement, but for nearly all the lawlessness and crime of the country, as well.

II

These men have as much right to go to Washington and demand justice at the hands of congress as bankers, railroad magnates and corporation attorneys have to go and lobby for measures by which to plunder the public; and if their rights are not respected there will be trouble; rest assured of that. Let the powers that be beware how they treat the Coxey army.

III

Who is it that is threatening violence to-day? An army of American citizens who have been forced into idleness by vicious republican methods are marching to Washington peaceably, and bearing the American flag, to ask of the national government that something shall be done for their relief. The commissioners of the District of Columbia have issued a manifesto warning these men to abandon the idea of invading the territory. In the meantime the Washington police and the national guard are drilling for service against them; and all the threats of violence that have been made, and all the demonstrations indicating that violence is intended by anyone have been on the part of the national and district authorities.

At the same time . . . we witness another demonstration. The manufacturers engaged in the protected industries in Eastern cities rig out a lot of their employes in guady raiment and send them up to the national capital in palace cars, as living witnesses of the prosperity of American workingmen under a republican tariff system, to protest against the horrid Wilson bill. Were these men headed off by the police and the national guard and forbidden to enter the sacred precincts of the capital? No, they were met by a brass band and nothing was too good for them. Even members of congress went down to the Baltimore & Ohio depot to greet them on their arrival.

40. The Right to Petition

The Lincoln *Wealth Makers,* again the *Farmers' Alliance* at a later date and with a new editor, was another major Populist voice raised in defense of the industrial armies. In this early editorial, it affirmed the right of petition and expressed the wish that all of the poverty-striken could assemble in Washington.

Have not peaceful American citizens a right to petition congress in person? And if obliged to go there and to the White House barefooted, ragged and hungry, may they not be received respectfully, their rights considered and their plan, or some other, better, adequate plan of opening up immediate work for the unemployed be thought out, discussed and put into operation by act of congress?

It is stupid or cruel to tell these men, these destitute starving millions, that they must right their wrongs at the ballot box. What are men sent to congress and to the White House for but to make laws to protect the weak, the poor, the preyed upon?

. . . For our part we wish that all the destitute, wretched, miserable millions of American citizens which unjust legislation has made, could camp around the Capitol at Washington and form an ever present conscience-accusing spectacle for our national lawmakers to face. We wish also that every monopolist in the land was obliged each day to see filing past his door a section of the poorest of our people who labor without gain that their oppressors may gain without labor, and who in the stagnation period of each usury cycle are not allowed to work at any price.

Reprinted from *Wealth Makers* (Lincoln), April 5, 1894. Nebraska Historical Society.

41. On Industrial Armies

Support for the Coxey movement can also be seen on the grass-roots level in Nebraska. Resolutions from local and county alliance meetings were sent to the secretary of the state Farmers' Alliance, as were several personal communications. One more humorous than the others informed her about a coming picnic: "There Will be Vocal and Instrumental music and Speaking and a Good Time Generally all are Invited and no one Will Be *arested* for Steping on The Grass or Caring Banners." But most of the statements were deadly serious. The first resolution comes from Oak Valley Alliance number 1354 in Lancaster County and the second from a special meeting of the Burt County Alliance. The third selection is a letter from a woman in Cambridge, Nebraska.

I

The following resolutions were adopted.

We view with just alarm the excited condition of our people, over the Common-Weal army now marching to Washington.

We believe it is a right and dutie of these men at this time to go to Washington the capitol of our common country, the Congress of the U. S. being now in session, and there pesent a living petition of their poverty and suffering

While thus in persuit of their lawful wright of petition, and their further natural writes to life, liberty, and the persuit of happiness,

to their support we pledge our lives, our fortune's and our sacred Homes.

Resolutions of Oak Valley Alliance, May 5, 1894, and of Burt County Alliance, June 9, 1894; Ella Whitman to Luna E. Kellie, May 7, 1894, all contained in Nebraska State Farmers' Alliance Records, box 1, Nebraska Historical Society. The letter quoted above is from H. F. Wasmund, president of the Sheridan County Alliance, to Mrs. Kellie, May 14, 1894, *ibid*.

While we desire peace and an honorable adjustment of the difference's that so widely seperate labor and capital,

Still bleving the demands of labor to be just, we will not receed one attom from those demands.

II

Resl. adopted at a spicial meeting of the Burt co. F. all— June 9, 1894

Whereas, we believe the ranks of the commonweal army are filled by honest laborers & loyal american citizens who are peaceably striving to petition congress in the interests of the unemployed, & laboring people generally. Therefore Resolved, That we warmly sympathize with Gen. Coxey & his followers, & that we severely cirtisise the actions toward them by the authorities at Washington.

Res. That we warmly commend our representatives in congress for their faithful efforts in behalf of the producing classes of our country, & especially do we commend Senator W. V. Allen for the noble works he is doing in the U.S. senate, & for the eloquent, patriotic speech, in defence of Gen. Coxey & his army, & our constitutional liberties[.]

III

We are all stired up with the report of Coxey and the treatment and arrest of his commanders The brutal treatment of men, women, and children by the hireling police. Inocent spectators knocked down and trampled under foot of their horses If these are Self evident truths they should Suffer the penalty of the law in thus attacking a peaceable gathering We are proud of Coxey and the manner he behaved by report[.]

42.   Machinery and the Worker

Through the close of 1894 and the first half of 1895 the *Advocate* continued its discussion of tramps, industrial armies, and the introduction of labor-saving machinery, but by this time it was drawing increasingly radical conclusions from the events it had been witnessing. Of the three editorials that follow, the first represents a succinct statement of the *Advocate*'s beliefs concerning industrial capitalism, while the second refers to the social consequences of unemployment. In the third, the *Advocate* comments on a report issued by the New York State Bureau of Labor Statistics, which deals with "the decrease of the working force by the use of machinery."

I

Machinery has made it possible for women and children to do the work of men, and . . . they are employed in the place of men at from one-half to one-fourth of men's wages. It is thus that things which should afford the richest blessings to humanity, are converted, by a false and malicious industrial system, into instruments of the greatest evil.

What is the remedy? Ours is public control of these means of production and a sufficient reduction of the hours of labor to afford every willing hand an opportunity to work, thereby giving the benefits of improved methods to labor rather than permit capital to absorb vast profits and turn labor out to starve.

Reprinted from *Advocate* (Topeka), Nov. 14, 1894, Feb. 6, April 10, 1895. Kansas State Historical Society.

II

Men and women reduced to helpless want by the cruel conditions of our glorious social and industrial system, are thus shuffled about from place to place day after day—told to move on when they have no place on earth to go to, as though they were not recognized as human beings.

Where, in God's name, are these people to go, and what are they to do? What a glorious Christian civilization we are living under, to be sure, and yet the American people are contributing millions of dollars every year to send missionaries to heathen lands to convert them to this same blessed Christian civilization. Oh, blessed humbug!

III

Under the existing monopoly system of industry capital owns and controls all this labor-saving machinery, and derives all the benefits resulting from its use, while labor is forced into idleness and compelled to beg, steal or starve. At the same time we are told that state and national governments are powerless to provide employment to these enforced idlers or assist them in any way to supply the necessities of themselves and families, because to do so would be paternalism. There is no way in which idle men and women can be aided by government until after they have become criminals. Then places are provided for them where they are fed and clothed and where the products of their labor are brought into competition with those of free labor. Isn't it a system to be proud of? While such a state of things exists, the evils and disadvantages of which are generally acknowledged, every person who has the temerity to suggest that changes are possible by which a better state of society might be secured, is denounced as an impractical visionary and a crank.

43. Public Works for the Unemployed

Populists were not content to denounce the industrial system for creating tramps. They went further. In the many commentaries on the problem, there were often references to the powers of government to rectify the situation. In one statement of this character, Annie L. Diggs of Kansas urged a Populist congressman in that state, John Davis, to introduce a bill calling for the recruitment by the federal government of one-half million unemployed men to work on conservation, construction and other public projects. This program, which can be regarded as a forerunner of the Civilian Conservation Corps of the New Deal, received little or no attention in Washington.

A bill to provide for the enlistment and maintenance of an industrial army, for issuing and maintaining a sufficient and equitable volume of currency, and for other purposes.

Whereas the lack of employment for a vast number of workingmen in this country, caused by a contraction of money and falling prices, is productive of untold distress and of manifold demoralization. . . .

Be it enacted by the senate and house of representative . . . That the secretary of war shall be empowered and instructed, immediately upon the passage of this act, to enlist, as fast as practicable, five hundred thousand men in an industrial volunteer army to serve for the period of one year after enlistment.

That this army shall be enlisted, clothed, fed, and paid under the same rules and regulations as to physical soundness, comfort, and military discipline required of recruits in the regular army.

Reprinted from *Advocate* (Topeka), May 16, 1894. Kansas State Historical Society.

That . . . the industrial army shall be employed on works of public improvements, such as canals, rivers, and harbors, irrigation works, public highways, and such other public improvements as congress . . . shall provide.

44. An Opportunity to Work

A farmer in Madison, Kansas, writing to Ignatius Donnelly in mid-1892, suggested a more comprehensive rule-of-thumb on what the government's role should be in combatting unemployment. In the form of a resolution to be appended to the People's party platform, the writer advanced the principle that all men had the right to be gainfully employed in the United States, and hence, that jobs must be created by the government when this proves necessary. As for the kinds of projects he thought appropriate, the early portion of the letter is devoted to the problem of slum clearance.

Recognizing the Slums of our great? cities as a disgrace to the nation, the existence of which should mantle our brows with deeper shame than ever did the institution of American Slavery[.]
Recognizing also that true heroism consists in doing for others—especially for those whose needs are the greatest, we implore from on high such a baptism with "the enthusiasm of humanity" that we cannot rest until such environments are completely wiped out, and every child born into the world has a chance to grow heavenward in body mind & heart.
. . . Recognizing enforced & involuntary idleness as the parent of voluntary idleness trampism & crime.
We demand that the state furnish as necessary to every man an opportunity to work (to invest his God given capital

---

John B. Thomson to Ignatius Donnelly, June 30, 1892. Donnelly Papers, Minnesota Historical Society.

of heart brains & hands) at something useful to himself & his fellow man.

God furnished this opportunity when he gave to man the earth and the fullness thereof, and until this birth-right is restored society should at least give him a chance to work at fair pay that his mess of pottage be not entirely cut off— or worse doled out to him as charity.

45. The Suppression of Tramps

Charles C. Post had already established himself as a novelist and reformer in Michigan before coming to Georgia to aid Thomas E. Watson on the *People's Party Paper* and as the congressman's political lieutenant at home. Yet he did not remain. Whether Post's recent arrival and northern background generated suspicion, or his views were mistaken for being more radical than they actually were, he soon found himself in the center of political controversy and a target for abuse. After an unpleasant incident at the start of the 1892 campaign, Post without fanfare suddenly left the state. For the present purposes, however, he is less important as a supporter of Watson than as the author of a popular novel of 1891 entitled *Congressman Swanson*. At two points in this work Post interrupts the narrative to discuss the significance of tramps. He uses the depression of the mid-1880's as the basis for his remarks.

I

Two millions of unemployed men sought in vain for a chance to exchange their labor for bread, while eight millions of women and children waited and prayed, suffered and hoped and despaired.

The country began to be overrun with tramps.

Reprinted from Charles C. Post, *Congressman Swanson* (Chicago: Charles H. Sergel and Company, 1891), pp. 179-182, 264-266.

Men out of employment and seeking it, out of money and stopping to beg a meal and permission to sleep in barns, or out-buildings, began to be seen daily, and many times a day, on all roads leading from one manufacturing town to another.

Then the states began to pass laws for the suppression of tramps.

Pennsylvania led off; and was quickly followed by other states; and before long it came to be known that a man out of work and seeking it could no longer safely ask for the gift of a crust at any house within the limits of an incorporated town, or even at a country farm-house if an officer of the law happened to be within hearing of the request.

Even to ask for the proverbial "cup of cold water," if the appearance of the person asking it was such as to indicate poverty and suffering, was liable to be followed by arrest and incarceration in a felon's cell, or a ball and chain with labor upon the public streets.

Such enactments and such arrests were demanded by the rich and respectable.

For now, while the masses were daily growing poorer and poorer, while enforced idleness and rapidly falling prices were eating up, or had already consumed the savings of millions of the wealth producers of the land, the few who had directed the legislation of the country to this end, and for this purpose, were rolling in wealth and daily growing richer by a large portion of that which the business and producing classes were losing, and these men demanded protection of the law.

"Our property," they said, "and possibly our lives are endangered by the presence of these lazy and lawless characters, these tramps who roam about the country pretending to want work but in reality preferring to beg." And as the machinery of legislation was in their hands, or the hands of their dupes and tools, the politicians, "Tramp laws" were passed, and it became a crime for a man out of employment and out of money to ask for bread.

Then greed, the meanest of all the passions, greed which consumes the souls of men as a leprosy the body, showed itself among the smaller politicians; and those who were in office began to emulate the example of their political superiors and of the greedy souls that were back of them and had dictated the legislation that had brought such awful calamnities upon the people and filled the land with suffering and woe.

Petty officials, sheriffs, city marshalls and town constables began the nefarious work of arresting men in search of work and clapping them into jail for the sake of the profit that they made off the city or county on a few meals of victuals furnished to the poor fellows whom they had thus transformed from honest men into "jail birds."

A favorite way of these petty officials—these caricatures upon decent humanity—these jackdaw emulators of the larger birds of prey that were feeding off the vitals of the people, was to arrest as many "tramps" as was possible late on Saturday, so that they could not be brought before the mayor or justice before Monday; and were thus compelled to live in jail from Saturday afternoon until Monday, which enabled their captors to charge up their board for that length of time.

As the board necessarily furnished to "tramps" was not of the best, while the pay allowed for it by the Ring which run the affairs of the town or city, was, of the best, the profit on such transactions was considerable—depending largely upon how energetic and successful the officers were in making arrests.

As the arrested party had no remedy, even though found, on trial, to have a few shillings on his person, and not yet to have been reduced to the necessity of begging, it was a perfectly safe as well as a paying business to "run them in;" and in many towns a regular and systematic business was made of it.

The result was what alone could follow.

Honest men were transformed into criminals by the thousands and tens of thousands.

To-day a manufacturing establishment failed and five hundred men were thrown out of employment.

They sought it elsewhere in their own town or city and were unable to obtain it.

All the other manufactories had closed or were running on half time and there were no vacancies for any one to fill.

For weeks and months they sought for work; living, in the meantime, themselves and their families, upon their previous savings, or upon what they could get for odd jobs—cleaning the side-walks from snow—splitting a bit of wood—carrying a load of coal up-stairs—any thing for which some kindly disposed person would give them a dime or a quarter, and then, when all their savings were exhausted, a rumor that some manufacturing establishment in the next town was going to start up again—a rush of many to get a job, disappointment to all or a portion of the eager seekers for work, and, out of money, with clothes old and worn, they continued their tramp in search of employment and fainting with hunger, begged for bread and—were given it in a cell of some county or city jail.

A night, a day, two nights perhaps, a prisoner in a prison cell.

Then the arraignment in court.

The charge, "vagrancy, too lazy to work and caught begging." The verdict: "Thirty days on the streets," and the hellish work is done.

II

"The Sheriff of our county has adopted a new and somewhat unique method of dealing with the tramps that have of late infested our city and the country lying round about. Too lazy to work these miserable wretches have, during the recent severe weather, drifted into the city in large numbers and through their presence and their persistance in begging have become so great a nuisance that many of our best citizens, so our worthy sheriff informs us, have complained to him and urged upon him the necessity of adopting some means of abating it, and them.

"Fines and locking up in the calaboose or city jail does no good—is in fact, just what they desire as they are thus secured from both cold and hunger, since it is not yet considered quite the proper thing to shut them up and starve them to death, though that might, after all, be the easiest and most humane way of settling the question of what to do with these outcasts, to whom society really owes nothing.

"However, our very efficient sheriff, thinks he has found the proper way of dealing with them and we have no doubt that if not interfered with, he will speedily rid the community of their presence.

"On Saturday morning he, with the assistance of several deputies, gathered up such of the tramp fraternity as he could readily lay hands on, took them to the outskirts of the city, and after lashing each and every one of them in turn, with a good black-snake whip, laying it on thoroughly and well, until, in fact, the miserable wretches begged and plead to be let off and promised never again to be seen in the city or vicinity, they were allowed to go; but with the assurance that if they ever returned, the dose would be doubled at the very least.

"This may not be a strictly legal way of abating the tramp nuisance, but we repeat that it is likely to prove an effectual one and we do not doubt that our best citizens will sustain the sheriff and his deputies in any measures which they may find necessary to accomplish this much-to-be desired result."

The foregoing editorial appeared in one of the leading daily papers of the Capital city of one of our central western states; and was as well a statement of that which actually occurred as an expression of the sentiment of the editor of the paper, and, it is fair to suppose, of a considerable number of other citizens of that community.

The tramps were taken as was stated, to the city limits and "well and thoroughly lashed."

They had been guilty as charged of having flocked to the city and for the most part with but one purpose and one hope—that of being arrested and confined in some penal institution where they would be protected from the terrible inclemency of the weather and supplied with sufficient food to stay the cravings of hunger until the severe cold should abate. Most of them had already served at least one sentence of ten days in the calaboose; but as when they were released, the cold was still intense, making it quite impossible to sleep out of doors or in barns and straw-stacks, they still lingered about, begging or purloining from the citizens of the place such articles of food or clothing as opportunity offered, or charity would give, hoping thereby to sustain life until warmer weather made its appearance once more, or until again arrested and sentenced to another term in the county jail.

But against this, numbers of the "best citizens" had protested, going to the sheriff with their complaints.

If it had been summer time, if the ground had not been frozen so as to make it quite impossible to carry on repairs upon the streets, these wretched caricatures of prosperous humanity might have been made to earn their board and lodging by being put to work; but as it was, anything done to prolong their existence but added to that which must be raised by a levy upon the property of the citizens of the county and city; and against this the "best citizens" protested.

PART FOUR

JUSTICE FOR THE OUTCAST:

II

THE NEGRO

The second case study presented here concerns the Populist attitude toward the Negro. One must recognize at the outset that there are variations: Different states had different patterns, and within each state instances of divergent viewpoints can be found. But the dominant theme, occurring sometimes to the exclusion of all else, is that Populists sought to extend political justice to Negroes and to stand for policies which would benefit both races. On these two points, as Professor Woodward has observed, Populists were considerably in advance of other social movements and political forces in the South throughout its history up to that time, and perhaps since that time as well. To be sure, there is still not sufficient evidence to indicate whether Populists enlisted the support of Negroes in order to use them to get elected, or whether such support was founded on a genuine desire to extend a hand of friendship and justice for its own sake. In the case of Thomas E. Watson, the present writer believes that the latter is true. In fact, in very few instances anywhere in the South does one find indications that expediency rather than principle underlay the Populist response to the Negro. Too much was at stake for this possibility to occur. For any defense of the Negro's rights, any move—as was the case in Texas —to place Negroes on the party's state executive committee, any campaign where Negro and white speakers shared the same platform, could not have been made but at very great personal and political sacrifice. Under the circumstances where not simply social ostracism but beatings and murder awaited the white person who challenged the existing system, and where lynching awaited the Negroes who refused to be intimidated, it is difficult to take Populist sentiments at any but face value. This does not mean that all Populists were friendly to Negroes or that the extent of their friendship did not differ; some Populists were anti-Negro, and many Populist newspapers at one time or another defensively pointed out that Grover Cleveland invited Frederick Douglass, the distinguished ex-slave, and his white wife to the White House, and criticized the president for doing so. Yet, from the evidence thus far gathered, the exceptions hardly cast doubt on the generalization stated above.

46. The Negro Question in the South

Tom Watson saw the issue in a clearer, more comprehensive light than did others in the movement. But southern Populists as a whole, because they faced similar circumstances, reached essentially the same position that he did by a less articulate route. Writing for the *Arena* in 1892, Watson presented this core statement of the Populist view: Dominant groups in the South encouraged racial animosities to prevent poorer whites and Negroes from combining together to challenge existing economic arrangements. Watson's well-known contention, that "you are kept apart that you may be

---

Reprinted from Thomas E. Watson, "The Negro Question in the South," *Arena*, VI (October 1892), pp. 540-550.

separately fleeced of your earnings," is based on his belief that the cry of "Negro domination" heard incessantly during these years was designed to keep the poorer whites in line. They were being forced to submerge their interests in the name of white solidarity, with the result that economic grievances could not be raised and acquiescence to oppressive policies was insured. This appeal to race, then, was nothing more or less than a device to forestall conflicts between the lower and upper classes in the white community.

Watson attacked this edifice of artificial race hatred at its roots. In effect, he was denying that patterns of discrimination were founded on intrinsic psychological antipathies. Instead, he argued that these patterns were exactly *that*—artificial, man-made strategems to keep the two races from working together. For Watson, there was indeed hostility which had been built up, but this hostility could be broken down once the Negroes and the poorer whites understood the situation. His constant theme here was that class interests cut across racial lines; since both groups had identical material interests, there was an objective basis for common action. And through common action would come greater understanding and mutual respect. Thus, Watson proposed political equality as the necessary step to liberate the lower classes of both races. Each could not help its own interests without helping those of the other. Watson asserted in the article which follows, just as he did when speaking in Thomson, Georgia, that the Negro was a citizen and entitled to full equality in the legal and political realm. As for social equality, he stated, "That is a thing each citizen decides for himself." On other occasions in the very same year, he rejected social equality outright. Yet, a step had been taken toward racial justice. It was a bold one for the time.

I

The Negro Question in the South has been for nearly thirty years a source of danger, discord, and bloodshed. It is an ever-present irritant and menace.

Several millions of slaves were told that they were the prime cause of the civil war; that their emancipation was the result of the triumph of the North over the South; that the ballot was placed in their hands as a weapon of defence against their former masters; that the war-won political equality of the black man with the white, must be asserted promptly and aggressively, under the leadership of adventurers who had swooped down upon the conquered section in the wake of the Union armies.

No one, who wishes to be fair, can fail to see that, in such a condition of things, strife between the freedman and his former owner was inevitable. In the clashing of interests and of feelings, bitterness was born. The black man was kept in a continual fever of suspicion that we meant to put him back into slavery. In the assertion of his recently acquired privileges, he was led to believe that the best proof of his being on the right side of any issue was that his old master was on the other. When this was the case, he felt easy in his mind. But if, by any chance, he found that he was voting the same ticket with his former owner, he at once became reflective and suspicious. In the irritable temper of the times, a whispered warning from a Northern "carpet-bagger," having no justification in rhyme or reason, outweighed with him a carload of sound argument and earnest expostulation from the man whom he had known all his life; who had hunted with him through every swamp and wooded upland for miles around; who had wrestled and run foot-races with him in the "Negro quarters" on many a Saturday afternoon; who had fished with him at every "hole" in the creek; and who had played a thousand games of "marble" with him under the cool shade of the giant oaks which, in those days, sheltered a home they had both loved.

In brief, the end of the war brought changed relations and changed feelings. Heated antagonisms produced mutual distrust and dislike—ready, at any accident of unusual provocation on either side, to break out into passionate and bloody conflict.

Quick to take advantage of this deplorable situation, the politicians have based the fortunes of the old parties upon it. Northern leaders have felt that at the cry of "Southern outrage" they could not only "fire the Northern heart," but also win a unanimous vote from the colored people. Southern politicians have felt that at the cry of "Negro domination" they could drive into solid phalanx every white man in all the Southern states.

Both the old parties have done this thing until they have constructed as perfect a "slot machine" as the world ever saw. Drop the old, worn nickel of the "party slogan" into the slot, and the machine does the rest. You might beseech a Southern white tenant to listen to you upon questions of finance, taxation, and transportation; you might demonstrate with mathematical precision that herein lay his way out of poverty into comfort; you might have him "almost persuaded" to the truth, but if the merchant who furnished his farm supplies (at tremendous usury) or the town politician (who never spoke to him excepting at election times) came along and cried "Negro rule!" the entire fabric of reason and common sense which you had patiently constructed would fall, and the poor tenant would joyously hug the chains of an actual wretchedness rather than do any experimenting on a question of mere sentiment.

Thus the Northern Democrats have ruled the South with a rod of iron for twenty years. We have had to acquiesce when the time-honored principles we loved were sent to the rear and new doctrines and policies we despised were engrafted on our platform. All this we have had to do to obtain the assistance of Northern Democrats to prevent what was called "Negro supremacy." In other words, the Negro has been as valuable a portion of the stock in trade of a Democrat as he was of a Republican. Let the South ask relief from Wall Street; let it plead for equal and just laws on finance; let it beg for mercy against crushing taxation, and Northern Democracy, with all the coldness, cruelty, and subtlety of Mephistopheles, would hint "Negro rule!" and the white farmer and laborer of the South had to choke down his grievance and march under Tammany's orders.

Reverse the statement, and we have the method by which the black man was managed by the Republicans.

Reminded constantly that the North had emancipated him; that the North had given him the ballot; that the North had upheld him in his citizenship; that the South was his enemy, and meant to deprive him of his suffrage and put him "back into slavery," it is no wonder he has played as nicely into the hands of the Republicans as his former owner has played into the hands of the Northern Democrats.

Now consider: here were two distinct races dwelling together, with political equality established between them by law. They lived in the same section; won their livelihood by the same pursuits; cultivated adjoining fields on the same terms; enjoyed together the bounties of a generous climate; suffered together the rigors of cruelly unjust laws; spoke the same language; bought and sold in the same markets; classified themselves into churches under the same denominational teachings; neither race antagonizing the other in any branch of industry; each absolutely dependent on the other in all the avenues of labor and employment; and yet, instead of being allies, as every dictate of reason and prudence and self-interest and justice said they should be, they were kept apart, in dangerous hostility, that the sordid aims of partisan politics might be served!

So completely has this scheme succeeded that the Southern black man almost instinctively supports any measure the Southern white man condemns, while the latter almost universally antagonizes any proposition suggested by a Northern

Republican. We have, then, a solid South as opposed to a solid North; and in the South itself, a solid black vote against the solid white.

That such a condition is most ominous to both sections and both races, is apparent to all.

If we were dealing with a few tribes of red men or a few sporadic Chinese, the question would be easily disposed of. The Anglo-Saxon would probably do just as he pleased, whether right or wrong, and the weaker man would go under.

But the Negroes number 8,000,000. They are interwoven with our business, political, and labor systems. They assimilate with our customs, our religion, our civilization. They meet us at every turn,—in the fields, the shops, the mines. They are a part of our system, and they are here to stay.

Those writers who tediously wade through census reports to prove that the Negro is disappearing, are the most absurd mortals extant. The Negro is not disappearing. A Southern man who looks about him and who sees how rapidly the colored people increase, how cheaply they can live, and how readily they learn, has no patience whatever with those statistical lunatics who figure out the final disappearance of the Negro one hundred years hence. The truth is, that the "black belts" in the South are getting blacker. The race is mixing less than it ever did. Mulattoes are less common (in proportion) than during the times of slavery. Miscegenation is further off (thank God) than ever. Neither the blacks nor the whites have any relish for it. Both have a pride of race which is commendable, and which, properly directed, will lead to the best results for both. The home of the colored man is chiefly with us in the South, and there he will remain. It is there he is founding churches, opening schools, maintaining newspapers, entering the professions, serving on juries, deciding doubtful elections, drilling as a volunteer soldier, and piling up a cotton crop which amazes the world.

II

This preliminary statement is made at length that the gravity of the situation may be seen. Such a problem never confronted any people before.

Never before did two distinct races dwell together under such conditions.

And the problem is, can these two races, distinct in color, distinct in social life, and distinct as political powers, dwell together in peace and prosperity?

Upon a question so difficult and delicate no man should dogmatize—nor dodge. The issue is here; grows more urgent every day, and must be met.

It is safe to say that the present status of hostility between the races can only be sustained at the most imminent risk to both. It is leading by logical necessity to results which the imagination shrinks from contemplating. And the horrors of such a future can only be averted by honest attempts at a solution of the question which will be just to both races and beneficial to both.

Having given this subject much anxious thought, my opinion is that the future happiness of the two races will never be assured until the political motives which drive them asunder, into two distinct and hostile factions, can be removed. There must be a new policy inaugurated, whose purpose is to allay the passions and prejudices of race conflict, and which makes its appeal to the sober sense and honest judgment of the citizen regardless of his color.

To the success of this policy two things are indispensable—a common necessity acting upon both races, and a common benefit assured to both—without injury or humiliation to either.

Then, again, outsiders must let us alone. We must work out our own salvation. In no other way can it be done. Suggestions of Federal interference with our elections postpone the settlement and render our task the more difficult. Like all free people, we love home rule, and resent foreign compulsion of any sort. The Northern leader who really desires to see a better state of things in the South, puts his finger on the hands of the clock and forces them backward every time he intermeddles with the question. This is the literal truth; and the sooner it is well understood, the sooner we can accomplish our purpose.

What is that purpose? To outline a policy which compels the support of a great body of both races, from those motives which imperiously control human action, and which will thus obliterate forever the sharp and unreasoning political divisions of to-day.

The white people of the South will never support the Republican Party. This much is certain. The black people of the South will never support the Democratic Party. This is equally certain.

Hence, at the very beginning, we are met by the necessity of new political alliances. As long as the whites remain solidly Democratic, the blacks will remain solidly Republican.

As long as there was no choice, except as between the Democrats and the Republicans, the situation of the two races was bound to be one of antagonism. The Republican Party represented everything which was hateful to the whites; the Democratic Party, everything which was hateful to the blacks.

Therefore a new party was absolutely necessary. It has come, and it is doing its work with marvellous rapidity.

Why does a Southern Democrat leave his party and come to ours?

Because his industrial condition is pitiably bad; because he struggles against a system of laws which have almost filled him with despair; because he is told that he is without clothing because he produces too much cotton, and without food because corn is too plentiful; because he sees everybody growing rich off the products of labor except the laborer; because the millionaires who manage the Democratic Party have contemptuously ignored his plea for a redress of grievances and have nothing to say to him beyond the cheerful advice to "work harder and live closer."

Why has this man joined the PEOPLE'S PARTY? Because the same grievances have been presented to the Republicans by the farmer of the West, and the millionaires who control that party have replied to the petition with the soothing counsel that the Republican farmer of the West should "work more and talk less."

Therefore, if he were confined to a choice between the two old parties, the question would merely be (on these issues) whether the pot were larger than the kettle—the color of both being precisely the same.

III

The key to the new political movement called the People's Party has been that the Democratic farmer was as ready to leave the Democratic ranks as the Republican farmer was to leave the Republican ranks. In exact proportion as the West received the assurance that the South was ready for a new party, it has moved. In exact proportion to the proof we could bring that the West had broken Republican ties, the South has moved. *Without* a decided break in both sections, neither would move. *With* that decided break, both moved.

The very same principle governs the race question in the South. The two races can never act together permanently, harmoniously, beneficially, till each race demonstrates to the other a readiness to leave old party affiliations and to form new ones, based upon the profound conviction that, in acting together, both races are seeking new laws which will benefit both. On no other basis under heaven can the "Negro Question" be solved.

IV

Now, suppose that the colored man were educated upon these questions just as the whites have been; suppose he were shown that his poverty and distress came from the same sources as ours; suppose we should convince him that our platform principles assure him an escape from the ills he now suffers, and guarantee him the fair measure of prosperity his labor entitles him to receive,—would he not act just as the white Democrat who joined us did? Would he not abandon a party which ignores him as a farmer and laborer; which offers him no benefits of an equal and just financial system; which promises him no relief from oppressive taxation; which assures him of no legislation which will enable him to obtain a fair price for his produce?

Granting to him the same selfishness common to us all; granting him the intelligence to know what is best for him and the desire to attain it, why would he not act from that motive just as the white farmer has done?

That he would do so, is as certain as any future event can be made. Gratitude may fail; so may sympathy and friendship and generosity and patriotism; but in the long run, self-interest *always* controls. Let it once appear plainly that it is to the interest of a colored man to vote with the white man, and he will do it. Let it plainly appear that it is to the interest of the white man that the vote of the Negro should supplement his own, and the question of having that ballot freely cast and fairly counted, becomes vital to the *white man*. He will see that it is done.

Now let us illustrate: Suppose two tenants on my farm; one of them white, the other black. They cultivate their crops under precisely the same conditions. Their labors, discouragements, burdens, grievances, are the same.

The white tenant is driven by cruel necessity to examine into the causes of his continued destitution. He reaches certain conclusions which are not complimentary to either of the old parties. He leaves the Democracy in angry disgust. He joins the People's Party. Why? Simply because its platform recognizes that he is badly treated and proposes to fight his battle. Necessity drives him from the old party, and hope leads him into the new. In plain English, he joins the organization whose declaration of principles is in accord with his conception of what he needs and justly deserves.

Now go back to the colored tenant. His surroundings being the same and his interests the same, why is it impossible for him to reach the same conclusions? Why is it unnatural for him to go into the new party at the same time and with the same motives?

Cannot these two men act together in peace when the ballot of the one is a vital benefit to the other? Will not political friendship be born of the necessity and the hope which is common to both? Will not race bitterness disappear before this common suffering and this mutual desire to escape it? Will not each of these citizens feel more kindly for the other when the vote of each defends the home of both? If the white man becomes convinced that the Democratic Party has played upon his prejudices, and has used his quiescence to the benefit of interests adverse to his own, will he not despise the leaders who seek to perpetuate the system?

V

The People's Party will settle the race question. First, by enacting the Australian ballot system. Second, by offering to white and black a rallying point which is free from the odium of former discords and strifes. Third, by presenting a platform immensely beneficial to both races and injurious to neither. Fourth, by making it to the *interest* of both races to act together for the success of the platform. Fifth, by making it to the *interest* of the colored man to have the same patriotic zeal for the welfare of the South that the whites possess.

Now to illustrate. Take two planks of the People's Party platform: that pledging a free ballot under the Australian system and that which demands a distribution of currency to the people upon pledges of land, cotton, etc.

The guaranty as to the vote will suit the black man better than the Republican platform, because the latter contemplates Federal interference, which will lead to collisions and bloodshed. The Democratic platform contains no comfort to the Negro, because, while it denounces the Republican programme, as usual, it promises nothing which can be specified. It is a generality which does not even possess the virtue of being "glittering."

The People's Party, however, not only condemns Federal interference with elections, but also distinctly commits itself to the method by which every citizen shall have his constitutional right to the free exercise of his electoral choice. We pledge ourselves to isolate the voter from all coercive influences and give him the free and fair exercise of his franchise under state laws.

Now couple this with the financial plank which promises equality in the distribution of the national currency, at low rates of interest.

The white tenant lives adjoining the colored tenant. Their houses are almost equally destitute of comforts. Their living is confined to bare necessities. They are equally burdened with heavy taxes. They pay the same high rent for gullied and impoverished land.

They pay the same enormous prices for farm supplies. Christmas finds them both without any satisfactory return for a year's toil. Dull and heavy and unhappy, they both start the plows again when "New Year's" passes.

Now the People's Party says to these two men, "You are kept apart that you may be separately fleeced of your earnings. You are made to hate each other because upon that hatred is rested the keystone of the arch of financial despotism which enslaves you both. You are deceived and blinded that you may not see how this race antagonism perpetuates a monetary system which beggars both."

This is so obviously true it is no wonder both these unhappy laborers stop to listen. No wonder they begin to realize that no change of law can benefit the white tenant which does not benefit the black one likewise; that no system which now does injustice to one of them can fail to injure both. Their every material interest is identical. The moment this becomes a conviction, mere selfishness, the mere desire to better their conditions, escape onerous taxes, avoid usurious charges, lighten their rents, or change their precarious tenements into smiling, happy homes, will drive these two men together, just as their mutually inflamed prejudices now drive them apart.

Suppose these two men now to have become fully imbued with the idea that their material welfare depends upon the reforms we demand. Then they act together to secure them. Every white reformer finds it to the vital interest of his home, his family, his fortune, to see to it that the vote of the colored reformer is freely cast and fairly counted.

Then what? Every colored voter will be thereafter a subject of industrial education and political teaching.

Concede that in the final event, a colored man will vote where his material interests dictate that he should vote; concede that in the South the accident of color can make no possible difference in the interests of farmers, croppers, and laborers; concede that under full and fair discussion the people can be depended upon to ascertain where their interests lie—and we reach the conclusion that the Southern race question can be solved by the People's Party on the simple proposition that each race will be led by self-interest to support that which benefits it, when so presented that neither is hindered by the bitter party antagonisms of the past.

Let the colored laborer realize that our platform gives him a better guaranty for political independence; for a fair return for his work; a better chance to buy a home and keep it; a better chance to educate his children and see them profitably employed; a better chance to have public life freed from race collisions; a better chance for every citizen to be considered as a *citizen* regardless of color in the making and enforcing of laws,—let all this be fully realized, and the race question at the South will have settled itself through the evolution of a political movement in which both whites and blacks recognize their surest way out of wretchedness into comfort and independence.

The illustration could be made quite as clearly from other planks in the People's Party platform. On questions of land, transportation and finance, especially, the welfare of the two races so clearly depends upon that which benefits either, that intelligent discussion would necessarily lead to just conclusions.

Why should the colored man always be taught that the white man of his neighborhood hates him, while a Northern man, who taxes every rag on his back, loves him? Why should not my tenant come to regard me as his friend rather than the manufacturer who plunders us both? Why should we perpetuate a policy which drives the black man into the arms of the Northern politician?

Why should we always allow Northern and Eastern Democrats to enslave us forever by threats of the Force Bill?

Let us draw the supposed teeth of this fabled dragon by founding our new policy upon justice—upon the simple but profound truth that, if the voice of passion can be hushed, the self-interest of both races will drive them to act in concert. There never was a day during the last twenty years when the South could not have flung the money power into the dust by patiently teaching the Negro that we could not be wretched under any system which would not afflict him likewise; that we could not prosper under any law which would not also bring its blessings to him.

To the emasculated individual who cries "Negro supremacy!" there is little to be said. His cowardice shows him to be a degeneration from the race which has never yet feared any other race. Existing under such conditions as they now do in this country, there is no earthly chance for Negro domination, unless we are ready to admit that the colored man is our superior in will power, courage, and intellect.

Not being prepared to make any such admission in favor of any race the sun ever shone on, I have no words which can portray my contempt for the white men, Anglo-Saxons, who can knock their knees together, and through their chattering teeth and pale lips admit that they are afraid the Negroes will "dominate us."

The question of social equality does not enter into the calculation at all. That is a thing each citizen decides for himself. No statute ever yet drew the latch of the humblest home—or ever will. Each citizen regulates his own visiting list—and always will.

The conclusion, then, seems to me to be this: the crushing burdens which now oppress both races in the South will cause each to make an effort to cast them off. They will see a similarity of cause and a similarity of remedy. They will recognize that each should help the other in the work of repealing bad laws and enacting good ones. They will become political allies, and neither can injure the other without weakening both. It will be to the interest of both that each should have justice. And on these broad lines of mutual interest, mutual forbearance, and mutual support the present will be made the stepping-stone to future peace and prosperity.

47. The Cause of Both

Tom Watson did not reserve his views on cooperation between whites and Negroes for a Boston reform magazine, but expressed

Reprinted from *People's Party Paper* (Atlanta), March 17, 1892. Library of Congress.

them openly in his *People's Party Paper.* The selection which follows, written some six months before the *Arena* article appeared, is
a sketchy formulation of the subsequent piece.

Why should not a colored farmer feel the need of the same
relief as the white Farmer?

Why is not the Colored Tenant open to the conviction that
he is in the same boat as the white tenant; the colored laborer
with the white laborer?

Why cannot the cause of one be made the cause of both?

Why would this be dangerous?

I can see very well where it is dangerous to Ring Rule, to
Bossism, to the iron rule of the Money Power, but I can see no
reason why I am any less a white man—true to my color, my
rights, my principles—simply because the black people are
convinced that our Platform is a fair one, and vote for me
upon it.

The man who alludes to Social Equality in that connection,
insults the intelligence of those to whom he talks.

Social Equality is a question which every citizen settles for
himself. The law never did, and never can, interfere with it.

48. Fair Play Irrespective of Color

On August 9, 1892 Watson returned home to Thomson to begin his
bid for reelection. He had remained in Washington throughout the
congressional session, and was deeply hurt by reports that many
constituents were defecting and that the opposition party had already mounted a strongly vituperative campaign. Discouraged and

---

Reprinted from *People's Party Paper* (Atlanta), August 12, 1892.
Library of Congress.

physically exhausted, Watson was greeted by a crowd of six thousand, and proceeded to give one of the better speeches of his career. After two hours, he was forced to stop at the point of near collapse. Toward the beginning of the speech, Watson indicated that he would at some point discuss matters of interest to the Negroes in the audience, and after a long analysis of his voting record, turned to the topic of Negro rights. It is interesting to note here an element of *noblesse oblige* or stewardship in Watson's attitudes.

Now, my friends, I wish to discuss fairly and plainly, some of the facts in this campaign. I am glad to see so many of the colored people here, for I have something to say to them. I have never made a campaign in the Tenth District that I did not have something special to say to these colored people, and today I am going to read them a few lines of good doctrine. [Great applause, in which the colored people joined.]

. . . Fellow-citizens, I must hurry on. I want you colored citizens to draw near that you may hear what I have got to say, for I have something to say to you especially. [A voice, "Come up close; come Nicodemus; glory hallelujah!"] I have been here practicing law, for both white and black, some fifteen years, and if there is a black man in all this audience who can say that he ever trusted me with his case and I did not attend to it with the zeal and fidelity that I did for the whitest man in the county, let him say it here and now. [Several voices, "They cannot say it; nobody will say it."] Have I not always, when you put your cases in my hands, fought for you as if you were the whitest man in the country? [Cries of "Yes, yes, you have."] The first fee I ever received was from Zip Taylor, a black man; the first five dollars I ever made was paid by big-hearted Jack Roberts, and the first work I ever did when I was in the clerk's office was for Zip Taylor, and the records will show that I put him in possession of a little homestead and took him in out of the weather. [A voice, "We all know that; it's the God's truth."] It is a well known fact that when I ran for the Legislature in 1872, the black people supported me almost to a man. Why? Because it had sunk deep into their hearts that I tried to do right between man and man, and did not stop on account of color. [Cries from the colored, "Bless the Lord! We colored people knows that."] You know how I was hounded down and abused by some of the men who are now seeking your votes because I stood up at the courthouse and thanked you for giving me your support. [A voice: "We all know that; we doesn't forget."] You know that I said that I could see no reason why, because a man was colored, he should not have his say so as to who was the representative from McDuffie county as well as the proudest white man in the county. [A voice, "Go it, Tom; good-bye, Jim."] I will ask you this question: Has there ever been a time since you supported me and helped to elect me that the poorest black man in the county, if he had me representing him, would not trust me as quickly and as far as any white man in the county? [Cheering.]

On my plantation there are some black men working to-day who were my grandfather's slaves, and the foreman on my grandfather's farm was my foreman, and remained there in that position until the old man was too feeble to hold the hoe,—to lead the gang. Does not that speak well for the justice with which I have tried to treat your people? [A voice: "It does."] Do you not know that every colored man living on my place feels just as secure when I pass my word for anything as if I had drawn up the bond and signed the paper? [Cries of "That's so."] One of the last cases that I tried was that of a poor, unfortunate colored man, who was supposed to have committed murder. He did not have any friends, or if he did have they did not make themselves very numerous when he stood face to face with the gallows; he had no money and the judge assigned me to defend him, and I went into the case with all the power that God Almighty gave me; because naturally sympathizing with the poor and the oppressed, I thought that if there was a reasonable doubt it would be better for the county and for society at large, and for humanity that he should have it, and when Dennis Reese walked out of the Court House a free man it was to the astonishment of all the good people both white and colored in the county. [Cries of "Yes, yes, we remember all about that!"] I defended him because I had compassion for the poor, the old, the helpless and the friendless. [A voice: "That's so, Tom. We know you!"] Don't you know that I have always sympathized with the unfortunate and the poverty stricken? If ever a tramp was turned away from my door without anything to eat, it was done without my knowledge or consent or the knowledge or consent of my wife. I challenge the production of such a case. [A voice: "There ain't none."] Well, I remember another case. A poor colored woman, whose name I cannot remember, was up on the charge of stealing and Judge Roney in the kindness of his heart, remitted her sentence and told her to go home, putting her on good behavior. She had no home to go to, but she had three little children crying for bread, and you all know that I made an appeal in her behalf and passed the plate around up here in the court house, and said to the kind-hearted people, "Let us make up some money for this poor creature" [great applause and cries of "that's so"], and the result was that that woman went home with more money than she had, I reckon, since her freedom. [Renewed cheering.]

    . . . Now, I want to say another thing to you; and what I say to you I want to say in public in the blaze of day, so that all may hear it. I do not want to say anything to my white friends that I do not want the colored people to hear, and I do not want to say anything to the colored people that I would hide from my white friends. Now, what I want to say is this: I pledge you my word and honor, as a man and as a representative, that if you stand up for your rights and for your manhood, if you stand shoulder to shoulder with us in this fight, you shall

have fair play and fair treatment as men and as citizens, irrespective of your color. [Great cheering.]

I know that it has been said that I have raised a barrel of
money in Augusta to buy votes. I have no money to buy votes;
nor do I wish to buy the vote of any man, either white or
colored, even if I could, but I make this appeal to you—I ask
you this question: Is it not the most deadly insult to your color
to say that I, or anybody else, can buy you just as you were
bought and sold on the block in slavery? [Cries of "They cannot do it."] I know they say that they are not going to buy you
direct, but they say that they are going to sugar up a leader or
two, and that those leaders, with the sugar in their pockets,
will deliver you without dividing the sugar. [Derisive
laughter.]

What have we done, I ask you? We have broken away from
our leaders because they have not treated us right. Will you do
it too? [Cries of "Yes, we will!"] Let every man stand upon
his manhood; let every man say, "I am not a vassal;" let every
man put his fist between the eyes of the man who tries to buy
him; when these leaders who have always been such good
republicans, and have always so hated the democrats that they
can see no good in them come around and tell you that they
have discovered all at once that it is such a good party, say to
them as we say to ours, "We work for peace and harmony, for
mutual good will, and to wipe the color line out in politics."
Stand for your rights, and let every man be a man in politics.
[Voices: "We will, we will!"] You are doing nobly in the way
of educating your children; your daughters are beginning to
dress nicely and behave themselves decently, and be respected,
and now will you tear down, in one campaign, all the virtue,
morality and honesty that your schools have been trying to
inculcate because your leaders have been sugared and accepted by the leaders of the democratic party in the cities?
[A voice: "We will never do it."] My friends, this campaign
will decide many things, and one of the things it will decide is

whether or not your people and ours can daily meet in harmony, and work for law, and order, and morality, and wipe out the color line, and put every man on his citizenship irrespective of color. [Great cheering.]

49. The Prevention of a Lynching

Watson's 1892 campaign in Georgia was conducted along interracial lines: Not only did he enlist the support of Negro voters, but he often shared the platform with Negro speakers. In the closing weeks there was a dramatic incident which served as a test not only of Watson's courage, but of his determination to defend the rights of Negroes. The details, as related in Professor Woodward's biography of Watson, are as follows. A young Negro minister, H. S. Doyle, had worked actively in Watson's behalf, making no less than sixty-three speeches during the campaign. When Doyle's life had been threatened in late October he sought protection at Watson's residence, and was put up at a house on the grounds. Watson made it known to the lynch mob, who intended to come at night painted in blackface to take Doyle away, that he would defend Doyle with his life if that proved necessary. Watson then appealed for help, and many armed farmers came immediately into Thomson the next morning. As Woodward, in masterful understatement, observes: "The spectacle of white farmers riding all night to save a Negro from lynchers was rather rare in Georgia." And one might add, it was a spectacle which infuriated Watson's opponents, and raised him even higher in the Negroes' estimation. Watson and Doyle again shared the same platform, but this time surrounded by armed Populists. In the two editorials which follow, Watson first places the attempted lynching into a larger perspective, and then recounts some of the

---

Reprinted from *People's Party Paper* (Atlanta), Oct. 28, 1892. Library of Congress.

immediate events. His support of Doyle goes beyond the protection of a political ally; Watson demonstrates his awareness that lawlessness corrodes the entire society. He is not simply against lynching, but more positively, he is in favor of law and order.

I

The leaders and newspapers of the Democratic party have touched a depth of infamy in this campaign which is almost incredible. They have intimidated the voter, assaulted the voter, murdered the voter. They have bought votes, forced votes and stolen votes. They have incited lawless men to a pitch of frenzy which threatens anarchy. They have organized bands of hoodlums of both high and low degree to insult our speakers, silence our speakers, rotten-egg our speakers, and put lives in danger.

In the Tenth district this plan of campaign has had the fullest swing and has reached a desperate crisis. Mr. Watson has been repeatedly insulted, repeatedly howled down under a shower of the most odious epithets, and his life repeatedly threatened.

For this state of things the Democratic newspapers and leaders are directly responsible. They have lied about him in every conceivable way. They have lashed the rank and file into a condition of frenzied hatred against him personally. In this mad carnival of lies, misrepresentations and urging-on of violence, the Augusta Chronicle has been conspicuous. With a malignity which only one of Joe Brown's bribe-takers could show, they have hounded Mr. Watson from the opening speech of the campaign down to the shocking falsehoods concerning the meeting at Stellaville.

So far has this thing gone that the average Democrat believes that Mr. Watson is an enemy to his race and ought to be dealt with accordingly. Men have been heard to say on the streets of Augusta that he ought to be killed. They said the same thing on the night of the attempted meeting in the capital, when Judge Hilyer is said to have led the howlers.

There is no doubt on earth that there are large numbers of Democrats in every town who harbor this murderous idea. They are the blind and pitiable dupes and tools of the Augusta ring.

In no place has this lawless feeling been more continually fanned than in Thomson, where a small band of men with nothing to lose have been doing the dirty work of their Augusta bosses. These men have little standing and small following, but acting suddenly and desperately they were capable of embroiling better men in a deadly feud where the lives and fortunes of conservative people would be sacrificed as a consequence of the delirium of these reckless tools of the Augusta politicians.

Rev. H. S. Doyle, a colored preacher, was chased away from Sparta on the day of the State election. An account of the outrage has already been published in these columns. He came to Thomson for protection. A crowd of Democrats visited the house where he was stopping with the declared purpose of beating him. He was away. On his return he was arrrested in Augusta and thrown in jail upon the charge of carrying concealed weapons. Rev. W. J. White and Judson W. Lyons, learning of his situation, secured his release until next Thursday. He then came on to Thomson. He had scarcely touched the ground before the bootlicks of the Augusta ring began to send runners for their men. They had already said that Doyle should be expelled.

Doyle came to Mr. Watson's yard and asked protection. He got it. He was told to take up quarters in a negro house on the lot, and that no man should molest him save by warrant of law.

In the meantime the Democratic gang had gathered. About twenty of the bitterest had congregated, and the mutterings of the storm were in the air. Mr. Watson took two friends and went to the mayor and told him of the situation, and asked that official (who is a Democrat) to say to the band that Doyle was on his lot and would remain there, and if they came on the lot and offered him violence somebody would get hurt. The mayor at once took steps to dissuade the gang from their purpose. That purpose was well known. No secret was made of the fact.

On Sabbath night these Democrats proposed to raid the premises of Mr. Watson, seize the person of this poor colored man who had sought asylum in the yard of his Congressman, and commit whatever violence was necessary in order to carry out their purpose. They knew quite well that Mr. Watson would defend Doyle with his life. They were coming armed to the teeth and with sufficient force to crush Mr. Watson's resistance, and capture the fugitive whose only offense was that he had dared to make speeches for the People's party.

If it had been necessary to kill Mr. Watson to get Doyle, then Mr. Watson would have been shot down like a dog in his own door yard, under the eyes of his wife and children.

To this extent has the Augusta ring, with its whisky, its money and its lies, infuriated men who wear white skins over hearts which were not always murderous.

By a providential incident a colored man found out what was going forward among the Democrats on yesterday's quiet Sabbath evening and gave the alarm to a trusted friend of Mr. Watson. In less time than it takes to tell it the brave men of the People's party were notified. They came. They always come. And when the Democrats found that they must clash with twenty-five as resolute men as ever faced an enemy they washed the black paint off their faces and turned the right sides of their coats out again.

Nothing but the fact that we were ready, and they knew it, prevented as cowardly an outrage as was ever committed in Georgia. Had it not been for timely warning, as black a deed as the annals of political murder contain would have been done last night; and we can prove it!

The Democrats have said that Doyle should be run away from here, and should not speak here. He is now on Mr. Watson's lot. He is going to stay there. Mr. Watson will speak here Tuesday. Doyle will speak here Tuesday.

That's all.   T. E. W.

II

To all white men we submit this view: Democratic lawlessness is willing to stain the Sabbath day with riot and bloodshed in order to wreak vengeance on a man who, if he has committed any crime whatever, is accessible to the law. Not only this, they are willing to jeopardize the life of your representative and his family in carrying out their unlawful designs. In their furious partisanship they are willing to violate the sanctity of God's day; the sanctity of a citizen's home, and the sanctity of a citizen's right to free speech and free action.

If these are Democratic principles then God save the people from Democracy.

To the colored people we submit this view:

One of your race has been shot away from the polls, hounded from the parsonage where he should have been safe, chased from his home and his county, by those Democrats who profess to so love the negro. He has been pursued into the county where he took refuge. With his enemies hot upon his heels, he has gone to the home of his Congressman and appealed for safety. He has promptly received all Mr. Watson could give. As fully as Mr. Watson could protect himself he stood ready to defend the man to whom he gave shelter.

The People's party friends of Mr. Watson gave him their prompt co-operation. They came at the word. They felt that the cause of the poorest man in the Tenth district was the cause [of] us all.

We were determined to give asylum and protection to the weakest of our men, just as we would to the strongest.

Presenting this firm front to our enemies, they recoiled as they always will recoil. They know they were wrong and that we were right.

They could not face resolute men who were not only armed with Winchesters, but also with the more powerful weapons of right.

Therefore they painfully washed the black off their faces and sneakingly crept to bed.

Men of the People's party! Show to the world that we mean to commit no wrong, and to suffer none!

Show that we will defend ourselves and our friends in all that is right.

Show that the humblest white man and the poorest colored man in the Tenth district is as much an object of our care as the proudest leader we have got.

Show that the man who wrongs one of us wrongs all, and that we all will endeavor to right that wrong.

In this way we inspire confidence in our friends and check violence in our enemies.

Let none of us be the aggressor.

Adhere strictly to the lines of self-defense. . . . With God's approval always in mind, stand to your rights like men, fearing nothing except to do wrong.

50. Equal Justice

The Louisiana People's Party further illustrates the Populist insistence on equal justice for whites and Negroes. William Hair, in a recent dissertation on agrarian protest in that state, quotes from the initial address issued by the state party when it was established in October 1891: "You colored men . . . must now realize that

Reprinted from *People's Party Paper* (Atlanta), March 10, 1892. Library of Congress.

there is no hope of any further material benefit to you in the Republican party, and that if you remain in it you will continue to be hewers of wood and drawers of water in the future as you have been in the past." Significantly, the document was entitled, "Address to the People of the State of Louisiana . . . Irrespective of Class, Color, or Past Political Affiliation." Hair points out that of the 171 delegates who attended the party's nominating convention in February 1892, twenty-four were Negro, and that two Negroes were placed in nomination on the state ticket. They withdrew their names in the belief that the time for such a move was not ripe, and were instead made members of the People's party state executive committee. The following selection is taken from the platform which emerged from that meeting.

We declare emphatically that the interests of the white and colored races in the South are identical, but that both would suffer unless the undisputed control of our government were assured to the intelligent and educated portion of the population.

Legislation beneficial to the white man must, at the same time, be beneficial to the colored man.

Equal justice and fairness must be accorded to each, and no sweeping legislation should be allowed bearing unjustly on either.

51. A Negro at the State Convention

A writer who signed himself "Hayseeder" wrote to the organ of the Georgia State Farmers' Alliance that Populists must continue to encourage Negroes to participate in the movement. He discounts

Reprinted from "Hayseeder" to editor, *Southern Alliance Farmer* (Atlanta), Aug. 2, 1892. University of Georgia Library.

Democratic criticism as an attempt to keep both races apart, and thereby maintain one-party rule.

Why is it that the bosses have raised such a howl because John Mack, the negro, went to the state convention held in Atlanta on the 20th to represent his race, and also seconded the nomination of W. L. Peek for governor? Are they not citizens of the State, holding the same rights under the law that the white man does? If so, isn't it better to give them representation in the convention, that they may know for whom they are voting thereby getting them to vote with the white people at home than to ignore them till the day of election and then try to buy or force them to vote, thereby driving them into the Republican party, which the Democrats have so recently found out is an honorable party? Is not all this howl because the bosses see that their little game is played and the negroes of this county are going to vote with the People's Party?

52. An Equal Share of Benefits

In a remarkably frank and detailed letter, a Populist from Alabama presented a viewpoint which on paper is not terribly different from the ones noted thus far: Negroes must be accorded full political equality; they share with poorer whites the same material interests; only by banding together can the lower classes effectively challenge the power structure. Indeed, he even argues that the Democrats deliberately stir up prejudice to prevent such a coalition from taking form. Yet, unlike many of the views found above, this Populist not only denies the possibility of social equality but goes out of his way

Reprinted from John C. McLeran to editor, *People's Weekly Tribune* (Birmingham), May 28, 1896. Alabama Department of Archives and History.

to underscore that denial. Using Booker T. Washington's formulation as his point of departure, the writer insists upon a sharp distinction between political and social equality, while at the same time urging that the poor of neither race can advance unless the poor of both do.

The only argument on which the Democrats depended for result in '92 was the Force Bill. They have repealed the law and are now reduced to appeals to the prejudices of the whites against the colored people. Hoping to control the people through these prejudices to vote against their interests, they enter the campaign.

Booker Washington said at the Atlanta Exposition that upon all questions of a social character the two races could be as separate as the fingers but one as the hand on all questions involving their material welfare. This was heralded as a solution of the race issue. . . . Well, we the Populists are simply making a practical application of this sentiment. We are co-operating with the Republicans for the purpose of restoring the purity of the ballot box, of having once more honest elections and majority rule. If this is not a question involving the material welfare of both races then in heavens name what would be such a question? A cause must be weak indeed, that has no loftier argument than appeals to the prejudices of the whites against the negroes; and in fact the argument is in keeping with the cause of "organized" Democracy. Their talk about our going into the Republican party or leaning towards social equality bothers no intelligent Populist. We know that they know such a charge to be false when they make it. In fact we are farther from advocating or practicing social equality, than any ballot box stuffer alive. Our objection does not relax at the going down of the sun. We have got no children at the Tuskegee normal school or kindred there.

There is no danger of a contingency of choice between the

old parties. We must first down this hydraheaded monster of corruption called "organized" Democracy and then we will have a battle of the ballots with the Republicans. In that contest we hope to have the assistance of the colored voter because we are the only party that is in fact a friend to the colored race and we are so, not from choice but from necessity. The colored man is a factor in the problem which we cannot eliminate if we would. The Populists represent the industry side of the question. The two old parties represent the usury side of it. Whatever victories we may win, whatever we may accomplish for the benefit of agriculture or productive industry, from the very nature of the case, the colored man will have an equal share with us in those benefits. We cannot prevent it if we would. Likewise if we are defeated, the colored man will have an equal share with us in the woes of that defeat. No matter with which party he votes, he cannot prevent that. This may be truly said about all classes engaged in productive industry.

This has nothing whatever to do with social equality. It is a question of the material interests of both races.

The time has been when the negro had twenty thousand majority in the State. He had just been freed, was entirely ignorant and irresponsible. With this majority and in this condition the right of suffrage was thrust upon him. It did look at that time, that any means under heavens to thwart that majority was the lesser of two evils. But now, all this is changed. A generation has passed away. The whites have now a majority of sixty thousand in this State. The danger from negro supremacy at the polls has passed away forever. The negroes vote was stolen or miscounted in the beginning with the excuse that it was for the security of a white man's government. Now the votes of both white and black are stolen in the interest of a white rascal's government! The whole moral tone of society from Statesman to the rum seller is blighted with the curse of this crime.

53. The Negro Is a Man and a Citizen

That Populists in Georgia were forthright in calling upon Negroes for support, rather than in accepting such support reluctantly or secretly, can be seen from an editorial in the Gracewood *Wool Hat*. These remarks were prompted by the announcement of a prominent Negro that he was endorsing the People's party. The paper contends that only Populism encourages Negroes to act independently instead of as an object to be manipulated.

It is taken for granted that [the] Republican party will not place a ticket in the field for the state campaign, and the choice of the voters will be between the Populist and Democratic parties. Aside from the platform of the two parties, and the measures advocated by them, which should certainly influence any honest, intelligent man who loves justice and desires prosperity to smile upon the country, to vote the Populist ticket, there [is] to the colored citizens the additional consideration of how each proposes to treat the negro voter.

The Democrats treat him as a brute. Ever ready to raise the cry of "Negro Domination" they seek to obtain the negro vote by the most debasing means, by corruption and debauchery, snubbing them publicly and secretly pandering to their lowest instincts. All this that by the help of his vote they may be placed in power which when obtained they use to enact laws which oppress and rob the masses, both white and colored.

The Populists recognize that the negro is a man and a citizen. They want him to see that his ballot is a sacred trust put into his hands to assist in shaping the destiny of the nation and not something to be bartered to designing demagogues

---

Reprinted from *Wool Hat* (Gracewood, Georgia) as quoted in *People's Party Paper* (Atlanta), June 22, 1894. Library of Congress.

who have the longest purse and the largest jug. The Populists will not resort to meetings in dark alleys or make secret promises which will not bear the light of day. On the question of social equality they stand where all other sensible men stand, irrespective of party or race, for to invade the sanctity of home and family by legal enactments would be the ruin of both races. But in the enjoyment of the rights granted to every citizen by the constitution the Populists advocate equal and exact justice to all men, and to again secure which they invite the negroes to vote with them by treating them as men and not as brutes.

54. Voluntary Colonization

As stated earlier, it would be incorrect to suggest that all Populists sought a coalition with Negroes, and respected them as human beings. There may well be cases of outright hostility, but a more likely departure from the general position is one showing varying degrees of ambivalence. In the following selection, two planks pertaining to Negroes in the 1894 state platform of the Jeffersonian Democratic-Populist fusion group, there is a strong declaration in favor of political rights and fair treatment for Negroes; but there is also a stand taken in favor of voluntary colonization to lessen the number of Negroes in the state.

7. As Thomas Jefferson was opposed to any restriction upon the suffrage of men, so are we, except it be for some grades of crime, among which we would place the purchase or sale of a vote, or other interference with the honest expression of the will of the people at the ballot box.

Reprinted from *Daily News* (Birmingham), Feb. 8, 1894. University of Alabama Library.

. . . 10. We would discourage the spirit of emigration among the colored people, and encourage them to be honest and industrious by dealing fairly with them and according to them their rights under the law. We are in favor, however, of having the general government set apart sufficient territory to constitute a State, given exclusively to the colored race, to which they may voluntarily go, and in which they alone shall be entitled to suffrage and citizenship.

55. On Negro Participation

A more clearly anti-Negro statement can be seen in the *People's Weekly Tribune* of Birmingham. While the paper did not promote racial antagonisms, it did in this instance boast that no Negroes have held positions of responsibility in the state party. Further, in commenting on the Democrats' claim that theirs was the party of white supremacy, the paper felt that they were not *sufficiently* in favor of white supremacy.

. . . Let us try them by it. In 1891 their Registrars did all they could to get the negroes to register while the opposition did all it could to prevent registering by the negro. How does that fact tally with white supremacy? In 1894 the negroes in the black belt of this District were most solemnly assured if they would then vote for Underwood they would be cheerfully admitted to the Democratic primaries of this year. How does that fit white supremacy? No negro was ever promised any political position by the Populists. Mr. Cleveland gave the best paying office in the United States, except his own, to a negro, besides

---

Reprinted from *People's Weekly Tribune* (Birmingham), June 4, 1896. Alabama Department of Archives and History.

others of high honor. No negro ever held a seat in any Populist Convention in Alabama. Every beat in Oates' county sent a negro delegate to the county Democratic Convention. Every Judge of Probate, Sheriff and Clerk of the Circuit Court in the black belt uses the negro's right to vote to set up State and county government calculated to suppress and negative the white vote.

56. An Alliance of the Common People

Yet the *People's Weekly Tribune* could and did feature the letter of a Negro from Eufala, Alabama, calling upon all Negroes to join the Populist movement. For William Drewry Jackson, Populism was the hope and not the enemy of Negroes. It represented the cause of all underprivileged people, farmer and worker, Negro and white.

In my opinion, it would be the heighth of wisdom and of superlative importance were the Afro Americans to repudiate both the old parties, and renounce all of their allegiance and fidelity thereto, and switch in and ally themselves with the rank and file of those who are endeavoring, bona fide, to devise some plans by which to substantiate a popular government, a government of the people, for the people and by the people.

. . . I hope the day is not far distant when the common masses of the common people, including the laborers of towns and cities, as well as the great body of yeomanry, will wake up to a sense of duty, come together and vote in a common cause to throw off and exonerate themselves from the yoke that

Reprinted from letter of William Drewry Jackson, *People's Weekly Tribune* (Birmingham), March 19, 1896. Alabama Department of Archives and History.

has been pinching their necks for the last decade, for in reality they are only serfs and vassals used by the demagogues to fill the coffers of the magnates and money kings.

57. A Chance to Earn a Home

A Negro in Georgia likewise endorsed the Populist movement, although for reasons which were the direct counterpart of those advanced by many white Populists: social equality was an irrelevant issue; the focus must be on economics and not race. In his view, Negroes had more important things on their minds than integrated schools and churches, for they wanted to rise out of poverty and carve out a decent life.

Editor People's Party Paper:

Ever since the reform movement began, we colored people have had more advice given us by the democrats than we have had before or since freedom. Their advice is for us to stick to the republican party.

In the race between Cleveland and Blaine they did not give us such advice; nor in the Cleveland and Harrison campaign did they tell us to vote the republican ticket. But now, since the laboring men of the north, south and west have seen their families in want of food and raiment and their children growing up without education, they have looked into the causes of their poverty. They have petitioned congress for some measure of relief, but congress has laughed at their petitions and told them to go home and work harder and eat less. We have gone home and worked harder and eat less, and find ourselves in a worse condition than before.

Reprinted from S.D.D. to editor, *People's Party Paper* (Atlanta), June 3, 1892. Library of Congress.

Now we are told that we are naked and hungry because we worked too hard and made too much cotton in the south and too much wheat, corn and meat in the west.

Now, since we could see no hope of better times through the old parties, and have got together and formed a new party—a People's Party—the democrats are kicking terribly; for Colonel Livingston says it will bring about negro supremacy—it will wipe out the color line.

Now, let me tell you, Mr. Editor, we don't want to rule the government; we don't want to come into your family; we don't want to enter your schoolhouses or your churches. But I tell you what we do want: We want equal rights at the ballot-box and equal justice before the law; we want better wages for our labor and better prices for our produce; we want more money in circulation to pay for our labor or our produce; we want to lift the mortgage from the old cow and mule which they have carried till they are sway-backed; we want to school our children, and we want a chance to earn a home.

We can never realize these wants without more money in circulation.

Our old people have been working for twenty-seven years and have not got a dollar laid by for old age. But the gold-bugs are laying up money every day and plenty to spare to carry elections.

The democrats have hired such of our ministers as they could to go to work among our people to save the old republican party. Who ever heard the like before—white democrats hiring colored men to vote the republican ticket?

They call the republicans their enemies, yet they hire colored men to bring out candidates and vote the republican ticket. The object is to defeat the People's Party, so if the democrats are beaten the republicans will win, because they know they will be brothers when they get to Washington anyway.

It seems to be a hard thing for us colored men to give up

the republican party, but let us stop and consider: We are living in another man's house, working another man's land, and our smoke house and meal-tub are in town.

Let us quit the old party and vote for wife and children and a chance for a home.

S.D.D.

58. Equal Opportunities in Education

In presenting evidence on Populist attitudes toward Negroes, the writer is constantly reminded of how these responses differ not only from that of many southerners in the 1890's, but throughout the twentieth century up to and perhaps including our own day. Populists were not afraid to face the issue of race relations. They did not sweep it under the rug, nor did they try to deny its existence by dinning into each other's ears the cry of white supremacy. If their confrontation with race was limited, it was also honest. And it was also courageous. Poorer whites and their leaders understood the aspirations of the Negro people; they did not ridicule these aspirations or the men who held them. Today, the South has forgotten that hard-core segregationist views were not always a part of southern history. There have always been exceptions, sometimes in the case of isolated individuals, sometimes large-scale social movements, and these exceptions must be brought to light by the historian so that all will realize there has never been a monolithic, psychologically ingrained view governing the attitudes of whites to Negroes and Negroes to whites. It would seem inconceivable at the time of this writing that a southern white leader could denounce racial injustice in Philadelphia, Mississippi. Yet, Frank Burkitt, the leader

---

Speech of Frank Burkitt, July 31, 1895, quoted in William D. McCain, *The Populist Party in Mississippi* (unpub. M.A. thesis, University of Mississippi, 1931), pp. 46, 48.

of Mississippi Populism, told a Philadelphia audience in September 1895 that he refused to sign the 1890 state constitution because of the clause disfranchising "50,000 of the best citizens of the state." The difference between the two periods marks the difference not only in race relations but in the total outlook on man's dignity and capabilities. In the following selection, Burkitt discusses the public schools in his acceptance speech as the People's party nominee for governor in 1895.

In the face of this damnable record [3,000,000-acre land give-away that was supposed to be the property of the public schools], it is now proposed by gentlemen who are expecting high official preferment at the hands of the Democratic convention which assembles one week hence, to so change our school laws as to practically destroy the colored schools of the state and when this is done it will require one more step to abrogate the schools of the poor whites in the country. . . .

It will be our purpose to maintain free public schools for at least four months in a year for equal benefit of all the children of the state without regard to race, color or condition in life, and if the present law, honestly enforced, does not meet this, then such changes will be made as may be necessary to give every child in the state equal opportunities to attain a common school education.

59. Jefferson's Creed

Tom Watson's Douglasville, Georgia, speech of July 4, 1893 affirmed the Jeffersonian position on equal justice to all men, and then went on to deny that such a position could lead to the domination

Reprinted from *People's Party Paper* (Atlanta), July 7, 1893. Library of Congress.

by Negroes over whites. The speech appears to reflect the argument of Anglo-Saxon superiority, and perhaps that was Watson's intent. Yet, Watson lists so many features of specific power which whites possess in American society that one might place a different interpretation on his remarks: The cry of "Negro domination" does not hold because, if anything, it is the whites who control the power structure and have always controlled it. Through the cumulation of examples, Watson conveys the impression that injustice has been done to the Negroes.

I believe in the Jeffersonian creed with all my heart, and think that all the aims of good government can be covered by that one sentence.

EQUAL AND EXACT JUSTICE TO ALL MEN!

To the rich and to the poor, to the farmer and the merchant; to the Banker and the miner; to the scholar and the ditcher. And I emphasize here what I have been so misrepresented and blamed for saying before, that this Republic will never reach its true grandeur as long as a dead line is drawn between one section and another, one color and another.

I yield to no man in my pride of race. I believe the Anglo-Saxon is stronger, in the glorious strength of conception and achievement, than any race of created man. But from my very pride of race springs my intense scorn of that phantasm, manufactured by the political boss, and called "Negro domination"!

Socially, I want no mixing of races. It is better that both should preserve the race integrity by staying apart. But when it comes to matters of law and justice, I despise the Anglo-Saxon who is such an infernal coward as to deny legal rights to any man on account of his color for fear of "Negro domination."

"Dominate" what? "Dominate" how? "Dominate" who?

It takes Intellect to dominate: haven't we got it?

It takes Majorities to dominate: haven't we got them?

It takes Wealth to dominate: haven't we got it?

It takes social, financial, legislative, military, naval, ecclesiastical and educational establishments to dominate: haven't we got them?

For a thousand years the whites, the Anglo-Saxons, have had all these advantages. Armed with the garnered wealth of ten centuries, equipped with all the mental advantages of school systems hoary with age; holding all the land, all the avenues of commerce, all the sources of political power, outnumbering the blacks eight to one, and continually gaining on them, what words can paint the cowardice of the Anglo-Saxon who would deny "equal and exact justice" to the ignorant, helpless, poverty-cursed Negro in whose ears the clank of chains have scarcely ceased to sound—upon the ground that he feared:

"Negro domination."

Away with such contemptible timidity of counsel!

For twenty-five years the Eastern democracy has whipped Southern and Western democracy into repulsive positions by the threat of helping Republicans "put the Negro over us!"

In the name of common sense, let us throw off this yoke and be men.

No power on this earth will ever reverse the decree of God!

60. The Curse of Intolerance

Watson's attack on intolerance brings this section to a fitting close. A front-page editorial in mid-1894, it pleads for a willingness to entertain new ideas and to fight for those ideas in the face of social pressures. Fears on race, as the last sentence suggests, constitute an important form of intolerance.

Reprinted from *People's Party Paper* (Atlanta), July 20, 1894. Library of Congress.

If we were asked to name the most paralyzing hindrance to the progress of any people, we would say intolerance.

No country ever thrived under it; no people ever improved under it.

Tyranny uses it as a prop; malice uses it as a deadly weapon.

Wherever its iron hand has ruled, progress has been halted, mental achievement ceases and human happiness disappears.

Wherever church and state have gone hand in hand, compelling all minds to accept one creed, as an escape from persecutions worse than banishment or death, independence gives way to blind servility, hypocrisy takes the place of manly openness, and cowardice becomes more common than courage.

Whenever any people has been cursed with intolerance, either political or religious, its ruinous effects can be traced in the history of national decay and death.

The reason is plain. The nation prospers most where the largest number of individuals prosper.

The individual cannot prosper unless you allow him freedom of action. When you compel a man to hide his manhood, his opinions, his actions, he becomes a hypocrite and a coward. And hypocrites and cowards never did open a way to national greatness and never will.

It takes brave men to make a country great. And to have brave men the community must not combine to crush the individual who dares to have personal independence. If Jones is born into the world with no chance to think and act for himself; if he has got to go to his neighbor to get his opinions just as he goes to the tailor for clothes, then Jones will never have a mental equipment which lifts him above the ape, simply because there is no need for him to investigate any subject whatsoever. If he is obliged to adjust himself to the opinions which already prevail, there is no reason for losing time in studying them. If to differ from those opinions would bring down upon his head the intolerant persecution of the whole community, then the instinct of self-preservation will keep him from mental investigation.

Thus the mind of Jones never develops because it never investigates.

And, inasmuch as the community is made up of Joneses, the community has no mental progress because it never investigates.

The calm of the Dead sea rests over the surface of society, and progress halts because no man dares to lead it.

Intolerence was the curse of Spain.

Intolerance was the curse of Ireland.

And intolerance is the curse of the south today.

PART FIVE

THE BRUTALITY OF CAPITAL:

POPULIST SUPPORT

FOR THE WORKING CLASS

While the Populist movement was predominantly agrarian in composition, this did not mean that it confined its vision of a better
society simply to improved conditions for the farmer. On the contrary, Populists were strongly pro-labor, and regarded the industrial
worker not as a rival but as a natural ally who was oppressed by
the same economic forces and who shared the same goals of social
justice and an equitable distribution of wealth. Only through united
action, they reasoned, could there be an effective challenge to the
dominant groups in American society. Hence, their attempts to
effect a farmer-labor coalition were founded on economic necessity
and political reality, and not on the desire to restore the lost world
of producer values where all laborers were enveloped by the same
physiocratic cloak. Appeals to the working class for a common front
looked to the future, indeed to the belief that agrarian radicalism
and the labor movement constituted the chief means, perhaps the
only means, to attaining the democratic transformation each had

been seeking on its own. And these appeals demonstrated not only sympathy for the plight of labor, but a very real awareness of the significance of the industrial warfare during the period. For Populists, strikes signified far more than the goal of higher wages and lower hours: Homestead, Pullman and other scenes of conflict represented the desperate stand of desperate men to preserve their unions and to keep themselves from being driven down to the subsistence level of existence. Populists followed these struggles closely, arguing that labor's fight was also their fight because the degradation of one necessarily meant the degradation of the other. They maintained that the right to organize was crucial, for workers were powerless as individuals when resisting the policies of large corporations. Accordingly, Populists defended the principle of unionism, and opposed all policies of brutality—such as the use of Pinkertons and troops—which were designed to destroy labor organizations. The lines were becoming tightly drawn, and Populists made clear where they stood.

61. Millionaires Against Miners

In "an open letter to the millionaires," Henry D. Lloyd in the first selection describes the circumstances surrounding the lockout in the coal mines of Spring Valley, Illinois. For Lloyd, the campaign of systematic impoverishment found here was not an atypical instance, but rather served as a case study of the irresponsibility of corporate practices prevalent throughout the United States during the late 1880's. He points in this analysis to the way a policy of intimidation operates: Far more men are recruited for the mines than are needed, so that the miners will be forced to fight against each other for the available jobs. The wage level is depressed to below a sub-

Reprinted from Henry D. Lloyd, *A Strike of Millionaires Against Miners* (Chicago: Belford-Clarke Company, 1890), pp. 10–16, 19, 26–27, 32, 34–38, 48, 51–52, 57–59, 79–83, 85, 96–99, 105–112, 121, 247.

sistence standard, and the men have the choice of working on the company's terms or not at all. When the mines are shut down without warning or explanation, when starvation and sickness become living realities, the will to resist is broken down and the men finally submit to the proffered arrangements—not only low wages but the destruction of their union. Lloyd sees this as a disciplinizing process, designed to insure total control over the lives of the workers. These were the kinds of facts Populists recognized quite early, and these were the kinds of facts they sought to change.

. . . I have selected the story of Spring Valley for narration because I have come to know it; not because there has been anything there in your conduct as capitalists and corporations specially worse than what has been done elsewhere. On the contrary, I believe, from my investigations, that the case of Spring Valley is fairly representative of the relations between miners and mine-owners throughout the country—and that is the worst feature of it all. If Spring Valley were exceptional, we could dismiss it as a mere aberration of the commercial conscience of some particularly depraved pot-hunter, and let it go. But when, by reading official documents like the report of the Ohio legislative committee of 1885 on the Hocking Valley strike, the report of the congressional committee of 1887 on the coal strikes in Pennsylvania, and other authorities, we come to realize that Spring Valley is but one case out of a multitude—but one pustule of a disease spread through the whole body—we begin to get an idea of the seriousness of our social condition.

The story of Spring Valley needs but a change of names and a few details to be the story of Braidwood, Ill., where babies and men and women wither away to be transmigrated into the dividends of a millionaire coal-miner of Beacon street, Boston. It needs but a few changes to be the story of Punxsutawney—where starving foreigners have eaten up all the dogs in the country to keep themselves loyally alive to dig coal again when their masters re-open the coal kennels; and of Scranton, and the Lehigh Valley, where the hard, very hard coal barons of Pennsylvania manufacture artificial winter for twelve months of every year. It needs but a few changes to be the story of Brazil, Ind., where the Brazil Block Coal Company locked out their thousands of miners last year until their wives and children grew transparent enough to be glasses through which the miners could read, though darkly, the terms of surrender which they had to accept. It needs but a few changes to be the story of the Hocking Valley, where Pinkerton gunpowder was burned to give the light by which Labor could read "the free contract" its brother Capital wanted it to sign—or the story of the Reading Collieries, where, as stated in the report of the congressional committee of 1887–1888, the employer provoked the miners to riot, and then shot the rioters "legally." The story of Spring Valley needs not many changes to be a picture of what all American industry will come to be if the power of our Bourbons of business, such as you have shown yourselves to be at Spring Valley, develops at its present rate up to the end of the nineteenth century.

. . . Four legal dummies, or fictitious "persons," were the creators of Spring Valley. These were the four corporations, the Chicago & North-Western Railroad, the Spring Valley Coal Company, the Spring Valley Town Site Company, and the Northwest Fuel Company of St. Paul, behind which you who were the real persons are masked. According to any right standard of morals and law, every one of you who is a stockholder in those corporations must bear his share of the responsibility for what was done, just as each of you gladly receives his share of the profits. At the beginning, Spring Valley and its miseries and wrongs were the conception and achievement of but one or two among the leading owners of the railroad and the other companies. These few did the planning, secured the approval of the board of directors, and the active officers of the railroad, let in "on the ground floor" the influential men whose help they wanted, got the special freight rates needed to enable the "enterprise" to steal the business of its competitors, bought the coal land, and invented the various details of the scheme by which fortunes for you and themselves were to be made out of the public need for coal, the workingmen's need for employment, and the misuse of the powers of the common carrier. At the inception of the "enterprise," as Ali Baba would have us call it, some of the directors and most of the stockholders of the railroad, if not those of the other corporations, could plead that they had no actual knowledge of what was going on, and so no real responsibility for it. But the press and other indignant protestants when the iniquities of years culminated in the "lockout" made the whole matter, ending in this strike of the millionaires against the miners, a common scandal. But so far as the public know, not one of you, the directors, not one of you, the stockholders, in whose name and for whose profit the campaign of starvation and slander was carried on, has disavowed or discouraged it. You all seem to have accepted unprotestingly your share of the guilt—and gilt; and, if you have had any other anxiety than that the millionaires should succeed in their strike against the miners so that you might have more gilt, you have never let the public become aware of it. Not one of you, so far as known, sent a word of sympathy, or a mouthful of food, to the thousands who were being ground to powder by your agents for your benefit. Just who you are, accessories of the original willing sinners, the people cannot learn, for the names of the stockholders of our public corporations are kept in closest secrecy as one of the prerogatives of the private ownership of public highways. The laws of the State of Illinois require its railroads to keep records in Chicago, in which the transfers of stock are noted. Even that is not done by these bundles of men—so powerful because so well tied together. They think it of no ill omen to themselves, who get their vast wealth from the control of roads given them by the law, to set a public example of flagrant nullification of law. The corporation, which the great political economist Adam Smith predicted would never come into general use, has grown to be the almost universal instrument of modern business. It has become greater than government, and it shrouds its members in a secrecy, under the dark protection of which they can, with impunity, give rein to passions of power and greed. They have the cloak of invisibility, and they use it as men of prey and lust would use the darkness of our streets if cities put out their lights and went back to mediaeval gloom and crime. The public cannot penetrate into the anonymity which protects most of you who are responsible for Spring Valley.

. . . A common personality runs through the ownership of the railroad, the coal mine, the town lots, and the fuel company's business. Through this mutual element an identity of interest was established for all the associated capitalists of these enterprises, who represent upward of $500,000,000 at the least. The identity of interest has been practical, not nominal. They have accepted the results, still possess them, and are expectantly waiting for more. Through the easy machinery of the corporation, which is your kind of labor union, there has been a concert of action, with a common design, for a common object. The profits on the sale of farms as city lots to laborers and tradesmen, on the transportation of the coal, on the use of it for the locomotives of the road, on the buying and selling of it, on the sales of supplies to the miners, have gone to one or another of you to whom this letter is addressed.

[Lloyd then discusses how these companies artificially boomed the town of Spring Valley, bought acreage and subdivided the land into town lots, lured the miners in with promises of jobs at high wages, and left the town improvements to be paid for by the people themselves.]

. . . The Spring Valley *Gazette* of November 14, 1885, said: "What makes Spring Valley different from other coal towns is the fact that the contracts for the coal were made before the fields were open. It is to supply the Chicago & North-Western and the vast coal-using country tributary to that system. The coal company is the largest soft-coal corporation in the country, having a paid-up capital of $1,500,000. The selling of lots began in July last, and at the present time (July to November) about 1,000 lots have been sold. The price of lots ranges from $150 to $300." According to these figures, which were probably furnished to the *Gazette* by the agent of the town-site company to help the "boom," the total sales in the first six months had been about $200,000 for land which had cost less than $20,000.

From the coal-mining places in Illinois and the neighboring States miners who could move did so. It was by the best of their class that the skillfully prepared bait was taken. It was not the lazy miners who took the trouble to move themselves to the new industrial center. It was not the poor workers who could not get out of debt where they were—it was not the thoughtless and intemperate, who had saved no money with which to make the transfer. The men who came to Spring Valley were picked men—selected out of the whole number of the coal miners of the country by their intelligence, their thrift, their habits of industry. These men read the statements published by the Chicago & North-Western Railway, the Spring Valley Coal Company and the Town Site Company, and, seeing that the leaders of the enterprise were of the best business talent of America, and able, with their hundreds of millions of capital, to carry out any enterprise they undertook, decided, without a second thought, "Spring Valley is the place for us and our families."

[Agents of these companies, Lloyd continued, even roamed over Europe, encouraging miners to come to Spring Valley.]

. . . The "supply" of labor is in this way made to overrun the "demand," and the sacred character of the "immutable law of supply and demand" is given an illustration which workingmen understand, even if political economists do not. The "unchanging" law, when worked in this way, increases the number of the customers who buy goods at the "pluck-me" stores kept by the company, makes wages low by the under-bidding of the unemployed against the employed; it keeps the men poor, humble, and submissive to all your regulations and exactions. This method of regulating "supply and demand" is not a native product of Illinois. It is an importation from Pennsylvania. The select committee of Congress which investigated the labor troubles in Pennsylvania in 1888, say:

"Many thousands of surplus laborers are always kept on hand to underbid each other for employment, and thereby force the men to submit to whatever treatment the company may impose."

[Describing his personal interviews with the miners, Lloyd found that not wrath but patience characterized their responses. This led him to make the following statement on the nobility of the masses, and how they, and not their oppressors, retain a sense of dignity and autonomy.]

. . . I was amazed and humbled. It seemed to me that, had I been thus made the victim of inhuman greed for "more," had I and my home and my life been butchered—not "to make a Roman holiday," but an American dividend—I would have thought a lifetime too little to give to a crusade of retribution. The truth then first really dawned upon me, that there is a sanctification which comes, however unconsciously, to the victims of wrong and injustice, and that it is the master, not the slave, who receives the double curse of oppression.
. . . The miners, under the promise of steady employment, bought your lots on monthly payments, and began to build homes, getting their lumber and material on credit. The miners

had to buy their lots under arrangements which forfeited all they had paid, and the lot, too, if at any time they discontinued their monthly payments, no matter how near the end of their indebtedness they might have got. This forfeiture could be declared by the company without notice to the poor miner, and without any legal proceedings in which he might defend his rights. But the miners were brave-hearted; they loved to have homes of their own, and they made these razor-edged agreements and went in debt for lumber, believing all would come out right, since there was to be "steady employment."

Upon inquiring among these trusting men for copies of the deeds or contracts executed between the seller and these simple-minded buyers, I cannot find any. But I do find cases in which the company sold lots without giving the working-man who bought, a shred of title to attest their rights. Taking sometimes 33 per cent. of the price in cash, it charged them with the balance, and took part of their pay every month to wipe it off. All that such buyers had to show for their money and title were a receipt and an entry on the seller's books, and what is an entry worth when it is in the books of men who deal thus with poor and inexperienced "brothers"? Not one of you would buy ten cents' worth of land in that way.

[Lloyd next turns to the question of wages.]

. . . Sometimes it was a fall of rock in the roadway; sometimes a lack of cars to take away the coal; sometimes a suspension on account of a dull market; sometimes a man's room or place in the vein would be shut off by a new road, and he would have to wait until another place could be had. Sometimes it was one thing, sometimes another; but the upshot of it was that, mostly, when the miner came to settle with the company for the preceding month's work, he found that, after paying for his oil, and the sharpening of his tools, his rent or his monthly installment on the lot he had bought, his monthly contribution to the doctor, and his bill at the company's store, there was nothing left. He had just made ends meet; perhaps he was a little behind. Take it by the year, doing well one month, idle the whole of the next, the men could not make much more than about $30 a month. That is to say, they got for their lives and labor a scanty allowance of food, clothing, roofing, but not enough; and practically nothing of the many other things which people must have who are to keep up their health and strength—nothing for their old age, and nothing to help them for their duties as fathers and citizens.

[After citing the findings of the special commissioners appointed by the governor and providing examples from his own interviews, Lloyd narrates the events of the unannounced work stoppage at the beginning of winter.]

. . . Without notice! This has a familiar look again. It is the Pennsylvania plan, which is being introduced into the industries of the free West. Like the means, some of which have been hinted at, by which the wages of the miners were cut into and cut down, this unannounced stoppage of work is one of the well-worn practices of railroad and coal-mining combinations of Pennsylvania to "break" in the men.

[This order affected two shafts; in the spring, all of the miners were discharged.]

On Monday, April 29th, the men in the mines were told, that, when they quit work for the day, they could take out their tools, as the mines would be closed until further notice. In one afternoon, again without previous notice, all the miners of the town were deprived of their livelihood. They had not struck; they had not asked for any increase in wages; they had made no new demands of any kind upon their employers. Simultaneously with the closing of the mines, the company's store was closed. The company did not intend that any of its groceries should help to feed, nor any of its woolens warm, the people. No explanation was vouchsafed as to when the mines would be re-opened. The men were simply told to take out their tools at the close of the day, and not come back until they were bid. They were locked out. It was a strike, but it was a strike of millionaires against miners. It was a strike of dollars against men; of dollars which could lie idle one year, two years, longer if necessary, and be dollars still, against men who began to fade into nothingness the next day. It was a strike of rich men against poor men. It was a strike in violation of every pledge, tacit and expressed, which these rich men had given when they built their railroad, and sold the land, and opened the mines, and called in the men from other work far and near. It was a strike which brought woe and want upon innocent thousands for the sake of extra profits on stocks and bonds. To "make more money," disease and starvation were invited to come to Spring Valley, and they came.

[Lloyd then recounts the facts of suffering, malnutrition, and the lack of medical care.]

. . . This word "starvation" is obnoxious to you and other gentlemen who cut off the livelihood of working people by light-fingering the "laws" of supply and demand. It grates on your ears. You laugh at it over your weary and heavy-laden dinner tables. You pooh-pooh it when it gets into the newspapers or the appeals for relief. You quiet your conscience, and the generosity of others, by declaring that there is no want, that the people have saved piles of money out of the munificent wages you have paid them, and that they could all go to work to-morrow, and "earn $2 and $3 a day if it were not that they preferred charity to work." This is a mightily important point with you, and you maintain it with a stiff upper lip. Everywhere this sort of talk scattered by you through parlors, bank directors' rooms, counting-houses, and among your acquaintances, has tremendous influence. It buttresses you and your kind of "business" men in their determination to believe that the workingmen can neither do good nor feel wrongs. It shuts many hands and pockets ready to contribute to the relief which partly defeated your attempts to make the people so faint with want that their "supply" would yield to your "demand." Success in making the public believe the mystery that your workingmen continue to have plenty to eat after you have cut off all their means of buying food is vital to you, and you know it well. The public endures the things that are being done all over this country to whole communities of workingmen, only because it does not understand them. Even when they are explained, it cannot believe that the strong would so ill use the weak. It has not come to see that our market morality has overgrown all other morality, and has brought men who would be good but for business, down to the depravity of believing that "the Golden Rule" is that any rule is right which puts gold into their pockets.

There is one fatal flaw in your nervous talk about these poor people preferring, as you say, charity to work. They worked up to the last minute you kept your mines open. It was only when you drove them out that they began to beg. If you had any sense of shame, even any sense of humor, grim as it would be here, you would not make yourselves targets for public indignation and ridicule, by throwing slanders so obviously untrue at the heads of the people who came to Spring Valley to get the "steady work" you advertised, and who worked until you stopped them.

[After the documentation continues at some length, Lloyd states:]

. . . Why did not this evidence, volumes of which have been laid before you by the daily press of all parties and opinions, melt your hearts? Has the bourbonism of the "divine right" of buying cheap and selling dear become so fanatical that you think you have a right to grind up the very bodies of the poor for "six per cent. on the capital"—watered capital at that? Have your riches and your use of agents to deal with your employés and customers, borne you so far away from the people that you do really not believe that they have hearts that can ache as yours can, bodies that can suffer as yours can? Don't you believe that they love their wives and children as you do yours? that their hearts sink as yours would, when, without warning, they are dispersed, penniless, into strange parts for work, leaving wives and babies behind, perhaps to starve? Don't you believe that want of food weakens their bodies as it would yours—that hope and success and sympathy are as essential to their well-being as to your "finer" natures?

If you don't like to lose one per cent. out of your six per cents., how do you think it makes poor men feel to have you cut off all their income? If you like to take your wives and children with you to the sea-shore or to Europe, how do you think a workman feels when you force him to tramp hundreds of miles away from his family, leaving them to charity, while he hunts for work, as if that, too, were charity? Is it having three good meals a day that has made you believe that to live on twenty-one cents worth of pork and meal a week is not "starvation"?

. . . The local press chronicled your lock-out in a curt six-line paragraph, closing with the statement that "the wages for the next year is the question now to be decided." That was the question, but it was not to be decided by the ordinary and decent processes of bargaining between two free parties. It was to be decided by a commercial attack of the strong upon the very lives of the weak. These were to be made helpless, then asked to make a *free* contract. You who could live in luxury indefinitely without giving employment took employment away from the workman, who must die without it. You took hope, too, away. When you were boomers, you fed the people on hope in lieu of the good wages you had promised; but, when you changed this rôle and began to play the Doomer, it was necessary for success in bringing down the people that despair should be added to disease and starvation. Dark hints were circulated from headquarters as to what the millionaires had done in other cases and would do in this. The leader in this war on the workingmen, it was said, had utterly destroyed one mining town which had resisted his will, and he would do so here to obtain what he wanted. Meanwhile what he wanted remained like the secret of the sphinx—uncommunicated. "The Coal Company," said the Spring Valley *Gazette* of May 8th, "are as yet non-committal, and have made no offer to the men." At a mass-meeting of the miners June 1st, the resolutions began with this preamble, which corroborates the above: "WHEREAS, The Spring Valley Coal Company, have locked us out since April 29th without having given us any information why they did so." The coal company's office gazed out upon the town, blankly through its two great plate-glass eyes, and made no sign. The workingmen wrote letters to the company asking when and how they could get work, but could obtain no answer. They offered arbitration, but in vain. They sent committees to the office, but were told that positive instructions had been given that the men should be dealt with only as individuals, never again through representatives.

. . . From April 29th until August 23d your contemptuous silence in the face of all inquiries as to the cause and prospects of the lock-out was maintained—five heart-sick months for the people of Spring Valley. Then the company posted in its windows at Spring Valley an offer to them of thirty-five cents a ton, instead of ninety cents, which they were receiving when the mines were closed.

[And as part of the offer, the men had to give up their union.]

. . . You do all your business through a union, and by walking, or more correctly sitting delegates, and through committees of directors, and you keep a large staff of "professional agitators" constantly busy on your behalf in courts and legislatures and stock exchanges. But because you are rich and think you have the power, you determined to take away the same rights from these poor men. By this demand of August 23d, for the surrender of their union, the men learned that, worse than a reduction of wages, the destruction of their union had been decreed. This meant the destruction of their power to make a free contract, and to protect themselves against violations of the contract when made. It meant that the tasks, hours of work, the pay, the personal liberty, the treatment at the hands of overseers, settlement of disputes, and other matters, which lay at the very foundations of livelihood and rights, were to depend on the will of the employer —harder than that, on the will of the overseer. It meant that the men were to be denied the benefit of any gift of leadership—always too rare—that might develop itself among them. It meant that any man so gifted, who should have the heart to speak against the abuse of his fellows, who should have the brain to see how they could make better bargains for themselves, and the tongue to get the idea into their heads, and to speak for them, should be banished at the will of the employer. It meant that the workmen could have work only at the price of dumb submission and disunited helplessness.

The employers, rich, remote, independent, could bring their combined power operated through an agent, to bear resistlessly on the men, poor, dependent, anchored to the spot by family responsibilities and lack of the means to get away. The employers, although strong enough to stand alone, were united together in a union the wealth and discipline of which were far beyond anything possible to the workingmen, and yet announced that they were going to take away the same right of union from their men.

The company's vein of coal is so thin that the men have to

work all day on their knees or lying down, but you insist that in addition to this they shall come on their knees when they make their application for work, and not like American citizens acting through a committee or attorney, if that suits them better than coming one by one. You have in the mines a class of useful and docile animals in the mules which stay in the depths for years, and sometimes never come back to the surface. You always treat with them "individually." If your plans succeed, it will not be long before you will have the power to keep your miners like your mules—down below from year's end to year's end. There will be nothing left them worth coming to the surface for, because, if you can make them give up their unions, you can make them give up everything. "Unite or Die" said Franklin to the American colonies. The unorganized workman, says Prof. Thorold Rogers, cannot make a free contract. John Morley, the great English statesman, said recently to the miners of Durham: "We all know what the labor union has done for the working people. It has made men of them." You, with so many millions you could not count them if you counted all your life like clerks of the treasury, instead of helping to make men of your workingmen, seek to dehumanize them for "more" millions.

[Contending that mine owners are buying the men "below cost," that they are driving the men *below* the level of subsistence merely for the profit involved, Lloyd makes the following observations.]

. . . It was for this these poor men were seduced into leaving homes and employment elsewhere to settle in "your town;" that they were snared in the meshes of land purchase on monthly installments without a title, making the purchase of a home a means of slavery instead of the refuge and support it should be. It was for this the labor market was overstocked by bringing in superfluous miners from Belgium, France, Italy, and all parts of America; that one-third of the mines were shut down in December, and the rest in April, without notice; that having promised "steady employment," your agent refused for five months to give the arbitrarily disemployed men any explanation or any chance to work at any price; that he then offered them less than half what neighboring mines, poorer than yours, are paying; that he refused to arbitrate; that he would not receive the men when they came offering to work at the prices paid elsewhere, which he had sworn in public you would pay and better; that he dragged the men about from conference to conference at La Salle and Joliet and Chicago for a compromise which he had no thought of making; that he demanded the abandonment of their union by men who, without union, were but brittle sticks to be broken by you one by one at your pleasure. It is for this that the homes of the poor have been broken up, and the men, leaving wives and children to face the terrors of starvation, have been driven forth in heartbreak to seek work where a million unemployed were tramping ahead of them.

[Lloyd next examined the meaning of the "free" contract.]

. . . The arrangements under which the miners went back to work for you are called "contracts."

It is of the essence of contracts that they should be free; and to be free, they must be the voluntary agreements of equal parties, made without duress, and with a full understanding of all the obligations assumed and imposed. The means taken by the "party of the first part" to prepare the minds and bodies of the "parties of the second part," at Spring Valley, to accept the terms of the iron-clad printed contract offered them, were of a kind not to be found recommended in any of the law books. They were such as these:

Months of disemployment and of intimidation; refusal to give explanations why work had been stopped or when it would be resumed; the application of the torture of famine and of compulsory exile; systematic slander and misrepresentation through public and private channels; threats that the idleness might be prolonged for years; the public and repeated menace that other workingmen would be brought in to take their livelihood away from them, by force, "If it takes all the power of the State to do it," said the figure-head of the millionaires; the terrifying assertion that the pay was to be reduced from 90 cents to 35 cents a ton; threats of evictions and of forfeiture of all the earnings invested in the purchase of lots and building material bought from the company on the installment plan.

These were the influences used to prepare the men to make a "free" contract.

When the men broke their ranks, and ran to the company's office to "settle," they stood in a long file, hundreds of them passing one by one before the clerk's window to "sign." The paper given them, the "contract," was two pages, foolscap size, of fine print. They had no time to read it. Not one of them would have dared to ask to be allowed to read it before signing at the risk of finding his name on the black list when he came back. It would have done none of them any good if they had read it. They couldn't have understood its full scope, its provisions, carefully conned over by and woven together at their leisure by shrewd business men with the help of the best legal advice, embodying all the latest decisions of the courts in the phrasing of the different clauses. If they could have understood it, they couldn't have got it changed. Oliver Twist asking for "more" was nothing of a spectacle in comparison with a miner who should dream of suggesting some alterations to suit him in the "contract" he was about to sign. Imagine him, the "free" party of the second part, his clothes hanging limp over the cavities in his person caused by seven months enforced idleness, his wife and children at home waiting for what he will bring, the relief contributed by the public stopped by the news that work has begun. Imagine this "citizen" standing up to the five hundred million dollars which looks out at him over the counter through the supercilious eyes of the clerk. Try to fancy his saying: "This contract suits me, all but this and that; make that so-and-so, and we will call it a bargain!"

Of the men who scrambled over each other to get to the windows to "sign," a great many could not read at all; a great many, being French, Belgian, Italian, German, Polish, could not read English. No one read the contract to them; no one explained it. As fast as they could sign their names or make their mark, they passed on.

As each one came up he gave his name. The clerk, before presenting the "contract" for him to sign, it was observed, always glanced down to his desk. "What's your name? Brown?" Looks down. "That's all right, Brown; put your name here. Now, then, next!"

Here is one of the faithfulest members of the relief committee in the line. "What's your name? Bourke, you say? I'll see." Looks down. "B—B—B—Bourke. Ah! yes, Bourke. I haven't any contract for you. You will have to see the superintendent. Next."

It is the "black list" which lies on the clerk's desk. Bourke of the relief committee is on the list. He will get no work. He will have to go far from Spring Valley before his waiting wife and children get any earnings of his for the purchase of food. He is a "free" man—free to leave, free to hunt work, free to go into exile.

Here is the so-called contract. It binds the company to nothing but that while it keeps the man at work it will pay him so much a ton. The miner is bound to work usually from May to May, in this case from December to May, but the company is not bound to give him work. The miner cannot discharge the company for any cause, but they may discharge him whenever they see fit. The miner makes his payment, which is in coal, to the company every day, but the company makes him wait two weeks to six weeks for every dollar it owes him. However starveling may be his wages, the miner has to bind himself to join no combination to better them. If he even smiles upon any such combination, it is under the penalty of losing all the company owes him for work, and the company is the judge whether or not he has smiled an insubordinate smile. Meanwhile, the company may join any conspiracy it chooses to put down the wages of the men, or put up the price of coal. If the pit boss is a tyrant, and oppresses the miner, as he has hundreds of ways of doing, the miner has the privilege under the "contract" of appealing for redress to this pit boss who has wronged him. The miner who knows that all of his associates have under compulsion signed away their right to defend him by the only power that could help him, the power of the union, and that he stands in the darkness of the pit simply as an individual, is not likely to antagonize the petty despot of the mines. But if he has the rare courage to do so, and gets an adverse decision, he has one privilege more. He can appeal from the pit boss to the superintendent, whose appointee the pit boss is!

All of which amounts to this: that the miner, the weaker party, agrees to leave all disputed questions to the decision of the other party, opposed to him in interest at all points. No wonder the workingman has to be locked out and starved before he feels "free" enough (of food and manhood) to make such a bargain.

. . . The bald truth is that this yearly contract is slavery. It is slavery in yearly installments. Put together, year by year, it is a slavery for life. The miners, in submitting to it, and we, in allowing them to submit to it, degrade their manhood, and that of the republic. Slavery, in no matter how small a spot, among a free people, is like a spark in a cargo of cotton, a leak in a ship. It cannot be so insignificant that it does not imperil the whole. The miners, to a man, ought to resist this slavery, and the public should sustain them in doing so at any cost. Relief given these men in such a struggle would not be "charity;" it would be an investment for the defense of the

liberties and the homes of the whole people, all of which are
in peril, if any are in peril!

[Lloyd draws the following conclusion from his analysis.]

. . . If you continue your war on the miners, if you pocket
the profits that success will bring you, the public will sooner
or later declare to all of you that you have vitiated your title
to your rights and properties at their very roots. Political economy gives you private property only that the interest of all
may be served by your self-interest; the law gives you your
franchises and estates only for the general welfare and the
public safety; religion holds you to be only stewards of your
riches. If you usurp for your private profit all these trusts and
grants, if you withdraw yourself from serving and protecting
the public and take to oppressing and plundering them from
your points of advantage, you will but repeat the folly of your
mediaeval exemplars whose castles now decorate a better civilization with their prophetic ruins.

62. A Labor Day Message

Speaking to the Brotherhood of Locomotive Firemen in Augusta,
Georgia, on Labor Day 1891, Thomas E. Watson took the position
that labor and not capital is the creator of wealth. In stating this
labor theory of value, he maintained that throughout history there
has been a concerted effort to deny to labor an equitable share of
the products it creates. Indeed, he asserts, legislation, such as the
caste system in India and the English laws on vagabondage, has
been directed to keeping the laboring classes in a subordinate position. Watson does not, however, move from this position to a condemnation of capital. He wants "a just harmony" between the two

Reprinted from *People's Party Paper* (Atlanta), November 26, 1891.
Library of Congress.

classes, one in which capital cannot have undisputed sway over profits or over the lives of the working class.

There is one point, I wish to stress. It is this: the cause of labor is the same everywhere, whether in fields or factory, in rail-roads, mines, storehouses, or dock yards.

What is the labor question? In a nutshell it is this: Labor asks of capital, "Why is it you have so much and do so little work, while I have so little and do so much?"

That is about the size of it. You may use learned phrases, but after all, the sum and substance is that labor thinks it gets too little pay for housing, clothing and feeding the world.

What is capital and what is labor? Originally they were the same, to the extent that cause and effect are the same. There was a time when there was no capital. There never was a time when there was no labor. Capital is the child of labor. Work done today produces wheat, corn, bricks, steam engines, parlor cars, houses, furniture.

The process of production is labor. The thing produced is capital. Labor creates wealth, but the very moment it is created it becomes capital.

Once upon a time every dollar of the Vanderbilts lay in the muscles of the arms of labor and had not been created.

The national wealth of this country is some sixty-five billion dollars, yet when Capt. John Smith landed at Jamestown, none of that vast aggregate was here save the muscle and land.

Where was it then? It lay in the muscles of the laborers yet unborn, in the brains of the thinkers yet to be. This is literally true. No man denies it. Yet there is this queer thing. Every-body wants labor protected when it becomes capital, while most people laugh you to scorn if you propose to protect it while it is still labor.

Let me illustrate: Capital consists of money, lands, stock,

provisions, goods, chattels, etc. Protective legislation provides for their welfare.

What produces them? The labor of yesterday. But when you propose to throw protective legislation around the labor of to-day (which has not yet become capital), clamor at once arises and you are denounced as a fanatic and a demagogue.

Tell me, Mr. Lawmaker, why it is that you so carefully shelter and feed capital, the child of labor, while you "turn out to graze," as best it may, labor, the daddy of the child?

Take off your plug hat and study the question, for it is a vital one, and we are going to make you answer it. The natural reward of labor is that which it produces. If labor gathers rushes and makes a basket, the basket is the pay. If labor gathers palmetto and weaves a hat, that hat belongs to labor.

This is labor in its simple state, where it supplies itself with material and furnishes all the work. It is only when we advance and get to a stage where material may be furnished by one while labor is supplied by another that trouble begins. When different capitals furnish different materials and many laborers and many kinds of labor enter into production, the true wages of labor become a matter of doubt, of fraud, of deception, and of robbery.

How much ought labor to get? No man can be more definite than this: "It should get all that it makes after due allowance for material and the use of the capital."

But we can be perfectly definite on this point. It does not get a fair share now. Eight million bales of cotton flood the markets of the world, and have hammered the price down to zero. Yet millions of laborers haven't decent clothes to wear!

Corn was made in the West so plentiful that people burned it for winter fires because it would only bring twelve cents per bushel. Yet millions of laborers hunger, and some of them starve.

The earth quivers every second with the falling of the majestic pines as the lumberman seeks rafter, and joist, and sill, and planking, and never before were hurrying cars so laden with lumber, yet thousands of laborers shelter their families in wretched hovels, through whose sunken roof patters the rain, and through whose gaping cracks steal the bitter cold.

They tell us the country is suffering from overproduction of food! Then why do men go hungry through your streets? Overproduction of goods? Then why do shrinking women and feeble children go shivering down the icy sidewalks so scantily clad that suffering speaks in every line of pinched and haggard features? Overproduction? I will tell you where the overproduction is. It is in the cold-hearted and hard-hearted men who will not see any thing which does not belong to their class! It is in the men who consider the mere getting of gold the gospel of life; it is in the men who have grown proud and cruel because they possess capital (the thing which was labor yesterday), but utterly despise the labor of today.

In a world where all capital was produced by labor and where all the increase of that capital and all the necessaries of daily life are being created by labor, I hold it to be a plain truth that labor is entitled to these things, viz:

A sufficiency of food, clothing and lodging for the needs of today; a sufficiency of leisure from daily toil to preserve the strength of the body and to cultivate the capacity of the mind; the shortening of the hours of labor so that a man or a woman may not become a mere beast of burden, but will be a citizen, who, like other citizens, has a portion of the day for recreation, for social intercourse, and for self-improvement. But further still, I believe that he should have his fair proportion of the profits made by his labor to constitute a surplus for his time of sickness or old age and to transmit to his children, so that the condition of the producer may prosper in just proportion to the amount of his production.

This is a puzzling job for the legislator, but I firmly believe the law can be so framed if the government is to escape revolution.

There has always been a great reluctance to legislate in behalf of labor.

There has always been eager desire to legislate against it. If I were to give you a sketch of labor in the kingdoms of ancient times, you would be astonished at the infinite blackness of the tyranny with which capital crushed it and fattened on its sufferings.

The old caste system of India was but the law which capital made to keep the rich forever rich, and the poor forever poor: to guarantee to him who enjoyed privilege that it should never be destroyed and to discourage him who did not have it from ever aspiring thereto—killing the ambition by locking the road.

The Brahman was the legalized aristocrat of the Hindoos. He held the power, the privilege and the capital. The great body of the Indian people were called Sudras. They were, as usual, the yellow dogs of the social system. If one of the common people took a seat by the side of a Brahman it was a crime. If he spoke disrespectfully of one of these aristocrats, his mouth was to be burned; if this common man insulted this Brahman the tongue of the offender was slit. If he struck a Brahman, death was the penalty. The common people had no learning. The high-class had it all and kept it.

If one of the common people, yearning for knowledge, listened to the reading of the sacred books, burning oil was poured into his criminal ears. If he committed any of their contents to memory the punishment was death. Marriage between the upper and lower classes was prohibited under the awfulest penalties, and a law of the realm declared in plain terms that the laborer should not acquire wealth and that his name, laborer, should be an expression of contempt. Such were the hideous regulations by which those who had the advantage sought to keep it, and they kept it. I have been particular in specifying these things because the code of the Hindoos is perhaps the oldest of which we have any clear account, and because I wish to emphasize this fact: the code of every other nation has had substantially the same inhuman laws against labor.

Our scholars amuse themselves by curious study of the ancient caste system of the Hindoos. Let them look deeply and soberly into every social system and the same features will be seen again and again. Many a code of laws which the common people supported because they thought them wise and just, were nothing in the world but systems of rules by which those who held the power arranged to maintain it, and those who had the capital contrived to perpetuate its influence and accumulation.

But I have no time to go further into the subject. I will merely give some outline of the English system of labor legislation; not the ancient system, but the modern. Let us see how England treated her producing classes, not in times of feudal ignorance or of savage anarchy, but in modern times, when education spoke from her universities, and Christianity knelt in her temples.

They say the laws of Draco were written in blood. Perhaps they were, and perhaps that's where the fashion started. All the succeeding codes have been written in the same ink, among them, that of England.

Possibly in no other modern code can you find such an infamous law as this: "The laborer must serve the first who asks him, and be contented with the low wages which prevailed previous to the Great Plague of London." If he refused to do so, he was a criminal and must go to jail.

The "sturdy beggar" who was hungry or cold and asked alms, committed a crime for which he was publicly flogged. If he still remained hungry and cold after the flogging, and asked aid, his ears were cropped. If his distress happened to be of that unquestionable and obstreperous kind which was

not relieved by ear-cropping, and he again intruded his necessities upon the notice of the community, he was put to death.
. . . If the English capitalists combined to put up the profits
of capital, the law encouraged them. If English labor combined to put up the price of labor or to shorten its hours, they
were criminals and were punished as such. This outrageous
law was not repealed till 1824.

The English laborer had no voice in legislation. He had no
vote, could reach no office, could acquire no political or social
influence. The land laws made it practically impossible for him
to ever own the soil he tilled. Time and again the under classes
got themselves in protest and petition—protest against the
wrong, petition for the right.

Generally the movement ended by the hanging of the leaders and the beating back into sullen silence of the suffering
petitioners. History has not been written by the laborer. It has
usually been written by his enemy. Therefore we only catch
glimpses of the truth from time to time.

[After discussing the conditions under which colliers lived and
worked in England, and how their attempt to protest was brutally
suppressed, Watson made the following observations.]

. . . The picture is an old one, I know. Pardon me for dwelling on it. I suppose I get it from my mother to side with the
weak. I may lift my hat to the victor, but more frequently my
hand goes out to the vanquished.

I think less about Nelson, dead in the arms of success, than
of the English prisoner who laid in jail thirty-five years without
trial, without a known prosecutor, who was liberated at last
by chance, and faced a world which had forgotten him—his
family lost, his hopes gone, his future a blank, his past a horror
—and who did not even have the poor satisfaction of knowing
who had been his enemy or what had been his fault.

I think much less of William Pitt, dying at the summit of
a glory he had bought by a base surrender of his better prin-

ciples, than I do of that poor bridegroom who was snatched away from his bride on their way home from the marriage, was kidnapped into the navy, was forced to serve during the entire war between England and France, was discharged a battered veteran, came home to meet again the bride he had left weeping at the church door, and found that she was long since dead and he himself utterly forgotten in the home of his youth.

In the annals of crime there is no sadder incident than this, and it occurred under the sanction of law—a law which had existed in England over four hundred years and was not repealed till 1835.

In order that dissatisfaction with this law and others like it might not take definite shape and assume formidable proportions, public meetings were virtually prohibited, lectures and debates made penal, reading rooms were declared criminal and classed among "disorderly houses," while the press was so completely shackled it could strike no blow at abuses.

These were some of the laws of William Pitt, whom our boys have been taught to honor.

Studying such regulations and the cruelty with which they were enforced, we are lost in admiration of the courage which finally threw off the yoke.

In 1819 the people held a mass meeting at Manchester to consider their grievances. The orator of the day arose to speak. The moment he did so he was arrested and sent to jail—for no crime on the face of the earth. The military rode at the crowd and dispersed it—trampling beneath the feet of their horses men, women and children.

Why? Because they had dared to peaceably assemble to complain against misrule!

In 1830 the lower classes determined to have some share in government. They demanded redress of wrongs. They demanded representation.

All men now concede that the demand was moderate, was just, was indispensable. All men now concede that those who opposed it were selfish, narrow and unjust in their oppression. The nobility and the king put themselves against the people. The cause which is admitted to have been wrong, trampled down the cause which is admitted to have been right. Great excitement followed. Great riots broke out. They were crushed cruelly, relentlessly. Four apostles of the right were hung at Bristol by the defenders of the wrong. Three men who were of those demanding the right thing were hung at Nottingham, by those who were maintaining the wrong thing.

Then the martyrs, having been duly buried, the cause was allowed to triumph! The very things which those dead men had vainly asked for were conceded. Why? Because the nobility and the king grow pale before the frowning specter of civil war.

Yet they crushed the riots in blood—giving no punishment whatever to those selfish nobles who had caused the riots.

Thus it is that the cause of the common people progresses. Every step has been a struggle, every concession has been stained with blood. No chain has been struck from the limbs of fettered labor save at the cost of some brave man's life.

In ancient times no great thing was undertaken, till sacrifice was made. The altar must be erected, the victim chosen and garlanded, the sacrificial fire lit.

Then the blood of the offering having been shed, the waiting fleet unfurled its sails and stood out to sea, or the chieftain said to his halted columns, "Forward, march!"

How strangely these old customs reappear, the ceremonial altered, but the substance preserved.

No vessel ever lifted anchor to bear the liberties of the people through stormy seas to sunlit havens, no army marshaled to redeem the lost provinces of freedom, ever yet made successful venture without the altar and the victims—without the splendid heroism which offers the one, and inexorable custom which exacts the other.

What is the condition of labor in this land today? Bad.

Capital is protected by law from outside competition. Labor

is not. The pauperism of the universe is at liberty to come and drive it from the home market.

To competitive capital there is a tariff wall which is practically impassable and which says "Stay out." To competitive labor there is an open gate and a chronic invitation, "Come in."

If the manufacturer orders a lockout, labor is cut off from the help of foreign labor. If labor goes on a strike, capital brings in Chinamen, Hungarians, Italians and every other kind, and beats down home labor with foreign competition.

If capital says to Congress, "England threatens us," that assembly of agents and attorneys promptly obeys its master by building a tariff wall, which shuts English capital out. If labor says to the government, "Protect me from the inroads of pauper competition," Congress merely crosses its esteemed legs and contentedly picks its false teeth.

The gigantic trust is confessedly framed to limit and control the output of any industry. It is a highly fashionable affair. It has its managers in House and Senate. The railroads assist it and the courts get out of its way. It does its work by force and its success is a crime.

Suppose labor combines to do substantially the same thing, to control labor and say when it shall work and who for? It is a "conspiracy" and must be put down.

Ah, me! how alarmed we all grow when frantic laborers, ruin staring them in the face, derail some freight car or thump one of Pinkerton's toughs with a stick. We hold up our delicate hands in feigned horror, and cry, "Put it down!"

Yet we are the same people who exult in the piracy which our ancestors committed on the English tea ships. The same people who acquired this land from its owners by a long series of fraud, murders, and violating treaties; who made a president out of old Andrew Jackson, the executioner of prisoners.

We are the same people who made a heroine of Charlotte Corday, the murderess of Marat, and who imagine we see patriotism in the cowardly manner in which the rich senators of Rome hemmed up the unarmed Caesar in the Senate's house and cut him to pieces with their knives.

We say in those cases that the end justifies the means. I do not commit myself to the doctrine, but I say this: it is a strange thing the mantle of charity is cut so long for some folks and so short for others.

In New York they have a board of arbitrators to settle such disputes. It was framed by the sovereign State for the very purpose of deciding who was right and preventing bloodshed. A short while ago there was a great strike on the New York Central Railroad. Excited crowds filled the streets; the workmen said they had not been treated right; the railroad authorities denied the charge; the State board of arbitrators saw that strife was threatened; they wished to prevent it; they proposed to arbitrate and asked both sides to submit the question; the workmen consented; the railroad refused; riots followed, blood was shed.

In the eyes of all impartial men the fearful responsibility for that bloodshed must rest upon the railroad, for they refused a peaceful settlement before a legally constituted tribunal.

Let it be remembered that labor said, "I will submit to the law," while capital said, "I am a law unto myself."

If the earth is only a battle field in which the divine Creator intended that the strong battalion should always trample down the weak, then the success of the plan is gratifying.

Society, law and government are so framed that they almost inevitably carry out the scheme.

The great tendency of the present system is to keep at the top those who are above, and keep at the bottom those who are below.

But if this earth was intended by a common Father as the home of His children, and it was His Divine purpose that each of those children should find food and raiment and shelter in return for his labor—then this plan is at present a failure.

In Christendom are some three hundred fifty million people.

Statistics show that one-third of the number never have enough to eat.

Read the account of destitute laborers in the New York tenement houses; read of the squalor of the Pennsylvania mines; read of the hardships of New England factory operatives; and read of those bent and feeble sewing women of New York City, crouched in dreary garrets and plying their needles.

> Stitch—stitch—stitch—
> In poverty, hunger and dirt;
> Sewing at once with a double thread
> A shroud as well as a shirt.

It is said these wretched creatures get thirty-seven cents for making an entire suit of clothes!

How cheap! if flesh and blood, justice and mercy be worth a moment's thought.

Don't understand me to be making war upon capital as such. I am but denouncing that capital which is used tyranically. I recognize the fact that without capital there can be no progress. If labor consumed its products day by day, and there was no surplus collected anywhere, advance would be an impossibility.

There must first be a surplus somewhere (capital) before there can be a leisure class to devote themselves to science, to music, painting, bookmaking, law-making, school-teaching.

Without capital accumulated in the hands of some citizen, there could be nothing but the simplest manual labor—there could be no manufactories, no railroads, no steam boats, no foundries, no merchants and no bankers.

The healthy, happy prosperous community is not that which consists either of capitalists alone, or of laborers alone. Neither can do without the other.

The truly prosperous community is that in which a just harmony is preserved between the two, and they become allies instead of enemies. Every class has its legitimate work and cannot be dispensed with. The banker is as natural a part of the business system as the borrower. In fighting an abuse in the banking system I do not wage war on banking itself—for some poor man will always want to use the surplus of the rich one, and if he can do so on equitable terms, both are benefited.

The manufacturer is a necessity to his countrymen—working up into finished fabric the cruder material of a simple laborer. In making war upon an advantage which he unjustly holds as against others, I do not for a moment forget that his prosperity is absolutely essential to national welfare.

In this age of speed and progress, who can undervalue our railroads? I never in my life watched a train of cars without some thrill of pleasure—so instinctive and typical is it of man's power and skill and success! Yet when I see the railroads so frequently used for illegitimate purposes; when I see them become the mere "chips" in the great game of colossal gamblers; when I see them used to crush out this city and build up that; to bottle up this great harbor and develop that; to help the monopoly (like the Standard Oil Company) to beat down its competitor; when I see them bribing newspapers, and Senators, and Representatives to aid them in perpetrating wrongs upon the balance of the community, then it is that I find it impossible to refrain from denouncing the manner in which the magnificent blessing of the railroads is sometimes turned into a blasting curse!

I long to see public sentiment change on this labor question. I hope to see the problem studied and discussed more frequently among us. I hope to see all ranks meet the difficulty in a spirit of fairness and conciliation. You are a laborer. Remember that it is possible you may be a capitalist tomorrow.

You are a capitalist. Remember you may be a laborer tomorrow. This is the spirit in which serious issues should be adjusted. The man who despises the poor simply because they are poor, is too contemptible to be blamed for it. The man who hates the rich, simply because they are rich, has sinned just as much. It is the injustice and wrong which ought to be combated, whether among rich or poor.

I believe the evils of our present system can be remedied. How?

1. By co-operation among the laborers. You must organize, agitate and educate. Organize yourselves to get the strength of unity; agitate the evils and the causes thereof to arrest public opinion; educate yourselves and the public upon the principles underlying the issue in order that there be a proper understanding of the abuses complained of and the remedies proposed.

2. By a radical change in our laws. I firmly believe that before co-operation among laborers can secure complete success, we must have legislation which either takes from the tyrannical power of capital, or adds to the defensive strength of labor. We must make capital lay down its pistol, or we must give labor a pistol, too. When each man knows that the other has a "gun" and will use it, they get exceedingly careful about fingering the trigger.

3. By a change of public opinion, which will bring the irresistible power of moral support to the side of labor as against the unreasonable exactions of capital. Every pulpit, every newspaper, every leader of thought in every profession, should give to this question earnest attention and then speak out. I dwell on this because I regard public opinion as omnipotent. It cannot be seen, but its pressure is despotic. The bravest man quails before the silent aversion of hostile public opinion. The stoutest leader weakens before the frowning face. It changes policies, customs, manners. It enforces an unwritten law, and the criminal who violated it swings from a limb! It nullifies a written law and bears home in triumph the man who broke it.

You think you hold your life at the mercy of the law! You do nothing of the kind. You hold it at the mercy of public opinion. In a democracy or a republic it is at once the strength and the weakness of the system. Hence I say you must get this enormous power on your side. Once you get it—the way broadens and the light shines upon it.

How can you get it? By showing the public that you are right. Spread before the people facts which call aloud for attention; arguments which challenge reply; principles which defy criticism. Let the mistreated laborer show his wounds and ask sympathy; lift up his chains and ask freedom; hold on high, yes on high, the white face of his little child, hungry and sick, wasted and wan, and strike a thrill of pity through the great heart of the world!

Minister of God! You are appalled at evils of intemperance. Well may you be. You denounce the effects of the evil in the severest terms.

Well you may do so. But when you say intemperance causes poverty I respectfully beg you to consider whether you haven't got your cart at the wrong end of the horse! In seventy-five cases out of a hundred it is poverty which causes intemperance!

How can men love their homes when these homes are leaky hovels lit up by no comforts, but filled with wretchedness, sickness and want?

How can men lift themselves, when they have no leisure to improve the mind, to recuperate the body and to frame those moral and social relations which elevate men above the brutes?

Help us remove the cause—the effects will then disappear.

Fellow-citizens, my heart goes out to you in sympathy at your effort to better your condition. It has not been so long since I was as poor as the poorest man here. It has not been so long since I went weary up and down your streets asking for work and finding none. It has not been long since I knew what it was to have no place to lay my head when the night came upon me, and when today lost some of its gloom in the great fear that tomorrow might be darker.

The horror of that dreadful time I shall never forget. It has left its mark on my mind and on my heart. It has shaped my convictions and controlled my feelings. When the easy owner of inherited wealth or position sneers at the warmth of my utterances upon this subject, I beg to remind him that it is the man who has been burned who can best describe the pain of the fire.

Press on, workmen, in your worthy efforts. Whenever I can help you, call me. Preach the sublime doctrine of right. Demand it of others and practice it yourself. The time will surely come when the producers of wealth must share equally its benefits, when the bounteous results of your toil will not all turn in at the gates of the palace, but a portion thereof will pass on down to the cottage and lift that humble tenement into dignity, comfort and happiness of a home.

63. The Tendency of the Times

The Topeka *Advocate* regarded the strikes of the early 1890's as a reaction against the increasingly unequal distribution of wealth. The question was less that of lower wages than utter destitution or barely enough to continue one's existence. Here, the newspaper placed industrial unrest into the larger context of an economic system which maintains a reserve army of labor, so that there would always be a pool of unemployed from which to draw.

The strikes at Homestead and in the mines of Idaho are only indications of the general unrest that everywhere pervades

Reprinted from *Advocate* (Topeka), July 20, 1892. Kansas State Historical Society.

society throughout the world. In nearly every country upon the globe the rapid concentration of wealth in few hands is constantly widening the gulf between the patrician and the plebeian classes. . . . The tendency of the times is to constantly lower the standard of wages paid to labor in order to constantly add to the accumulations of the non-producing classes. The strikes that occur from time to time are merely local protests against this general policy. In every instance almost organized labor is defeated. There is always to be found a sufficient number of idle men who have either been formerly forced into idleness in consequence of the depressed condition of all industrial pursuits, or have been imported from the idle hordes of foreign countries for the purpose, to displace organized labor, always at lower wages than have been formerly paid. The Pinkerton army, or if need be the state militia or the army of the United States, under the pretense of protection to vested rights, can always be relied upon to assist in the displacement and to see that it is accomplished to the satisfaction of the employers of labor. . . . Labor is never conceded to have any rights that capital or government authorities are under any obligation to respect. . . .

How long the great producing masses will thus submit to be defeated in detail remains to be seen. The hope that the great industrial revolution now pending may be peaceably accomplished at the ballot box seems frequently to be overshadowed by serious doubt. That the revolution is to come in one form or another is as certain as that God's eternal justice must eventually prevail among men. The arrogance and greed of the Shylock classes may force a repetition of the French revolution; and should they do so, on them must rest the terrible responsibility. Of one thing they may rest assured; as sure as the blood of the patriot fathers flows in the veins of their worthy sons they will not long submit to the system of robbery that the last quarter of a century has imposed upon them.

64. The New York Central Strike

Taking a railroad strike in 1890 as the basis for its remarks, the *Farmers' Alliance* points to the uneven conflict between capital and labor and to the power of the former to overcome the resistance of the workers. Government, the editorial holds, should be but is not responsive to the needs of labor.

In this case the right of labor to organize is attacked by the best organized capitalistic force of the country. While we fully realize that a strike is unfortunate at any time, it is justifiable and in fact necessary under such circumstances as these. Until public opinion reaches the point when labor and its interests form the first care and duty of the government, as it properly should and some day will, labor must fight its own battles, and fight them with the only weapon it has at hand.

. . . Consider for a moment the monstrous inequality between capital and labor as illustrated by the relations between the N. Y. Central railroad and its striking employes. On one hand a corporation worth hundreds of millions, sharing the sovereignty of the state in its right of eminent domain, granted the franchise of a public highway in perpetuity, organized industrially in the most perfect manner—organized also to control legislatures and enact or repeal laws, and to advise and aid the courts in the execution of them, we see the most complete, the most tyrannical and the most powerful force known to modern society. On the other hand we find a multitude of atoms—mere individual men, necessary to the corporation certainly, but with no rights the corporation is bound to re-

---

Reprinted from *Farmers' Alliance* (Lincoln), August 23, 1890. Nebraska Historical Society.

spect, or if bound nominally to respect their rights having power enough to practically ignore them. . . . And yet the atoms are the ones who produce the wealth—who have created the capital which the controllers of the N. Y. Central are turning into an engine of oppression.

65. The Destruction of the Union

The Populist newspaper in Lincoln treated the Homestead strike as centering on the question of the very survival of the labor organization. It charged that once unions are destroyed, employers can play the individual workers off against each other and force down wages. This consideration, felt the paper, was what prompted the strategy of the Carnegie Company in the conduct of its policies during the strike.

The contest now on between Carnegie & Co. and their employes is not so much over the scale of wages, as it is over the destruction or perpetuation of the amalgamated association, one of the leading labor unions of the country. The capitalists have determined on a war to the death against this organization. The laborers will resist this warfare with all their power. It is not a matter of mere sentiment with them. They realize that their only protection against the tyranny of capital lies in their union. Once this is broken up, the capitalist will only have the individual laborers to deal with. He can then use the laborers to beat down their own wages through competition for employment.

Reprinted from *Alliance-Independent* (Lincoln), July 28, 1892. Nebraska Historical Society.

66. Corporations and a Surplus of Idle Men

In a pair of editorials on the same day concerning a railroad strike in Brooklyn, the *Advocate* presented its overall analysis of the labor situation, particularly on how workers were compelled to renew their own dependency by fighting for the available work. It saw the Pinkertons as a strikebreaking force and as the coercive instrument used by capital to prevent the formation of unions. Above all, the *Advocate* returned to the theme which characterizes much of its discussion of industrialism: the creation of a reserve army of labor to insure a submissive working class.

I

These Pinkerton thugs and hired assassins are always at the service of arrogant corporations. They constitute a private army under the command of neither state or national authority, but always at the service of capital in its every contest with labor. Do the people of this country see no danger from a force of this character?

It is to the interest of these corporate employers of labor that there shall always be an army of idle men in the country upon the very verge of starvation who may be relied upon to take the places of strikers in all difficulties of this kind. Without such an idle force, no corporation could hope to succeed against any labor strike. A strike occurring with no such force in reserve would simply mean a recognition of the rights of labor, or a stoppage of business, and hence the employers of labor encourage the conditions that produce idleness as a means of security to their own arbitrary designs. Does the reader see no danger in the continuance of such conditions?

Reprinted from *Advocate* (Topeka), Jan. 30, 1895. Kansas State Historical Society.

The demand of the Brooklyn strikers is simply for a ten hour day, whereas they have been required to work from fourteen to sixteen hours. The company deny this demand to their old employes, but hire new men through the Pinkerton pimps, agreeing to pay them $2.50 for ten hours' work. How long after this difficulty is settled would they adhere to this agreement? Starving men are ready to take the places of the strikers now upon the terms offered, but as soon as quiet is restored, these men will be subjected to the same conditions against which the old employes have gone out. The men themselves must realize this, but what can they do?

II

As in the case of every other controversy between labor and corporations, the plutocratic press and the upper crust of society can see no wrong except on the part of the strikers. No matter if men are required to work fourteen or sixteen hours per day at starvation wages, if they strike nothing is heard of these abuses, but great stress is laid upon the duty of government to protect "the rights of the people" against interference by strikers. "The rights of the people" are always spoken of as though the strikers themselves were no part of the people, and as though they have no rights that are to be considered.

67. Ripe for Socialism

A letter to the *Farmers' Alliance* contended that workers and farm tenants have a common material basis in society, and that the condition of each is but little short of precarious. The correspondent suggested that these similarities will lead the two groups to an acceptance of the same goals.

Reprinted from H. H. Haaff to editor, *Farmers' Alliance* (Lincoln), June 7, 1890. Nebraska Historical Society.

Illinois has two classes of men who are ripe for socialism. The poor of the cities. The men who labor with their hands. There are over three hundred thousand of these in Chicago alone; and most of them know that no steady job awaits them the year along. They know that six to eight months labor is all that they can reasonably expect to get and hence they combine and strike for all they can get during that time. . . . Those men are ripe for socialism. The farm renters of Illinois are fast approaching that same condition. Of what value is it to them that they repair houses or barns, cribs or fences. "Only just enough to carry us through the year and safely house us, our animals and our crops." The idea of home love is out side the pale of their dreams. How can they ever expect to purchase a $50.00 per acre farm. Where can the $5000 or more come from for that purpose, since they can scarcely raise the rental? These men, too, are fast, very fast ripening for socialism. The line between land lord and tenant is being forcibly put as the line of demarkation is now drawn in the cities between boss and employe.

68. The Lowest Living Wages

Not only did Populists follow closely many of the strikes occurring throughout America in the early 1890's, but they sometimes took notice of labor problems in Europe as well. In this selection, the *Farmers' Alliance* viewed the situation in Germany as being essentially the same as that in the United States, with the unemployed serving in both cases as the lever by which capital depresses the wage scale. The newspaper endorsed the idea presented in Germany of a public works program to aid labor.

Reprinted from *Farmers' Alliance* (Lincoln), March 3, 1892. Nebraska Historical Society.

It is in the interest of the capitalist class to have as many men as possible out of work and seeking it in order to keep and force wages down by making competition fierce between those seeking work and those employed. But unemployed, hungry men are an exceedingly dangerous element to society, as Emperor William of Germany has been finding out during the last week. Last Thursday for several hours a mob of several thousand unemployed working men was in practical control of the city.

. . . The people, by hunger made desperate, were beaten down with batons, the flat of swords and rifle stocks.

. . . The proposition of the socialist deputies, members of the Reichstag, that the government give work to the unemployed, seems a most reasonable plan, and in fact the only way to help them. They do not want charity, they are ready and anxious to work; they are strong and capable; but the capitalists, whom they are now at the mercy of, make it to their own advantage to have a large number of the poor unemployed, in order that their hunger and nakedness may lead them to accept the lowest living wages.

69. The Labor Contract

When the Illinois Supreme Court found unconstitutional the section of the state's antisweatshop law declaring "no female shall be employed in any factory or work shop more than eight hours in any one day, or forty-eight hours in any one week," the Topeka *Advocate* took the position that the notion of a free contract was fictitious, and that the worker in reality had to accept whatever terms were offered. The editorial then went on to chide the working class for not being sufficiently radical. Labor, it asserted, had not been supporting its own interests.

Reprinted from *Advocate* (Topeka), March 20, 1895. Kansas State Historical Society.

. . . The ground of the decision is that "woman has the same rights as man to make contracts, and that it is an infringement of her rights guaranteed by the constitution to say that she cannot work as many hours in a day as she may be inclined to."

It is remarkable what a high regard the courts have for the constitutional rights of labor in certain cases. The right of contract, for instance, must not be interfered with, though everyone knows that the right of contract means the right of capital in all cases to impose any conditions it may desire upon labor, simply because labor, unprotected, is powerless to reject the provisions of such contract, whatever they may be. In the present state of society, with a limited market for labor and thousands of idle men and women anxiously seeking opportunity to earn bread, there is no such thing as freedom of contract in the ranks of labor, and it is worse than nonsense to talk about it.

Everyone knows that all the laws of every state limiting the hours of labor have been enacted at the instance of labor, and not at the instance of capital; and the hypocritical pretense that the decision in question is in the interest of the overworked women in the sweat shops is too apparent to need to be pointed out. Was the case in which this decision was rendered carried up to the supreme court by any of the women affected by the law? Was it carried up at the instance of any laboring man or woman, or by any number of them combined? Not by any means. It was carried up by a proprietor of one of the Chicago sweat shops, who was so solicitous for the constitutional rights and privileges of his employes that he could not think of their being denied the right of "freedom of contract" and the court shared the solicitude of the sweat-shop proprietor and declared that this constitutional privilege should not be abridged. In this, as in other things, however, labor is getting what it has been voting for, and it has no right to squeal.

70. Homestead: A Paternal System

A Populist newspaper in Columbus, Nebraska, criticized Andrew Carnegie for exerting control over the lives of the Homestead workers, and for making large profits under a system of class legislation. As in the case of the *Advocate* in the preceding selection, this paper felt that workingmen were turning their backs on a farmer-labor coalition to bring about basic changes.

. . . Give any man such power and he will become a tyrant, and Carnegie is one, made such by laws that filch from one class to enrich another. If wages were proportionate to the profits of the rich manufacturers, there would be no strikes and lockouts and riots. But they are not. Here as well as in the old country wage workers are largely at the mercy of their employers, who are willing to pay just what they are obliged to and no more. The entire system of paternalism is based upon a paternalism as rank as that which prevailed in England at the time when the crown bestowed upon its favorite henchmen the landed properties belonging to the humble peasantry. So the great army of toilers in the south and west are made to pay toll, tribute and custom to the money kings of the east, and many of them howl for the system, under the false impression that what further enriches a millionaire manufacturer in Massachusetts, must benefit a ragged-backed corn-grower in South Dakota. For a fact, this ought to be a campaign of education.

Reprinted from *Platte County Argus* (Columbus, Neb.), July 1, 1892. Nebraska Historical Society.

71. Homestead: A War of Extermination

For the president of the Fourth Congressional District Alliance in Kansas, the events at Homestead signified capital's drive to suppress unions and undermine the bargaining power of labor. He points to the Pinkertons and state militia as the agents in this policy of coercion.

. . . When they ["iron barons of Pennsylvania"] wish to enforce a reduction of wages, they call to their aid an armed band of hired Hessians, under the command of Pinkerton, for the purpose of driving out the American workmen who belong to the union, and introducing a gang of non-union workmen. . . . Our workmen fly to arms and repel the Pinkerton invaders, the riot act is read and the state militia is called out, not for the purpose of restoring peace and arresting the treasonable organization of Pinkerton thugs, but for the purpose of intimidating the union workingmen, protecting capital and crowding down wages through the introduction of non-union men. . . . Thus the iron barons use the taxing power of the government to oppress the consumers of their products, and the military power to oppress the laboring men. . . . Capital has been incorporated. Our statutes are loaded with special legislation in its interest. Capitalists are now waging a war of extermination against labor organizations with a view of reducing the individual workers to a state of abject servitude.

Reprinted from J. R. Detwiler to editor, *Advocate* (Topeka), Aug. 3, 1892. Kansas State Historical Society.

72. Resolutions on Homestead and Pinkertons

The resolutions passed by a county Alliance in Kansas provide some indication of grass-roots sentiment concerning the Homestead strike. Here the farmers see all labor, agricultural and industrial alike, as being oppressed by the same economic system, and hence that they too are involved in what happens elsewhere on the labor scene.

We heartily sympathize with the union laborers at Homestead, Pa., in their determined, just and sacred efforts to be protected as wage earners as fully as the protected manufacturers, and condemn our present industrial system which subjects the laborer in the field, in the shop or mine, to the merciless and soulless moneyed corporations as to what he is to receive for the products of his labor, believing that the time has arrived when all who earn their daily bread by the sweat of their brow ought effectively to demand the worth of their labor. . . . We demand of our present congress the immediate passage of the anti-Pinkerton bill . . . to the end that the present oppressive hireling standing army used by the already overly wealthy to enslave American labor may be speedily demolished.

73. Homestead: Social Cannibalism

The best-known female orator and campaigner in the Populist movement, Mary E. Lease of Kansas, strongly criticized Andrew

Adopted by Mitchell County (Kansas) Alliance, July 1892, and reprinted in *Advocate* (Topeka), July 27, 1892. Kansas State Historical Society.

Reprinted from Mary E. Lease to editor, *Advocate* (Topeka), July 27, 1892. Kansas State Historical Society.

Carnegie and just as strongly supported the striking men at Homestead. Mrs. Lease maintained there are no basic antagonisms between farmers and workers, and urged the people of Kansas to
extend aid to the strikers by sending them food.

To-day the world stands aghast at the murderous attempt of
a Scotch baron entrenched and fortified by Republican legislation, to perpetuate a system of social cannibalism, and force,
by the aid of Pinkerton cut-throats, the American laborers to
accept starvation wages. . . . We have been told by those who
deal in misrepresentations that the farmers were not in sympathy with the wants and demands of laborers in town and
city. Let us hurl this falsehood back, and show to the world
that the farmers of Kansas are imbued with the spirit of 1776,
and in sympathy with the toilers and oppressed humanity
everywhere by sending from this state such a train load of
wheat and corn to our Homestead brothers as will make hungry mothers and their little ones laugh with glee.

74. Aid for Homestead

Three weeks after Mrs. Lease made her appeal, the Topeka newspaper could report that farmers were already sending food to Homestead. For the *Advocate*, all forms of labor must maintain a common
front against the elimination of labor unions.

We are glad to see the farmers of Kansas sending provisions
to the locked-out Homestead laborers. The fight at Homestead
is only the beginning of the battle against organized labor.
What has been done there will be repeated in detail in every

Reprinted from *Advocate* (Topeka), Aug. 17, 1892. Kansas State Historical Society.

great plutocratic establishment now employing union labor in the United States. . . . In this fight the labor forces in all departments must stand together.

. . . Let the aid to Homestead go forward. It is "bread cast upon the waters." Let it go in abundance.

75. The Oppressor Is the Aggressor

One Kansas correspondent to the *Advocate* rooted the causes of the Homestead strike in the nature of the economic system itself. He argued that unless there is a transformation of that system, labor strife will become intensified, with capital bearing responsibility for the unrest.

We confidently assert that "The hour is at hand," and there are but two methods to pursue now as of old—the ballot or the bullet. If we do not strike down the system that breeds and nourishes lockouts, strikes and anarchy, we must expect them to multiply. If you would destroy these evils and their effect you should operate upon the causes that produce them. No sensible man would . . . hope to terminate riots and anarchy by punishing or hanging a few of their leaders. This remedy was sought seven years ago at Chicago, but instead of destroying it multiplied anarchy perhaps ten-fold. We condemn anarchy, but we detest the causes that produce it even more. These evils are all the legitimate children of the oppression of capital, and again the oppressor is the aggressor. Capital has been waging war on labor for years. . . . We shall continue to hope for a peaceable solution of these differences, but we fear the haughty tyranny of capital will persist in its resort to war measures by the use of Pinkertons and militia beyond the point of endurance.

Reprinted from W. H. Bennington to editor, *Advocate* (Topeka), Aug. 10, 1892. Kansas State Historical Society.

76. Homestead: A Mere Incident

In a succinct statement, the *Alliance-Independent* summed up the prevailing mood on Homestead. For Populists, the events had significance over and above their face value: These developments reflected the larger confrontation between capital and labor brought about by unjust laws and undesirable conditions.

All who look beneath the surface will see that the bloody battle fought at Homestead was a mere incident in the great conflict between labor and capital; and they will place the real blame with the men who have misgoverned this country. They will blame the parties and the policy which have permitted existing conditions to arise. They will blame the so-called statesmen of this country who have betrayed the people in the interests of organized wealth.

77. The Pullman Strike

The *Advocate,* warmly defending the American Railway Union in the Pullman strike, stated on July 18, 1894, that federal intervention was unwarranted and that "disturbance is deliberately created by the companies and by the deputies and the military sent ostensibly to preserve the peace, in order to manufacture sentiment against the strikers." The following week, in the first editorial below, it renewed the charge and went on to indicate what it believed to be the broader significance of Pullman. Further, it once again

---

Reprinted from *Alliance-Independent* (Lincoln), July 14, 1892. Nebraska Historical Society.

Reprinted from *Advocate* (Topeka), July 25, Sept. 19, 1894. Kansas State Historical Society.

urged labor to recognize that no hope lay with the two major political parties. In a second editorial on that same day, the paper announced that food was being sent to the strikers and that more was needed. Then, two months later, the *Advocate* commented on the treatment of Eugene V. Debs by the Chicago courts.

I

It has taught lessons that nothing else could have taught. Thousands of people to-day see the absolute necessity of government ownership and operation of railroads who never saw it before. . . . Another of the lessons . . . has been of especial service to railroad employes themselves. They have seen that in a contest of labor against the encroachments of capital the republican and democratic parties are on the side of capital, and the press of both parties has been arrayed solidly against the interests of labor. They have seen that their only political friends in this country to-day are the Populists.

. . . The managers of the several railroads established headquarters at Chicago and were in constant consultation. They enlisted the press of the republican and democratic parties solidly in their support; and one of the methods adopted to the injury of the cause of labor was the constant and persistent misrepresentation of their claims and of their acts. Bums and hoodlums were employed by the railroad managers to incite riots and commit lawless acts, which the press at once attributed to the strikers in order to create prejudice against them in the minds of the people. These lawless acts were also designed to afford a pretext for police and military interference, and the promptness with which this was secured on demand of the corporations has been observed by everyone. It has become apparent in this contest that in any difference between capital and labor the courts and all the civil and military authorities are at the service of organized capital. Labor has no right that capital or its allies are bound to respect.

. . . As the men affected in this case are poor men, there is no likelihood of there being any constitutional bar to their punishment discovered. Laws are made now-a-days to shield men of wealth—not poor men; and the interstate commerce law is no exception to the rule. Neither that or the so-called Sherman anti-trust law were ever designed to operate against the interests of organized capital. They were designed solely as covers for legislation by which organized capital should be enabled to make further conquests over labor.

II

The railroad strikers . . . have made a brave fight, and as a consequence many of them will be displaced by a more servile class of employes. These strikers and their families are liable to see close times for a while, and we are glad to see the farmers of the country who are blessed with an abundance of food for which there is no profitable market, disposed to share it with their brother workingmen who need it. A wagon load was delivered at the headquarters in this city from the Meriden Populist club on the 19th inst. Let the good work go on.

III

Anyone who reads without preconceived bias, the report of court proceedings in Chicago in the Debs contempt case cannot escape the conclusion that the case is prejudged, and no matter what the testimony may be, no American Railway union man can hope for justice in a Chicago court.

. . . In the contempt case above referred to, it has been the policy of the government to simply establish the fact of the commission of violence during the continuance of the late strike, and without offering an iota of testimony to connect the officers or members of the American Railway union with this violence, to infer their responsibility and punish them accordingly.

. . . Put a corporation upon one side and a poor man upon the other and the courts will see to it that there is sufficient latitude to the law to satisfy the utmost demand of the corporation.

78. On Eugene V. Debs

These brief statements from the Populist papers in Lincoln, Broken Bow, and Wahoo, Nebraska, indicate the favorable treatment accorded Eugene Debs in the agrarian press. The first editorial makes clear that this was the case even before the Pullman strike, for Debs was already regarded as a leading reformer who was sympathetic to Populism. The remaining editorials deal with the imprisonment of Debs and his qualities as a leader. It should be noted that Debs returned the feeling in kind, endorsing the Populist movement publicly and in his correspondence. In a letter to Henry D. Lloyd (August 15, 1894, Lloyd Papers), for example, Debs wrote: "The Peoples Party will come into power with a resistless rush as did the Republican party a little more than 30 years ago."

I

Debs is not only leading the railway employes to organize for mutual assistance and resistance to tyranny, but he is with great ability educating them to vote intelligently and independently. He has built up a great magazine, a magazine which is filled with the light of advancing truth. Its contributors include not the old school professional, but the real economists and moral teachers of the time. In behalf of our

Reprinted from *Alliance-Independent* (Lincoln), Jan. 18, 1894; *Custer County Beacon* (Broken Bow, Neb.), Nov. 21, 1895; *Saunders County New Era* (Wahoo, Neb.), Feb. 20, May 21, 1896. Nebraska Historical Society.

people in Nebraska we reach out earnest hands of brotherhood to those whose co-operative and educational lines of
labor converge and agree with ours. The interests of the
producing classes are one and indivisible.

II

A grand reception will be tendered to Eugene V. Debs next
month at Chicago, on the occasion of his return from Wood-
stock. It will be under the auspices of the labor unions, as
a protest against judicial and corporate tyranny. . . . Debs
stands higher today in the hearts of the masses than any
labor leader in America. All friends of humanity and justice
delight to do him honor.

III

The malicious imprisonment of Eugene V. Debbs has led to
an inquiry in congress as to the power of the courts, and to
see if any legislation was necessary to protect citizens from
the courts. Here is a new phase of things; we had supposed
the courts were for the protection of the citizens, but now the
citizens has to be protected from the courts? Oh, this higher
civilization of the grand old party is something appalling!

IV

Eugene V. Debs was named for the presidency of the United
States by the Chicago Labor congress Saturday. . . . The
congress expressed the belief that Eugene V. Debs is best
fitted to become the leader of the industrial classes. An effort
is being made to combine all the labor organizations in the
country on Mr. Debs for the purpose of running him for this
position. Should the organization be effected Mr. Debs will
enter the race with the strongest following to start on of any
candidate of any party in the field.

79. Kansas Alliancemen and the Pullman Strike

In the early stages of the Pullman strike, a farmer from Larned, Kansas, wrote to Governor Lewelling describing agrarian sentiment about this issue.

Believing that the present strike of the great railway unions, is of stupendous importance in the widest possible sense, I feel anxious lest the F.A. and I.U. [Farmers' Alliance and Industrial Union] of Kansas shall fail to perform its part in the conflict.

. . . Unquestionably, nearly, if not quite, all Alliance people are in fullest sympathy with these striking men, and it seems to me that the present is an opportune moment to take such action as may be taken in order to render assistance in a struggle that bids fair to be fought to the bitter end on both sides.

80. Lewelling's Position on Pullman

In Kansas, support for the strikers was expressed by leaders of the People's party right up to and including the governor. As a case in point, the county central committee of the party in Kansas City resolved as early as June 30, 1894, "that we sympathize with the American Railway Union in its fight with the Pullman monopoly and that we approve of the attitude of Governor Lewelling as shown by an interview published in to-days Kansas City papers." From the selection that follows, a resolution passed by Local 49 of the American Railway Union in Argentine, Kansas, one can see

---

W. M. Goodnes to Lorenzo D. Lewelling, July 4, 1894. Lewelling Papers, Kansas State Historical Society.

Adopted by Local 49, American Railway Union, July 4, 1894. Lewelling Papers, Kansas State Historical Society.

not only that some unions greeted Populist overtures with enthusiasm, but also that there was an interaction between agrarians and laborers in the farming states.

Whereas his Excellency L.D. Lewelling, Govenor of the State of Kansas has taken occassion through the Public Press to Express his disapproval of the methods of the Pullman Car Co in the treatment of their Employes and whereas he has depreciated the Methods and Utterances of Federal Officers and others in dealing with the Labor Question and has shown and expressed a feeling of fraternal interest toward the Honorable efforts of Laboring Men to better their Condition, entirely at variance with that of the Plutocratic Press, Railroad Magnates, Money Power Representatives and some Federal officers. Therefore be it Resolved that the American Railway Union of Argentine *in Mass Meeting* assembled do hereby take *this* occassion to Publicly express their hearty appreciation of the Manly and honorable sentiments expressed by their Governor and trust the day may come when men like his excellency, L D Lewelling will hold the highest offices in the gift of the People of this Nation.

81. A Military Despotism

In Populist discussions of economic trends in the 1890's, attention was invariably called to the Pinkertons and militias as the concrete embodiment of the repressive practices found in industrial capitalism. In this selection, the *Advocate*, referring to the increase of large military posts in the vicinity of railroad and commercial centers, suggested that capital was relying on armed force to serve as a warning to the lower classes.

Reprinted from *Advocate* (Topeka), Oct. 31, 1894. Kansas State Historical Society.

The companies and regiments organized to occupy these city bastiles and equipped with the latest improved instruments of death constitute a private army directly under the command of capitalists of these cities, and ready, at their instance, to suppress any uprising of the common herd.

In addition to these forces we must not forget the 30,000 Pinkertons, who constitute another private army, larger even than the present army of the United States, and also under the direct and immediate command of corporations and capitalists. These forces have for years stood ready at the call of the railroads and other large employers of labor to suppress strikes and carry terror into the ranks of the oppressed and discontented.

. . . But this is not all. The railroad companies themselves are organizing forces of their own, and equipping them with arms of the most approved patterns, thus constituting still another private army. . . .

The excuse for the maintenance of a standing army in the United States has been the necessity of protection to the frontiers and the harbors and cities of our seaboards; but the policy now is to withdraw the troops from the frontiers and concentrate them near the large inland cities.

. . . It would seem sufficiently clear to the unbiased mind from these facts that we are even now far on the road to the establishment of a military despotism in this country.

82. Pinkertons and the New York Central Strike

As early as 1890 the Lincoln newspaper treated the use of Pinkertons as a manifestation of the unchallenged position of corporations

Reprinted from *Farmers' Alliance* (Lincoln), Aug. 30, 1890. Nebraska Historical Society.

in American life. Power was being exerted in realms, contended
the Populists, where the government should have been supreme.
Not only the rights of labor but the very principles of democratic
government were being undermined.

The most notable and alarming feature of the business is the
indifference of all local authorities to the glaring violation of
law and infringement of all sound constitutional principles
involved in the employment of this force; or worse, the sub-
serviency of the authorities to the corporations which employ
it. . . . There has never been a place where the Pinkerton's
have been employed as an armed force to protect private property where the police could not have legally arrested, disarmed
and imprisoned them. And yet we have never heard of a
case where the authorities have taken this view, which is the
only proper one.

. . . The people of this country . . . will not much longer
endure . . . the arbitrary and despotic sway of an overgrown
corporate power which says to the great plain people, "you
shall not organize," while itself organizing, and which arro-
gates to itself all dominion and functions which belong to the
people.

83. Pinkertons: An Armed Mob

The following terse indictment of the Pinkertons can be found in
the minutes of an alliance meeting in Texas. In that state, where
there had already been major railroad strikes in the 1880's, agrarians
had established close ties with members of the Knights of Labor
and the American Railway Union.

Gillespie County (Texas) Alliance Minutes, April 8, 1892. The University of Texas Library, Texas Archives Division.

We regard the Pinkerton Dectives as an armed mob, under the employ of the money power of the U.S. for the purpose of intimidation labor. Therefore be it resolved, That we call upon our representatives in Congress to legislate them out of existence.

84. To Overthrow a Law of Kansas

In his governor's message before leaving office, Lorenzo D. Lewelling described how corporations in Kansas had challenged the sovereign powers of the state by maintaining private armies. He went on to proclaim that during his term of office the state militia was not used to put down labor. Significantly, Cherokee and Crawford—the two counties mentioned in his message—were mining areas and among the banner Populist counties in the state.

The act of the last legislature concerning the screening of coal was not, by its terms, to take effect till September 1, 1893; but the generous operators could not endure the delay, and decided to put it into operation at the very beginning of summer. They tendered to the miners, months in advance, a new scale of wages to take away the benefits the new law was designed to confer. In short, they entered into a conspiracy to overthrow and nullify a law of the state. In depositions now on file in the United States circuit court at Fort Scott, operators admitted, under oath, that the deliberate object of the conspirators in tendering the new scale of wages when they did was to provoke the miners to strike. Having accomplished this purpose, the operators of Cherokee and Crawford counties proceeded to erect private forts, garrisoned with conscienceless mobs armed with Winchester rifles, intended to commit murder in resisting mere trespasses upon

Reprinted from *Advocate* (Topeka), Jan. 9, 1895. Kansas State Historical Society.

lands; an offense which, under the statutes, constitutes man-slaughter. Men assembled for such an unlawful purpose to the number of three or more constitute an unlawful assembly —a riotous body; and when armed as those were, constitute a dangerous mob, and menace the peace of the community. As was to have been expected, these lawless desperadoes were not long in finding a coveted occasion for using the weapons which had been put into their hands, and an exciting affray occurred. The executive sought to obtain accurate information as to the situation of affairs, and determined to refuse military aid to corporations engaged in an armed revolt against the law of the state, and determined, also, that the only forts on Kansas soil should be those erected by the constituted authorities of the state or of the general government.

85. The Cripple Creek Strike

The most direct ties between farmers and laborers occurred, however, in mountain Populism, and more specifically in Colorado under the leadership of Davis H. Waite, one-term Populist governor of that state. Waite was the editor of the strongly pro-labor *Aspen Union Era* before assuming the governorship, and had a long career of varied activities including politics, law, teaching, election to the state legislatures of Kansas and Wisconsin, and involvement in the labor movement, to the extent even of serving as secretary of a local assembly of the Knights of Labor. In his view, mountain Populism stood for a great deal more than the silver issue; financial contraction, railroad discriminations, absentee land ownership and labor's inability to organize were uppermost in his mind. Arguing that Colorado was under the control of corporations, he felt that only a firm coalition of farmers, workers and miners could effec-

Reprinted from Colorado *House Journal*, Tenth Legislative Session (1895), pp. 55-57.

tively challenge the business domination of the state. As Leon W. Fuller pointed out in the *Mississippi Valley Historical Review* (December 1934), the state had indeed become "a pocket borough of the corporate oligarchy," for it was heavily dependent upon outside capital, had totally ineffective regulation of railroads and public utilities, and was one of a dozen states that did not place legal curbs on usury. Moreover, within the state itself, bankers and other business leaders dominated local government to the exclusion of all other interests. In a setting such as this, Waite said, in his famous statement of July 11, 1893, that Colorado was engaged in a war "which must always be waged against oppression and tyranny to preserve the liberties of man—that eternal warfare of monarchy and monopoly against the rights of the people to self-government." He further asserted that if changes could not be brought about peacefully through the ballot, then "we will meet that issue when it is forced upon us, for it is better, infinitely better that blood should flow to the horses' bridles than our national liberties should be destroyed." While this was not as revolutionary as it may sound, for Waite always emphasized political processes and public opinion, one should not be surprised to find an interesting turnabout in the practices of that period. Thus, militias had been used in most other states against the workers, but in Colorado the governor used his forces in their behalf. In the selection that follows, Waite, summarizing his tenure in office, explained to the state legislature what his role was in the second Cripple Creek strike, of mid-1894. He not only acted as the arbitrator for the miners, but also placed the national guard between them and a large force of local citizens who had been deputized to take action on behalf of the owners.

During the month of April and to the 20th of May, quiet existed in the Cripple Creek district. The largest producing mines were, however, closed, and many miners idle, although three-fourths of all the mines had continued in operation with eight hours for a day's work and $3 a day pay. The closed

464 The Populist Mind

mines belonged to non-resident owners and were voluntarily shut down, as it is claimed, in order to save $3 freight on ore per ton to the railroad terminal.

Meanwhile the sheriff of El Paso county, with the knowledge and authority of the county commissioners of El Paso county, was engaged in enlisting men, and swearing them in as deputy sheriffs, until he had enlisted about 1,200 men, divided into infantry, cavalry and artillery. About May 20, 1894, of this illegally organized force, nearly 200 were sent by way of Pueblo and Florence to take forcible possession of the mines near Victor, and thus the right to levy war, which neither the governor of a state and the general assembly combined, nor even the president of the United States can lawfully do, was usurped by the county of El Paso. This department of 200 men did not make the contemplated attack. The El Paso county troops, however, constantly concentrated and drew nearer to the mining district, and it was evident that hostilities could not much longer be delayed. Mr. Hagerman and two other gentlemen from Colorado Springs attempted to arbitrate the matters of difference in the Cripple Creek mining district, but the attempt failed. On the 27th of May, by the courtesy of E. T. Jeffery, president of the Denver & Rio Grande railway, a gentlemen for whom I desire to express my most sincere admiration and respect, I was sent by special train by night, Denver to Victor. On the 28th I held a conference at Altman with the miners and was chosen sole arbitrator for them. I telegraphed to Mr. Hagerman to meet me at Colorado Springs, but owing to the floods at that time I did not reach Colorado Springs until June 2. I had no difficulty in making terms of arbitration with Mr. Hagerman, but outside parties—lawyers and politicians—prevented any settlement, and I returned [the] same night (Saturday) to Denver. Next morning the daily papers contained the news that bands of armed men were assembling in many mining camps of the state, to aid the miners of Cripple Creek. On

Sunday I was informed that many gentlemen representing the most important business interests of the state had become anxious for a settlement. Another arbitration conference was held on Sunday, at which the governor appeared for the miners and Messrs. Hagerman and Moffat for the mine-owners. A fair and just arbitration was agreed upon, but so inflamed had become the minds of a majority of the people of Colorado Springs, and so determined were the politicians of the state that these difficulties should not be settled, that the governor issued his proclamation and called out all the national guards of the state to preserve the peace. On the 6th of June General Brooks marched between the opposing forces—the El Paso troops attacking and miners defending—and notified Sheriff Bowers that he (General Brooks) was ordered to prevent bloodshed, to restore quiet and to enforce the law; that no further advance by the deputies would be permitted, and that all further operations were to be under his (Brooks') command, to which Sheriff Bowers agreed. Notwithstanding this the entire force of deputies, the following morning, left their camp in three columns, moving towards Bull Hill. General Brooks and his staff pursued the deputies, overtaking first Sheriff Bowers' column. The sheriff offered as an excuse for breaking the agreement, that "he had no control over his men." Another column was under the nominal command of one Adams, who was told that the national guard would fire upon them if they did not return. This alternative was communicated to all the deputies, and within a short time they all returned to their camp in Beaver Park.

The miners peaceably surrendered to the national guard, and on the 9th of June the deputies, to the number of 1,100, broke camp at Beaver Creek and returned to Cripple Creek and afterwards to Colorado Springs, where they were paid and discharged. The national guard, with the exception of a small detachment, kept near Victor, returned to their homes. Peace and quiet was restored, and, thanks be to Almighty God, without the loss of a single life at the hands of the national guard.

I desire in the name of the state of Colorado, to tender to each and every member of the national guard, both officers and privates, the thanks of the commander-in-chief for their prompt obedience to orders, their bravery in the field, and their patriotism and loyalty to the state.

PART SIX

EPILOGUE:

A TRANSFORMATION OF

SOCIAL VALUES

Populists contended that the American economy did not fulfill its potential to overcome poverty and create widespread abundance. While the factors necessary to the elimination of hardship and privation were present, the economic system moved in the direction of a maldistribution of wealth. For Populists inequality became the central fact of the age. Moreover, they maintained, the growing disparities in income, power and living conditions were buttressed by the prevailing ideologies of the period. Hence, they criticized both the economy and the values which justified its existence.

Populists rejected the explanations offered by the success myth, social Darwinism, and laissez-faire for the concentration of wealth on one hand and impoverishment on the other. It seemed to them cruel as well as incorrect to say that such conditions stem from the individual's laziness or moral shortcomings, or from the operation of blind, impersonal forces. They could find nothing inevitable about low crop prices, mortgages, monopolies, unemployment, and subsistence wages for many who were fortunate to find jobs. Still less, they believed, did these problems reflect any deficiencies of character in the man who bore the brunt of the hard times. Populists dissented from the dominant strands of thought in this crucial respect: They insisted that poverty was socially created. Further, it could be eradicated only by the common effort of all through an attack on its roots. While the success myth urged clean living, thrift and hard work as the way to get ahead, and while social Darwinism urged unrelenting competition to the same end, Populists saw in such doctrines no more than sterile materialism and the gratification of one's needs at the expense of others. Nor did the assumption of laissez-faire, that the pursuit of self-interest somehow promoted the common good, appear to take the individual's mind away from climbing the ladder for its own sake. For Populists the emphasis in all three ideologies was antisocial in nature. And worse, by focusing on the role of the individual, these ideologies shielded the economic system itself from any criticism for existing grievances. If the isolated individual must fall back on his own devices, the attitude becomes one which denies the necessity for social protest.

Populists opposed this entire pattern of thinking as representing no more than the enshrinement of selfishness. In its place they proposed a social ethic in which competition is replaced by cooperation, and in which the point of departure is the belief that the economic system *was* amenable to human control. Social consciousness rather than self-interest was held to be the desired goal. The issue at stake therefore was that of individual versus social responsibility as the proper response to existing problems and to social change. Populists took the position that the industrial system must be made more democratic, and that an important means for achieving this end was the reliance on governmental action.

Yet to alter the economic framework could not be an end in itself. For unless this alteration was accompanied by a change of values, there was no assurance that the old arrangements would not be eventually reinstated. Economic democracy was for Populists as much a matter of ethics as of economics. Not only must there be structural changes to correct contemporary abuses, but there must also be an ethical content incorporated into these changes if they are to be secured on a solid footing.

The first three selections that follow are taken from the novels of Ignatius Donnelly. Because of his far-ranging interests, his brilliant mind, his inability to avoid political controversies, and his colorful personality, Donnelly has been perhaps the least understood leader in the Populist movement. Fortunately, the biography of Martin Ridge (see Bibliography) helps us to see discernible patterns where before there was seeming chaos. Whatever may be said for Donnelly's dubious ventures (these will be noted momentarily), it is clear that he was a consistent and courageous reformer for three decades. His early career, after removing from Philadelphia to Minnesota, gave little indication of the independent path he was later to follow. As a congressman during the Civil War period Donnelly was quite at home in the Republican machine politics of the state. But at the beginning of the next decade—in his Red Wing speech of July 1871, for example—it became clear that he had taken a new course, one to which the term antimonopolism can be applied for the next thirty years. Donnelly was involved in virtually every reform endeavor during that period in Minnesota, and certainly by the late 1880's was regarded as a leading agrarian spokesman in the western Midwest. Donnelly was a Granger, Greenbacker, Allianceman, Populist and many more things besides, but throughout his career one finds his continuous opposition to the railroads, millers and bankers, and his continuous defense of the small farmer and industrial laborer. In the mid-1880's he tried to effect a coalition between the Northern Alliance and the Knights of Labor but was finally unsuccessful in this attempt. During this period he served briefly in the state legislature (Donnelly's independency was maintained at great political sacrifice, for he never again rose to the position he held in the 1860's), where he fought for stricter railroad regulation, an anti-usury law, and the destruction of the marketing combinations of the millers in Minneapolis. As the 1890's began, he served both as president of the state Alliance and as a member of the Minnesota upper house. At the Cincinnati Conference Donnelly was a driving force in the establishment of a national committee which would lead to the formation of the third party. He was also the chairman of the resolutions committee of the convention.

In the four or five months preceding the Cincinnati meeting it generally became known that Donnelly was the author of *Caesar's Column,* an exciting reform novel which had been published under a pseudonym in the spring of 1890, and because of this he achieved greater recognition in national reform circles. Such recognition was long overdue, but be that as it may, Donnelly came into his own in 1892 as the author of the famous preamble (see Document 24) to the Omaha Platform, and as one of the People's party's outstanding orators. Also in that year he helped to identify the Alliance more explicitly with the People's party in Minnesota, and ran for governor in that campaign. Yet, because Donnelly had been regarded as something of a Don Quixote on the Left for so many years in his own state, he was respected and consulted in Minnesota and in the national councils of the People's party, but was never taken altogether seriously. As a man who prepared the way for Populism and who in the mid-1890's sought to keep the movement intact as a third force in American politics, Donnelly might well have been considered for the first or second spots in 1892 or 1896, but this did not happen. He was simultaneously beloved and underestimated by the people he served for so long.

This was the case in great part because of the man's self-righteousness; he was a "loner" in politics and had certain messianic qualities about him. And yet, as Mr. Ridge shows, Donnelly was quick to forgive, even when the actions by others toward him were downright treacherous, and he was willing to swallow his pride when his political opportunities came into conflict with the larger principles he wanted at all costs to see achieved. Though

Donnelly was a difficult person to work with, this only partially explains why he was not taken seriously by contemporaries. The more basic reason concerns his vast undertakings during the 1880's in the fields of scientific writing and literary criticism. It is almost impossible to convey to the reader the scope of Donnelly's interests, the breadth of his reading, and the audacity and quickness of his thinking. He accomplished the work of several men in one lifetime, and this even if one were to leave his political career wholly out of the picture. That Donnelly could be up to his neck in fights in the state assembly at the very time that he was carrying on an international correspondence on Shakespeare gives some indication of his multiple lives.

In these nonpolitical activities he was thought by many to be, and perhaps correctly so, at best as a born dissenter and at worst as a thoroughly engaging quack. Thus in the space of two months in 1881 he wrote a full-scale defense running to nearly five hundred pages on the existence of the lost continent of Atlantis. While distinguished Atlantean scholars even to this day, such as Edgerton Sykes, take *Atlantis: The Antediluvian World* seriously (Harper and Brothers republished it in 1949), there is ample justification for Mr. Ridge's conclusion that Donnelly did not examine his sources in a critical light. Then the very next year (1882) Donnelly, in an even shorter time, wrote *Ragnarok: The Age of Fire and Gravel*, which ventured into the realms of prehistory to assert that the earth's mineral and soil formations were caused not by the work of glaciers but by a comet colliding with or coming near to the earth. Finally, and most memorable, Donnelly immersed himself deeply in the Bacon-Shakespeare controversy, writing *The Great Cryptogram* to suggest that a series of ciphers in Shakespeare's plays pointed to Francis Bacon as the author of these works.

It is this background of quasi-scientific and literary scholarship which surrounded the name of Ignatius Donnelly, and which prevented his political principles and record from gaining a fair hearing in their own right. The temptation has been great, for contemporaries and later historians alike, simply to merge the two sides

to Donnelly, and from that to conclude that his was a politics of irrationality. Mr. Ridge helps us to see that such an analysis is far too simplistic, for it enables one to discredit Donnelly's reform position without examining it closely. That he was not an anti-Semite, as recent critics charge, has already been pointed out (see Introduction and Bibliography). That he *was* humane in outlook will be seen in the selections from *Caesar's Column* (1890), *Doctor Huguet* (1891), and *The Golden Bottle* (1892).

These three novels, as well as *The American People's Money* (1895), can properly be regarded as stemming directly from his political efforts rather than from his scientific and literary interests. Each story relies on a highly imaginative gimmick to provide the backdrop for a statement of the need for reform principles. As Donnelly states in *The Golden Bottle,* he is using this medium "to explain and defend, in the thin disguise of a story, some of the new ideas put forth by the People's Party." Hence, these works are political tracts, and as such provide an indication of Donnelly's thinking. Because the present writer is concerned with the social values expressed in these books, and not with their literary merits and demerits, he will omit the running commentary found in section two which provided continuity (in this case of plot), and turn instead to the statements themselves. It is sufficient to note here that the plots are exceedingly melodramatic and sometimes quite intricate.

86. There Is Nothing Sacred on Earth but Man

Donnelly uses the device of a future setting in *Caesar's Column* to suggest what will happen if *existing* trends in the society remain unchecked. In that sense, the book is not a utopian novel, for

---

Reprinted from Ignatius Donnelly (Edmund Boisgilbert, *pseud.*), *Caesar's Column* (Chicago: F. J. Schulte and Company, 1890), pp. 3-5, 20-22, 40-41, 44-46, 79, 82-84, 122, 129-132, 212-216.

Donnelly is in reality describing the oppression and impoverishment of his own time. The horrible climax, in which millions die (many to be encased in cement—Caesar's column—as a reminder to future generations of what can happen when grievances become too intolerable to bear), is written as a warning directed to the present generation. Far from being nihilistic or from welcoming upheaval and bloodshed, Donnelly attempts to shock his readers and make them aware of the seriousness of the growing disparities in wealth. He wants to avoid rather than encourage a possible conflict, and in doing so, he points to the way out through a set of economic reforms and a highly affirmative statement of values. His own self-image in writing the book can be gathered from the quotation by Goethe he selected for the title-page: "The true poet is only a masked father-confessor, whose special function it is to exhibit what is dangerous in sentiment and pernicious in action by a vivid picture of their consequences."

The two leading characters, who appear in the passages below, are Gabriel and Max, the former a young traveler from Uganda who speaks for Donnelly and narrates the story in a series of letters to his brother at home, and the latter, a friend of Gabriel who is a leader of the Brotherhood of Destruction but who nonetheless dissents from that organization's quest for destruction and hopes to guide the coming revolution into constructive channels. Both flee to Uganda when the revolution runs amuck, and set up there a society based upon reform principles.

[At the outset Donnelly explains his reasons for writing *Caesar's Column*.]

. . . It must not be thought, because I am constrained to describe the overthrow of civilization, that I desire it. The prophet is not responsible for the event he foretells. He may contemplate it with profoundest sorrow. Christ wept over the doom of Jerusalem.

Neither am I an anarchist: for I paint a dreadful picture

of the world-wreck which successful anarchism would produce.

I seek to preach into the ears of the able and rich and powerful the great truth that neglect of the sufferings of their fellows, indifference to the great bond of brotherhood which lies at the base of Christianity, and blind, brutal and degrading worship of mere wealth, must—given time and pressure enough—eventuate in the overthrow of society and the destruction of civilization.

I come to the churches with my heart filled with the profoundest respect for the essentials of religion; I seek to show them why they have lost their hold upon the poor,—upon that vast multitude, the best-beloved of God's kingdom,—and I point out to them how they may regain it. I tell them that if Religion is to reassume her ancient station, as crowned mistress of the souls of men, she must stand, in shining armor bright, with the serpent beneath her feet, the champion and defender of mankind against all its oppressors.

The world, to-day, clamors for deeds, not creeds; for bread, not dogma; for charity, not ceremony; for love, not intellect.

Some will say the events herein described are absurdly impossible.

Who is it that is satisfied with the present unhappy condition of society? It is conceded that life is a dark and wretched failure for the great mass of mankind. The many are plundered to enrich the few. Vast combinations depress the price of labor and increase the cost of the necessaries of existence. The rich, as a rule, despise the poor; and the poor are coming to hate the rich. The face of labor grows sullen; the old tender Christian love is gone; standing armies are formed on one side, and great communistic organizations on the other; society divides itself into two hostile camps; no white flags pass from the one to the other. They wait only for the drum-beat and the trumpet to summon them to armed conflict.

These conditions have come about in less than a century; most of them in a quarter of a century. Multiply them by the years of another century, and who shall say that the events I depict are impossible? There is an acceleration of movement in human affairs even as there is in the operations of gravity. The dead missile out of space at last blazes, and the very air takes fire. The masses grow more intelligent as they grow more wretched; and more capable of co-operation as they become more desperate. The labor organizations of to-day would have been impossible fifty years ago. And what is to arrest the flow of effect from cause? What is to prevent the coming of the night if the earth continues to revolve on its axis? The fool may cry out: "There shall be no night!" But the feet of the hours march unrelentingly toward the darkness.

Some may think that, even if all this be true, *"Caesar's Column"* should not have been published. Will it arrest the moving evil to ignore its presence? What would be thought of the surgeon who, seeing upon his patient's lip the first nodule of the cancer, tells him there is no danger, and laughs him into security while the roots of the monster eat their way toward the great arteries? If my message be true it should be spoken; and the world should hear it. The cancer should be cut out while there is yet time. Any other course

> "Will but skin and film the ulcerous place,
> While rank corruption, mining all beneath,
> Infects unseen."

Believing, as I do, that I read the future aright, it would be criminal in me to remain silent. I plead for higher and nobler thoughts in the souls of men; for wider love and ampler charity in their hearts; for a renewal of the bond of brotherhood between the classes; for a reign of justice on earth that shall obliterate the cruel hates and passions which now divide the world.

[In this passage Donnelly captures the feeling of alienation in modern industrial society. Suicide, he suggests, is the logical result of such a society, where life has become so utterly devoid of meaning. The bitterness of his writing points up his rejection of materialistic values.]

. . . Would you believe it, my dear brother, in this city they actually facilitate suicide! A race of philosophers has arisen in the last fifty years who argue that, as man was not consulted about his coming into the world, he has a perfect right to leave it whenever it becomes uncomfortable. These strange arguments were supplemented by the economists, always a powerful body in this utilitarian land, and they urged that, as men could not be prevented from destroying themselves, if they had made up their minds to do so, they might just as well shuffle off the mortal coil in the way that would give least trouble to their surviving fellow-citizens. That, as it was, they polluted the rivers, and even the reservoirs of drinking-water, with their dead bodies, and put the city to great expense and trouble to recover and identify them. Then came the humanitarians, who said that many persons, intent on suicide, but knowing nothing of the best means of effecting their object, tore themselves to pieces with cruel pistol shots or knife wounds, or took corrosive poisons, which subjected them to agonizing tortures for hours before death came to their relief; and they argued that if a man had determined to leave the world it was a matter of humanity to help him out of it by the pleasantest means possible. These views at length prevailed, and now in all the public squares or parks they have erected handsome houses, beautifully furnished, with baths and bed-rooms. If a man has decided to die, he goes there. He is first photographed; then his name, if he sees fit to give it, is recorded, with his residence; and his directions are taken as to the disposition of his body. There are tables at which he can write his farewell letters to his friends. A doctor explains to him the nature and effect of the different poisons, and he selects the kind he prefers. He is expected to bring with him the clothes in which he intends to be cremated. He swallows a little pill, lies down upon a bed, or, if he prefers it, in his coffin; pleasant music is played for him; he goes to sleep, and wakes up on the other side of the great line. Every day hundreds of people, men and women, perish in this way; and they are borne off to the great furnaces for the dead, and consumed. The authorities assert that it is a marked improvement over the old-fashioned methods; but to my mind it is a shocking combination of impiety and mock-philanthropy. The truth is, that, in this vast, over-crowded city, man is a drug,—a superfluity,—and I think many men and women end their lives out of an overwhelming sense of their own insignificance;—in other words, from a mere weariness of feeling that they are nothing, they become nothing.

[In a conversation between Gabriel and Max, Gabriel tells of how "mankind has become wise in breadth of knowledge, and sweet and gentle in manner." Max, in replying, acquaints his friend with the conditions existing in American society.]

. . . "Yes; it is the greatest of pities that so noble and beautiful a civilization should have become so hollow and rotten at the core."

"Rotten at the core!" I exclaimed, in astonishment; "what do you mean?"

"What I mean is that our civilization has grown to be a gorgeous shell; a mere mockery; a sham; outwardly fair and lovely, but inwardly full of dead men's bones and all uncleanness. To think that mankind is so capable of good, and now so cultured and polished, and yet all above is cruelty, craft and destruction, and all below is suffering, wretchedness, sin and shame."

"What do you mean?" I asked.

"That civilization is a gross and dreadful failure for seven-tenths of the human family; that seven-tenths of the backs of the world are insufficiently clothed; seven-tenths of the stomachs of the world are insufficiently fed; seven-tenths of the minds of the world are darkened and despairing, and filled with bitterness against the Author of the universe. It is pitiful to think what society is, and then to think what it might have been if our ancestors had not cast away their magnificent opportunities—had not thrown them into the pens of the swine of greed and gluttony."

"But," I replied, "the world does not look to me after that fashion. I have been expressing to my family my delight at viewing the vast triumphs of man over nature, by which the most secret powers of the universe have been captured and harnessed for the good of our race. Why, my friend, this city preaches at every pore, in every street and alley, in every shop and factory, the greatness of humanity, the splendor of civilization!"

"True, my friend," replied Maximilian; "but you see only the surface, the shell, the crust of life in this great metropolis. To-morrow we will go out together, and I shall show you the fruits of our modern civilization. I shall take you, not upon the upper deck of society, where the flags are flying, the breeze blowing, and the music playing, but down into the dark and stuffy depths of the hold of the great vessel, where the sweating gnomes, in the glare of the furnace-heat, furnish the power which drives the mighty ship resplendent through the seas of time. We will visit the *Under-World*."

[Gabriel then describes the miserable existence of the working class.]

   . . . What struck me most was their incalculable multitude and their silence. It seemed to me that I was witnessing the resurrection of the dead; and that these vast, streaming, endless swarms were the condemned, marching noiselessly as shades to unavoidable and everlasting misery. They seemed to me merely automata, in the hands of some ruthless and unrelenting destiny. They lived and moved, but they were without heart or hope. The illusions of the imagination, which beckon all of us forward, even over the roughest paths and through the darkest valleys and shadows of life, had departed from the scope of their vision. They knew that to-morrow could bring them nothing better than to-day—the same shameful, pitiable, contemptible, sordid struggle for a mere existence. If they produced children it was reluctantly or unmeaningly; for they knew the wretches must tread in their footsteps, and enter, like them, that narrow, gloomy, high-walled pathway, out of which they could never climb; which began almost in infancy and ended in a pauper's grave—nay, I am wrong, not even in a pauper's grave; for they might have claimed, perhaps, some sort of ownership over the earth which enfolded them, which touched them and mingled with their dust. But public safety and the demands of science had long ago decreed that they should be whisked off, as soon as dead, a score or two at a time, and swept on iron tram-cars into furnaces heated to such intense white heat that they dissolved, crackling, even as they entered the chamber, and rose in nameless gases through the high chimney. That towering structure was the sole memorial monument of millions of them. Their graveyard was the air. Nature reclaimed her own with such velocity that she seemed to grudge them the very dust she had lent them during their wretched pilgrimage. The busy, toiling, rushing, roaring, groaning universe, big with young, appeared to cry out: "Away with them! Away with them! They have had their hour! They have performed their task. Here are a billion spirits waiting for the substance we loaned them. The spirits are boundless in number; matter is scarce. Away with them!"

I need not tell you, my dear brother, of all the shops and factories we visited. It was the same story everywhere. Here we saw exemplified, in its full perfection, that "iron law of wages" which the old economists spoke of; that is to say, the reduction, by competition, of the wages of the worker to the least sum that will maintain life and muscular strength enough to do the work required, with such little surplus of vitality as might be necessary to perpetuate the wretched race; so that the world's work should not end with the death of one starved generation.

[Donnelly definitely does not glorify the Brotherhood of Destruction, but rather sees it as being a negative force. In this passage he once again makes clear his belief that an upheaval must be prevented.]

. . . There is no bigotry so blind or intense as that of caste; and long-established wrongs are only to be rooted out by fire and sword. And hence the future looks so black to me. The upper classes might reform the world, but they will not; the lower classes would, but they cannot; and for a generation or more these latter have settled down into a sullen and unanimous conviction that the only remedy is world-wide destruction. We can say, as one said at the opening of the Cromwellian struggle, "God help the land where ruin must reform!"

. . . I tremble, my brother, I tremble with horror when I think of what is crawling toward us, with noiseless steps; couchant, silent, treacherous, pard-like; scarce rustling the dry leaves as it moves, and yet with bloodshot, glaring eyes and tense-drawn limbs of steel, ready for the fatal spring. When comes it? To-night? To-morrow? A week hence? Who can say?

And the thought forever presses on me, Can I do nothing to avert this catastrophe? Is there no hope? For mankind is in itself so noble, so beautiful, so full of all graces and capacities; with aspirations fitted to sing among the angels; with comprehension fitted to embrace the universe!

[Gabriel dedicates himself to trying to head off the conflict, and speaks at meetings of the Brotherhood.]

. . . More than once I have spoken to them in these dim halls; and while full of sympathy for their sufferings, and indignant as they themselves can be against their oppressors, I have pleaded with them to stay their hands, to seek not to destroy, but to reform. I preach to them of the glories of civilization; I trace its history backward through a dozen eras and many nations; I show them how slowly it grew, and by what small and gradual accretions; I tell them how radiantly it has burst forth in these latter centuries, with such magnificent effulgence, until to-day man has all nature at his feet, shackled and gyved, his patient logman. I tell them that a ruffian, with one blow of his club, can destroy the life of a man; and that all the doctors and scientists and philosophers of the world, working together for ages, could not restore that which he has so rudely extinguished. And so, I say to them, the civilization which it has taken ten thousand years to create may be swept away in an hour; and there shall be no power in the wit or wisdom of man to re-establish it.

[While discussing concrete reform proposals—abolishing interest rates, limiting the size of wealth and landholdings, and the like— Gabriel presents his positive alternative to the contemporary situation. He calls for a comprehensive program directed to human welfare.]

. . . Government is only a machine to insure justice and help the people, and we have not yet developed half its powers. And we are under no more necessity to limit ourselves to the governmental precedents of our ancestors than we are to confine ourselves to the narrow boundaries of their knowledge, or their inventive skill, or their theological beliefs. The trouble is that so many seem to regard government as a divine something which has fallen down upon us out of heaven, and therefore not to be improved upon or even criticised; while the truth is, it is simply a human device to secure human happiness, and in itself has no more sacredness than a wheel-barrow or a cooking-pot. The end of everything earthly is the good of man; and there is nothing sacred on earth but man, because he alone shares the Divine conscience."

[Then, after coming out for an international system of paper money and other proposals, Gabriel replies to a question concerning remedies in these terms.]

. . . "Government," I replied; "government—national, state and municipal—is the key to the future of the human race.

"There was a time when the town simply represented cowering peasants, clustered under the shadow of the baron's castle for protection. It advanced slowly and reluctantly along the road of civic development, scourged forward by the whip of necessity. We have but to expand the powers of government to solve the enigma of the world. Man separated is man savage; man gregarious is man civilized. A higher development in society requires that this instrumentality of co-operation shall be heightened in its powers. There was a time when every man provided, at great cost, for the carriage of his own letters. Now the government, for an infinitely small charge, takes the business off his hands. There was a time when each house had to provide itself with water. Now the municipality furnishes water to all. The same is true of light. At one time each family had to educate its own children; now the state educates them. Once every man went armed to protect himself. Now the city protects him by its armed police. These hints must be followed out. The city of the future must furnish doctors for all; lawyers for all; entertainments for all; business guidance for all. It will see to it that no man is plundered, and no man starved, who is willing to work."

[As part of the same discussion, Gabriel is critical of the success myth and of the drive to emulate others.]

. . . "Men work at first for a competence—for enough to lift

them above the reach of want in those days which they know
to be rapidly approaching, when they can no longer toil.
But, having reached that point, they go on laboring for vanity—one of the shallowest of the human passions. The man
who is worth $100,000 says to himself, 'There is Jones; he is
worth $500,000; he lives with a display and extravagance I
cannot equal. I must increase my fortune to half a million.'
Jones, on the other hand, is measuring himself against Brown,
who has a million. He knows that men cringe lower to Brown
than they do to him. He must have a million—half a million is nothing. And Brown feels that he is overshadowed by
Smith, with his ten millions; and so the childish emulation
continues. Men are valued, not for themselves, but for their
bank account. In the meantime these vast concentrations of
capital are made at the expense of mankind.

. . . "And thus, under the stimulus of shallow vanity," I
continued, "a rivalry of barouches and bonnets—an emulation of waste and extravagance—all the powers of the minds
of men are turned—not to lift up the world, but to degrade
it. A crowd of little creatures—men and women—are dis-
played upon a high platform, in the face of mankind, parading
and strutting about, with their noses in the air, as tickled
as a monkey with a string of beads, and covered with a glory
which is not their own, but which they have been able to
purchase; crying aloud: 'Behold what I *have got!*' not, 'Behold
what I *am!*' "

[In the chapter entitled "A Sermon of the Twentieth Century,"
Donnelly attacks the materialistic values of his day. The sermon,
presented in social Darwinian terms, justifies poverty and praises
unrestrained competition and the resulting inequalities. After can-
vassing recent scientific developments, the minister states the following.]

. . . "Nature," he continued, "is as merciless as she is prolific.
Let us consider the humblest little creature that lives—we

will say the field-mouse. Think what an exquisite compendium it is of bones, muscles, nerves, veins, arteries—all sheathed in such a delicate, flexible and glossy covering of skin. Observe the innumerable and beautiful adjustments in the little animal: the bright, pumping, bounding blood; the brilliant eyes, with their marvelous powers; the apprehending brain, with its sentiments and emotions, its loves, its fears, its hopes; and note, too, that wonderful net-work, that telegraphic apparatus of nerves which connects the brain with the eyes and ears and quick, vivacious little feet. One who took but a half view of things would say, 'How benevolent is Nature, that has so kindly equipped the tiny field-mouse with the means of protection—its quick, listening ears; its keen, watchful eyes; its rapid, glancing feet!' But look a little farther, my brethren, and what do you behold? This same benevolent Nature has formed another, larger creature, to watch for and spring upon this 'timorous little beastie,' even in its moments of unsuspecting happiness, and rend, tear, crush and mangle it to pieces. And to this especial work Nature has given the larger animal a set of adjustments as exquisitely perfect as those it has conferred on the smaller one; to-wit: eyes to behold in the darkness; teeth to tear; claws to rend; muscles to spring; patience to wait; and a stomach that clamors for the blood of its innocent fellow-creature.

"And what lesson does this learned and cultured age draw from these facts? Simply this: that the plan of Nature necessarily involves cruelty, suffering, injustice, destruction, death.

"We are told by a school of philanthropists more numerous in the old time, fortunately, than they are at present, that men should not be happy while their fellow-men are miserable; that we must decrease our own pleasures to make others comfortable; and much more of the same sort. But, my brethren, does Nature preach that gospel to the cat when it destroys the field-mouse? No; she equips it with special aptitudes for the work of slaughter.

"If Nature, with her interminable fecundity, pours forth millions of human beings for whom there is no place on earth, and no means of subsistence, what affair is that of ours, my brethren? We did not make them; we did not ask Nature to make them. And it is Nature's business to feed them, not yours or mine. Are we better than Nature? Are we wiser? Shall we rebuke the Great Mother by caring for those whom she has abandoned? If she intended that all men should be happy, why did she not make them so? She is omnipotent. She permits evil to exist, when with a breath of her mouth she could sweep it away forever. But it is part of her scheme of life. She is indifferent to the cries of distress which rise up to her, in one undying wail, from the face of the universe. With stony eyes the thousand-handed goddess sits, serene and merciless, in the midst of her worshipers, like a Hindoo idol. Her skirts are wet with blood; her creation is based on destruction; her lives live only by murder. The cruel images of the pagan are truer delineations of Nature than the figures which typify the impotent charity of Christendom—an exotic in the midst of an alien world.

"Let the abyss groan. Why should we trouble ourselves. Let us close our ears to the cries of distress we are not able to relieve. It was said of old time, 'Many are called, but few chosen.' Our ancestors placed a mythical interpretation on this text; but we know that it means:—many are called to the sorrows of life, but few are chosen to inherit the delights of wealth and happiness. Buddha told us, 'Poverty is the curse of Brahma;' Mahomet declared that 'God smote the wicked with misery;' and Christ said, 'The poor ye have always with you.' Why, then, should we concern ourselves about the poor? They are part of the everlasting economy of human society. Let us leave them in the hands of Nature. She who made them can care for them.

"Let us rejoice that out of the misery of the universe *we* are reserved for happiness."

. . . "On with the dance!" shouted the preacher, "though we dance above graves. Let the very calamities of the world accentuate our pleasures, even as the warm and sheltered fireside seems more delightful when we hear without the roar of the tempest. The ancient Egyptians brought into their banquets the mummied bodies of the dead, to remind them of mortality. It was a foolish custom. Men are made to feast and made to die; and the one is as natural as the other. Let us, on the other hand, when we rejoice together, throw open our windows, that we may behold the swarming, starving multitudes who stream past our doors. Their pinched and ashy faces and hungry eyes, properly considered, will add a flavor to our viands. We will rejoice to think that if, in this ill-governed universe, all cannot be blest, we at least rise above the universal wretchedness and are reserved for happiness."

87. The White Man Is But a Bleached Negro

In the novel *Doctor Huguet* (1891), Donnelly attacks racial discrimination head-on in one of the most sympathetic works on the Negro in the latter nineteenth century. The central character, Huguet, is an aristocratic physician living in the post-Civil War South. Although he wants to help Negroes, Huguet does not maintain his convictions with any determination, and he is suddenly punished by God for not having gone far enough. His mind and soul are placed in the body of a Negro in the vicinity, and through this transformation Huguet realizes for the first time what it means to be a Negro in America. As the story unfolds, one has the impression that Donnelly feels his way more and more into Huguet's

Reprinted from Ignatius Donnelly, *Doctor Huguet* (Chicago: F.J. Schulte and Company, 1891), pp. 60-61, 63-65, 80, 163, 166, 200-201, 289-290, 308-309.

role in that the author increasingly grows in understanding. For once the transformation occurs, Donnelly treats the degradation of the Negro people with great sensitivity. There is some ambiguity on that score in the beginning. Huguet, engaged in a long conversation with his southern friends, comes out for political but not social equality. Yet even when he refers to white supremacy, there is reason to believe that in the context of the story Huguet is only making concessions to his friends in order to win their approval for political justice for the Negro. Thus, he subjects to ridicule many stock segregationist responses of that period and later ("because a man votes beside me at the polling-place, it does not follow" that he will marry my daughter), which suggests that he is seeking leverage for basic political rights. Huguet also poses the most thoroughgoing equalitarian question one can ask, a question pointing to the essential unity of mankind. "If the white man is but a bleached negro, what right has he to mock his dark progenitor?" And this conversation takes place *before* Huguet's transformation. Afterward, there is no question about Donnelly's position. He concludes by calling upon southern Negroes to align with the poorer whites in a new political movement. Donnelly's book contains almost the same formulation on the economic character of segregation as that stated by Thomas E. Watson (see Document 46) the following year.

[When asked whether he thought that "negroes should have the same political rights as the whites," Huguet replied:]

. . . "Why not? Political equality does not imply social equality, or physical equality, or moral equality, or race equality. When you go to the ballot-box to vote you find a group assembled of white men, originally of different nationalities— Yankee, French, German, Irish, Scotch—of different complexions, conditions, mental power, education and knowledge. No two are alike; no two are equal in any respect, and yet they all peacefully unite in expressing their political prefer-

ences. The right to participate in the government, in a republic, is like the right to breathe the atmosphere. No man feels
degraded because the air he inhales has already passed
through the lungs of his fellow-man, differing from him in
every respect and condition. We must all breathe to live, and
we must all vote if the republic is to live. Because a man
votes beside me at the polling-place, it does not follow that
I must take him into my house, or wed him to my daughter,
any more than those results follow because we breathe the
same air."

[When asked later in the conversation whether the white race was
superior, Huguet turns the discussion into a plea for an attitude
of *noblesse oblige*.]

. . . "Granted, Major," I replied; "granted that the white
race is the masterful race of the globe; and, in the presence
of their tremendous achievements, no man—black, brown,
red or yellow—can doubt it. They are the biggest-brained, the
boldest-hearted, the most capable subdivision of mankind
that has ever dwelt on the planet. I grant you all that. But
are we to do justice only to our superiors, or our equals?
If so, it yields us no honor, for our superiors and our equals
are able to enforce justice from us. Generosity can only be
exercised toward those less fortunate than ourselves. Power
has no attribute grander than the god-like instinct to reach
down and lift up the fallen. If we can plainly perceive in
the progress of humanity the movement of a great Benevolence, every year adding to the comfort and happiness of
mankind, why should we not, to the extent of our little
powers, aid Him in His tremendous work? How divine a
thought is it that we are participating in the purposes and
work of the Almighty One! That, as he has dragged man up
from reptilian barbarism to this splendid, this august era of
peace and love, we are able to help the flagging footsteps
of the laggards and stragglers who have dropped behind in

God's great march! In such a work we become the very children of God—fired with his zeal, illuminated by his smile. How base and brutal it would be if we were willing to be fed with all the countless fruits of God's beneficence, and, in the midst of our full content, commend only poison to the lips of those whose sole offense is that Heaven has not given them our blessings!"

[At another point Huguet is asked to comment on the need to keep Negroes out of government and to prevent them from going to the polls.]

. . . "The present system, practiced in some places, of brutally killing a man because he attempts to peacefully exercise the right which the laws of the land confer upon him, is, to my mind, revolting and dreadful, and a disgrace to the Southern people. To fill a man with lead, to tear his vitals to pieces, simply because he attempts to put a piece of paper in the ballot-box, when the law says he shall have the right to do so, is a horrible travesty on our civilization and Christianity; and I am glad to know that our best people repudiate it."

[When the girl he intends to marry asks him to make a statement in favor of white supremacy, Huguet responds with this comment.]

. . . "It is not white domination they [politicians] seek, but negro degradation; they are not satisfied to rule the blacks —they must ruin them; not content to deny the colored people leadership, they would reduce them to beasts. I do not speak of the whole people, but of a faction, who rise to office on the shoulders of public prejudice. They are not teachers of the people, but betrayers of humanity."

[All of the foregoing statements occurred *before* Huguet's mind and soul were placed into the body of a Negro. In what follows, Huguet describes his early reactions to the discrimination he has encountered as a Negro.]

. . . The day darkened as I sat and thought, but it was nothing to the profound darkness that settled on my soul. My head sank into my chest; my shoulders drooped. I seemed to cringe into myself, as if the very props of life had been withdrawn from within me. Night came, but, with its stars, it was as daybreak to the moonless and starless night that reigned within me. Never before had I realized the glory of my *white life*. Never before had I understood what "honor, love, obedience, troops of friends," meant. Never before had I comprehended the dreadful burden of disqualification and disability borne by the colored people of America.

[With such thoughts running through his mind, Huguet "cried out aloud:"]

. . . "Oh, my white brethren! Little do you appreciate what a glory it is to belong to the dominant caste; what a hell it is to fall into the subject caste!"

[Rebuffed at every turn, Huguet was determined to get a job so that he could "lead the negroes to better things."]

. . . It was a long time before I could get to sleep. The high hopes and aspirations with which I had started out in the morning were all blasted and withered. I began to lose confidence in my own theories. The Archimedean lever would not work. I could not find a fulcrum for it. It seemed to me that the eloquence of Daniel Webster or the learning of William E. Gladstone, wrapped up in a black hide, would amount to nothing. . . . The world is a wretched-looking object viewed from below, but grand and gaudy as stage scenery to him who can contemplate it from above.

[Huguet does become a respected Negro minister, and in his last sermon before being lynched, calls upon the southern Negroes to break away from the Republican party and form a coalition with the poorer whites.]

. . . "*Let the black men break ranks!* Let them dissolve into the community. Let them divide politically on other lines than those of color. Great economic questions are arising which have nothing to do with the old struggles. A tidal wave—a great passionate cry for justice, for prosperity, for liberation from the plunderers, for each man's share of happiness and the fruits of civilization—sweeps, high-mounting, through the hearts and brains of the whites of the South. They are gathering in a vast army, with principles for banners and ballots for weapons. The black man's interests are the same as theirs. He needs prosperity, growth, opportunity, happiness. So do they. He wants to see the robbers struck down. So do they. He desires all that civilization can give him—all that belongs to him. So do they. Will he join with his white brethren to rescue the land from poverty and ruin? Or will he stand afar off, in solid, unreasoning, sullen, threatening array, to perpetuate the race-prejudices which are destroying him? When he breaks his own ranks and moves, in solid column, with part, at least, of his white friends and neighbors, they will perceive that his ballots are bullets, as potent as their own to kill injustice. Their own interests will compel them to defend his rights. The day of persecution and cruelty will end. In every intelligent white man the intelligent black man will find a defender; and the reign of peace and love and brotherhood will begin in the South, yea, in the whole land."

[In the last two pages of the book, Huguet, whose mind and soul had been returned to his body at the time of the lynching, ponders the meaning of the experience and how what he has gone through will govern his future conduct.]

. . . Have I forgotten the lessons I have learned?

No; no; they will never depart from my memory. My heart is softened by the miseries I have endured and the scenes I have witnessed. I have walked in the Valley of the Shadow of Death. I understand now, as I never did before, the feelings of the proscribed and wretched.

Mary [his future bride] and I have talked it over. . . .

There, hand in hand, we agreed that I should devote my fortune and my life to the up-building of the negro race in this great America—this grandest and noblest of nations.

. . . I shall erect school-houses, I shall provide teachers, I shall employ good men and women to work goodness in the land. I shall labor to enlighten minds, to enkindle souls, to sweeten tempers, and to lift both races out of the slough of bigotry and intolerance. I shall preach mercy and good will and peace on earth to men, for the great Gospel of Brotherly Love is the true solvent in which must melt away forever the hates of races and the contentions of castes.

88. Man Is the Only Thing Worth Considering

The Golden Bottle is the most hastily written and avowedly political novel of the three presented here. Donnelly makes no attempt to hold his imagination in check, and the result is a simple, direct, impulsive story which probably reflects his spontaneous thoughts. The central character, Ephraim Benezet, is a young Kansas farmer whose family is about to be thrown off the land. Then Benezet discovers a magic bottle (it turns out that this is a dream, and at the end he must come to grips with poverty again) which enables him to convert ordinary metal into the finest gold. Hence, Benezet has literally unlimited sources of wealth at his command. From this point on Donnelly simply unwinds and all good things happen: Benezet becomes the president of the United States and enacts the People's party platform into law; poverty is eliminated and an ethic of cooperation and fellowship predominates. He next encourages the oppressed peoples of the world to overthrow their rulers, and leads an army to accomplish that end. Again the Peo-

Reprinted from Ignatius Donnelly, *The Golden Bottle* (New York and St. Paul: D. D. Merrill Company, 1892), pp. 125, 128, 171, 269-271, 291. The portions quoted in the headnote are on pp. 269, 280-281.

ple's party platform becomes the basis for organization, and these other nations now have nationalized railroads, an equitable distribution of landholdings, and universal religious toleration, a point Benezet always insisted upon. Finally a world government is established to secure the peace, encourage economic development, and provide for national self-determination along constructive lines.

For those who see anti-Semitism in Donnelly's works, it is significant that Benezet "restored Palestine to the Jews" as a national homeland. He states: "It seems to me that this great race, the Israelites, from whom we had derived our religion and so much of our literature, should have some share in the awakening of the world." Benezet then creates the new Jewish state. "I gave orders that all Jewish emigrants to the Holy Land should be carried free, with their effects, over the government railroads; that the land should be divided among them; houses built; railroads and ships constructed; a national convention held at Jerusalem, and financial help extended to make them at once a great and prosperous people." The following observation is added:

> And out from all the lands of hatred and persecution the poor afflicted Hebrews, with their wives and little ones, poured in a steady stream into the old lands of their race; wealthy Israelites helped them, and natural leaders sprang up among them; and it will be but a short time until the Jews, too, shall have a nation and a flag, illustrious and honored in the world; while the smoke of their steamers shall ascend from every sea and every harbor on the globe.

The two dominant themes in *The Golden Bottle* concern, first, the social gains that can be accomplished through an adequate supply of money and a dynamic government willing to control the financial system and promote creative programs, and second, the ethical underpinnings that will encourage men to move in this direction. For Donnelly religion must, unlike the sermon in *Caesar's Column*, actively support and reinforce a spirit of toleration and brotherhood. Its motto should be: "*Love God with all thy heart and thy neighbor as thyself.*"

[Ephraim Benezet, before becoming president, addresses the following words to the United States Congress.]

. . . "Statutes, ordinances, customs; banks, bonds, money; beliefs, theories, religions; philosophies, dogmas, and doctrines, are only valuable as they conserve the happiness of mankind. Whenever they conflict with it, they must fall to the ground. Man is the only thing worth considering in this great world. He is the climax of the creative force; the ultimate object for which this planet was made; a little god working out the purposes of the great God. To set up anything—any device or invention of man, any belief or form or theory, statute or custom, against the welfare, happiness, development, of man —is a species of horrible blasphemy against the Everlasting One, whose child and instrument man is."

[Later in the speech Benezet presents his notions on the powers of government, and adds at the end a twist similar to the remark contained in *Caesar's Column* about man as a drug.]

. . . *"Keep the land in the hands of the many.* [Cheers.]
"Limit the amount that any man may own. [Cheers.]
"See to it that the working-men obtain homes. [Great cheers.]
"Use the powers of government for the good of the governed. [Cheers.]
"Open the post-offices as savings banks, as other countries have done. There is little difference between depositing fifty dollars, as we do now, in a post-office, and receiving an order payable at any other post-office, and depositing that same fifty dollars and receiving a government agreement to repay that sum any time after thirty days, at any post-office in the United States, with two per cent per annum interest added. [Great applause.]

"There are now one billion and a half dollars in the savings banks of this country. Do this, and every dollar of it would in a short time be deposited in the post-offices, with billions more which the people do not dare to trust to the banks, but have hidden away or buried in the earth.

"But what will the government do with all this vast sum, many times larger than our whole national debt? The answer is plain. Lend it out to the farmers and working-men on real-estate security, at two per cent per annum, to enable them to save or obtain homes; to break the backs of the usurers, and prevent the transformation of this country from a republic into a despotism. [Tremendous applause.]

"Nay, go farther. Issue paper currency, legal-tender, to the amount of fifty dollars *per capita*. [Immense applause.] Man is now a 'drug,' and money is a god. Let us reverse it. Let us make money a 'drug' and man a god." [Great cheering.]

[Commenting on one of the many projects he plans to undertake with his unlimited source of wealth, Benezet poses the following questions.]

. . . "Why should not government expand its powers with the necessities of its surroundings? Has government any higher function than the relief of the human estate? And does not earthly power seem likest God's when it lifts up man and makes him contented, virtuous, and happy?"

[Toward the end of the book Benezet discusses the need for more vital religious beliefs promoting a feeling of mutual understanding. In the following paragraph Donnelly sets the stage, and this is followed by Benezet's speech to Christians throughout the world.]

. . . For what is man if not a creature of the spiritual world, temporarily loaned to the material world by its great Designer. The man who proclaims himself a brother of the beast, and no more, abases himself, not humanity. Who is so blind that he cannot see the tremendous spirit of man shining through the clay? Can clay think, reason, worship? No; not in a million years. That which is within the clay is that which thinks, reasons, worships; it is man; nothing else can be.

[Benezet states:]

"Law can prevent crime and insure justice, but it has its limitations. It deals not with thoughts, but acts. It can regulate the opening and shutting of the doors of the temple of the soul, but it cannot enter in and purify the polluted chambers. Only that which connects man with the vast spiritual brotherhood around him can do that mighty work. No reform of legislation is complete which is based on a beast-world, without conscience. Besides a fair division of the rights and goods of the world there must be a something vaster and profounder —man's love for his fellow—not merely a willingness to give him a fair show and a fair divide, but an *affection* for him, reaching from heart to heart."

[After discussing the social good brought about by Benezet's programs, in great part the People's party platform, Donnelly concludes on this note.]

Men worshipped God by helping their fellows.

89. The Old Self-Interest and the New

In the final selection, passages from the introduction and concluding two chapters of Henry Demarest Lloyd's *Wealth Against Commonwealth*, one finds an eloquent and at the same time systematic statement of the necessity for a new set of social values. Lloyd took six years to write this book, and it stands not only as his most important work but as a model for subsequent critiques of the corporate structure. While 450 pages are devoted to a meticu-

Reprinted from Henry D. Lloyd, *Wealth Against Commonwealth* (New York: Harper and Brothers, 1894), pp. 1-2, 6-8, 494-510, 514-518, 521-524, 527-536.

lous indictment of the Standard Oil Company, the chapters on social values at the end are by no means tacked on. For Lloyd's contribution in this book, as well as in his other writings (see Document 61), was to merge economics and ethics and, in the case of *Wealth Against Commonwealth*, fashion this into a new synthesis which would serve as a blueprint for social change. As Chester McArthur Destler, the leading scholar on Lloyd, wrote concerning the book, "Its first object was to make a realistic study of the pathological aspects of corporate capitalism." But, Destler added, Lloyd's "ultimate purpose was to secure a hearing for a new social philosophy that should supply the theoretical basis for effective democratic action in opposition to prevailing economic trends."

Perhaps the term "meticulous" used above has connotations of pettiness and "thorough" would be a better word, but the important point is that Lloyd used only the most authoritative sources to support his contentions. He could not afford to err, for more was at stake than an attack on monopoly. Lloyd wanted above all to make certain that the proposed social ethic receive a fair hearing. Although the following selection will not be concerned with his documentation on monopolistic practices, a word might be said at this point about Lloyd's bill of particulars on Standard Oil. He suggests among other things that independent refiners such as George Rice were hounded from market to market until every territory was closed to them, that rebates were secured and pools established, that pipelines were used to keep the railroads in line, that competition was eliminated, sometimes by the use of violence but more generally by simply forcing rivals out of business, that the tactics of espionage were perfected, that a United States senator was elected by corrupt means, and most important, that the railroads were the chief means used by Standard Oil to achieve a monopoly in the refining sector. Some historians, notably Allan Nevins, have disputed Lloyd's evidence, but it appears to the present writer that Mr. Destler (see the two books listed in the Selected Bibliography) has successfully defended Lloyd against practically all of the charges.

On the basis of his study Lloyd concluded that there was nothing "natural" or inevitable about monopolization. Quite to the contrary, this form of economic organization required the resort to questionable practices and dubious ethics. Furthermore, he contended, monopoly was not, as its supporters maintained, the most efficient way of carrying on business. Too much energy was directed to stifling possible competition, and too much thought was given to remaining on top instead of turning to the task of innovation and lowering consumer prices.

Lloyd begins by calling attention to the potential for abundance in America, but feels that the present industrial system does not permit the fulfillment of human needs. He then goes on to state that monopoly characterizes the age, and that he is exploring the operations of Standard Oil as a case study of the consequences of this economic form. His last two chapters are devoted to the new ethic, which in a speech that same year (1894) he referred to as the "divinity of humanity." (See Document 26.) These chapters represent a direct repudiation of social Darwinian values and of laissez-faire. Individualism, for Lloyd, can only be meaningful when realized through a humanistic concern for one's fellows. Freedom does not begin until that stage is reached. Only by acting selflessly can one reach a true knowledge of the self. Lloyd calls for a transformation of values, but he recognizes that this in itself is not enough. What is also needed is that these values are incorporated into new institutional structures, so that they can operate in a meaningful way.

Nature is rich; but everywhere man, the heir of nature, is poor. Never in this happy country or elsewhere—except in the Land of Miracle, where "they did all eat and were filled" —has there been enough of anything for the people. Never since time began have all the sons and daughters of men been all warm, and all filled, and all shod and roofed. Never yet have all the virgins, wise or foolish, been able to fill their lamps with oil.

The world, enriched by thousands of generations of toilers and thinkers, has reached a fertility which can give every human being a plenty undreamed of even in the Utopias. But between this plenty ripening on the boughs of our civilization and the people hungering for it step the "cornerers," the syndicates, trusts, combinations, with the cry of "overproduction"—too much of everything. Holding back the riches of earth, sea, and sky from their fellows who famish and freeze in the dark, they declare to them that there is too much light and warmth and food. They assert the right, for their private profit, to regulate the consumption by the people of the necessaries of life, and to control production, not by the needs of humanity, but by the desires of a few for dividends. The coal syndicate thinks there is too much coal. There is too much iron, too much lumber, too much flour—for this or that syndicate.

The majority have never been able to buy enough of anything; but this minority have too much of everything to sell.

Liberty produces wealth, and wealth destroys liberty. "The splendid empire of Charles V.," says Motley, "was erected upon the grave of liberty." Our bignesses—cities, factories, monopolies, fortunes, which are our empires, are the obesities of an age gluttonous beyond its powers of digestion. Mankind are crowding upon each other in the centres, and struggling to keep each other out of the feast set by the new sciences and the new fellowships. Our size has got beyond both our science and our conscience. The vision of the railroad stockholder is not far-sighted enough to see into the office of the General Manager; the people cannot reach across even a ward of a city to rule their rulers; Captains of Industry "do not know" whether the men in the ranks are dying from lack of food and shelter; we cannot clean our cities nor our politics; the locomotive has more man-power than all the ballot-boxes, and mill-wheels wear out the hearts of workers unable to keep up beating time to their whirl. If mankind had gone on pursuing the ideals of the fighter, the time would necessarily have come when there would have been only a few, then only one, and then none left. This is what we are witnessing in the world of livelihoods. Our ideals of livelihood are ideals of mutual deglutition. We are rapidly reaching the stage where in each province only a few are left; that is the key to our times. Beyond the deep is another deep. This era is but a passing phase in the evolution of industrial Caesars, and these Caesars will be of a new type—corporate Caesars.

. . . What we call Monopoly is Business at the end of its journey. The concentration of wealth, the wiping out of the middle classes, are other names for it. To get it is, in the world of affairs, the chief end of man.

There are no solitary truths, Goethe says, and monopoly—as the greatest business fact of our civilization, which gives to business what other ages gave to war and religion—is our greatest social, political, and moral fact.

The men and women who do the work of the world have the right to the floor. Everywhere they are rising to "a point of information." They want to know how our labor and the gifts of nature are being ordered by those whom our ideals and consent have made Captains of Industry over us; how it is that we, who profess the religion of the Golden Rule and the political economy of service for service, come to divide our produce into incalculable power and pleasure for a few, and, partial existence for the many who are the fountains of these powers and pleasures. This book is an attempt to help the people answer these questions. It has been quarried out of official records, and it is a venture in realism in the world of realities. Decisions of courts and of special tribunals like the Interstate Commerce Commission, verdicts of juries in civil and criminal cases, reports of committees of the State Legislatures and of Congress, oath-sworn testimony given in legal proceedings and in official inquiries, corrected by rebutting testimony and by cross-examination—such are the sources of information.

. . . To give the full and official history of numbers of these combinations, which are nearly identical in inspiration, method, and result, would be repetition. Only one of them, therefore, has been treated in full—the oil trust. It is the most successful of all the attempts to put gifts of nature, entire industries, and world markets under one hat. Its originators claim this precedence. It was, one of its spokesmen says, "the parent of the trust system." It is the best illustration of a movement which is itself but an illustration of the spirit of the age.

THE OLD SELF-INTEREST

. . . The corn of the coming harvest is growing so fast that, like the farmer standing at night in his fields, we can hear it snap and crackle. We have been fighting fire on the well-worn lines of old-fashioned politics and political economy, regulating corporations, and leaving competition to regulate itself. But the flames of a new economic evolution run around us, and we turn to find that competition has killed competition, that corporations are grown greater than the State and have bred individuals greater than themselves, and that the naked issue of our time is with property becoming master instead of servant, property in many necessaries of life becoming monopoly of the necessaries of life.

We are still, in part, as Emerson says, in the quadruped state. Our industry is a fight of every man for himself. The prize we give the fittest is monopoly of the necessaries of life, and we leave these winners of the powers of life and death to wield them over us by the same "self-interest" with which they took them from us. In all this we see at work a "principle" which will go into the records as one of the historic mistakes of humanity. Institutions stand or fall by their philosophy, and the main doctrine of industry since Adam Smith has been the fallacy that the self-interest of the individual was a sufficient guide to the welfare of the individual and society. Heralded as a final truth of "science" this proves to have been nothing higher than a temporary formula for a passing problem. It was a reflection in words of the policy of the day.

When the Middle Ages landed on the shores of the sixteenth century they broke ranks, and for three hundred years every one has been scurrying about to get what he could. Society was not highly developed enough to organize the exploration and subjugation of worlds of new things and ideas on any broader basis than private enterprise, personal adventure. People had to run away from each other and from the old ideas, nativities, guilds, to seize the prizes of the new sciences, the new land, the new liberties which make modern times. They did not go because the philosophers told them to. The philosophers saw them going and wrote it down in a book, and have believed themselves ever since to be the inventors of the division of labor and the discoverers of a new world of social science. But now we are touching elbows again, and the dream of these picnic centuries that the social can be made secondary to the individual is being chased out of our minds by the hard light of the crisis into which we are waking.

"It is a law of business for each proprietor to pursue his own interest," said the committee of Congress which in 1893 investigated the coal combinations. "There is no hope for any of us, but the weakest must go first," is the golden rule of business. There is no other field of human associations in which any such rule of action is allowed. The man who should apply in his family or his citizenship this "survival of the fittest" theory as it is practically professed and operated in business would be a monster, and would be speedily made extinct, as we do with monsters. To divide the supply of food between himself and his children according to their relative powers of calculation, to follow his conception of his own self-interest in any matter which the self-interest of all has taken charge of, to deal as he thinks best for himself with foreigners with whom his country is at war, would be a short road to the penitentiary or the gallows. In trade men have not yet risen to the level of the family life of the animals. The true law of business is that all must pursue the interest of all. In the law, the highest product of civilization, this has long been a commonplace. The safety of the people is the supreme law. We are in travail to bring industry up to this. Our century of the caprice of the individual as the law-giver of the common toil, to employ or disemploy, to start or stop, to open or close, to compete or combine, has been the disorder of the school while the master slept. The happiness, self-interest, or individuality of the whole is not more sacred than that of each, but it is greater. They are equal in quality, but in quantity they are greater. In the ultimate which the mathematician, the poet, the reformer projects the two will coincide.

Our world, operated by individual motive, is the country of the Chinese fable, in which the inhabitants went on one leg. Yes, but an "enlightened self-interest"? The perfect self-interest of the perfect individual is an admirable conception, but it is still individual, and the world is social. The music of the spheres is not to be played on one string. Nature does nothing individually. All forces are paired like the sexes, and every particle of matter in the universe has to obey every other particle. When the individual has progressed to a perfect self-interest, there will be over against it, acting and reacting with it, a correspondingly perfect self-interest of the community. Meanwhile, we who are the creators of society have got the times out of joint, because, less experienced than the Creator of the balanced matter of earth, we have given the precedence to the powers on one side. As gods we are but half-grown. For a hundred years or so our economic theory has been one of industrial government by the self-interest of the individual. Political government by the self-interest of the individual we call anarchy. It is one of the paradoxes of public opinion that the people of America, least tolerant of this theory of anarchy in political government, lead in practising it in industry. Politically, we are civilized; industrially, not yet. Our century, given to this *laissez-faire*—"leave the individual alone; he will do what is best for himself, and what is best for him is best for all"—has done one good: it has put society at the mercy of its own ideals, and has produced an actual anarchy in industry which is horrifying us into a change of doctrines.

We have not been able to see the people for the persons in it. But there is a people, and it is as different from a mere juxtaposition of persons as a globe of glass from the handful of sand out of which it was melted. It is becoming, socially, known to itself, with that self-consciousness which distinguishes the quick from the dead and the unborn. Every community, said Pascal, is a man, and every man, said Plato, is a community. There is a new self-interest—that of the "man called million," as Mazzini named him—and with this social motive the other, which has so long had its own way, has now to reckon. Mankind has gone astray following a truth seen only partially, but coronated as a whole truth. Many civilizations must worship good men as gods and follow the divinity of one and another before civilization sees that these are only single stars in a firmament of humanity. Our civilization has followed the self-interest of the individual to learn that it was but one of the complex forces of self-interest.

The true *laissez-faire* is, let the individual do what the individual can do best, and let the community do what the community can do best. The *laissez-faire* of social self-interest, if true, cannot conflict with the individual self-interest, if true, but it must outrank it always. What we have called "free competition" has not been free, only freer than what went before. The free is still to come. The pressure we feel is notice to prepare for it. Civilization—the process of making men citizens in their relations to each other, by exacting of each that he give to all that which he receives from all—has reached only those forms of common effort which, because most general and most vital, first demanded its harmonizing touch. Men joining in the labors of the family, the mutual sacrifices of the club or the church in the union of forces for self-defence and for the gains of co-operation on the largest scale in labors of universal concern, like letter-carrying, have come to be so far civilized.

History is condensed in the catchwords of the people. In the phrases of individual self-interest which have been the shibboleths of the main activities of our last hundred years were prophesied: the filling up of the Mississippi by the forest-destroying, self-seeking lumber companies of the North; the disintegration of the American family—among the rich by too little poverty; and among the poor by too much; the embezzlement of public highways and public franchises into private property; the devolution of the American merchants and manufacturers into the business dependants—and social and political dependants, therefore—of a few men in each great department of trade, from dry-goods to whiskey; the devolution of the free farmer into a tenant, and of the working-man into a fixture of the locomotive or the factory, forbidden to leave except by permission of his employer or the public; and that mêlée of injunctions, bayonets, idle men and idle machinery, rich man's fear of poor man and poor man's fear of starvation, we call trade and industry.

Where the self-interest of the individual is allowed to be the rule both of social and personal action, the level of all is forced down to that of the lowest. Business excuses itself for the things it does—cuts in wages, exactions in hours, tricks of competition—on the plea that the merciful are compelled to follow the cruel. "It is pleaded as an excuse by those" (common carriers) "who desire to obey the" (Interstate Commerce) "law that self-preservation drives them to violate it because other carriers persist in doing so," says Senator Cullom. When the self-interest of society is made the standard the lowest must rise to the average. The one pulls down, the other up. That men's hearts are bad and that bad men will do bad things has a truth in it. But whatever the general average of morals, the anarchy which gives such individuals their head and leaves them to set the pace for all will produce infinitely worse results than a policy which applies mutual checks and inspirations. Bad kings make bad reigns, but monarchy is bad because it is arbitrary power, and that, whether it be political or industrial, makes even good men bad.

A partial truth universally applied as this of self-interest has been is a universal error. Everything goes to defeat. Highways are used to prevent travel and traffic. Ownership of the means of production is sought in order to "shut down" production, and the means of plenty make famine. All follow self-interest to find that though they have created marvellous wealth it is not theirs. We pledge "our lives, our fortunes, and our sacred honor" to establish the rule of the majority, and end by finding that the minority—a minority in morals, money, and men— are our masters whichever way we turn. We agonize over "economy," but sell all our grain and pork and oil and cotton at exchanges where we pay brokerage on a hundred or a thousand barrels or bushels or bales of wind to get one real one sold. These intolerabilities—sweat-shops where model merchants buy and sell the cast-off scarlet-fever skins of the poor, factory and mine where childhood is forbidden to become manhood and manhood is forbidden to die a natural death, mausoleums in which we bury the dead rich, slums in which we bury the living poor, coal pools with their manufacture of artificial winter—all these are the rule of private self-interest arrived at its destination.

A really human life is impossible in our cities, but they cannot be reconstructed under the old self-interest. Chicago was rebuilt wrong after the fire. Able men pointed out the avenues to a wider and better municipal life, but they could not be opened through the private interpositions that blocked the way. The slaughter of railway men coupling cars was shown, in a debate in the United States Senate, to be twice as great

as it would be if the men were in active service in war. But
under the scramble for private gain our society on its railway
side cannot develop the energy to introduce the improved appliances ready to hand which would save these lives, all young
and vigorous. The cost of the change would be repaid in 100-
per-cent. dividends every year by the money value alone to us
of the men now killed and wounded. But we shall have to
wait for a nobler arithmetic to give us investments so good
as that. The lean kine of self-interest devour the fat kine. The
railroad stockholder, idolater of self-interest, lets himself be
robbed—like the stockholder of all the railroads in this story—
either because he is too rich to mind, too feeble to make himself heard, or too much implicated elsewhere as principal in
the same kind of depredation to care or dare to stir what he
knows to be a universal scandal. He has become within himself the battle-ground of a troop of warring devils of selfishness; his selfishness as a stockholder clutched at the throat by
his selfishness as a parasite, in some "inside deal," feeding on
the stockholder; some rebate arrangement, fast-freight line,
sleeping-car company, or what not. And, as like as not, upon
this one's back is another devil of depredation from some
inner ring within a ring. Torn at the vitals, the enlightened
swinishness of our *leit-motif* is hastening to throw itself into
the sea.

We are very poor. The striking feature of our economic
condition is our poverty, not our wealth. We make ourselves
"rich" by appropriating the property of others by methods
which lessen the total property of all. Spain took such riches
from America and grew poor. Modern wealth more and more
resembles the winnings of speculators in bread during famine
—worse, for to make the money it makes the famine. What we
call cheapness shows itself to be unnatural fortunes for a very
few, monstrous luxury for them and proportionate deprivation
for the people, judges debauched, trustees dishonored, Congress and State legislatures insulted and defied, when not

seduced, multitudes of honest men ruined and driven to despair, the common carrier made a mere instrument for the creation of a new baronage, an example set to hundreds of would-be commercial Caesars to repeat this rapine in other industries and call it "business," a process set in operation all over the United States for the progressive extinction of the independence of laboring men, and all business men except the very rich, and their reduction to a state of vassalage to lords or squires in each department of trade and industry. All these —tears, ruin, dishonor, and treason—are the unmarked additions to the "price marked on the goods."

Shall we buy cheap of Captain Kidd, and shut our ears to the agony that rustles in his silks? Shall we believe that Captain Kidd, who kills commerce by the act which enables him to sell at half-price, is a cheapener? Shall we preach and practise doctrines which make the Black Flag the emblem of success on the high seas of human interchange of service, and complain when we see mankind's argosies of hope and plenty shrink into private hoards of treasure, buried in selfish sands to be lost forever, even to cupidity? If this be cheapness, it comes by the grace of the seller, and that is the first shape of dearness, as security in society by the grace of the ruler is the first form of insecurity.

The new wealth now administers estates of fabulous extent from metropolitan bureaus, and all the profits flow to men who know nothing of the real business out of which they are made. Red tape, complication, the hired man, conspiracy have taken the place of the watchful eye of the owner, the old-fashioned hand at the plough that must "hold or drive." We now have Captains of Industry, with a few aides, rearranging from office-chairs this or that industry, by mere contrivances of wit compelling the fruits of the labor of tens of thousands of their fellows, who never saw them, never heard of them, to be every day deposited unwilling and unwitting to their own credit at the bank; setting, as by necromancy, hundreds of properties, large and small, in a score of communities, to flying through invisible ways into their hands; sitting calm through all the hubbub raised in courts, legislatures, and public places, and by dictating letters and whispering words remaining the master magicians of the scene; defying, though private citizens, all the forces and authorities of a whole people; by the mere mastery of compelling brain, without putting hand to anything, opening or closing the earth's treasures of oil or coal or gas or copper or what not; pulling down or putting up great buildings, factories, towns themselves; moving men and their money this way and that; inserting their will as part of the law of life of the people—American, European, and Asiatic—and, against the protest of a whole civilization, making themselves, their methods and principles, its emblematic figures.

Syndicates, by one stroke, get the power of selling dear on one side, and producing cheap on the other. Thus they keep themselves happy, prices high, and the people hungry. What model merchant could ask more? The dream of the king who wished that all his people had but one neck that he might decapitate them at one blow is realized to-day in this industrial garrote. The syndicate has but to turn its screw, and every neck begins to break. Prices paid to such intercepters are not an exchange of service; they are ransom paid by the people for their lives. The ability of the citizen to pay may fluctuate; what he must pay remains fixed, or advances like the rent of the Irish tenant to the absentee landlord until the community interfered. Those who have this power to draw the money from the people—from every railroad station, every street-car, every fireplace, every salt-cellar, every bread-pan, wash-board, and coal-scuttle—to their own safes have the further incentive to make this money worth the most possible. By contracting the issue of currency and contracting it again by hoarding it in their banks, safe-deposit vaults, and the government treasury, they can depress the prices of all that belongs to the people. Their own prices are fixed. These are "regular prices," established by price-lists. Given, as a ruling motive, the principles of business—to get the most and give the least; given the legal and economic, physical and mechanical control, possible under our present social arrangements, to the few over the many, and the certain end of all this, if unarrested, unreversed, can be nothing less than a return to chattel slavery. There may be some finer name, but the fact will not be finer. Between our present tolerance and our completed subjection the distance is not so far as that from the equality and simplicity of our Pilgrim Fathers to ourselves.

Everything withers—even charity. Aristocratic benevolence spends a shrunken stream in comparison with democratic benevolence. In an address to the public, soliciting subscriptions, the Committee of the United Hospitals Association of New York said, in December, 1893: "The committee have found that, through the obliteration of old methods of individual competition by the establishment of large corporations and trusts in modern times, the income of such charitable institutions as are supported by the individual gifts of the benevolent has been seriously affected."

Franklin pricked the bubble of the lottery by showing that to buy all the tickets and win all the prizes was to be most surely the loser. Our nascent common-sense begins to see that the many must always lose where all spend their lives trying to get more than they give, and that all lose when any lose. The welfare of all is more than the welfare of the many, the few, or the one. If the few or the one are not fine enough to accept this truth from sentiment or conscience, they can find other reasons as convincing, though not as amiable. From the old régime of France, the slave-holders of the South, the death-rate of tyrants, the fear of their brothers which the rich and the great of to-day are printing on their faces, in fugitive-slave treaties with Russia, and in the frowning arsenals and armories building in our cities for "law and order," they can learn how to spell self-interest.

If all will sacrifice themselves, none need be sacrificed. But if one may sacrifice another, all are sacrificed. That is the difference between self-interest and other-self interest. In industry we have been substituting all the mean passions that can set man against man in place of the irresistible power of brotherhood. To tell us of the progressive sway of brotherhood in all human affairs is the sole message of history. "Love thy neighbor as thyself" is not the phrase of a ritual of sentiment for the unapplied emotion of pious hours; it is the exact formula of the force to-day operating the greatest institutions man has established. It is as secular as sacred. Only by each neighbor giving the other every right of free thought, free movement, free representation which he demands for himself; only by calling every neighbor a friend, and literally laying down his life for his friend against foreign invasion or domestic tumult; only by the equalization which gives the vote to all and denies kingship to all, however strong or "fittest"—only thus is man establishing the community, the republic, which, with all its failings, is the highest because the realest application of the spirit of human brotherhood. Wonderful are the dividends of this investment. You are but one, and can give only yourself to America. You give free speech, and 65,000,000 of your countrymen will guard the freedom of your lips. Your single offer of your right arm puts 65,000,000 of sheltering arms about you. Does "business" pay such profits? Wealth will remain a secret unguessed by business until it has reincorporated itself under the law which reckons as the property of each one the total of all the possessions of all his neighbors.

Society could not live a day, the Bishop of Peterborough said, if it put the principles of Christ into practice. There is no rarer gift than that of eyes to see what we see. Society is society, and lives its day solely by virtue of having put into actual routine and matter-of-fact application the principles of Christ and other bringers of the same message. Imperfect and faulty though the execution, it is these principles which are

the family, the tribe, the sect, the club, the mutual-benefit society, the State, with their mutual services, forbearance, and guarantees. The principles of Christ are the cause and essence of society. They are not the ideal of which we dream; they are the applied means with which we are working out our real life in "the light of common day." They have not been so much revealed to us by our inspired ones as best seen and best said by them. Insurance for fire, accident, sickness, old age, death —the ills that flesh is heir to—has the same co-operation for its innermost forces. Limited now by the intervention of the selfishness of profit-seeking, it needs only to be freed from this, and added, as in New Zealand, to the growing list of the mutualities of the general welfare operated by the State to be seen as what it is. The golden rule is the original of every political constitution, written and unwritten, and all our reforms are but the pains with which we strive to improve the copy.

In the worst governments and societies that have existed one good can be seen—so good that the horrors of them fall back into secondary places as extrinsic, accidental. That good is the ability of men to lead the life together. The more perfect monopoly makes itself the more does it bring into strong lights the greatest fact of our industry, of far more permanent value than the greed which has for the moment made itself the cynosure of all eyes. It makes this fair world more fair to consider the loyalties, intelligences, docilities of the multitudes who are guarding, developing, operating with the faithfulness of brothers and the keen interest of owners properties and industries in which brotherhood is not known and their title is not more than a tenancy at will. One of the largest stones in the arch of "consolidation," perhaps the key-stone, is that men have become so intelligent, so responsive and responsible, so co-operative that they can be intrusted in great masses with the care of vast properties owned entirely by others and with the operation of complicated processes, although but a slender cost of subsistence is awarded them out of fabulous profits. The spectacle of the million and more employés of the railroads of this country despatching trains, maintaining tracks, collecting fares and freights, and turning over hundreds of millions of net profits to the owners, not one in a thousand of whom would know how to do the simplest of these things for himself, is possible only where civilization has reached a high average of morals and culture. More and more the mills and mines and stores, and even the farms and forests, are being administered by others than the owners. The virtue of the people is taking the place Poor Richard thought only the eye of the owner could fill. If mankind, driven by their fears and the greed of others, can do so well, what will be their productivity and cheer when the "interest of all" sings them to their work?

This new morality and new spring of wealth have been seized first by the appropriating ones among us. But, as has been in government, their intervention of greed is but a passing phase. Mankind belongs to itself, not to kings or monopolists, and will supersede the one as surely as the other with the institutions of democracy. Yes, Callicles, said Socrates, the greatest are usually the bad, for they have the power. If power could continue paternal and benign, mankind would not be rising through one emancipation after another into a progressive communion of equalities. The individual and society will always be wrestling with each other in a composition of forces. But to just the extent to which civilization prevails, society will be held as inviolable as the individual; not subordinate— indeed inaudible—as now in the counting-room and corporation-office. We have overworked the self-interest of the individual. The line of conflict between individual and social is a progressive one of the discovery of point after point in which the two are identical. Society thus passes from conflict to harmony, and on to another conflict. Civilization is the unceasing accretion of these social solutions. We fight out to an equilibrium, as in the abolition of human slavery; then upon this new level thus built up we enter upon the struggle for a new equilibrium, as now in the labor movement. The man for himself destroys himself and all men; only society can foster him and them.

The greatest happiness of the greatest number is only the doctrine of self-interest writ large and made more dangerous by multitude. It is the self-interest of the majority, and this has written some of the unloveliest chapters of history. There have never been slaves more miserable than those of Sparta, where the State was the owner. American democracy prepares to repeat these distresses of the selfishness of the many, and gives notice to its railway employés of a new divine right— "the convenience of the public"—to which they must forego every right of manhood. No better definition of slave could be found than one who must work at the convenience of another. This is the position into which recent legal decisions and acts of the Federal executive force railway men. These speak in the name of Interstate Commerce, but their logic can be as easily applied by State judges to State commerce, and all working-men are manifestly as necessary, each in his function, to the convenience of the public as the men of the rail. The greatest happiness of all must be the formula. When Lamennais said, "I love my family more than myself, my village more than my family, my country more than my village, and mankind more than my country," he showed himself not only a good lover, but the only good arithmetician.

Children yet, we run everything we do—love or war, work or leisure, religion or liberty—to excess. Every possibility of body and mind must be played upon till it is torn to pieces, as toys by children. Priests, voluptuaries, tyrants, knights, ascetics —in the long procession of fanatics a new-comer takes his place; he is called "the model merchant"—the cruelest fanatic in history. He is the product of ages given to progressive devotion to "trading." He is the high-priest of the latest idolatry, the self-worship of self-interest. Whirling-dervish of the market, self, friends, and family, body and soul, loves, hopes, and faith, all are sacrificed to seeing how many "turns" he can make before he drops dead. Trade began, Sir Henry Sumner Maine tells us, not within the family or community, but without. Its first appearances are on the neutral borderland between hostile tribes. There, in times of peace, they meet to trade, and think it no sin that "the buyer must beware," since the buyer is an enemy. Trade has spread thence, carrying with itself into family and State the poison of enmity. From the fatherhood of the old patriarchal life, where father and brother sold each other nothing, the world has chaffered along to the anarchy of a "free" trade which sells everything. One thing after another has passed out from under the régime of brotherhood and passed in under that of bargainhood. The ground we move on, the bodies we work with, and the necessaries we live by are all being "exchanged," by "rules fetched with cupidity from heartless schools," into the ownership of the Jacobs of mankind. By these rules the cunning are the good, and the weak and the tender the bad, and the good are to have all the goods and the weak are to have nothing. These rules give one the power to supply or deny work to thousands, and to use the starvation terms of the men he disemploys as the measure of the cost of subsistence of all workmen. This must be near the end. The very churches have become mercantilized, and are markets in which "prophets" are paid fancy prices—"always called of God," as Milton said, "but always to a greater benefice"—and worshippers buy and sell knee-room.

Conceptions of duty take on a correspondingly unnatural complexion. The main exhortations the world gives beginners are how to "get on"—the getting on so ardently inculcated being to get, like the old-man-of-the-sea, on somebody's back. "If war fails you in the country where you are, you must go where there is war," said one of the successful men of the fourteenth century to a young knight who asked him for the

Laws of Life. "I shall be perfectly satisfied with you," I heard one of the great business geniuses of America say to his son, "if you will only always go to bed at night worth more than when you got up in the morning." The system grows, as all systems do, more complicated, and gets further away from its first purposes of barter of real things and services. It goes more under the hands of men of apt selfishness, who push it further away from general comprehension and the general good. Tariffs, currencies, finances, freight-rate sheets, the laws, become instruments of privilege, and just in proportion become puzzles no people can decipher. "I have a right to buy my labor where I can buy it cheapest"—beginning as a protest against the selfish exclusions of antiquated trade-guilds outgrown by the new times—has at last come to mean, "I have a right to do anything to cheapen the labor I want to buy, even to destroying the family life of the people."

When steaming kettles grew into beasts of burden and public highways dwindled into private property administered by private motives for private ends, all previous tendencies were intensified into a sudden whirl redistributing wealth and labors. It appears to have been the destiny of the railroad to begin and of oil to lubricate to its finish the last stage of this crazy commercialism. Business colors the modern world as war reddened the ancient world. Out of such delirium monsters are bred, and their excesses destroy the system that brought them forth. There is a strong suggestion of moral insanity in the unrelieved sameness of mood and unvarying repetition of one act in the life of the model merchant. Sane minds by an irresistible law alternate one tension with another. Only a lunatic is always smiling or always weeping or always clamoring for dividends. Eras show their last stages by producing men who sum up individually the morbid characteristics of the mass. When the crisis comes in which the gathering tendencies of generations shoot forward in the avalanche, there is born some group of men perfect for their function—good be it or bad. They need to take time for no second thought, and will not delay the unhalting reparations of nature by so much as the time given to one tear over the battle-field or the bargain. With their birth their mission is given them, whether it be the mission of Lucifer or Gabriel. This mission becomes their conscience. The righteous indignation that other men feel against sin these men feel against that which withstands them. Sincere as rattlesnakes, they are selfish with the unconsciousness possible to only the entirely commonplace, without the curiosity to question their times or the imagination to conceive the pain they inflict, and their every ideal is satisfied by the conventionalities of church, parlor, and counting-room. These men are the touchstones to wither the cant of an age.

We preach "Do as you would be done by" in our churches, and "A fair exchange no robbery" in our counting-rooms, and "All citizens are equal as citizens" in courts and Congress. Just as we are in danger of believing that to say these things is to do them and be them, there come unto us these men, practical as granite and gravitation. Taking their cue not from our lips, but from our lives, they better the instruction, and, passing easily to the high seats at every table, prove that we are liars and hypocrites. Their only secret is that they do, better than we, the things we are all trying to do, but of which in our morning and evening prayers, seen of all men, we are continually making believe to pray: Good Lord, deliver us! When the hour strikes for such leaders, they come and pass as by a law of nature to the front. All follow them. It is their fate and ours that they must work out to the end the destiny interwoven of their own insatiate ambition and the false ideals of us who have created them and their opportunity.

If our civilization is destroyed, as Macaulay predicted, it will not be by his barbarians from below. Our barbarians come from above. Our great money-makers have sprung in one generation into seats of power kings do not know. The forces and the wealth are new, and have been the opportunity of new men. Without restraints of culture, experience, the pride, or even the inherited caution of class or rank, these men, intoxicated, think they are the wave instead of the float, and that they have created the business which has created them. To them science is but a never-ending répertoire of investments stored up by nature for the syndicates, government but a fountain of franchises, the nations but customers in squads, and a million the unit of a new arithmetic of wealth written for them. They claim a power without control, exercised through forms which make it secret, anonymous, and perpetual. The possibilities of its gratification have been widening before them without interruption since they began, and even at a thousand millions they will feel no satiation and will see no place to stop. They are gluttons of luxury and power, rough, unsocialized, believing that mankind must be kept terrorized. Powers of pity die out of them, because they work through agents and die in their agents, because what they do is not for themselves.

. . . Two social energies have been in conflict, and the energy of reform has so far proved the weaker. We have chartered the self-interest of the individual as the rightful sovereign of conduct; we have taught that the scramble for profit is the best method of administering the riches of earth and the exchange of service. Only those can attack this system who attack its central principle, that strength gives the strong in the market the right to destroy his neighbor. Only as we have denied that right to the strong elsewhere have we made ourselves as civilized as we are. And we cannot make a change as long as our songs, customs, catchwords, and public opinions tell all to do the same thing if they can. Society, in each person of its multitudes, must recognize that the same principles of the interest of all being the rule of all, of the strong serving the weak, of the first being the last—"I am among you as one that serves"—which have given us the home where the weakest is the one surest of his rights and of the fullest service of the strongest, and have given us the republic in which all join their labor that the poorest may be fed, the weakest defended, and all educated and prospered, must be applied where men associate in common toil as wherever they associate. Not until then can the forces be reversed which generate those obnoxious persons—our fittest.

Our system, so fair in its theory and so fertile in its happiness and prosperity in its first century, is now, following the fate of systems, becoming artificial, technical, corrupt; and, as always happens in human institutions, after noon, power is stealing from the many to the few. Believing wealth to be good, the people believed the wealthy to be good. But, again in history, power has intoxicated and hardened its possessors, and Pharaohs are bred in counting-rooms as they were in palaces. Their furniture must be banished to the world-garret, where lie the out-worn trappings of the guilds and slavery and other old lumber of human institutions.

AND THE NEW

We have given the prize of power to the strong, the cunning, the arithmetical, and we must expect nothing else but that they will use it cunningly and arithmetically. For what else can they suppose we gave it to them? If the power really flows from the people, and should be used for them; if its best administration can be got, as in government, only by the participation in it of men of all views and interests; if in the collision of all these, as in democracy, the better policy is progressively preponderant; if this is a policy which, with whatever defects, is better than that which can be evolved by narrower or more selfish or less multitudinous influences of persons or classes, then this power should be taken up by the people. "The mere conflict of private interests will never produce a well-ordered commonwealth of labor," says the author of the article on political economy in the *Encyclopaedia*

Britannica. The failure of monarchy and feudalism and the visibly impending failure of our business system all reveal a law of nature. The harmony of things insists that that which is the source of power, wealth, and delight shall also be the ruler of it. That which is must also seem. It is the people from whom come the forces with which kings and millionaires ride the world, and until the people take their proper place in the seat of sovereignty, these pseudo owners—mere claimants and usurpers—will, by the very falsity and iniquity of their position, be pushed into deceit, tyranny, and cruelty, ending in downfall.

Thousands of years' experience has proved that government must begin where it ends—with the people; that the general welfare demands that they who exercise the powers and they upon whom these are exercised must be the same, and that higher political ideals can be realized only through higher political forms. Myriads of experiments to get the substance of liberty out of the forms of tyranny, to believe in princes, to trust good men to do good as kings, have taught the inexorable truth that, in the economy of nature, form and substance must move together, and are as inextricably interdependent as are, within our experience, what we call matter and spirit. Identical is the lesson we are learning with regard to industrial power and property. We are calling upon their owners, as mankind called upon kings in their day, to be good and kind, wise and sweet, and we are calling in vain. We are asking them not to be what we have made them to be. We put power into their hands and ask them not to use it as power. If this power is a trust for the people, the people betrayed it when they made private estates out of it for individuals. If the spirit of power is to change, institutions must change as much. Liberty recast the old forms of government into the Republic, and it must remould our institutions of wealth into the Commonwealth.

The question is not whether monopoly is to continue. The

sun sets every night on a greater majority against it. We are face to face with the practical issue: Is it to go through ruin or reform? Can we forestall ruin by reform? If we wait to be forced by events we shall be astounded to find how much more radical they are than our utopias. Louis XVI. waited until 1793, and gave his head and all his investitures to the people who in 1789 asked only to sit at his feet and speak their mind. Unless we reform of our own free will, nature will reform us by force, as nature does. Our evil courses have already gone too far in producing misery, plagues, hatreds, national enervation. Already the leader is unable to lead, and has begun to drive with judges armed with bayonets and Gatling guns. History is the serial obituary of the men who thought they could drive men.

Reform is the science and conscience with which mankind in its manhood overcomes temptations and escapes consequences by killing the germs. Ruin is already hard at work among us. Our libraries are full of the official inquiries and scientific interpretations which show how our master-motive is working decay in all our parts. The family crumbles into a competition between the father and the children whom he breeds to take his place in the factory, to unfit themselves to be fathers in their turn. A thorough, stalwart resimplification, a life governed by simple needs and loves, is the imperative want of the world. It will be accomplished: either self-conscious volition does it, or the slow wreck and decay of superfluous and unwholesome men and matters. The latter is the method of brutes and brute civilizations. The other is the method of man, so far as he is divine. Has not man, who has in personal reform risen above the brute method, come to the height at which he can achieve social reform in masses and by nations? We must learn; we can learn by reason. Why wait for the crueler teacher?

. . . Aristotle's lost books of the Republics told the story of two hundred and fifty attempts at free government, and these were but some of the many that had to be melted down in the crucible of fate to teach Hamilton and Jefferson what they knew. Perhaps we must be melted by the same fierce flames to be a light to the feet of those who come after us. For as true as that a house divided against itself cannot stand, and that a nation half slave and half free cannot permanently endure, is it true that a people who are slaves to market-tyrants will surely come to be their slaves in all else, that all liberty begins to be lost when one liberty is lost, that a people half democratic and half plutocratic cannot permanently endure.

The secret of the history we are about to make is not that the world is poorer or worse. It is richer and better. Its new wealth is too great for the old forms. The success and beauties of our old mutualities have made us ready for new mutualities. The wonder of to-day is the modern multiplication of products by the union of forces; the marvel of to-morrow will be the greater product which will follow when that which is co-operatively produced is co-operatively enjoyed. It is the spectacle of its concentration in the private fortunes of our day which reveals this wealth to its real makers—the whole people —and summons them to extend the manners and institutions of civilization to this new tribal relation.

Whether the great change comes with peace or sword, freely through reform or by nature's involuntary forces, is a mere matter of detail, a question of convenience—not of the essence of the thing. The change will come. With reform, it may come to us. If with force, perhaps not to us. But it will come. The world is too full of amateurs who can play the golden rule as an aria with variations. All the runs and trills and transpositions have been done to death. All the "sayings" have been said. The only field for new effects is in epigrams of practice. Titillation of our sympathies has become a dissipation. We shed a daily tear over the misery of the slums as the toper takes his dram, and our liver becomes torpid with the floods of indignation and sentiment we have guzzled without converting them into their co-efficients of action.

"Regenerate the individual" is a half-truth; the reorganization of the society which he makes and which makes him is the other half. Man alone cannot be a Christian. Institutions are applied beliefs. The love of liberty became liberty in America by clothing itself in the complicated group of structures known as the government of the United States. Love is a half-truth, and kissing is a good deal less than half of that. We need not kiss all our fellow-men, but we must do for them all we ask them to do for us—nothing less than the fullest performance of every power. To love our neighbor is to submit to the discipline and arrangement which make his life reach its best, and so do we best love ourselves.

History has taught us nothing if not that men can continue to associate only by the laws of association. The golden rule is the first and last of these, but the first and last of the golden rule is that it can be operated only through laws, habits, forms, and institutions. The Constitution and laws of the United States are, however imperfectly, the translation into the language of politics of doing as you would be done by—the essence of equal rights and government by consent. To ask individuals to-day to lead by their single sacrifices the life of the brother in the world of business is as if the American colonist had been asked to lead by his individual enterprise the life of the citizen of a republic. That was made possible to him only by union with others. The business world is full of men who yearn to abandon its methods and live the love they feel; but to attempt to do so by themselves would be martyrdom, and that is "caviare to the general." "We admire martyrdom," Mazzini, the martyr, said, "but we do not recommend it." The change must be social, and its martyrdoms have already begun.

The new self-interest will remain unenforced in business until we invent the forms by which the vast multitudes who have been gathered together in modern production can organize themselves into a people there as in government. Nothing but this institutionalization will save them from being scattered away from each other again, and it can be achieved only by such averaging and concessions and co-operations as are the price of all union. These will be gains, not losses. Soldiers become partners in invincibility by the discipline which adopts an average rate of march instead of compelling all to keep step with the fastest and stay with the strongest. Moralists tell men to love each other and the right. How, by doing what things, by leaving what undone, shall men love each other? What have the ethicals to say upon the morality of putting public highways in private hands, and of allowing these private hands to make a private and privileged use of them? If bad, will a mere "change of heart," uninstitutionalized, change them?

New freedoms cannot be operated through the old forms of slavery. The ideals of Washington and Hamilton and Adams could not breathe under kingly rule. Idle to say they might. Under the mutual dependence of the inside and outside of things their change has all through history always been dual. Change of heart is no more redemption than hunger is dinner. We must have honesty, love, justice in the heart of the business world, but for these we must also have the forms which will fit them. These will be very different from those through which the intercourse of man with man in the exchange of services now moves to such ungracious ends. Forms of Asiatic and American government, of early institutions and to-day's, are not more different. The cardinal virtues cannot be established and kept at work in trade and on the highways with the old apparatus. In order that the spirit that gave rebates may go to stay, the rebate itself must go. If the private use of private ownership of highways is to go, the private ownership must go. There must be no private use of public power or public property. These are created by the common sacrifices of all, and can be rightfully used only for the common good of all— from all, by all, for all. All the grants and franchises that have been given to private hands for private profit are void in morals and void in that higher law which sets the copy for the laggard pens of legislatures and judges. "No private use of public powers" is but a threshold truth. The universe, says Emerson, is the property of every creature in it.

[Lloyd then comments on the charge that reform will lead to the loss of individuality.]

. . . And "individuality." "You are going to destroy individuality." We can become individual only by submitting to be bound to others. We extend our freedom only by finding new laws to obey. Life outside the law is slavery on as many sides as there are disregarded laws. The locomotive off its tracks is not free. The more relations, ties, duties, the more "individual." The isolated man is the mere rudiment of an individual. But he who has become citizen, neighbor, friend, brother, son, husband, father, fellow-member, in one, is just by so many times individualized. Men's expanding powers of co-operation bring them to the conscious ability to unite for new benefits; but this extension of individuality is forbidden in the name of individuality. There are two individualities: that of the dullard, who submits to take his railroad transportation, his light, his coal, his salt, his reaping-machine at such prices and of such quality as arbitrary power forces upon him, and that of the shrewder man who, by an alliance of the individualities of all, supplies himself at his own price.

Time carries us so easily we do not realize how fast we move. This social debate has gone far beyond the question whether change there must be. What shall the change be? is the subject all the world is discussing. Exposure of abuses no longer excites more than a languid interest. But every clear plan how things might be rearranged raises the people. Before every revolution marches a book—the *Contrat Social*, *Uncle Tom's Cabin*. "Every man nowadays," says Emerson, "carries a revolution in his vest-pocket." The book which sells more copies than any other of our day abroad and at home, debated by all down to the boot-blacks as they sit on the curb-stones, is one calling men to draw from their success in insuring each other some of the necessaries of life the courage to move on to insure each other all the necessaries of life, bidding them abandon the self-defeating anarchy which puts railroad-wreckers at the head of railroads and famine-producers at the head of production, and inspiring them to share the common toil and the fruits of the toil under the ideals which make men Washingtons and Lincolns. You may question the importance of the plan; you cannot question the importance of its welcome. It shows the people gathering-points for the new constitution they know they must make.

In nothing has liberty justified itself more thoroughly than in the resolute determination spreading among the American people to add industrial to political independence. It is the hope of the world that good has its effects as well as evil, and that on the whole, and in the long-run, the seed of the good will overgrow the evil. "Heaven has kindly given our blood a moral flow." Liberty breeds liberties, slavery breeds slaveries, but the liberties will be the strongest stock. If the political and religious liberties which the people of this country aspired to set up had in them the real sap and fibre of a better life than the world had yet known, it must certainly follow that they would quicken and strengthen the people for discovery and obedience in still higher realms. And just this has happened. Nowhere else has the new claim to tax without representation been so quickly detected, so intelligently scrutinized, and so bravely fought. Nowhere else has this spreading plague of selfishness and false doctrine found a people whose average and general life was pitched on so high a level that they instantly took the alarm at its claims over their lives and liberties. It has found a people so disciplined by the aspiration and achievement of political and religious rights that they are already possessed of a body of doctrine capable, by an easy extension, of refuting all the pretensions of the new absolutism. At the very beginning of this new democratic life among the nations it was understood that to be safe liberty must be complete on its industrial as well as on its political and religious sides. This is the American principle. "Give a man power over my subsistence," said Alexander Hamilton, "and he has power over the whole of my moral being." To submit to such a power gives only the alternative of death or degradation, and the high spirit of America preferred then, as it prefers now, the rule of right, which gives life.

The mania of business has reached an acuter and extremer development in America than elsewhere, because nowhere else have bounteous nature and free institutions produced birthrights and pottages so well worth "swapping." But the follies and wickedness of business have nowhere been so sharply challenged as in free America. "Betake yourself to America," said Carlyle to a friend beginning a literary career; "there you can utter your freest thoughts in ways impossible here." It is to this stern wakefulness of a free people that the world owes it that more light has been thrown in America than in any other country on the processes of modern money-making. A free press, organ of a free people, has done invaluable service. The legislatures have pushed investigation after investigation into the ways in which large masses of the people have been deprived, for the benefit of single men or groups of men, of rights of subsistence and government. Through the courts the free people have pursued their depredators by civil and criminal process, by public and private prosecutions. Imperfect and corrupt, these agencies of press, courts, legislatures have often been; they have still done a work which has either been left undone altogether in other countries, or has been done with but a fraction of our thoroughness.

It is due to them that there exists in the reports of legislative investigations, State and national, in the proceedings of lawsuits and criminal trials, in the files of the newspapers, a mass of information which cannot be found in any other community in the world. There is in these archives an accumulation of the raw material of tragedy, comedy, romance, ravellings of the vicissitudes of human life, and social and personal fate, which will feed the fires of whole generations of literary men when once they awake to the existence of these precious rolls. In these pigeon-holes are to be found keys of the present and clews to the future. As America has the newest and widest liberty, it is the stage where play the newest and widest forces of evil as well as good. America is at the front of the forward line of evolution. It has taken the lead in developing competition to the extreme form in which it destroys competition, and in superfining the processes of exchange of services into those of the acquisition of the property of others without service.

The hope is that the old economic system we inherited has ripened so much more rapidly than the society and government we have created that the dead matter it deposits can be thrown off by our vigorous youth and health. "It is high time our bad wealth came to an end," says Emerson. It has grown into its monstrous forms so fast that the dullest eye can separate it from the Commonwealth, and the slowest mind comprehend its mischievousness. In making themselves free of arbitrary and corrupt power in government the Americans prepared themselves to be free in all else, and because foremost in political liberty they have the promise of being the first to realize industrial liberty—the trunk of a tree of which political liberty is the seed, and without which political liberty shrinks back into nothingness.

"The art of Italy will blossom over our graves," Mazzini said when, with true insight, he saw that the first artistic, first literary task before the Italians was to make their country free. Art, literature, culture, religion, in America, are already beginning to feel the restrictive pressure which results from the domination of a selfish, self-indulgent, luxurious, and anti-social power. This power, mastering the markets of a civilization which gives its main energies to markets, passes without difficulty to the mastery of all the other activities. When churches, political campaigns, the expounding of the law, maintenance of schools and colleges, and family life itself all depend on money, they must become servile to the money power. Song, picture, sermon, decrees of court, and the union of hearts must pass constantly under stronger control of those who give their lives to trade and encourage everybody else to trade, confident that the issues of it all will be that they will hold as property, in exclusive possession, to be doled out on their own terms, the matter by which alone man can live, either materially or spiritually.

In America, where the supreme political power and much of the government of church and college have been taken out of traditional hands and subjected to the changing determinations of popular will, it has inevitably resulted that the State, church, and school have passed under this mercantile aristocracy to a far greater extent than in other countries where stiffer régimes under other and older influences still stand. Our upper classes—elected, as always, by the equipoise of effort and opinion between them and the lower classes—are, under this commercial system, the men who trade best, who can control their features and their consciences so that they can always get more than they give, who can play with supply and demand so that at the end of the game all their brethren are their tributaries for life. It is the birthright-buying minds that, by the adoption of this ideal, we choose for our rulers. The progressive races have altered their ideals of kings with the indescribable advantage of being ruled by Washingtons and Lincolns and Gladstones instead of Caligulas and Pharaohs. We have now to make a similar step forward in another part of life. The previous changes expressed outwardly an inner change of heart. The reformer of to-day is simply he who, with quicker ear, detecting that another change of heart is going on, goes before.

Another great change is working in the inner mind of man,

and will surely be followed by incorporation in institutions and morals and manners. The social head and heart are both being persuaded that too many are idle—rich and poor; too many are hurt in body and soul—rich and poor; too many children are "exposed," as in the old Greek and Roman market-places; too many are starving within reach of too much fertile waste; too many passions of envy, greed, and hate are raging among rich and poor. There is too much left undone that ought to be done along the whole scale of life, from the lowest physical to the highest spiritual needs, from better roads to sweeter music and nobler worship. It cannot be long, historically speaking, before all this new sense and sentiment will issue in acts. All will be as zealously protected against oppression of the cruel in their daily labor as now against oppression from invader or rioter, and will be as warmly cheered in liberty to grow to their fullest capabilities as laborers—*i.e.*, users of matter for the purpose of the spirit—as they are now welcomed to the liberty of the citizen and the worshipper. Infinite is the fountain of our rights. We can have all the rights we will create. All the rights we will give we can have. The American people will save the liberties they have inherited by winning new ones to bequeath.

With this will come fruits of new faculty almost beyond calculation. A new liberty will put an end to pauperism and millionairism and the crimes and death-rate born of both wretchednesses, just as the liberty of politics and religion put an end to martyrs and tyrants. The new liberty is identical in principle and purpose with the other; it is made inevitable by them. Those who love the liberties already won must open the door to the new, unless they wish to see them all take flight together. There can be no single liberty. Liberties go in clusters like the Pleiades.

We must either regulate, or own, or destroy, perishing by the sword we take. The possibility of regulation is a dream.

As long as this control of the necessaries of life and this wealth remain private with individuals, it is they who will regulate, not we. The policy of regulation, disguise it as we may, is but moving to a compromise and equilibrium within the evil all complain of. It is to accept the principle of the sovereignty of the self-interest of the individual and apply constitutional checks to it. The unprogressive nations palter in this method with monarchy. But the wits of America are equal to seeing that as with kingship and slavery so with poverty—the weeding must be done at the roots. Sir Henry Sumner Maine says mankind moves from status to contract; from society ruled by inherited customs to one ruled by agreement, varied according to circumstances. Present experience suggests the addition that the movement, like all in nature, is pendulous, and that mankind moves progressively from status to contract, and from this stage of contract to another status. We march and rest and march again. If our society is settling down to an interval of inertia, perhaps ages long, we must before night comes establish all in as much equality and comfort as possible.

The aspirations are not new. We have had them since Plato. The knowledge of means for realizing them is not new. We have had it since Aristotle, and the history of civilization is but the record of the progressive embodiment of the ideals in institutions for the life together—sexual, social, spiritual. What is new in our moment is that mankind's accumulating forces are preparing for another step forward in this long processional realization of its best possible. Nothing so narrow as the mere governmentalizing of the means and processes of production. It is only the morally nerveless who ask government to do that which they will not rise to do. The conversion which is now working itself out within us, and perhaps is more nearly born than we suspect ("We shall not live to see slavery abolished," said Emerson, in 1859) is making itself felt on all sides of our life. In manners, in literature, in marriage, in church, in all, we see at work the saving ferment which is to make all things new by bringing them nearer to the old ideals. George Sand was revolted by the servile accent of the phrase of her day, "Madame est servie." Society has grown to the better fellowship her finer ear found wanting in these words, and is now told it is dinner, not madame or monsieur, that is served.

We are to have, of course, great political changes. We are to apply the co-operative methods of the post-office and the public school to many other common toils, to all toils in which private sovereignty has become through monopoly a despotism over the public, and to all in which the association of the people and the organization of processes have been so far developed that the profit-hunting Captain of Industry may be replaced by the public-serving Captain of Industry. But we are to have much more. We are to have a private life of a new beauty, of which these are to be merely the mechanical exhibitions on the side of politics. We are to move among each other, able, by the methodical and agreed adherence of all, to do what the words of Lamennais mean, instead of being able, as now, in most things, to afford only an indulgence in feeling them. We are to be commoners, travellers to Altruria.

We are to become fathers, mothers, for the spirit of the father and mother is not in us while we can say of any child it is not ours, and leave it in the grime. We are to become men, women, for to all about reinforcing us we shall insure full growth and thus insure it to ourselves. We are to become gentlemen, ladies, for we will not accept from another any service we are not willing to return in kind. We are to become honest, giving when we get, and getting with the knowledge and consent of all. We are to become rich, for we shall share in the wealth now latent in idle men and idle land, and in the fertility of work done by those who have ceased to withstand but stand with each other. As we walk our parks we already see that by saying "thine" to every neighbor we say "mine" of palaces, gardens, art, science, far beyond any possible to selfishness, even the selfishness of kings. We shall become patriots, for the heart will know why it thrills to the flag. Those folds wave the salute of a greater love than that of the man who will lay down his life for his friend. There floats the banner of the love of millions, who, though they do not know you and have never seen you, will die for you and are living for you, doing in a thousand services unto you as you would be done by. And the little patriotism, which is the love of the humanity fenced within our frontier will widen into the reciprocal service of all men. Generals were, merchants are, brothers will be, humanity's representative men.

There is to be a people in industry, as in government. The same rising genius of democracy which discovered that mankind did not co-operate in the State to provide a few with palaces and king's-evil, is disclosing that men do not co-operate in trade for any other purpose than to mobilize the labor of all for the benefit of all, and that the only true guidance comes from those who are led, and the only valid titles from those who create. Very wide must be the emancipation of this new self-interest. If we free America we shall still be not free, for the financial, commercial, possessory powers of modern industrial life are organized internationally. If we rose to the full execution of the first, simplest, and most pressing need of our times and put an end to all private use of public powers, we should still be confronted by monopolies existing simply as private property, as in coal-mines, oil lands.

It is not a verbal accident that science is the substance of the word conscience. We must know the right before we can do the right. When it comes to know the facts the human heart can no more endure monopoly than American slavery or Roman empire. The first step to a remedy is that the people care. If they know, they will care. To help them to know and care; to stimulate new hatred of evil, new love of the good, new sympathy for the victims of power, and, by enlarging its science, to quicken the old into a new conscience, this compilation of facts has been made. Democracy is not a lie. There live in the body of the commonalty the unexhausted virtue and the ever-refreshed strength which can rise equal to any problems of progress.

INDEX

535

Lynching, attempted against a
Negro Populist, 380–385

Major political parties, Populist
comments on, 55–56, 113,
280–283, 286–287, 288, 290,
292, 363–365, 453
Mankind. *See* Affirmation of man
Masses, conception of, 11, 23, 69–
70, 284, 410, 504, 520, 534
Materialism, sterility of, 468, 482–
483, 499–500
Money, Peffer's theories on,
105–107
"Moral insanity," Lloyd on,
516–517
Morgan, W. Scott, background
notes, 246
Mortgage indebtedness, 34–35, 36,
82, 88–91, 92, 145–146,
162–163, 260–262

National banks, 63, 144, 174–183,
264, 291–293, 315–321
Negroes, and Populism, xxvi, xlvii–
xlviii, 23, 50, 241, 284–285,
359–401, 486–492
"New mutualities," necessity for,
522–524
New South ideology, critique of, 24
Noblesse oblige, and Watson on
Negro rights, 377
Nugent, Thomas L., background
notes, 283–285

Overproduction, and discussion of
underconsumption, 15–16,
45, 103, 395, 426, 499

Peffer, William A., background
notes, 71
Phillips, Wendell, 118
Pinkertons, 65, 149, 186–192, 439,
442–443, 448–449, 450, 451,
459–461

Political parties. *See* Major political
parties
Post, Charles C., background notes,
352
Postal savings banks, 6, 9, 64
Potential for abundance, and actual
practices, 498–501
Prevailing ideologies, rejection of,
467–468, 482–486
See also Competition, Laissez-
faire
Price decline, concerning crops and
livestock, 74–80
"Progressive communion of equali-
ties," Lloyd on, 513–514
Progressive historical orientation,
xli–xliii
Public opinion, Watson on, 436–437
Public ownership, 58–59, 70, 192–
195, 214–215, 264, 279–280,
294–295, 348, 453
Public works, 445
Pullman Company, 309–310
Pullman strike, 452–455, 457–458

Racial animosities
artificial basis for, 360–361,
363–364
need to combat, 366–367
solution for overcoming, 368–374
Railroads, 18, 33–34, 58, 63, 87–92,
128–129, 130–131, 159–160,
170, 184–188, 192–195, 204,
205, 222, 250–251, 252–255,
263, 270–278, 294–295, 433,
453, 497
Reformers
hardships of, 280–281
historical role of, 297–305
Reprisals against Negroes, condemnation of, 489
Robinson, R. L., 333–334
Rockefeller, John D., 230–231,
234–235